PUBLICATIONS

OF THE

NORTH CAROLINA HISTORICAL COMMISSION

—————

THREE YEARS IN BATTLE

AND

THREE IN FEDERAL PRISONS

THE PAPERS OF

RANDOLPH ABBOTT SHOTWELL

EDITED BY

J. G. DE ROULHAC HAMILTON
WITH THE COLLABORATION OF
REBECCA CAMERON

VOLUME III

RALEIGH
THE NORTH CAROLINA HISTORICAL COMMISSION
1936

CONTENTS

THREE YEARS IN BATTLE

AND

THREE IN FEDERAL PRISONS

CHAPTER TWELFTH

Marion and Raleigh

Marion, McDowell Co., N. C., August 22nd, 1871.

Again I write from the interior of a filthy and crowded cage! Again my theme is of shameful ill-treatment, undeserved, unprovoked, unnecessary, barbarous! But let me in calm dispassionateness the tale unfold—the truth set down! My suspicions on Saturday evening that some unusual movement was on foot among the Mongrels proved to have been much better founded than I had any conception. It seems that in the very face of declarations that we were not to be removed until September, together with assurances that we should have "two or three days' notice" before any movement, the Mongrels were planning to drag us away within a few hours, and upon less than 20 minutes' notice! To be sure we deserve the discomfort occasioned by it, as a lesson for our silliness in believing anything the creatures pretended to assert. Of course they had no idea of giving us notice. All the day on Saturday the arrangements for our removal were being made; guards summoned, wagons ordered, shackles procured, etc., yet not a hint of it was permitted to reach us, although it was well known we were unprepared for any such sudden departure, and were relying on their assurances of "ample notice." Nearly every one had sent home his clothing to be washed; none of us were provided with money, travelling satchels, or any of the small articles of daily need and comfort, which we designed taking with us when we transferred to the distant place of trial; for Raleigh is as much out of communication with

1

Rutherfordton as with Richmond and Baltimore.   But let that pass.

On Sunday morning, the 20th, after the dirty dish-pan of boiled potatoes had been introduced into the usual greasy section of the floor, and the motley crowd were huddled around it, about to begin breakfast, Andy Scoggins threw open the door, and shouted, *"Shotwell, Cooley, Sweezy, and Padgett—get ready to start for Marion, in ten minutes!"*   Imagine our dismay!   We were taken totally by surprise; hence in utter unreadiness!   I had no means of even returning the borrowed books, magazines, kindly sent me by lady friends.   I could not so much as notify my father, and sister-in-law, that I was about to be borne away—perhaps never to return; though on second thought I should have been pleased, for their sakes, if they had known nothing of it all until we were afar away, and the trying spectacle of our removal unwitnessed by them.

The ten minutes were scarce elapsed when the tramp of a gang of men was audible in the ante-chamber, accompanied by an ominous clanking of chains!   John Cooley was first called out; then Sweezy; then Isaac Padgett; lastly myself. Each as he left the larger room bade a sad, but excited adieu to his fellow prisoners of the past two months, and there were almost tears in many eyes. On emerging into the box-like ante-room, I beheld a spectacle unparalleled in cowardly brutality as yet even in the annals of Mongrel Man-Hunting.   Forming a circle were half a dozen guards: Jim, Joe, or Bill Scoggins, Hodges, Callahan, McArthur, *et al*—all armed with seven-shooters.   Andy Scoggins acted as Brute-in-Chief; being assisted by a big *black* negro, (Scoggins was *white,* or mulatto-colored) named Charles Bryan, a well known leader in the Leagues. In the center of the group were Brother Addie, Will G. Edgerton, and the three who had preceded me, all with their wrists handcuffed to a chain!   Stop a moment! and reflect that these were all young men of known respectability, who had never given any trouble, never attempted to escape, and were not criminals, nor even *charged* with the more serious offenses, had never been allowed an examination, or any chance to establish their innocence, but after two months of torture in the vilest of prisons were now chained in pairs like savage dogs, or desperate slaves en route for the mart.

When I was brought out, Addie's indignation got the better of his judgment and he burst out, saying that it was a cowardly act—a piece of political spite—that the puppies felt very big in being able to handcuff gentlemen. It was the truth, but I urged him to be silent, as nothing was to be gained by talking so long as we were in their power; for of course they would be very brave while dealing with helpless prisoners. Jim Scoggins verified my words by assailing us all with his cowardly bluster and insolence, saying he wasn't afraid of anybody, "could lick ten such Rebels." For my part, on being told to hold out my wrist, I said, *"Sir, I cannot prevent your seizing my arm, but first I formally protest against this outrage; I have never been tried, convicted, or otherwise incurred this indignity.* Scoggins grasped my wrist, and the negro blacksmith quickly and roughly riveted around them the rudest, coarsest pair of shackles I ever saw. Thus the gang was made up, and six decent citizens of North Carolina stood, chained together, and surrounded by the lowest of the League leaders, armed and insolent, gloating over their superior, but unfortunate victims. At this moment the doors of the jail room were opened (the outer one) and as all the inmates crowded to the bars to look at us, I turned to them and said, *"Men, this sight shows you what our enemies would do with every true Southerner if they could! But be not intimidated! Time will bring to all of us an opportunity!"*

This speech was answered by murmurs of *"We'll remember, We'll see it out, etc., etc.,"* whereupon the Mongrels hurried us down the dark and dirty stairs.

At the foot of the staircase on the ground floor there was a dense gang of Mongrels and negroes, filling the hallway, and crowding around the door. All the low creatures in the village and adjacent country, including the drunken strumpets supported by several of the most zealous Mongrels, were assembled; showing that they had been privately notified, as it was too early for them to be in the village on a Sabbath morning.

I cared little for such spectators, but my feelings were about to be sorely tried. As we appeared at the head of the staircase, I saw father entering the jail door, and forcing his way through the throng to the foot of the stairs. He had been on the eve of starting to church to hold services when the intelligence reached him that his sons were being handcuffed, like felons, to be borne away! Naturally by the time he could walk to the jail the cowardly deed had been perpetrated; but the sight of us, thus chained, threw him into ungovernable excitement; and throwing the Mongrels right and left, he confronted those who were bringing us down, denouncing and protesting against the outrage in the sternest tones I ever heard him use. Indeed he barred the way, with cane uplifted, until I could drag my comrades down the steps, and beg him to go home: that all this scene was a delicious treat for the Mongrels; that they cared nothing for his denunciations, whereas the commotion was paining me, etc., etc. Finally he was prevailed upon to walk away with old General Bryan, and others, but still vehemently denouncing the utterly unwarrantable outrage. I made haste to clamber in the wagon with the others in order to get out of his sight as speedily as possible, as I knew he was liable to an apoplectic attack—(hereditary)—and I feared the effect of his overwrought feelings. Had he dropped lifeless in the base-born crowd, then indeed would my life have been ruined: for I should devote my years be they many or few to the pursuit of vengeance!

There was not the slightest excuse for the handcuffing. We were not desperadoes. We were not even accused of capital crimes. We had never been examined by any authority. The papers authorizing our arrest were never seen by any of our captors, if they ever had an existence anywhere. We had never been boisterous or unruly, or threatening. There were *fifty* heavily armed guards to watch *six men;* besides the scores of Mongrels, Pukes, and witnesses, riding with the train, all of whom were armed, and ready to assist.

Moreover, we were placed in low-covered wagons, with a guard at each end absolutely preventing escape had we been slippery as eels! No one will say that we were chained for *security;* it was merely a specimen of the Mongrel malice which has pursued us in all this business! This was shown by the remark of John M. Allen, one of the more moderate Loganites, (He runs a mill, and a miller has need to be moderate.) who rode up by the side of the wagon, and said, "Mr. Shotwell I am sorry to see this. I tried to persuade 'em out of putting them chains on you. It ain't my business, but I'm opposed to it." "There was not the slightest excuse for it; none of us desire to escape, unless it be to take revenge on the men who have maltreated us," I replied. "Yes," he responded in a rather low tone, as Cebern L. Harris and Jay Bird Carpenter rode by, feasting their eyes on the spectacle of six better men chained together in the bottom of a wagon, "Yes, I told 'em you'uns wasn't going to give any trouble, and I offered to take you to Marion by myself without a gun or a guard!" It is due John Allen to say that he made these statements in the presence of old Scoggins, the wagon driver. This reminds me that all the Scoggins tribe are now engaged in skinning the government and people. Nathan is U. S. Commissioner, Andy is U. S. Deputy Marshal, Joe, Bill, and Jim are either "Deputies" or "Acting Deputies," and the old man drives the wagon to haul the prisoners unlawfully seized by his Man-Hunting sons. Together they must pocket $50 per day as their squeezing from the government, not to speak of private operations!

'Squire Sweezy has just called my attention to the remark of Allen that orders had been issued to the guards to shoot us as we lay in the wagon if there were any demonstration to rescue us! I do not know if this be true, but I entirely believe it to be. Confirmatory, Ike Padgett reminds me that after we passed Dobson's on the road, two shots were heard some distance to the right (probably hunters) whereupon the drivers whipped up their horses and consolidated the train, while a gang of guards unslung their carbines, and rode near our wagons. We had no special fear, for had a rescue been attempted and a single volley fired at the Mongrels, every man of them would have fled like partridges. There is no bravery in a man who could illtreat a helpless prisoner.

The spectacle presented by our cavalcade, the wagons, the guards, the negroes trotting along side, the long procession of lawyers and witnesses in buggies and on horseback, was a strange one for the peaceful Sabbath. Perhaps there were similar scenes in Virginia during the war, when Sunday almost faded from recollection as a day of rest and decent demeanor. But the excuse of those days no longer exists and the desecration of today might have been easily avoided. It would have been perfectly easy to leave Rutherfordton at dawn on Monday, and reach Marion at 2 P. M. even if it were not well known that Court transacts no business on Monday. Probably the Mongrels thought there would be more people on the road going to and from church on Sunday, to see us than on other days. There was little likelihood of any service in Rutherfordton that day. As we slowly dragged through the main street, I saw not a single front door or window open—all the dwellings seemed tenantless—though it may be suspected that more than one pair of indignant eyes was peering from the lattice upon the shameful procession.

We had gone about seven miles, when I heard the rattle of wheels coming at Jehu speed, and saw father sitting bolt upright in his buggy and looking as stern as a Roman Senator. Swiftly passing without a word, he handed me a package of linen collars; as I had been hurried away half dressed. When he was gone by, Andy Scoggins came galloping up, and demanded the "secret paper" that had been handed me. I showed him the collars, and told him if he would look more closely he would see that the handcuffs were cutting the flesh of our wrists: Edgerton's especially showing blood! He replied indifferently, "Oh! I'll fix that when we git to a blacksmith's shop," as if it were a small matter that we were tortured at every jolt of the wagon. At Henderson Weaver's, where a brief halt was made, we found father and learned that his object in going to Marion was to see if a writ of *habeas corpus* could be obtained from Judge Brooks, who was expected to arrive on Monday to hold court. I could see no probability of success, nor of advantage at this stage of the game, for the Mongrels have now done their worst, and short of shooting me in the back can descend no lower in their cowardly brutality. But I made no objection to father's views, preferring that he should be stirring about, working with a hopeful spirit rather than remaining shut up in the parsonage study, brooding over the desolation and outrage which has come upon his home. At Weaver's, the ladies were kind and sympathetic, though somewhat timid in expressing their feelings, as nine-tenths of the crowd were Mongrels, and old Mr. Weaver, one of the most respectable and well-doing farmers in the region, has already been put to a thousand or twelve hundred dollars' expense for turning off some of his negro laborers after the election.

The distance from Rutherfordton to Marion is some 36 miles; the road the worst imaginable. It passes through the Brindletown region, once lively with gold miners; now barren and deserted, rendered even more desolate looking by the red-mud caves on the hills, and the gravel pits everywhere seen among the briars and laurels. Frowning mountain cliffs, and dark ravines, impenetrable thickets and roaring waterfalls, add to the wild loneliness of the region; and in many places the road runs directly up the bed of streams for miles, the horses walking in water over fetlocks, and the wagon jolting from innumerable stones.

As we were chained together in the bottom of the wagon-bed, with no springs to break the force of the jolting, it may be conceived that our weariness became very trying to the soul.

After passing the mountains we began to encounter large groups of negroes and "poor whites" of the Mongrel variety assembled at every cross road, blacksmithy, or country store. In some places as many as 40 persons were posted on each side of the road (an old woman with a yellow sunbonnet and short pipe, generally sitting upon the top rail of the fence) and all eager to "see dem Kluxes" go by! for it appears the intelligence was sent ahead in order that the Mongrels might enjoy the spectacle. Upon no other hypothesis can the general turnout be explained.

In the dusk of evening we approached Marion—a little village nestling in an amphitheatre of mountains, and which might have been expected to be quiet as a deserted country church at this twilight hour on Sabbath; whereas there was all the bustle and appearance of a large military encampment. All along the roads, as seen from the hilltop, a mile from town, were the numerous camp-fires of families bivouacking around their wagons. Every moment new trains turned off from the highway into the bushes, or fields, and soon had a roaring log fire, around which the women and children huddled while the men attended to the horses. Here and there were men and women trudging wearily along on foot, with blankets on their backs, and their food in satchels. The noise, cracking of whips, barking of dogs, whistling, calling, and uproar of rattling wagons, composed anything but a peaceful Sunday evening scene!

These wayfarers were citizens under indictment, or summoned as witnesses, all coming to attend the so-called Federal Court. Too poor to pay for hotel lodgings, they are obliged to bivouac in the fields around the village and are now exposed to a thunder storm as I write. Many of them have *walked* for upwards of thirty-one-two-three and -four miles, and through the rough region of which I have spoken. Hundreds of them have travelled all day, and a part of yesterday to come here as witnesses, some against, but the majority in favor of the prisoners, or indicted. And this is the *fourth time* many of the Rutherford citizens have been dragged to one point and another to save their friends or relatives. During a halt upon the hill, I heard this conversation between lawyer Jos. Carson and an old woman, who was seated on the tongue of a wagon awaiting the building of a camp-fire, for which a grey-haired old man was gathering logs; she looked worn out, and heartbroken. *Mr. Carson*—"Why, auntie, you are getting to be a regular attender of courts; I meet you, and the old man wherever I go." *Old Woman*—"Yes, Mr. Carson, it does seem like a body would never git done a-goin, and a-goin an' all for nothing. But our [boy] ain't got nobody but us ter prove he wus a bed ter home that night of the lickin' old Pukey Biggerstaff ketched. And we had to go along to Ruth'ferd, an' then to Shelby, an' Cherryville, and then here once afore, an' now agin, an' I wus just a tellin' pappy [her husband] we would hev' to be hauled in our beds next time, fur it seems like [I] would just lie down, an' die ef this pullin' and a haulin' is gwine ter go on much longer." (Then after a pause) "And I reckon it won't stop tell them Scoggins get all the money in the country."

Such is the persecution.

Driving to the little two-story brick-jail in Marion, Andy Scoggins marshalled his men, taking time enough to collect a large crowd, and disembarked us from the wagons. I heard a voice say: *"Isn't that a d—d piece of villainy; the rogues chaining decent men?"* Whereupon another voice said: *"Don't talk so loud! They'll have us all in jail if they can make an excuse."* We were marched up-stairs into the room we at present occupy; a small, low ceiled apartment with three windows. It is only about ten feet square and as filthy as a pig-sty. In the centre and occupying most of the room is a rusty old cage, similar to the one at Rutherford, but smaller, and filthier; besides having only a partial flooring. It seemed incredible that any man would think of crowding even four men into such a place; but Scoggins marched in the entire seven, in addition to an occupant placed here by the McDowell County authorities for stealing. His name is Sheehan, and he is said to spend the greater portion of his time in jail. His presence was a severe infliction from the first, as his personal habits are unclean to the last degree, and his slovenliness had filled the cage with filth, decayed vegetables, bones, etc., creating a sickening stench, and curtailing the surface for spreading our bedding to one-tenth the requisite allow-

ance.   My comrades kindly allowed me choice of space,
but it is so uncomfortable for all that few of us can
sleep more than an hour or so.

On being forced into the cage we were still handcuffed
together, and, as the rivets had been hammered tightly
by the negro blacksmith, part of the irons only were removed!   (These shackles were not the modern kind
which lock with a key, but were riveted around our
wrists, cutting the flesh with their rough edges).   My
wrists are still raw and sore.

Of course there was a large crowd of Mongrels to witness the spectacle of our incarceration.   I very foolishly
asked one of them if he would do me the favor to send
Col. Carrow, the United States Marshal for North Carolina, to see me, as I had heard he was a humane man,
and hoped he would at least allow us the liberty of the
room, as we must surely suffocate in the crowded cage.
The fellow grinned, but departed ostensibly to inform
Carrow, who I need scarcely say did not pay any attention to my request.   Bro. Addie, also, asked for the
use of a candle—"just two minutes"—to see what sort
of filth we were to sleep upon, but was denied it.   So
we sat, or squatted, in the darkness, while Sweezy and
——tugged and rattled their chains trying to get
free from them; which they finally accomplished with
some sacrifice of the skin of their hands.

At length "supper," so-called, was fetched in; a large
platter of cold "string" or "snap" beans, and some bits
of corn bread!   Neither "meat nor drink" of any kind!
And, will it be believed, this musty stuff was not passed
into the cage, as could have been done in a second, but
was placed on a bench outside the cage, compelling
those whose hunger forced them to it, to claw their food
through the narrow holes between the latticed bars, like
monkeys snatching chestnuts from outside pans in a
menagerie.   I went supperless to bed—Bah! to a six-
inch wide strip of dirty plank.

Finally the little poodle of a jailer slipped around to
a corner of the cage, and whispered in my ear that he
was "All right"—hoped "the boys wouldn't cause any
trouble"—anyhow he was "all right, and "would treat

us right." I told him if he had any such intentions it was about time to begin to manifest them; that we were gentlemen, not desperados, and it was cowardly to cage us in this way, and not even allow us to eat our food decently. He replied that we were "United States prisoners," and "Colonel" Scoggins (That's the tin-peddler on horse back!) made him do it, etc., but he would hereafter try, and give our meals inside!

Yesterday (Monday) the Mongrels flocked in from dawn till dusk to gloat over the sight of half a dozen *gentlemen* locked in a cage with a professional thief. But they turned back quite a number of our friends who desired to call upon us. Father, himself, was twice turned back on various pretexts. He looked sadly care-worn but is busy with the lawyers. He is a guest of Maj. Neal, whose good lady has sent a tray of delicacies to brother and me, yesterday and today. We, of course, divided with our comrades.

The jail is now surrounded by 50 Yankee soldiers.

5 P. M. We fancied that we had seen the worst in the way of ill treatment but our present experience is going somewhat ahead of even Rutherford "Black Hole." This afternoon five young fellows charged with violation of revenue laws in one of the trans-mountain counties were brought up from Raleigh, and placed in the same room with us. But they enjoy 10 per cent more liberty than we as they are outside of the cage, and can go to the windows, and talk with their friends outside. Unfortunately their privileges work to our detriment; they huddle at the window two in each, and thus cut off every breath of air we occasionally caught from that source. And the young fellows care nothing for our sufferings. They are all ignorant, uncouth mountaineers; as will appear from the fact that three of them are very proud of a coarse pair of breeches given them by the Federal authorities at Raleigh, and de-clare they are ever so anxious to "git home an' show my new rig." The clothing is worth about ten dollars a cart load!

August 23rd. I have just had a secret note which explains the presence of the blue-coats. They came up as a body-guard for Judge G. W. Brooks, of the U. S. Dist. Court, who arrived on Monday! Was anything so absurd ever before heard! The facts are as follows: On Saturday evening Capt. R. E. Wilson, a one-armed Confederate, learning that U. S. District Attorney Starbuck, a North Carolina Scalawag, was in the city, called at his room in the hotel and demanded satisfaction for certain personal grievances; telling Starbuck he must make an apology or settle the long-standing difficulty then and there within locked doors. Starbuck made some excuse, but said he would attend to the matter next morning (Sunday) at 8 o'clock. But at the appointed hour, he was half a mile away, impatiently awaiting the train. Capt. Wilson, accompanied by his friends, "Bull" Mitchell, and W. Beard, hastened to the depot, and denounced Starbuck for his conduct. Blows passed, and, of course, Messrs. Mitchell and Beard interferred, whereupon Judge Brooks, and Larkins his clerk, fell upon the two young men with sticks and clubs in an outrageous manner. Judge Brooks who was not molested, or even insulted, attacked Mr. Beard, and broke his heavy gold-headed cane over the young man's head, while the latter was not expecting the unprovoked assault! By this interference, the *five* arms were exposed to six arms, and a cane; but Starbuck and Larkins caught a good drubbing, and Brooks lost his cane, his spectacles, and studs—besides his dignity, and reputation for fair-mindedness, won during the Holden and Kirk war.

As soon as the crowd interfered, and stopped the row, the Judge spluttered furiously about "Ku Klux attacks," and telegraphed for a regiment of Yankees to "guard his court," though he knew there was not the least need of them, or if there had been—the army of "U. S. deputy marshals" would have sufficed to guard the court against a thousand Klans! But thus it goes! Every excuse, every private fracas, is magnified into the plea for "more troops!!" "more soldiers!!" "more men and more money!!"

The arrival of the military, however, has been a benefit to us prisoners from a personal point of view, as they have been just stationed as guards at the jail, both outside and within; relieving the Mongrels of the duty, and relieving us of their disagreeable presence. Not one of us but would prefer to be watched by Yankees rather than the base-born renegades who have treated us so barbarously. In fact I have always preferred a straight out Northerner to the Mongrel renegades. The soldiers are much more decent, and treat us more decently. The Yankee at the present moment on guard at the door is very friendly and says he has no sort of sympathy with men who could shut us up here.

In order not to do injustice I here add the account of the Salisbury fracas as recorded in the *Examiner* of that city, whose editor is an old citizen not at all in sympathy with the Klan, and who wrote with the facts fresh in his mind. No denial of the following account has been made so far as I can learn.

There was an old grudge existing between Capt. R. E. Wilson and Mr. District Attorney Starbuck. Capt. Wilson had long felt aggrieved by Mr. Starbuck's persistent and repeated persecutions, and had the previous evening called on him to bring about a settlement. This Mr. Starbuck refused; but told the Captain that he would attend to the matter the succeeding morning (Sunday) at 8 o'clock. On Sunday morning Capt. Wilson, accompanied by a friend, again called at Mr. Starbuck's room at the appointed hour, but found no one in. As it was known that Mr. Starbuck would leave on the western train for Marion that morning, the Capt. entered the omnibus and proceeded to the depot. On the way, Judge Brooks and Mr. Starbuck got in the omnibus. The party then consisted of Capt. R. E. Wilson, Mr. W. Beard, Mr. Luico Mitchell, Mr. Larkins, U. S. D. Court Clerk, Mr. Starbuck, and Judge Brooks, and perhaps one or two others. On arriving at the depot, Capt. Wilson reminded Mr. Starbuck of his promise made on the previous evening to settle the old difficulty, when some words passed and finally blows. Then were drawn in Mr. Beard, Mr. Larkins and Judge

Brooks, respectively. There were very few persons at the depot, and consequently, some of the parties (Mr. Starbuck, Mr. Larkins, and Mr. Beard) were considerably bruised before they could be separated, Mr. Beard being severely hurt by the blows inflicted by Judge Brooks, who had furiously attacked him with his gold-headed cane, which he broke to pieces—a great loss. It should be borne in mind that Judge Brooks was not struck, not a hand being uplifted against him except to get him out of the way, notwithstanding his disgraceful attack upon Mr. Beard. No one intended any indignity to or wished to hurt the Judge, though his undignified temerity cost him a valuable cane and a gold stud from his shirt collar.

It will thus be seen that the whole affair grew out of an old unsettled difficulty between Capt. Wilson and Mr. District Attorney Starbuck; and was simply *an affray, and the parties to it amenable to the Municipal and State laws for this breach of the peace*. And why, we would most respectfully ask, were not each and all arrested and bound over to Court? This should have been done at all hazards. Has the power to keep the peace been taken from our Municipal and State functionaries? Or has timidity taken possession of their souls? If they have been deprived of the power to perform a plain, and, in better days, an imperative duty, then, they should no longer attempt to keep up appearances, but throw up their commissions, and submit, at the advice of the timid, to whatever breaches of the peace may befall us. How humiliating the spectacle!

Our people generally entertain a high regard for Judge Brooks, but they are almost unanimous in their condemnation of his course in this matter. The Judge is a sworn officer of the law—a conservator, and should not be a disturber of the peace. To say the least, it was very undignified for him to take part in a street fight.

Again, it is generally conceded, as this was

merely an ordinary affray of which the *State Courts alone have jurisdiction,* that the conduct of the Judge in binding three of the combatants over to the Federal Court and allowing the others to go scot free, is arbitrary and unjust.

The Judge himself was not exempt from arrest. He took part in an *affray,* he used an unlawful weapon, he is guilty and is amenable to the offended law—no matter if he was about to start to his Court. Judges, Jurors, Members of Congress, and Legislators, are protected against *civil* processes, while on their way to duty; but suppose one of these, while *en route* to his place of business get into an affray and kill a man, will any one say that he is exempt from arrest? There is a distinction made in the laws with regard to such cases, and this is not in favor of Judge Brooks.

The whole matter is deeply deplored by our citizens, and it is believed that Judge Brooks, after the excitement under which he seems to have been laboring, will release the gentlemen whom he has placed under arrest.—[*Salisbury Examiner.*]

Basket with very acceptable delicacies, dinner, etc., from Miss N. and Mrs. R.

August 24th. Having received no answer from my verbal message, I today addressed a formal note to Col. S. T. Carrow, U. S. Marshal for North Carolina, requesting him to call at the jail (just across the street from his hotel) that I might explain to him our terrible situation. All the day yesterday I awaited his coming, but there was a political meeting, and he made a very violent, and abusive speech, from the steps of the Court House, but paid no attention to my appeal—for it was in the nature of an appeal. Today I addressed a note to the commander of the troops in whose keeping we are, and he was enough of the gentleman to reply that he had no authority to make any change in our situation, but would personally wait upon Col. Carrow to ask an examination of the matter.

This evening Carrow came swaggering in, accompanied by all the Scogginses, the other Mongrel deputies, and a crowd of his followers, who filled the room, and crowded around the cage until we seemed shut up in a vault—one of those hectacombs, which run underground throughout all Paris, and are walled up with rows of grinning skulls! Carrow waited until all his gang were in position, then asked what I wanted with him.

"Sir," I replied, "if you will observe for yourself you will see that we are undergoing unnecessary and outrageous tortures for lack of room, of air, of food and water—yes, even sleep, for we cannot sleep, packed as we are, eight grown men in this small space!"

Carrow began to mumble that he always treated his prisoners well; that no man could say he was hard on prisoners, etc., etc.

"Throw open the door!" he cried, in *ore rotundo* voice, to the "caitiff" who handles the keys, and who now began to bustle about to bring water, and remove the slops. Carrow entered, and expressed surprise at seeing young men of our appearance in such a place. I replied that it was through no fault of our own; but that I had asked him to come that he might learn by ocular, and odorous demonstration how abominably we were treated. All I asked was the poor privilege of being allowed the use of the entire room, so that we could get near the windows, and escape the stench of the foul cage, and the fouler bucket placed outside the cage—too indecent to relate here! I pointed out that as there was a Federal soldier on guard inside the door, and a squad of them in the room opposite, and a regular guard all around the jail, there was not the least chance for escape; therefore this confinement in the cage was altogether unnecessary even from his point of view.

"Desparate cases require desparate remedies," he replied, with a look at his followers and deputies which resulted in a snicker. He then began to say that we ought to be ashamed, that we had ruled it over Rutherford, making good men live in terror of their lives, etc. But I interrupted him, saying he was uttering that which was not the fact; and he had no right to hector us as criminals, when as yet we had never had any sort of examination, or any opportunity to face our accusers, etc.

He then launched into a stump speech—recalling, no doubt, his declamation of the previous day—supposing, *I* suppose, that it would be a good time to "show off" before his mountain deputies. Referring to the members of the Order, who have left the region, he burst forth in more of the *rotundo*—"Yes, and you too no doubt think you will escape, but I tell you, sirs, the country is aroused—the government is aroused!—its eye is upon you!—you cannot escape!—flee though you may to the frozen snows of Canada, or the waving chapparal of Mexico—the omniscient eye of the government will search you out—and the strong right arm [Carrow and company—I suppose] will drag you back to the bar of retributive justice!" Whereupon he swelled after the fashion of a toad with a goose-egg in its belly, and his henchmen applauded.

To say that I was disgusted with this senseless diatribe from a man who knew nothing of our cases save by hearsay, and who had no right to inflict the additional torture of his speech upon us, even had we been deep-dyed assassins, will hardly be necessary. Yet, as I had heard him spoken of as a kindly dispositioned man, and had hopes of his alleviating our condition, I repressed my indignation, and even assumed a conversational tone with him—much to my after disgust.

Carrow now ordered us to *strip off our clothing,* that he might *search our persons,* saying he understood we had concealed weapons! It seems he had employed the Revenue defrauders (the five young men from_____ county) who were outside the cage, to watch us, and they spied Edgerton's knife which chanced to drop from his pocket. Edgerton handed over the knife; but Carrow caused two or three of the men to strip. I told him he could examine my pockets if he desired to do so, but I did not propose to be stripped for the amusement of his crowd, unless overpowered by brute force. He therefore contented himself with feeling in my pockets, and around my waist-belt, and in the tops of my shoes! Shame upon the cowards! All this was done— not to make sure of our having no weapons—for he did not examine our baggage, did not look beneath the loose boards of the flooring, where one knife was hidden, and 500 might have been, nor did he really care if we had a peck of knives, as he had no intention of releasing us from the cage, and even had he so released us, our knives could have been of no avail against the bayonets and revolvers of 50 armed Yankees!

Oh! fool that I was to be deceived by his promises of "I'll treat you well; I always treat my prisoners well!" and allow him to leave the cage without telling him how rascally he had already treated us, for he is responsible for every rascality of his agents or "deputies!"

Well, I accidentally obtained one important admission from him.   He remarked that the jail *was* rather small for so many prisoners, but he didn't build it, and could not enlarge it.   I then asked—"Why then, do you not remove us to Raleigh, where you say there is plenty of room?"   He replied, "Well, you see, I can't move you for a day or two; the *papers in your case aint come yet; but I sent a man after 'em, and he'll be back termorrer, or next day."*   Innocently I further asked, "I suppose you are sure you have them?" "Oh yes, I have them down at Raleigh.   I, some way, mislaid them—but they'll be here all right tomorrow."   Then I said with raised voice, *"So it seems I have been arrested, held for more than two months—caged like a felon—dragged here in handcuffs—while the capias for my arrest is still at Raleigh, 250 miles away!"*   "Desparate cases, you know," said Carrow, backing out of the cage, and going off, laughing and chuckling!

Of course not a particle of change has been made in our situation, and as I write these lines I occasionally must stop to catch breath, for the atmosphere is sultry and fetid in suffocating degree.   Think of eight grown men, packed in an iron cage—with five other men filling the three small, latticed windows outside of the cage, and the whole surroundings so filthy that constant stench pervades the small quantity of air circulating on this sultry evening!

Mrs. Col. H—s, kindly remembers us with a waiter of

supper, and Maj. Malone sends a number of news-papers which I am very glad to get.

August 25th. Capt. Plato Durham, and Maj. A. C. Avery, "Brethren of High Degree," came up about dusk last evening, and chatted a few moments, though there were scores of spies also hanging around to catch some word of "contraband" confab! Bah! the Mongrels imagine we are all on the Guy Fawkes, dark lantern, gunpowder plot order, continually making secret signs, and scheming to put "cold pi-sin" in their cups.

Father has just been up with Col. Burgess S. Gaither, who, in conjunction with other lawyers attending the Federal Court, has drawn a petition for the writ of *habeas corpus* for Bro. Addie, and I, to be presented to Judge Brooks. We signed the petition; though only because father wished it, and to show how maliciously the Mongrels are acting toward us. It is openly boasted by the Scoggins gang that if Judge Brooks should grant the writ they will re-arrest me on other charges, and continue to do so until there is "not enough property in Western North Carolina to go bail." For my part, I have reached the point where I am superior to all the tortures my foes may inflict. And as for asking any man to go as my surety, I shall never even hint such a thing no matter if I die in this cage. If my friends are disposed to go upon my bail-bond they will not need to be asked to do so; and if they are not so disposed; I am too proud to ask it as a favor.

Mrs. Maj. Neal sends welcome reminder that all men are human, and have an "inner man," whose fondness for good living is remarkable. Mrs. Maggie has shown a real interest and sympathy which Bro. and I can never forget. Indeed the ladies of Marion have all been exceedingly kind; at least all of whom I have any knowledge. Their kindness is the more to be prized, because it manifests itself spontaneously and in practical alleviation of the needs of young men, with none of whom they are personally acquainted, unless I except a few acquaintances of Bro. Addie's. The food sent to us, we divide equally among our five fellow-prisoners, hence the whole party of seven are made glad thereby.

August 26th. Judge Brooks, after hearing Col. Gaither's argument in Chambers, refused to grant the writ of *habeas corpus,* but ordered the Marshal to admit us to bail in the sum of six thousand dollars—$2,000, and $4,000! We thank him for nothing! It is adding insult to injury to grant us at the last moment, after keeping us in cages and handcuffs, for two months, and dragging us 40 miles from home into a strange community, to at length offer us the privilege of giving enormous bail—merely to release the government of the expense of carrying us to Raleigh. I don't think I would accept it now, if my friends were to come in troops. But there is no danger of that. The Federal Court adjourned today, and nearly all the Rutherford people started home yesterday afternoon. Some of the Mongrels came in just now to bid us good by. Hodges and Callahan looked ashamed, and offered me their hands, which I took; for I could not be rude to them.

Capt. Huffmaster of Rutherford ran in just now with a gallon of brandy which he and other friends desired to leave with us in case we should become thirsty. The whole party were seized with sudden thirst including the guards (Yankees) who indulged in sundry remarks not complimentary to the Mongrels.

All the lawyers and Court attendants have returned home, including more than half a dozen acquaintances of mine—and for whom I have battled boldly in my paper at Asheville and Rutherfordton, yet who would not walk across the street to pay me a visit of sympathy, or inquire of my needs, now that I am caged like a felon, and for no other crime than the outspoken advocacy of Democratic-Conservative principles! Ah! well, I was young and absurdly enthusiastic: not yet versed in the gratitude of politicians and public leaders.

August 27th. No movement yet, although all the court officials have departed. I suppose the warrant, or capias, in our case has become lost, or has never been issued, and the Grantizaries are in trouble about it.

Mrs. Dr. Gilkey sent breakfast, and Mrs. Col. Halliburton dinner. Two young men doing business here sent some cigars, and writing material—the latter very acceptable to me, and the cigars to the others. I shall always hold in kind remembrance the people of Marion, more especially the ladies, who have given us, daily, *practical* testimonials of their sympathy and good will. How wonderfully the weaker, gentler sex come out strong and fearless in times of great trouble and oppression like the present! I verily believe the South would have succumbed to Yankee coercion twelve months earlier but for the indomitable spirit of the women. I believe the South would have gained her independence had our leaders paid more regard for public opinion—made, as it was in large measure, by the wives, mothers, and sweethearts, at home. Just so long as the latter were encouraged and appealed to, they cast their influence in favor of resistance till the last. But when their spirit became dampened by long continuance of utter disregard of them, when they saw their husbands and brothers treated as mere machines— when they saw fine fledged birds flitting about on ostensible errands, bombproofs, etc.—while the army was starving on 1-8 of a pound of meat and a pint of sour meal per day—the women lost heart, and wrote such letters to their "boys in the army" as took life and hope out of many of them. I have read letters from women, which made me almost shed tears, though I was in no wise interested either in the writer or the recipient.

[*August 28th.*] On the train—at Company Shops, tediously awaiting the "up"-train. About 9 A. M., in a drenching rain we bade adieu to Marion jail, and surrounded by Yankees with bayonets fixed, were marched to the depot. Ladies crowded the balconies, and saluted us with waiving handkerchiefs, many of which were seen waiving from residences in different parts of the village as we drew out thereof. 'Twill be many a long day I doubt not, ere I again shall see these friends, though the pleasant memory goes with me.

The party of prisoners are in charge of Lieut. Quinan,[1] and a detachment of the 4th Artillery, U. S. A.,

---

1 William Russell Quinan, of Maryland, who had graduated from West Point the preceding June.

who appears to be a gentlemanly person. He and a young doctor, attached to the company, have shown a very friendly disposition toward me; and their treatment is so in contrast with the brutality of the Mongrels, that I can understand poor Paddy's remark, "Thank ye, Mr. Sheriff, really now, *'tis quoite a pleasure to be hanged by ye!"*

At Morganton Capt. Willoughby Avery, and W. F. McKesson boarded the train to call upon us, and the former whispered to never mind the weather. At Hickory, Maj. Jas. H. Foote (if I caught the name) a burly old gentleman came aboard, and talked very pleasantly. Carrow seeing that some attention was shown us, bustled in the car, and handed to Edgerton a 25 cent flask of bad whiskey saying, "Drink it up, Boys!" then turning to Foote, "I always treat my prisoners cleverly, so long as they behave." I turned away, and resumed my newspaper, not caring to seem to endorse the utterance, even by silence.

At Statesville quite a number of persons were upon the depot platform merely for gratification of their curiosity I suppose. I have no personal acquaintance in the town.

At Salisbury, we found a large assemblage, among whom were Capt. R. E. Wilson, A. H. Boyden, Luico Mitchell, and others, who came to the car window, and manifested much interest in us. Speedily the news spread and a vast crowd of negroes gathered around the cars, jabbering and cursing, until Lieut. Quinan, fearing some disturbance, ordered his men to fix bayonets, and drive back the "black cloud" o'erhanging us. The soldiers did not wait for second orders, but were using their points in an instant making the darkeys run like sheep. Strange that the Regular Army, while antagonistic to the negroes, and only too glad of an opportunity to show their antipathy, allow themselves to be used as the facile tools for trampling upon the Caucasian, and holding him subject to the African!

After an hour's delay at Salisbury, we took the North Carolina train, and are now within a couple of hours ride from Raleigh;—very weary, and depressed, I need hardly say. At Greensboro there were hundreds of people upon the depot platform, and among them dozens, if not scores, of members of the Order; judging by the constant signals given me. It would have been easy to raise a cry, a row, a rescue; and as the night was very dark and the throng around the guards too dense for them to use their weapons, we could all have decamped. But I felt that we owed something to the leniency of the Federals, who had trusted largely to our sense of gratitude (allowing me to move about the car as I saw fit), and, indeed, after suffering all the indignities and hardships my enemies could invent, I would not now run away even if the doors were thrown open.

To show the feeling at Greensboro, one of the Federal lieutenants in stepping down from the cars shoved against one of the bystanders who instantly whipt out a revolver and cursed the officer in violent language—much to the amusement of the crowd.

September 10th. For two of the longest, dreariest weeks of my existence, I have made no entry in my journal; humiliation and sorrow become mute when they pre-dominate in the mind over all other feelings. Besides I could not write coherently until the freshness of our experiences here were dulled by constant usage. Let me now briefly state that we arrived in Raleigh at 2 o'clock A. M. on the 29th of August, and were marched to jail, which is directly behind the Court House, on Fayetteville Street, opposite the Yarborough Hotel. The building is of brick, two stories, surrounded by a high plank fence; its dirty walls, and rusty barred windows giving to the general appearance a repulsiveness perceptible even at night. The jail, both as to its exterior and interior, is a disgrace to the Capital of the State.

For some reason we were conducted through the jailer's apartment, up-stairs, and through a small trap door (3 feet square) into the narrow corridor of the prison proper, very much as persons climb into the aperture of a cave before descending to its shadowy depths.

Our party was now sixteen in number, having been re-
cruited by nine others at Marion, and the entire 16 were
crowded into a small dark room, less than sixteen feet
square, if I can judge aright. When all the prisoners
are stretched upon the floor there is no room to step
between sleepers, and the crowding is suggestive of sheep
huddled under a shelter in stormy weather. But I
would endure even closer packing if the place were rea-
sonably cleansed. No one who has never seen the interior of an ante-bellum negro-jail can have any conception of this "Black-Hole." I did not dream that such
places were in existence, as I have discovered in Rutherfordton, Marion, and in Raleigh. This room has recently been occupied by negro vagabonds, whose slovenliness still disfigures the floors and window ledges. The
walls are battered and stained, and, where the plastering
is not peeled off, it is frescoed with obscene charcoal
sketches; the two small windows, are without glass, but
heavily latticed with rusty bars of iron, with a sheet-iron
hood overhanging them; the filth, stains, and accumulated tobacco quids of successive occupants line the
washboards all round the room; while a disgusting tub
in one sloppy corner (without even a screen, until I
stretched a blanket before it) adds not a little to the
nauseating squalor, and wretchedness of the interior.
Yet my annoyance from the crowding, the noise, the
stench, the vermin, of all kinds, (for there are flies and
fleas, mice and mosquitoes, lice and lizards, spiders and
chinches), and the dirty surroundings, is often forgotten in the depression arising from reflections relating
both to the *past,* and the future. Looking from the
narrow window this evening, noting the dismal per-
spective—a foreground of horse stables upon a horizon
of negro cabins, shoemaker shops, etc.—I recalled with
deep melancholy the changes in my situation since my
last visit to Raleigh, when I was constantly surrounded
by friends (the State Democratic Convention being in
session, and I being one of its Secretaries, as well as a
member of several important committees) ; and also, enjoyed myself in a social way going to ride, or to dine,
every evening of my stay. Alas! the intervening two

years and a half, were in many respects worse than thrown away. Better had they never been! And now, how many other years must be added to these lost ones to satiate the spitefulness of my scalawag foes!

I have suffered physically during the past fortnight more than any one, even my fellow-prisoners, could imagine. Long confinement rendered me very bilious, and the 200 miles of railroad travel, with changes of food and water, threw me into a condition of semi sea-sickness, which my too frequent resort to cheap, mean liquor—the only kind to be had—served to allay only for a brief period, succeeded by increased disorders. Pride upheld this silly course for several days after I came here, because I felt that if I succumbed, the daily visiting spies of the Mongrels would report me *broken down, and self-distressed,* as they did when I was sick at Rutherford. At length I could keep upon my feet no longer, and wrapping in my single blanket, crawled into the corner to make a pillow out of a pair of boots and stretched myself upon the rough uneven plank for a spell of sickness. Brother tried to obtain some medicine for me, but failed; the negro to whom he threw the money from the jail window never returned. He then asked Maguire to send for a physician, but was told that Dr. Jas. McKee held the post of county physician to attend prisoners in the jail. It was supposed the Doctor would be sent for, but it was not until some time after night (upon my second application) that Dr. McKee appeared, and prescribed some slight medicine; whether tonic or sedative, I am unable to say. But suffice it of this topic—I passed the two or three subsequent days and nights in utter wretchedness. While in this condition J. C. L. Harris, son of Ceburn and nephew of George Logan, came into the corridor, and talked through the bar-door with brother Addie, seemingly friendly disposed. He is the brother-in-law of Tim Lee, the sheriff of Wake, in whose keeping we are; therefore, might do much to alleviate our discomfort; but of course we do not expect it. I think he is naturally kind-hearted, but politics have been his bane.

Very much to our surprise we find in the last *Cleveland Banner,* the following:—

> Yesterday evening some of the ladies of Shelby
> came by our office soliciting contribution for the six
> prisoners who were taken in handcuffs from the
> Rutherfordton jail to Raleigh, and who are now
> there suffering the horrors of another loathsome
> prison. The ladies, we understand, collected fifty,
> or sixty, dollars for the six [seven] gentlemen. The
> true ladies of our country cannot remain inactive
> when they know that many of the prisoners have
> *been thrown into that dirty jail without even a
> hearing* on the side of justice! All Honor to you,
> noble ladies, you have in days past shown your
> tender sympathies for your suffering country; and
> although you may be insulted by fiends now, the
> day is not far distant when we shall be enjoying the
> sweets of liberty and good government.

The last remark I fear will prove to be merely the
wish fathering the thought; who the patriotic and
generous-hearted ladies were, who originated the movement above described, I know not, but their kindness will
never be forgotten. I confess it caused me a wince or
two, on first reading it, because it happens to be *the
bald fact* that such assistance will really come most opportunely and this very consciousness is a little galling
to one's sensitiveness. But all this quickly fades away
on reflecting that our noble friends were so thoughtful
of our comfort, and so fearless in manifesting their sympathy. I doubt if any other town in the South has ever
witnessed a parallel case, refined ladies taking the street
to solicit "aid and comfort" for men, who (except brother and I) were almost, if not altogether, total strangers to them, and who had been dragged 300 miles away
in irons like felons or slaves. "All honor to these noble
ladies of Shelby!"—say I, too; for, in truth, the gentler
sex alone seem to have the majority of spunk and manliness—or, let us say, *fearlessness of consequences*—now-
a-days! It may be that I am unduly suspicious, unduly
sensitive of slights; but assuredly there are very many
men whom I have known in other days, yea, men for

whom I have given my humble labors as an editor; who "pass by on the other side"—really, and figuratively—now that I have "fallen among thieves." There are dozens of men in town today—some of them within pistol shot of me at this moment—who have never even inquired for me at the jail door. There are scores of others who "swore to befriend"—to the "best of their ability"—every "brother in distress," yet, who never utter a word in condemnation of the outrages heaped upon my head, and, from all that I can learn, even join with the time-servers in saying with long visages, "Yes, this Ku Klux business was all wrong; Shotwell and his gang have acted recklessly—very badly. I really cannot apologize for him, he must have known better. I'm sorry for him but as a man makes his bed, so must he lie in it," etc., etc.

Ah me! I hope to God, such talk may not drive me into some "recklessness" sure enough!

Happily I am able to make numerous exceptions; there are many who feel no fear of the Grantizaries; and many kind ladies who do not forget the "sick, needy, and in prison." Dr. Geo. W. Blacknall of the Yarborough has been especially kind, a very "Prince of Good Fellows." Thrice already has he sent over a large waiter of edibles, with his compliments; and though addressed to me, the contents sufficed to give all my fellow-prisoners a share, much to our enjoyment. Dr. B. wrote a note with the viands as follows:—

> My Dear Sir: I send you dinner which you will please accept. Whatever success I have had in life is partly attributable to my editorial friends, and whenever in my power it gives me much pleasure to add to their comfort. Trusting you may soon be out, and with us, I am Sir, With High Regards,
> Yours very truly,
> G. W. B.

Considering the circumstances, this was very neatly done for the Doctor, and I shall hope one day to do him "a good turn." It was the more creditable in him from the fact that he knows perfectly well that I shall *not* "be out soon," and that not many will know of his kindness except among the Mongrels, some of whose patronage he may lose thereby.

Rev. Dr. Drury Lacy has also interested himself in our behalf (brother and I) and has twice called; once while I was sick and could not go down to the gate, and again when the keeper refused to give him admittance. I am told that several callers have been turned back in like manner; the object being to deprive us of even the consolation of feeling that we have a few staunch friends left!

By Dr. Lacy's influence probably, and the kind offices of young Brainard Whiting (a brother of the lamented Gen'l W. H. C. Whiting, and a most deserving young gentleman) who has himself brought the articles to the jail gate, we have received, either in tray, or basket, a liberal present of "Dinner," or "Supper," from those estimable families, Dr. Burwell, Col. C. C. Crow, the Misses McPheeters, Mrs. Prof. Kerr, Mrs. Dallas Haywood, and two "unknown friends." These good gifts of "goodies" for the "inner man" (sixteen samples of him!), though coming at intervals of several days; and, while plentiful *for two,* dividing into small shares; were nevertheless, so timely and useful, that I do not know how we should have gotten on without them; and I trust I never shall be so ungrateful as to forget those for the which we are indebted.

Our prison food thus far has been simply unendurable by any than an ostrich's stomach, which is said to digest nails, pebbles, and horse-shoes. For example, we receive at breakfast a small "chunk" of cornbread baked from sour corn-meal of the roughest quality. Frequently it is so soggy and sour as to seem mixed with *sooty-*water; and rarely is it *cooked.* This morning it was scarcely *warmed through;* consequently very repulsive to the taste. For meat, we are given a small slice of "rusty" bacon—with an unbearable odor and the white carcasses of "skippers" everywhere visible in it! The third, and last article, is a table-spoonful of half-boiled cow-peas! Once or twice these have been exchanged for white beans, which, if clean and *fully cooked* and supplied at more than two thimblesful per meal, might prove of some service. But the sour bread, rusty bacon, and half boiled cow-peas, are dished out on dirty, fire-blackened, and battered tin plates, which leak, and stain the floor, and inspire disgust at first sight. Yet this repulsive dish is all that we receive for either *dinner* or *breakfast*—these paltry meals, at nine A. M., and two P. M., being our allowance for 24 hours! Think of it! And think of the shame which attaches to men who can coop-up sixteen respectable citizens in one small room—filthy and stinking; at all times a torture to the hapless inmates—and then half-starve them upon food which a dog would turn aside from! We have prepared a statement to publish in the *Sentinel*. But I am loath to send it, because it will do no good, and will gratify my malicious enemies, while paining my friends. Besides, have I not resolved *not* to complain, no matter what happens?

By the way, I am glad to hear that the State papers are kindly copying my card, printed in the *Sentinel* last week. Mr. Shelman writes that it has appeared in the Greensboro *Patriot,* Salisbury *Watchman, Southern Home,* and *Cleveland Banner;* the last of which comments upon it in a bold-spoken, generous manner.*

Raleigh Jail, Sept. 4, 1871.

Messrs Editors Sentinel. In the Greensboro Republican of recent date I find an extract from the Asheville *Pioneer* as follows:

"Shotwell, ex-editor of the *Citizen,* is still in jail, and waiting for his friends outside to release him but in vain. Since Durham's testimony in Washington before the outrage committee, Shotwell has become despondent and declares now that he is chief of Rutherford county, and intends to expose the whole matter; that there are 400 members in Rutherford county, 800 in Cleveland, 200 in Henderson, 200 in McDowell, and that when he gave up his editorship and left Asheville there were 400

*The Card, and comments were as given above. I now (1878) regret the publication, because undignified, and too vehement. But it was written in great haste, under excitement, and indignation, wrought up by repeated and persistent slanders, and abuse, of a nature to damage me severely among strangers; not to speak of my feverish condition physically, I having just arisen from my hard couch in the corner for the first day in four or five. However I said nothing, but the truth, and Truth can spare some of the niceties and elegancies of rhetoric, when slanders are denounced.

organized K. K. in this (Buncombe) county, and
that he is ready to give names. Mr. Justice has evidence that proves beyond doubt that Shotwell was
in command of the klan on the night of the destruction of the *Star* office and the assault upon himself.
The authorities have now secured the names of
many of the prominent actors, and others are being
obtained daily. Operations have been commenced
in Cleveland county, when new developments are
looked for."

Similar misrepresentations have been made by
the Newbern *Republican* and other radical prints,
I have been informed.

Now, in reply, I have to say that there is not one
particle of truth in any of these statements. It is
false that I could not give bail; but my friends were
given to understand that I would not be admitted
to bail. It is false that I ever declared myself chief
of Rutherford county, and intended to expose the
whole matter; I have nothing to expose. It is false
that I said there were 400 Ku Klux in Rutherford;
so far as I know there never were half so many.
It is false that I ever made an estimate of the number of Ku Klux in Cleveland, Henderson, Buncombe and McDowell. So far as I know, there
never has been any organization in either of these
counties. While in Asheville I knew of no such
organization, nor do I believe there was any.

It is false that I was in command of the Klan
which made a martyr of the infamous Jim Justice
and committed the depredation on the *Star* office.
I have never gone in disguise, nor intentionally injured a human being except in lawful warfare.

In fine these malicious falsehoods are of a piece
with the incessant spewings of the radical press
during the recent campaign. Nor is it the first attempt to blacken my private character since my
arrest by the minions of the corrupt despot at
Washington. Every little cur whose antics I have
had occasion to rebuke while conducting a conserv-

ative newspaper, now hopes to yelp his note of defamation at a safe distance.

Prominent in the pack may be named the editor of the *Pioneer,* who, with customary veracity, announced a few weeks ago that I was in great tribulation and had made no less than *three attempts to commit suicide.* This absurd lie I never corrected, feeling confident that my friends would not permit me to be "killed off" in any such manner. Mr. Rollins ought to unite his paper with the Rutherford *Star,* whose editor, J. B. Carpenter, threatened to shoot me on sight, and forgot to do so. Perhaps between them they could get up a spark of courage and a ray of truth now and then.

But I beg the Logans, the Scoggins, the Carpenters, and the Rollins, and others of that ilk, not to solace themselves with my declining health, spirits or influence. They have seen me arrested, they have seen me confined in a cage with murderers and negroes, they have seen me handcuffed and carried away like a convict, and they may see me arraigned at the judicial bar, yet they have never seen nor shall see me on a level with them in the estimation of the good people of Rutherford county and North Carolina.

Respectfully,
Randolph A. Shotwell.

The *Sentinel,* editorially comments on my card, as follows:— "Card from Capt. R. A. Shotwell. We invite attention to the card of Captain Shotwell, to be found in today's paper. It is disgraceful to see the efforts of certain papers to prejudice the case of this gentleman. Guilty or innocent, he is entitled to a fair and unbiased verdict, and it is cowardly to assail him with his hands tied and he confined in a common jail."

The *Sentinel* also republished the editorial remarks from the *Cleveland Banner,* the Shelby paper:

Capt R. A. Shotwell

We would especially call the attention of our readers and the public to the card in this issue of this gentleman, who is now suffering the horrors and pangs of another filthy and loathsome dungeon, in Raleigh.

Though the infamous radical organs all over the state are, by their never ceasing lying, endeavoring to hurl their invectives upon him, while bound, riveted to a dirty jail; yet the manly voice from the prison door comes in thundering tones defying the infamous blood-hounds to the very last.

Capt. Shotwell, as editor of a conservative newspaper, spoke out freely in defense of law and justice exposing the rascality of the radical party, without asking any quarter from their infamous clique. They are now endeavoring to wreak their vengeance upon him, while debarred the privilege of defending himself from their hellish persecutions.

This noble man has shown himself to be a true lover of liberty and his country, but now lies quietly bound, waiting for justice to be done.

Shall the innocent always suffer? Justice may sleep but never dies.

Here is one outspoken editor. Genl. D. H. Hill, writing for his Charlotte *Home,* thus comments upon the letter which Sheriff J. Z. Falls, of Cleveland County addressed to "Governor" Tod R. Caldwell, the man whom Holden's impeachment gave an accidental authority as so-called Chief Magistrate of N. C. [Sept. 5th.]

This gentleman, a former Sheriff of Cleveland county, has written a letter to Gov. Caldwell, protesting against the indiscriminate arrests made by the donkey-king of Rutherford and stating that many innocent persons were fleeing to escape arrest, thereby leaving their families in a destitute condition. The Governor replies in a lengthy claptrap article, intended for the Northern market; but is careful to say not a word in regard to his duty to protect innocent parties. On the contrary, he claims that flight is an evidence of guilt and quotes what he calls an old proverb, "The *guilty* flee when no

man pursueth." We would remind the Governor
that an old Book, called the Bible, which his party
has ignored as completely as it has the Constitution
of the United States, gives a different version of
this old proverb: "The *wicked flee* when no man
pursueth." The difference between the Governor's
"old proverb" and the Bible truth is infinite—the
one referring to a specific sin and the other to general depravity, such as can only be properly illustrated by the Governor's . . .[1]

But it is not true that flight is an evidence of
guilt in the realm of the donkey-king. Gov. Caldwell knows that thirty-nine men were carried to
Raleigh last Summer in the midst of the crop season, upon the oath of Aaron Biggerstaff's daughter, the much-swearing Mary Ann. These men had
been arrested four or five times before and, in all,
lost some sixty days out of their crops. It now turns
out that only one of the thirty-nine had anything
to do with the offense with which they were charged
—the whipping of that old sinner Aaron. Of the
innocence of thirty-eight of them, even Logan himself is satisfied. Would it not have been better for
these 38 men to have fled and worked in some other
State for the maintenance of their families than
thus to have left them exposed to want and suffering? Does not the Governor know that the organ
of the donkey-king boasts that an *alibi* cannot protect anyone charged with ku-kluxism? Does he not
know that the best and purest man in the State can
be arrested upon the oath of any depraved white
or ignorant black? Suppose he does prove his innocence after being confined for weeks and months
in Logan's Black Hole, what redress of grievance
has he? What damages will these thirty-eight men
ever recover for loss of time, loss of property and
personal suffering? Does not Gov. Caldwell know
that the perjured scoundrels, who under Logan's
orders, are causing all this distress, are wholly irresponsible persons?

---

1 A line, or more, is missing here.

The manly letter of Sheriff Falls is answered by a quibble and a shuffle, a misrepresentation of facts, and a misquotation of scripture. As the Governor is in the Biblical department, we commend to him the following passage:

"When the wicked beareth rule, the people mourn."

When Judge Logan makes wholesale arrests and Gov. Caldwell encourages his crimes, the people may well mourn and innocent men may run off, as they have done by the hundred in Rutherford.

This is entirely true, but falls short of the full truth. Several men of those alluded to, and who were dragged *four different* times, to different courts,—the last being 260 miles distant—were actually absent from the State at the time they were sworn to be present at old man Biggerstaff's.

So, in the case of *Captain Caswell Camp,* of Polk County, a gentleman of recognized integrity and high character; he was arrested upon the "charge" of a worthless negro, was thrown into jail, and though he brought *seven* of his *negro* servants, all Radicals of course, to prove an *alibi,* he was placed under heavy bonds to attend Raleigh Court, and only finally escaped by paying large sums; which, with his counsel fees amounted to almost the value of a plantation. Capt. C. was utterly *innocent* of the accusations: but he happened to be possessed of more than the average amount of property, for that region; and as he knew well enough the Mongrels meant to plunder him he preferred to pay directly to them, and avoid the loss of time and liberty, which he must undergo if he should insist upon his rights.

Rev. Thos. J. Campbell, now in the same room with me, is another case. He was never upon a "Raid," nor in any way incurred the frown of the law, yet here he lies, caged like a felon, half-fed, maltreated, and kept from his duties as a Christian minister.

Rev. Berry Rollins, well known throughout Western N. C., was twice arrested, bound over to appear at Raleigh Court, put to great trouble, expense, and indignity, utterly without cause.

Old "Uncle" Wiley S. Walker, aged 70, the reader will remember, and how narrowly he escaped suffocation, for lack of water while in Rutherford jail. No one had the slightest idea that "Uncle Wiley" was "guilty" (even according to Tod-dy Caldwell's criterion), but he owned a comfortable property; hence the persecution.

Jonathan Whitesides, who sits at my elbow, as I write, is a grey-haired farmer, a gallant ex-Confederate who left a leg in the trenches around Petersburg, and this worthy man, whom every one respects, is accused with midnight raiding, galloping "26 miles to Marion," etc. Of course when I add that he is able to pay $300 or $500, for his release the motive of his arrest and incarceration becomes apparent.

Nathaniel Thorne's innocence did not shield him from arrest, from abuse, from incarceration in Rutherford "Black Hole," from a week of annoyance, harassment, and indignity!

Jas. H. Sweezy, aged 56, positively privately declares to me that he is innocent of the charge alleged against him; yet he was dragged from home, thrust into the "cage" with murderers and negroes, forbidden to see, or speak to his wife (except from the 3rd story windows) after she had ridden a dozen miles to bring him some tobacco and clothing, was handcuffed to a chain (with myself, *et al*), dragged to Raleigh (so far away that his witnesses cannot come, he fears) and will shortly learn—what the Mongrel friends of the governor mean to do with him.

My card soon found its way into most of the Conservative papers of the State, and was favorably commented on by many of my friends, who were not too much frightened to express their sentiments.

About this time the ladies of Shelby gave a very unexpected and practical token of their sympathy for the victims of mongrel malice; to wit, a purse of 65 or seventy dollars to be divided among the six, who were handcuffed at Rutherford. Who originated the movement I know not, but it is said that a committee of ladies collected the funds—which were conveyed to us by Capt. Durham.

I confess I could not but feel somewhat sensitive on the subject as it showed rather publicly the poverty of our pockets. But I consoled myself with the reflection that the ladies wished merely to testify in an unmistakable manner that they were in earnest in their contempt for our persecutors and in their sympathies for us. In this view of the matter, it was a source of comfort, and, to me at least, the funds were very acceptable.

Unfortunately such bold expressions were extremely rare. Hundreds of members of the Order, and personal acquaintances of mine, were in the city; men who had taken a solemn oath to *"aid and assist all Brethren in distress."* Yet few of them came, even to inquire how I got on!

I am too old, too philosophic, to rail at inconstancy of friends. But I cannot help feeling vexed and mortified by the neglect and avoidance I have experienced from the hour of my arrest by those who profess to be my friends. Of course they will be able to excuse themselves on prudential grounds. Yet had they stood by me unflinchingly, and boldly denounced the outrages perpetrated on me, it would have been better for all parties. Because, there is no question that the Mongrels were emboldened to trample on law and justice as they did, chiefly by the little opposition they encountered, and the base sycophancy of many men, who did not scruple to "bow the knee that thrift might follow favoring." Many respectable and intelligent men fairly courted the favor of every Mongrel "deputy-marshal" in order to make sure his escape from prosecution. This of course is in accordance with human nature; but we are obliged to dispise it nevertheless.

CHAPTER THIRTEENTH

Convicted and Sentenced

Not having the stenographic reports of my trial, I omit the few notes made at the time, until I shall have obtained the necessary data from the files of the Raleigh newspapers.[1]

WAITING FOR THE VERDICT

The long afternoon wore away: listeners as well as speakers were fatigued, mentally and physically, yet the dense assemblage showed no sign of scattering: each looker on held his position in unsatiated curiosity, or from grim resolution to see the worst—the climax—the verdict!

Such scenes are not uncommon in the civil courts on occasions of great criminal trials; but in the present instance the proceedings derived special interest aside from the circumstances of the case, from the peculiar surroundings of the Court: the handsomely furnished Senate Chamber, with galleries and lobby crowded to their utmost, the Judges seated under the damask canopy of the speaker's dias, the clerks and reporters below, the lawyers occupying the desks of Senators—all served to recall the spectacle of a fashionable theatre with a tragic court scene upon the boards. Alas! 'Twas both *farce* and *tragedy* accompanied by all the usual features of bribery, treachery, villainy, and arbitrary injustice, except that the *denouement* failed to unmask and punish the traitor and the false Judge, as it should!

The prisoners, as heretofore, were hemmed in, in the corridor behind the Speaker's desk, by ropes drawn from the pillars to the walls; and guarded by half a dozen Mongrel marshal's deputies. They were the objects of constant observation and remark by the multitude; —often to *my* great mortification, as my companions were men of little education, less culture, and of the humbler walk of life, even in their own mountain region;

---

1 The Ku Klux trials are inadequately reported in Ho. Reports, 42 Cong., 2 Sess., No. 22, pt. 2, pp. 417-592.

hence many of my eastern friends, viewing me in apparent association, and jointly-accused, with them, (tho' I had never spoken to one of them previous to my imprisonment!) very naturally assumed that intemperance and recklessness had lowered me in every respect. It was foolish for one in my situation to be worried by such trifles, but the experience of all prisoners—at least those wrongfully confined—shows that these apparent trifles of ordinary life, are real grievances "behind the bars."

On the right of the Judge sat our counsel, Ex-Gov. Thomas Bragg, looking very infirm and feeble; Col. Geo. V. Strong, fresh and ruddy; ex-Judge Daniel G. Fowle, easy and yet watchful, Col. T. C. Fuller, busily writing, Capt. Plato Durham, serious and angry, Jos. L. Carson, ponderous and tired: Geo. M. Whiteside, *et als*.

On the opposite side of the Chamber, around a little stand, grouped "Jim" Justice, prosecutor, Virgil S. Lusk, Government Attorney, Samuel F. Phillips, guilty looking, Mark L. Erwin, rather "spirit"-ous, and Gov. Tod R. Caldwell, who scowled at me, as if gloating over the fact that I was soon to become a "convict."

It was one of the coincidences of life that all save one of these men who had so strenuously exerted their talents to send me to the Penitentiary were persons whom I regarded as deadly enemies.

Lusk, had grossly assailed me in the public prints because of my defence of certain unoffending citizens of Madison County—strangers to me personally. I caned him severely in the public street of Asheville, and he, being armed and prepared, slightly wounded me in two places.

Caldwell, I had convicted in my paper of promising to obtain a pardon for Col. Gaither, and others of his Morganton neighbors, and actually showing them a letter to Congress, asking the removal of their disabilities, while at the same time, mailing a *secret* letter (which Senator Nye very blunderingly read in the Senate) declaring that they were arrant Rebels, and ought not to be pardoned on any conditions. Gov. C. never forgave me for the exposure, and my indignant comments on his conduct. Consequently throughout the trial, he was an ever present "abettor," if not an "aide" to the pack of my unscrupulous pursuers.

Justice, I had repeatedly flayed in my paper, and never treated otherwise than as a Mongrel of the lowest order! Besides he was attempting to wrong me; and a man always *hates* him whom he has wronged, or tried to wrong.

Erwin I had more than once censured for his political turn coatism, and he, too, felt that he was conspiring against an innocent man.

I have said that all, save one, were enemies: perhaps I ought not to except Sam Phillips—for while he knew nothing of me personally, he had winced severely under the plain-speaking of my counsel, and was now enlisted against me, not alone by his big fee, but in hatred and malice. This will more clearly appear hereafter, in Addie's case.

Three of the Government's counsel against me, I have not mentioned; their names will suffice: Judge Hugh L. Bond, occupied the Bench: Judge George W. Brooks, though not of the Circuit Court,[1] sat by Bond to give him countenance (if that be not absurd in connection with a *face of brass!*) and the third, Attorney-General of the United States, Amos T. Akerman (like Phillips, a renegade Southerner) alternated between Judge Bond on the Bench and Judge Bond in his private room, spending three days in Raleigh to make sure that there should be no failure to carry out the plot! Worthy spectacle! a National Cabinet-Minister, leaving the Capital to come to a distant state, and cast all the power and influence of the government against a number of humble citizens on trial for their lives! Does any one believe that zeal for the good of the state actuated this trip! The purpose, and its success, was shown in the Presidential election a few months later. A thousand indications, and subsequent revelations, now establish the fact that the whole course of the Grant Administration in the North Carolina "Ku Klux trials," so-called, was the carrying out of careful plans for capturing the electoral

---

1 This is, of course, an error.

votes of the State, and other Southern states, without any regard for the ends of justice, or the rights of individuals.

But let us return to the court-room: Time has dragged upon leaden wings, and the jury are still "out" making a pretense of deliberating. It would not look well to return suddenly, as if the verdict were already written out when they retired. So the red sun crept down in the west, leaving a crimson flush dyeing the walls and bringing into relief the picture of Washington, directly behind and over, the group of government attorneys. The old patriot might well look sadly at them! At length, the gas was lit, and the crowd, which had thinned somewhat at supper-time became reinforced by stragglers from the streets attracted by the brilliant windows of the Capitol. For all the jam, it was noticeable that there was little noise, no loud talking, and the scarcely audible hum of many voices was in that subdued tone used at funerals, or in the presence of a great tragedy. The clock points to half-past nine: the Judges resume their seats: the door of the jury room opens, and a straggling line of guilty looking jurors—the darkeys at the rear—files into court. Indignant glances shoot at them from all sides, for every one knows what will be their verdict. They would not be where they are, for any other purpose than to execute the orders of their masters and *payer*, by bringing in a so-called verdict of Guilty!

THE VERDICT

"We find," quoth foreman Manliff,[1] "the following persons *not Guilty* (quite generous!—as there was not one bit of evidence against them!) Frederick Addison Shotwell, Calvin Teal, and Wm. Tanner. We find the following persons *Guilty:* Randolph A. Shotwell, Adolphus DePriest, Wm. McIntyre, George Holland, Amos Owens, David Collins, Wm. Teal, and Wm. Scruggs."

Two of the prisoners included in the count, S. K. Moore, and Doc. B. Fortune, were seduced into pleading *guilty* early in the trial, on promise of light sentence.

---

1 Manliff Jarrell, a Guilford County distiller, was foreman of the grand jury not of the trial jury.

My brother's counsel now arose, and asked in the usual
forms that he, and the two other men acquitted, should
be discharged from custody. Bond began to give the
necessary order—"The marshall will release the pris"—
when Sam Phillips, jumping up, very red-faced and
angry—bellowed—"Not so! your Honor; *we have other
charges against him!*" The Judge looked surprised, as
if wondering what new scheme his confederate had in
view; but ordered my poor brother once more back to
the filthy Raleigh jail. I will here remark, par paren-
theses, that I do not believe Phillips had any other
charge against Addie; but knowing the sentence soon
to be imposed on me, he hoped that its severity would
cause many poor devils to try to save themselves by
manufacturing evidence against their neighbors, and
that in the meshes of this net, Addie might be taken. He
was accordingly remanded to jail—held for nearly two
weeks—and *then*—discharged, *informally* without the
promised "other charges" ever appearing outside of
Sam Phillips' malicious head.

Intense silence for one minute followed these proceedings; then a murmur of suppressed indignation,
with an occasional hiss, ran around the lobbies: yet it
was a shudder rather than a protest, for nearly one-third
of the audience were directly or indirectly interested in
the trial—being themselves members of the Secret Order, consequently liable to similar, or approximate, maltreatment.

A PETTY ATTEMPT TO HUMILIATE

When a portion of the multitude had vacated the
Senate Chamber, leaving the main aisle clear, U. S. Marshal Carrow waddled to a corner, where I had seen him
deposit a rope early in the evening, (showing that the
verdict of the jury was well known, and prepared for,
in advance) and calling me out, in front of the Speaker's stand, in full view of the crowded Chamber, *roughly
bound my arms behind my back,* like a slave tied for the
mart!

Let it be remembered that I had never signified in
word, or deed, the least intention to escape, the least
truculence or turbulance, nor had been in the least offen-

sive to my keepers, even while lying among the robbers, thieves, and red-handed murderers in Rutherford and McDowell county jails. Hence this humiliation was inflicted in sheer spite, to gratify the low malice of the Logans, Scoggins, Lusks, Caldwells, and Justices among Carrow's accomplices.

So *unnecessary* was this indignity that Capt. R. T. Bosher, one of Carrow's most trusted "deputies" (a former Yankee soldier, and *Captain in Kirk's cut throat gang!*) actually sprang forward to stop the tying of my wrists, saying, *"Marshall, don't tie Capt Shotwell, there's no need of it; I'll engage to take him safely back to jail!"**

Carrow took hold personally to superintend the tying and drew the ropes so tightly, that for three or four days my arms showed dark purple rings in the skin to mark the coils of the cord.

This last indignity overcame my self-control (as I had weakened that self-control by taking several drinks during the noon-recess, and was therefore dry and *nervous,* now) and I could not deny myself the pleasure of saying to Carrow, "You cowardly hound! Cannot your brigade of armed deputies guard a half-dozen half-starved men, without tying them till you cut the blood from their arms! Shame!"

NEW QUARTERS

Down from the Capital, down Fayetteville Street, past groups of curious citizens, and astonished ladies, the cavalcade of bound-slaves, all tied to the same rope, like a gang of galley slaves, going to work, returns to the jail; where we find new evidence that the court-officials were well-informed of the verdict before its delivery. For it appears that shortly after noon—*before my counsel had finished the defence,* the jailor cleared the "strong-room," or "condemned cell" to receive us, and had our baggage removed therein! Our new quarters were about 12 x 15 feet square— filthier than those we left—and far more uncomfortable as there was a thick wooden door outside the iron one, so that we could hold no communication with our fellows, and were without air or

---

*Capt. B. has since my release frequently assured me that he was disgusted with the whole proceeding; and acknowledges that it was done to humiliate me.

light save that from two small windows, scarcely large enough for a man to crawl through, and heavily barred, besides being overhung and shaded by a tin water-shoot. Of course, the interior was gloomy, damp, and oppressive in extreme.

Here, too, I was denied any intercourse with brother Addison, though I could well rejoice that he was exempt from the torments we endured. The gloom and depression of that night, and the following day need not be described. For weeks and months I had been certain that the end would be just this very thing, yet now that it was come, the blow fell heavily. Half my solicitude was on account of my poor old father for whom I feared— feared!!

Sept. 21. I arose early; shaved and dressed as neatly as my scanty wardrobe would permit: expecting to be called to the Court room to receive sentence. It was my determination if opportunity occurred to address the assemblage and calmly, plainly detail my connection with the Klan, and give full statement of its origin and objects; as well as an account of the malicious persecution which had followed me, and was still pursuing me, for political effect. In short, I meant to vindicate myself, before the bar of public opinion, if not of "Jeffreys" Bond's court.

Alas! I was not called out, and the suspense became intolerable. Some one bribed a guard to get us a quart of liquor—very *mean,* it was, too, and ere night we had finished it; and unhappily it finished us, as well. My system being charged, and surcharged, with bile, from long confinement and excessive drinking was now in a condition of real fever, and danger. Shortly after lying down at night, I found myself *deathly sick,* and slept no more that night. Every other moment a qualm of sickness caused me to retch violently: then a raging fever forced me to drink water, which almost instantly produced more retching.

This state of things left me exhausted and dizzy at daybreak; so that I could not hold my head off the pillow.

SENTENCED

On the 22nd day of September ('71) was witnessed the crowning act and outrage of the vile political drama —the Judicial farce—which was to send me to a far Northern prison to drag out six of the best years of my life, at hard labor, in the garb of a felon!

Daybreak found me as already stated, seriously ill: —so nervous, weak, and dizzy-headed as to be unable to stand alone. It is impossible to conceive of one more wretched! Breakfast was brought in at nine o'clock but the very sight of it caused me to vomit. A dirty-battered, tinplate, containing two table-spoonsful of half boiled "cow-peas," a slim slice of 'rusty' bacon, too 'strong-smelling for even the stomach of an ostrich;' and a small chunk, or piece, of sour, sun-dried corn-dodger, hard as cocoanut shell, *twice a day* (at 9 A. M. and 3 P. M.) constituted the only food furnished us by the great and good government, whose helpless captives we were! No negro in the town lived half so poorly. While the men were eating this stuff, Capt. Plato Durham came in and kneeled on my blankets to urge me to get up, and prepare to go to the Capitol. I assured him I was not able, and could I obtain medical counsel, would, doubtless, have a certificate to that effect. But on his representing to me that my enemies would sneer, and say that after all I feared to face the sentence, I managed to muster sufficient pride to sustain me; and when called, promptly answered; though in going up Fayetteville street I was obliged to hold to the arm of Capt. Bosher, and another deputy, guarding me, as I reeled like a drunken man. Ah! what would I not have given for a gill of strong brandy then to settle my system! Men who talk *temperance* as a general thing are ministers and others who never drank to excess, if at all; hence do not know the nature of the ailment they wish to cure: therefore nine times out of ten fail lamentably, because thereof.

The prisoners were marched into the room of the Senate enrolling clerk to await call. Here Col. Carrow made his appearance, and quite familiarly addressed some of the men, as if the verdict of his packed jury had reduced us to the level of his complacent consideration. I turned my back upon him, and gazed out of the window. Mention is made of this incident prefatory to subsequent occurrences.

BEFORE THE BAR

Court having been opened, after some delay, I was summoned to receive sentence. It was a moment long anticipated (since no one supposed that anything less would result from Mongrel malice) yet it had never occurred to me that I should be so utterly prostrate, physically, at so important a time: and God knows, I would have sacrificed my right arm to have been in ordinary strength and composure! But there could be no hesitating or delay; and I followed the Mongrel into the vast assemblage, which packed every inch of standing room in the Senate Chamber. Calling all the pride and resolution of my nature to sustain me, I stood in front of the multitude, gazing *generally* at the mass of heads not daring to distinguish between faces and persons lest some expression of pity should melt my firmness. The ordeal was long and trying: worse than repeated gazing into the photographer's *camera!* For besides the natural embarrassment of my situation, I was deeply agitated by thoughts of the mistaken ideas that would be drawn from my nervousness and pallor. My friends, themselves, would argue that I felt *guilty* from the very tremors, and trepidation; the absence of bold, calmness, etc., etc. Whereas the truth is, I hardly thought, or remembered, that I was a prisoner about to receive sentence, but was worried beyond description by the mortification of being misunderstood, caught in the toils of circumstances! Perspiration poured from my forehead, and in spite of all that I could do, my hands and limbs shook with feverish nervousness, and in my agony of consciousness that I was giving a false impression I would cheerfully have submitted to double the sentence provided it were delayed until I could come before the Court, strong, composed, "clothed and in my right mind." Many persons will not comprehend this sensitiveness on my part, because they do not know the nature of the situation as it affected me, at the time. It is probable I exaggerated my own sensations, as the newspaper reports spoke of our demeanor as being very "quiet and stolid, even to indifference." But no such description could apply to my *feelings,* whatever were my looks.

In making this somewhat lengthy statement of my feelings and condition at the time of receiving sentence, I wish to explain the reasons why I failed to say more in my own defence, when allowed to do so. It had been my plain design to boldly and frankly avow my connection with the "Invisible Empire," stating the circumstances which induced me to join it, explaining the objects and ends of the Order, that I had never taken part in any raids or lawlessness, nor ordered the same, that my so-called "Chief"-ship was purely nominal, I having not the least authority over the reckless young country boys who were most active in "night-riding," whipping, etc., all of which was outside of the intent and constitution of the Klan, (except in certain cases, under orders of the Grand Council) with much other matter that would not only be new to many of my friends but must put a new phase on the whole affair. This, I say, was my long-cherished purpose, alas! in my prostrated condition I could only curse my own folly at having crippled myself, body and mind; throwing away an opportunity for not only vindicating myself in the estimation of the decent people of the State, but also, rescuing the good name of all my fellow members of the Klan from unmerited reproach.

While awaiting the action of the Court, Judge Fowle came to me, and whispered "You will need to summon all your strength and philosophy: Bond has decided to give you the full penalty of the law, six years at hard labor!" "I suppose so; they have meant it from the first. He will make a stump speech, I understand?" said I. "Yes, it is too good an opportunity for Bond to miss, he feels meanly, and will talk accordingly," quoth the Judge.

As a number of the lawyers, and others, were watching these proceedings and heard my remark, Carrow made a pretence of loosening the ropes but in point of fact, drew them if anything tighter than before.

Men who have known Sam Carrow as a good neighbor, and generous friend, are loath to believe this, and other instances of malicious cruelty, I shall have to record against him. But there is nothing strange in it. When at Marion he kept seven of us confined in a putrid cage gasping, day and night, for *air* and *water,* he was surrounded by Mongrels, his "deputy marshals," and he tortured us for *their* benefit. Here at Raleigh he was surrounded by similar scoundrels, and again tortured us as a side-show for *their* benefit.

"It is strange," says Sir James Macintosh, in writing of the French Revolution, "how *uniformly,* when *oppression rules the hour,* the tyrant, *be he who he may,* on the throne, or the lowest turnkey of a prison, contrives, and seems to *study to contrive,* how to *make cruelty more cruel*—add insult to injury, and inflict *new torments* and annoyances on those who must be necessarily, *already wretched!"*

Mr. Assistant (hireling) U. S. District Attorney Phillips, now prays the formal "Judgment" of his confederate on the Bench upon Randolph A. Shotwell *et al.* And with a view to palliate the enormity of the sentence which he knows will immediately follow, he reads a long letter written in 1869, two years earlier, by Wm. P. Bynum, Solicitor of the Lincoln District, not embracing Rutherford, addressed to Wm. H. Holden, and reciting certain instances of whipping of vagabond negroes, frightening of negro women, etc., etc., all of which occurred previous to the date of the letter, and had no sort of connection with my trial. This same letter, be it remarked, furnished a part of the grounds upon which Holden maneuvered his "Kirk's Lambs" (cut throats) for which he was impeached, convicted, and run out of the State. To add to the villainy of the thing, Sam Phillips at the time the letter was written, and first published, was a prominent leader in the Democratic party, and denounced the falsity of the charges in the letter fully as strongly as myself. Yet now he produces it, and makes it a part of the record against

me, and others—already doomed. But my indignation
at this attempt to manufacture prejudice against me by
means of a letter written two years before, and relating
to a section wherewith I had no sort of connection, was
destined to give place speedily to an overwhelming
sense of *mortification* and *anguish* from a most unexpected source, and all the more bitter, because an utterly, needless, ill-founded, and gross error of one of
my own counsel!!

Col. T. C. Fuller, who had been very active in fighting Lusk, Phillips, & Co., on the constitutional features
of the law, came to me just as court was opened remarking that he thought of making an appeal to the
Court. I was so dazed, bewildered, and sick—my mind
seemed paralyzed, and I did not once catch his idea, or
supposed the "appeal" was some sort of a legal process.
I supposed he meant a private appeal to be made for
the prisoners collectively, on the ground that the Klan
was now disbanded, and made no objection, though the
next moment I began to wonder how he could approach
the Judge to ask leniency when he must have known
all the vile measures taken by the prosecution to obtain
their ends. Hence when the speaker mentioned my
name, and continued to beg for mercy for me, I could
not credit my ears. What, then, was my amazement,
mortification, shame, when he began by saying he would
not question the propriety of the prisoner's conviction
as the Jury had convicted on the evidence before them
(yet Col. Fuller knew that the jury was "packed," and
the evidence "false!"). The Ku Klux organization was
broken up, the court could fairly infer that no fresh
crimes had been committed since the Justice affair, and
as the law had been vindicated no good purpose could
now be subserved by severe punishment. "Shotwell was
a young man, respectably connected, the son of an aged,
poor Presbyterian Minister, whose heart had often bled
for the indiscretions and recklessness of his son in these
transactions. He appealed to the clemency of the Court
for the sake of the prisoner and the aged father, and
asked them to deal tenderly with the boy. He knew he
must be punished, but as the object of the prosecution

had been accomplished by the conviction he prayed for mercy! mercy!! mercy!!"

Had the waters of the Deluge suddenly arisen around my feet, I could not have been more shocked—overwhelmed—agonized than I was on hearing these words! I was fairly paralyzed; for, though I tried to turn, and deny the speaker, my limbs seemed spell-bound, and voice deserted me. I could only glare at the Judge in dumb horror. Here was one of my own counsel, completely conceding all that I denied with scorn—completely giving up my defence—giving away my good name and reputation—vindicating all that had been done against me by my mortal enemies—accepting all as a righteous verdict of an impartial tribunal!! A thousand times during my long imprisonment I wept tears of bitterness over this most unkindest cut of all (though not unkindly meant!), the heaviest blow that yet had fallen upon my luckless head!

In the first place it was not true that my poor old father had ever grieved over my "indiscretions and recklessness in these transactions," for he, without knowing whether I had, or had not, a connection with the Secret Society of the Klan, often conversed with me, at table, or elsewhere, upon the impolicy, wickedness and lawlessness of the "raids" frequently occurring throughout the South, and we perfectly agreed that they should be suppressed as they could not result otherwise than unfortunately for our whole section. I say we were of one mind in regard to this whole subject, and I repeatedly assured him that so far as my influence went, I should exert it in accordance therewith. My father doubtless mourned at times over my intemperance; but he knew that I, drunk or sober, was a gentleman, and would not be guilty of galloping over the county at night in a red gown, horns, and tail! Col. Fuller, I assume, was misled and purposely, by a couple of pettifogging lawyers, of the up-country, who secretly hated me, wished me out of the way—and were recently angered against me by the free comments I never failed to make on their pusilanimity, and meanness in refusing their legal services, without tremendous fees *in advance* to poor fellows,

confined in jail, and without a dollar in their pockets.
I assume that they misled the Colonel, because he did
not know my father—his circumstances or anything
about him.

The appeal was a fine specimen of legal rhetoric—
very touching, and all that: it brought tears to many
eyes, and made Col. F. quite a reputation. But how
Judge Bond, and Caldwell and Lusk and Justice, and
the whole posse of Mongrels must have chuckled for
joy, at the virtual surrender of the case, and admission
that their charges, and lawless procedure was—*Right!*

My God! the recollection cuts me to the heart even
unto this day!

Why did I not then and there repudiate the appeal?
I was barely able to stand, my brain whirling, a thous-
and eyes staring at me, and a feeling of utter despair
creeping over my soul! It seemed as if all nature was
turning against me, and 'twere useless to struggle!

Col. Fuller's startling words were still ringing in my
ears, when Bond turned to Judge G. W. Brooks, of the
U. S. District Court, sitting with him on the Bench (a
voluntary participant in these infamous trials) and requested him to deliver the Judicial charge before sentence. Brooks began to read from a paper (showing
that everything in this business was cut-and-dried) of
which the following are a few of the salient points:

"That bad men should now be found to violate the
law, and even conspire together to violate the law, not
only by attacking the *most sacred rights of their fellow
men* [!] but their lives also. Not only so, but even more,
that men should be found to attack in this way, not only
those around them, and not content with that should
attack posterity by *treasonable acts with a view to destroy a government which had never punished* but *protected* them [the miserable old liar knew that there was
not one word of truth in all this, as even the suborned
government witnesses admitted that each member of
the Klan was *sworn* to "*uphold and defend the Constitution of the United States!*"] is not a matter of so much
surprise; for in looking into history, we find that at all

times there have been those who would committ such crimes. . . .

"That this association should have existed so long, and have drawn into its folds, so many men in any part of our State, is, we say without hesitation, the most damning blot upon the character of our State that history records. This association has not, so far as the Court can discover from the evidence the merit or excuse that vigilant committees ordinarily have" (what a lie!) "The purpose as stated by a majority of the witnesses" [bought and paid for] *"was not to punish crime* (!), or any acts forbidden by law [this was precisely what it was for!] but in the language of the witnesses [bought and paid for!] who were members of the organization, to 'put down the *radical* party and raise up the Democratic or Conservative Party.'. . .

"We do not entertain a doubt as to the validity of the 14th and 15th Amendments of the Constitution; and these being valid, then as to the Act of July 31st, 1870, and the 20th of April 1871—they also are valid. These laws oppress no one but are only so framed as to secure those from being oppressed, whom the more powerful and lawless [we may add the evil-disposed] may attempt to oppress."

Probably no Judge, making a deliberate utterance from the Bench ever was guilty of so false, malicious, spiteful, and utterly wicked an attempt to manufacture evidence to misrepresent and defame his fellow citizens, quote: "A peculiar feature, *clearly* developed by the evidence in this case is the cool and deliberate manner in which each individual member of the Society goes to work to execute, even in the most cruel and inhuman way, the orders of the chiefs, or committees of the Dens or clans by *torturing,* and even *taking the life of a fellow being* for no higher crime than the exercise of a privilege guaranteed to him by the constitution and laws of our common country: that is to vote for and advocate the election to office of any they may prefer and for reasons satisfactory to themselves."

Now Judge G. W. Brooks in assenting that the "evidence clearly developed" that "each individual member

goes about" "taking the life," or "torturing" any man or
men "clearly developed" the infamy of his own mind.
The evidence, false and suborned as it was, did not show
that any life had ever been taken by the order or any
of its members. It did not show that any man had ever
been molested for his political [opinions?]. One or two
instances were sworn to (falsely I am sure) where men
were cursed as "Radicals" just as men in anger might
say the "Damned Democratic thief" the politics of the
rascal being merely secondary to his theft. The truth is,
in the South since the advent of Brooks' party the difference between Radicalism is so imperceptible that to
denounce a rogue as a Radical is about equivalent to
calling him a rascal. But whatever may have been the
operations of the Klan in other regions, there was none
even of the shameless "pukes" who did Brooks' and
Bond's bidding that dared to swear the object of the
Klan was to punish men for their political opinions, or
that any man ever was molested solely on account of
politics. Brooks, therefore, *lied* and disgraced the Bench
by seeking to twist the false testimony more falsely to
make the northern people think the Klan was an organization to maltreat Republicans.

A BRUTAL ATTACK ON AN OLD MAN

I have said that the appeal for mercy gave this scoundrel an opportunity to insult me, and my aged father.
Here is a specimen of his insolence:

"In most respects it was cowardly, base and devilish.
And especially does it seem to have been so on the part
of the elder Shotwell, who seemed to be anxious to prepare himself to establish his innocence [alluding to my
published letter denying *in toto* the vile accusations of
the Mongrels] when in fact he was perhaps the most
prominent and active of the conspirators, and now for
him mercy is asked. If some good spirit hovering
round, *or a pious old father,* had whispered in his ear
the language of the poet—

Lord, that mercy I to others show
That mercy show to me—

it may be that he would not so cooly have entered into
the conspiracy for taking the life of a fellow being for

such an offence. Had he been admonished and still conspired then he was indeed as one lost."

In my statement of the testimony, and of my own connection with the Klan I have shown how utterly false and unjust were these imputations, specifically and general. But neither Bond, nor Brooks in the conduct of these trials showed the least regard for decency, justice, nor truth. Brooks continued, "The prisoners complain that the jurors were not Democrats. They would probably have complained of any who were not conspirators like themselves."

Here is another lie. The prisoners did not complain that the jurors were not Democrats. The honest portion of the community *did* complain at the shame and scandal of *first,* discharging the regularly paneled jury because it would not suit the government purposes; and *second,* selecting a jury composed *entirely of Radicals,* and not content with Radicals, adding two negroes, members of a race taught to regard the Klan as the opponent and suppresser of their own Leagues. Besides the marshal *confessed he consulted the prosecuting attorney* as to the men he should draw! Think of a public prosecutor selecting the jury to try cases, and picking men of his own party to try men accused of maltreating members of their party! But Brooks must go farther and fling venom on my poor brother Addison whom the jury had acquitted because there was not one among the depraved "Pukes" who dared swear he even belonged to the Klan. I say it with the testimony before me—there was not a word implicating him in any manner. Yet this disgrace to the Bench says, "If any doubt of the honesty of the jurors exists it should be dispelled after the acquittal of three of the parties against *all of whom* there was evidence of such a character as renders it questionable whether they should not have found them guilty also." What right had the old scoundrel to reflect on gentlemen whose little finger contains more honesty than his whole carcass!

Brooks closed by a gratuitous fling at my counsel composed of such men as Judge Fowle, Gov. Bragg, Geo. V. Strong, F. C. Fuller, and others. Truly it was a "stump-speech" from the Bench, disgraceful alike to the speaker, and the government which employed him.

SENTENCED

At the conclusion of Brook's harangue, Bond ordered me to stand up, and state anything I might have to say in mitigation of punishment.

Nervous and sick, I felt utterly unable to go into the statement I intended to make. Indeed it seemed useless; the tide ran so strongly against me that for the moment I lost the clearness to see I ought to speak for the benefit of my friends, no matter if it made no impression on the judges. Perhaps I should have made the attempt, physically weak and shaken as I was, had not Col. Fuller's cruel error so stunned and overwhelmed me. Naturally sensitive, and easily wounded, I had been for weeks in a state of deep humiliation and despondency at the abandonment of my acquaintances and so-called friends. Only a very few persons had paid me the least attention during the month I lay in the filthy prison though at the Yarborough Hotel, directly across the street were scores every morning and evening whose faces I recognized, and for whom I had worked as editor of the party papers at New Bern, Asheville and Rutherford. Again I had noticed that those friends, who had sent little delicacies of food etc., before the trial instantly ceased thereafter as if accepting the verdict of a packed jury and crediting the lies of low-born scoundrels who were forced to forswear themselves by threats of the Penitentiary on the one hand and seduced by bribes and promises on the other.

All these things gained weight and significance from the excessively bilious condition of my system which as is well known tends to give one depressed and gloomy views even where all personal affairs are in good trim. Hence instead of a lengthy vindication of myself and a refutation of the slanderous stories respecting the plans and purposes of the Klan, I simply exclaimed, looking the Judges in the eyes, "The testimony against me in many particulars has been utterly false; in some *ridiculously* false!"

Bond then said that, as a man of intelligence and a leader in the organizations, he regarded me as the most guilty of all, and would suffer no mitigation in my case. (He need not have stated it, for every one knew the government would not go such lengths to convict, if it had not determined to impose the full penalty of the unjust and unconstitutional law passed by the fanatics in congress for the very purpose.)

Sentence: "That the prisoner be imprisoned with hard labor for the term of six years, and pay a fine of five thousand dollars!"

A rustle, and murmur, of indignation, or approbation according to the politics of the spectator, ran around the crowded lobbies, on the announcement of the sentence but there was no outbreak of disgust and abhorrence as there would have been had not the reign of terror reached even to Raleigh, and the clutches of despotism rested upon these people, who once were wont to boast of being freeborn and inheritors of free speech!

"Remove the prisoner!" cried Bond, whose guilty eyes seemed to quiver under my steady, contempuous gaze. At this I gave him an ironical bow, and followed "Deputy" Scoggins into the small committee room on the right of the Judge's Bench. As we entered I said, "Will you please get me a glass of water, I am very sick?"

"No!, you shan't have any favors here," growled a rough voice behind me, and as I recognised Carrow, the U. S. Marshal, he added—"You think you're mighty big; wouldn't speak to me this morning; I'll know how to treat you hereafter." "Sir," said I, "Wait till I ask you for anything before you refuse me, I desire no favor at your hands."

However, after he had left the room, Scoggins had the decency to go and fetch a pitcher of water—the first and only kindness I ever had or wished for, from him. Subsequently, thinking of this episode I recalled the passage in Shakespeare

"Par—Sir, you give me most egregious indignity
Laf—Aye—*with all my heart,* and *thou art worthy
of it!*"

Amos Owens was next called, and given the same
sentence as myself.   Mr. Strong urged leniency in his
case as he was a middle aged man, in the humblest walks
of life, and, had seven or eight children dependent on
him.   He might have added that Amos could neither
read nor write—and actually took no part in the raid of
which he was convicted, though perhaps a participator
in others.

David Collins followed.   The shameful story of this
old man's arrest, after having fed and entertained his
captors, their enticing him away from home on pretence of showing them the road, their carrying him
away 40 miles to Rutherford in another state, leaving
his aged wife sick in bed without a soul to wait upon
her, his subsequent transfer to Raleigh 250 miles from
home, where he was dragged to trial without counsel,
friends, witnesses, or money, or education to teach him
how to make his own defence, his conviction notwithstanding that the only evidence against him showed
that a party of wild men, one night, forced him by
threats of a whipping, to let them take his mule and
shotgun to go on a raid; notwithstanding all this, I say,
Bond sentenced him to four years at hard labor and
$500 fine!

Collins, uneducated as he was, half crying, and bent
with the weight of 64 years, retained self-possession to
declare (truthfully) that he was not guilty, that he was
not in the raid, that he loaned his mule and gun because
he could not help it, and did not know to what purpose
they were to be put, etc., and he would not have justice
if punished.   How Bond must have *grinned* internally
at this!   Externally he frowned, and said angrily,
"Well you belonged to a den that has run every decent
man out of Spartanburg, and I'll not mitigate your
case." What a villainous liar he was can be testified
in Spartanburg today, where as everybody knows not
one single "decent man" was raided out, except when
Bond's master sent his Hessians to drive innocent men

into exile to escape lawless punishment such as he was now inflicting on Collins.

Wm. Scruggs aged 47, resident of Spartanburg—cannot read or write—said he didn't feel guilty but was sentenced to 3 years at hard labor and $500 fine.

Adolphus DePriest, aged 19 had nothing to do with the raid; though he had expressed a willingness to go with his neighbors had he been able to procure a horse. I have heard men who were on the raid swear that *he was not.* Yet he was sentenced to 2 years at hard labor, and $500 fine. (He died from the effects of imprisonment in the cold Northern Penitentiary.)

J. W. McIntyre, aged 21, can read and write, farm laborer, was sentenced to 2 years and $500.

George Holland, aged 23, can read and write, married with family dependent on him. Bond remarked that as it appeared from the evidence that he had not been on the raid he should sentence him to *only two* years at hard labor, and $500 fine! *Only two years!*

Wm. Teal, aged 25, ignorant, married, with two children dependent on him. This man was seduced by the Mongrels to turn state's evidence and forswear himself to assist in convicting some of his own acquaintance and neighbors. But he made the mistake of refusing to swear to some of the more palpable lies, and the Mongrels after *using* him, brought in a new charge and upon this he was now sentenced to 3 years at hard labor and $500 fine. He died in prison as will be hereafter stated.

D. B. Fortune, 24 years, after swearing to me privately that he knew nothing of the raid, became a "Puke," and made terms for himself. Though he confessed to being on the raid upon Justice, Bond permitted him to go with a sentence of *six months* in his own *county jail!*

Spencer R. Moore, one of the most active of the raiders, (Men have assured me that Fortune and Moore were the most troublesome and lawless of all the marauders in their settlement) also confessed or "Puked," and received the same mild sentence—six months incarceration at home, where they lived at ease, comfort, and

plenty, and even walked about on parole! Let it be remarked that these fellows, like many others, who were
similary excused, *confessed* to active participation in the
lawlessness, of which myself and others were not only
innocent, but had labored to suppress;—confessed I
repeat, and simply because they confessed, were let off
with a comparatively trivial sentence. Is it necessary
to add the explanation of this action of the government
or the Mongrels, for the Mongrels managed the government side of the trials? The design was to induce others
to confess; the guilty telling all they knew, and the innocent, *manufacturing* testimony against others equally
innocent, to purchase immunity from dreadful Penitentiary! Alas! as time rolls on, men who were not
spectators of this wonderful crusade, will deem it *impossible* that American citizens could be driven to such
conduct, or yield to fear so abject. But the fact that
I write this four years after the occurence, while many
spectators and participants are living is enough to convince my readers of its truthfulness. Now it may be
said the government had a right to show clemency to
those who humbly confessed their sins, and expressed
penitence therefore. But the government had no color
of justice in bribing men to forswear themselves. That
this was the intent of Bond, and the prosecution will be
fully shown hereafter, if it be not already establishhed
by the acts of the government "deputies." Knowing
that the ignorant mountaineers are fondly attached
to their homes, and look with mortal terror on any such
thing as a long imprisonment in a distant Penitentiary,
Bond imposed the full weight of an arbitrary law upon
me, and others while at the same time, letting off those
who confessed with a merely nominal punishment.
Hence every one of the accused (there were thousands
of them) had the choice of telling, or making up to tell,
a specious tale implicating as many new men as possible
(for the government would not excuse any one unless he
swore against some one not criminated by other
"Pukes") as the means of escape, or of standing firm,
and being dragged off to Albany, leaving wife and little
ones to starve, and perchance dying afar in the icy cell!

What wonder that so many succumbed, and with sinking hearts and bowed heads took upon their souls the stain of perjury and treachery to their friends! Jeffreys, in his "Bloody Assize" adopted the same method, and actually caused hundreds of innocent men to *criminate themselves* as the only way to escape death! If they confessed or "Puked" the Monster might simply *imprison* but if they proclaimed their innocence he caused them to be convicted, and death followed next day.

The succeeding days were full of mournful misery. The situation was particularly irksome to me. The entire party of nine adults were locked in the one small room, of which about a third was rendered unserviceable, by leakage from the slop-tub, not *improved* by copious distribution of lime and carbolic acid. Hence there was no space for those who were restless, and no quiet, or seclusion for those who, like myself, would gladly have sought to cheat misery with sleep. In the morning, and at meal hour, all were astir, but, there being nothing attractive in the view from the two small windows, with their sickening pools of tobacco spittle and other filth outside the rusty grating, and the chill wind whistling through the unglazed sashes, it generally happened that one by one the entire party went to bed. How I envied those who, like Scruggs and Collins, could neither read nor write, therefore felt no deprivation of intellectual occupation or amusement; and were free of the mental harassment, the vividness of imagination, that *would not,* and *could not be made* to lay aside its pencillings of the sombre future, and cease to fill my soul with horrible forebodings! To them the seriousness of our situation was mainly its personal discomfort, its separation from friends, its prospect of physical suffering. To which must be added, also, the sense of bitter wrong, and grievous injustice done to us, and which all felt in some degree varying with the intelligence of the individual.

Remembering that I had gone forth, in the morning, so weak and sick as to be forced to lean upon the arm of one of my keepers, it can be conceived how utterly prostrate I became on returning to the fetid atmosphere of the "Dark Room" after all the day—Judge Brooks' stump-speech abuse, and Bond's malicious sentence! I was really in sore need of medical treatment, but after having twice asked for a physician; and with my mind deeply wrought up by all the wrong that day done to me, and mine; I preferred death itself to any further requests of my captors. It is proper to say I do not know who was to blame for my failure to obtain medical attention. It may have been the negligence of the physician, or he may not have been notified by the jailer. Many of our requests were quietly ignored by the latter, who rarely failed to promise, but often to perform. The succeeding one or two days are a blank in my memory, and my note-book as well; our little party were closely "cribbed" in the "Dark Room" getting light and air from two small windows only, and they darkened by tin sheeting hoods, on the exterior; so that the wonder is we were not all prostrated by fevers. Some days later Maguire consented to leave open the heavy plank door between the room and the Hall, giving us more ventilation, and permitting conversation with our fellow prisoners in the other room, who were allowed the privilege of the Hall, and small yard around the jail. After 4 P. M. the wooden door was shut upon the iron-lattice one, leaving us to half suffocate until 8 A. M. next day.

It had been supposed we should be sent immediately to Albany, but as day on day elapsed it appeared the authorities were awaiting the issue of Capt Plato Durham's case, expecting to augment our convoy with a number of other well known Democrats thereby increasing the effect on the Northern mind.

My indisposition was much relieved by the contents of a large basket most unexpectedly received by me from the young wife of one of the best-known Republican State officials in the city; a daughter of another office-holder, who was the most decent of our carpet-baggers in North Carolina. I had little acquaintance with her, but happened one night in 1867 to be called by her in mortal terror to capture a negro who had broken into the room in which she, her sister, nurse and child slept.

I of course seized the robber, and delivered him over to the hotel watchman, whereupon the ladies were quite profuse in their expressions of thankfulness. I thought no more of the circumstance until now came this token of kind remembrance; bottles of champagne, a large chicken pastry, and other delicacies, most palatable, and very nourishing. A dainty note in a dainty napkin was full of womanly sympathy "To sympathize with you is futile—useless! Keep up. Don't allow yourself to become discouraged, or despondent: it will kill you! I am glad you look upon your sentence in the light you appear to do. You are young and be thankful! You have health, and can endure any punishment those dogs of Judges (pardon the language!) may put upon you. Let me know if there is anything whatever I can do to add to your comfort."

Alas! Poor woman, she had faults, but within a year after this note she sacrificed her life for others.

An editorial in the Daily *Sentinel* commenting upon the trial, etc., says:—

> The liberty of the citizen is well nigh if not altogether gone when he is arrested, ironed, imprisoned, and transported 300 miles for trial, especially if he is a poor man and not able to pay his witnesses to follow him to his uncertain place of trial. Three of the defendants [These were Bro. Addie, Wm. Tanner, and C. Teal] stand acquitted of any violation of law whatever. Yet they have been punished as felons, and are still held in durance the vilest! What says the Country? What says *Justice* to this Judicial Outrage!

Small use to appeal to Justice, or the popular indignation when daily and hourly the most abominable acts of tyranny and wrong were being perpetrated in defiance of either Justice or humanity, and almost without a remonstrance, save by a few. I doubt if modern history—American history at all events, can furnish a parallel instance of as general and as complete submission to governmental oppression, and usurpation of personal rights, as was witnessed in North Carolina from July to January, of the year of our Lord, 1871. The passage of the Ku Klux Bill, the defeat of Amnesty, the wholesale and lawless arrests, followed by shameless "confessions" of low-lived fellows, eager to swear away the liberty and reputation of any man, however pure-lived, who chanced to incur the hatred of the Grant rascals, had seemingly paralyzed the manhood of thousands of citizens, even of those who were never in any way connected with secret associations, and who had fought bravely during those earlier days when Grant was directing the organized hordes of hirelings of half the world to obtain the power of this very trampling upon legal and constitutional rights.

Sept. 29—Maguire was accompanied this morning by Rev. J. M. Atkinson, D. D. brother of Bishop Atkinson of the Episcopal Diocese, and pastor of the Raleigh Presbyterian church.   He had just returned from Marion, where Mrs. Neal kindly acquainted him with the truth in my case, (and that of brother Ad) leading him to call to pay his respects, and offer his services, whereinsoever he could be of service. I suggested that he drop a line to father who will be almost overwhelmed by the wrongs that are being heaped upon us.   I am grateful for Dr. A's kind attention.

Basket of cake, champagne etc., from "Incognito" who says Judge Bond was invited to dine at the____of____ but the moment she saw him enter the room she flounced out. Who would think that among the enemy I have so thoughtful a friend!   But her prediction that I shall be free in six months is the wish fathering the thought. W____, too, predicts that I shall return in a few months— and doubtless laughs in his sleeve at the knowledge that the months will lengthen into years before that occurs.

September 30th.   At last! At last the malicious wretches who make mockery of the machinery of justice on the part of the government, have released my innocent, foully wronged brother! Oh! Language! you fail me, you are clumsy and meaningless, to portray the villainy that is being practiced by the Mongrels, and their abettors, the representatives of usurper Grant. Look at the facts. On the 30th of June, three months ago this night, brother Addison, a youth of little [more than]

20 years, having ridden from his plantation nine miles to
the village to inquire the truth of rumors to the effect
that he had been indicted by the Grand Jury of the
Grant Court at Raleigh, was walking on the street
when two Mongrels (Deaver, the Asheville Revenue
fellow and Elias) sprang at him, with pistols covering
his breast, and marched him to jail without warrant,
without examination by magistrate or commissioner,
without allowing him to send for a negro to take his
horse off the street, or to send for a blanket to sleep
upon, when thrust in a filthy stinking hole already
crowded by similar sufferers. Here for two months
he lay without examination, without bedding, knives or
forks, chair or table, books or newspapers, without food
or water in satisfactory quantity or quality, and subject to daily, hourly insults from his jailors and other
enemies. During these months his plantation, which at
the time of the arrest gave excellent promise of a crop,
whose lowest valuation was $3000, became a prey of
thieving negroes, including the hands he had employed
who seeing no prospect of his release, stole what they
could and left the place. In short, the crop did not
return the seed planted in the spring. The loss crippled him, broke him up. At the end of two months
he was handcuffed to a chain, with myself and four
others, carried to Marion confined in a stinking cage,
with a common thief, without bedding or even a clean
floor to sleep on, without water, food, or air in sufficient
quantities (seven men packed in a cage 8 by 10 feet).
Sometimes clawing his food through the bars of the
cage like monkeys, etc.—then carried to Raleigh, 300
miles from home, friends, and witnesses, tried with a
batch of 14 others, of whom he knew only myself, accused by false witnesses, of being at a place he never
saw, yet so perfectly innocent that the bribed witnesses
would only swear they *heard* he was a member, but
couldn't recollect where they heard it, and finally acquitted by the packed jury. No! not finally for his
persecutors were not done with him. "We have other
charges against him," said Sam Phillips bristling with
rage at the thought of losing a single victim. He *lied;*

there were *no* other charges then, but the vile wretches hoped the severity of my punishment would lead many of the Ku Klux to "confess" and furnish evidence against Addie. Eight days have passed without supplying the testimony desired, and this evening brother has been turned loose. "Get your things," said Maguire, "you are a good fellow and we won't keep you any longer." So he is free and en route for home at this hour. He came in just before he started West and was in high spirits, says I have no idea how public feeling runs outside or I would not be low spirited. Alas! I *know* the froth of a passing excitement.

October 1st, 1871. Still locked in the convict-room of Raleigh jail. Rev. Dr. Lacy called yesterday, but being a true man, and gentleman, was forbidden admission.

The Daily *Sentinel* of this morning contains a leading editorial on Brother Addison's case, denouncing in broad language the maltreatment he has received at Mongrel and governmental hands. True he has been restored to liberty, but who shall restore to him time lost, crop lost, labor lost, health and spirits lost? Who shall clear his name from the stigma of the dungeon and the shackles? Who recompense him for liberty, *comfort,* society lost, and insults sustained? Oh the mockery of the so-called freedom and justice of this country.

Today was rendered one of very great bitterness of spirit to me, among other things by a package of extracts from an unfriendly newspaper, kindly clipped for me by some thoughtful (?) friend. Number one, of the clippings, was an editorial from the weekly *North Carolinian,* a newspaper just issued by Maj. W. A. Hearne, a bosom friend of Gov. Caldwell and formerly editor of the Radical organ under its various names of *"Telegram," "Era," "Register,"* etc. The tenor of the editorial may be inferred from its caption, *"Shotwell and his Accomplices";* and from its opening sentence, *"The general sentiment of the community accepts the punishment of Shotwell and his accomplices as just and reasonable."* To add poignancy to this uncalled for

disparagement at the moment of my melancholy departure from the State, I knew that a very large edition of
the paper was being scattered far and wide by the publishers to introduce the "New Democratic Organ," and
my heart ached as I reflected that possibly a copy might
fall into the notice of my sorely distracted father.

Now if I did not know that Hearne is not tolerated
in the better class of society in Raleigh, and moreover
is deemed a mere mouth piece for Governor Caldwell
who hates me with hatred natural in a man of his narrow
spirit, after being publicly exposed by me in an act of
deliberate falsehood and treachery to his nearest neighbors; if I did not know Hearne, as I do, I might feel
hurt at this article, which so foully and cruelly misrepresents me, and will spread that misrepresentation
in all parts of the state. Happily I have a note which
says that notwithstanding the terrorism that prevails
among all who ever had any knowledge of or connected
with the Klan, there are few who do not despise the Mongrels, and denounce the Mongrel Judges in unrestrained
terms, even though they do not know the full truth.
Hearne talks about my "confederates" and "associates"
though he must have heard many times that I never saw
nor spoke with, a single one of those who were convicted with me previous to being locked in jail with
them! Herein my enemies, through Judge Bond, had
me greatly at disadvantage since by refusing to try me
separately, and including me in a batch of a dozen, some
from another state, some from another county, all from
a different community than myself and all strangers to
me, they gave the impression that I was in close association and confederation with them, and was the direc-
tor of their several actions.

Will these facts ever be known to the public? Alas!
I fear not. It may be I shall not survive the long years
in the cold northern dungeons; at least I shall return
broken in health, heart, and mind. These transactions
will pass out of recollection and if I attempt to revive
them to correct them and lift the cloud upon my own
good name, people will charge me with bitterness, malig-
nity raking up old scores. Oh! the injustice that re-

quires a man to bear a load of infamy simply because to vindicate himself demands the revival, and exposure of former villainies by men whose wealth or duplicity has restored them to a measure of public approbation!

Amid my reproaches of those cowardly creatures who give me the cold shoulder, and dare not visit me lest they too should be tainted with suspicion, let me exempt that honorable and steadfast friend, Capt. Plato Durham, whose efforts in behalf of the helpless and innocent have already been noted in these pages. Durham is unceasingly active at present in aiding our poor fellows, borrowing money to lend them, to pay their board while awaiting trials, or to return home if acquitted or postponed for a term. He has been a friend in need for many a poor man—here without friends, and penniless as well; and he alone of my so-called friends has adhered firmly through good and, also evil, report. May his kindness recur to me if ever I am in condition to repay it.

Let me remember, also, Dr. G. W. Blacknall of the Yarborough who this evening has repeated his thoughtful care for our comfort by sending a tray of delicacies from his table. My companions were in very low spirits from having nothing since 3 o'clock, and the evening being dull, gloomy and depressing so that when I called all to come up and partake we made a lively party. Blacknall is styled the Prince of Hotelists—to which I shall add "Prince of Good Fellows."

I have forgotten to mention that yesterday evening there came a large dish of fried oysters from "an unknown friend" who ordered it from Pepper's saloon. Who my friend is, I cannot conjecture; though circumstances point to one of the very marshals who guarded me to and from my trial. Bro. A. told me he was told that several parties had sent me edibles, which were returned by the jailor without my knowledge and among them a tray from a "deputy marshal." Strange that men of that ilk should feel kindly towards persons whom they had assisted in foully wronging!

Extract Number Two, was from the Newbern *Journal of Commerce,* printed by my former partner Col.

Stephen D. Pool, with whom I had originally established the paper. The article professed to be horrified at the "atrocities" of the Rutherford Klans, and after regretting that Shotwell who had been well thought of in Newbern at one time had sunk so low, wound up with the consoling quotation—*"The way of the transgressor is hard."*

Col. P— doubtless afterwards regretted his haste to accept the lies of perjured "witnesses" as fact; for he sent me a telegram at Charlotte (on my return, two years later) expressing sympathy, and gratification at my release, etc., etc.

Indeed, I can scarcely blame either Pool or Hearne, because they as editors simply stated what many others were saying on the streets, and at their homes. But this only adds to the bitterness of the blows as they fell upon me in that hour of my wretchedness!

Clipping Number Three, was worse than either the others. It was a three column telegram to the Washington Chronicle, written by A. H. Dowell, formerly editor of the Radical and Ring organ at Asheville. He was one of half a dozen fellows ostensibly "government stenographers," selected by John Pool, and sent to Raleigh at the *expense of the National Treasury,* to write up the Ku Klux trials as campaign documents for the Radical party. I recognized Dowell among the reporters, and nodded to him pleasantly; for though a Radical editor he had come to me at Asheville in 1870, and gratefully thanked me for refusing to re-print in my paper an article from Brick Pomeroy's sheet assailing his personal appearance and moral character. Several persons brought me copies of the *Democrat* and urged me to copy the article; but I invariably replied that my opposition to the *Pioneer* and its editor, was upon political and moral grounds not from petty or personal spite.

For this, I say, Dowell professed to be exceedingly grateful and in his correspondence from Raleigh he takes care to repay my forebearance of the previous year by slandering and maligning me in all manner possible to his weak brains. After misrepresenting me in every way—misquoting and distorting the testimony false

though it is at best and exaggerating the cases of those
tried with me, that the reflection may be cast upon me
also—he describes me as a young man of splendid prospect, good social and political standing, some talent,
much pride, etc., who having descended to the degradation of a sot, and consented to play the murderer and
midnight marauder, have at length sunk beyond the
recognition of gentlemen, and must drag out my miserable existence a disgraced, despised, abject, felon—
a mark for scorn to point its unerring finger at, etc., etc.,
etc.

Ought I to feel annoyed or hurt by the palpable malice of the insignificant whelp who repays my forbearance by manufacturing downright lies to slander me?
Reason says not: yet with the almost total desertion of
friends, and the weight of six years sentence to the Peni-
tentary upon me, it is difficult to restrain the mingled
indignation and grief.

It may not be amiss here to mention a circumstance
illustrative of Radical Rule that about the time the Lit-
tlefield-Swepson Ring began to put in operation their
schemes for swindling the state of six or seven million
dollars on the Western Railroad, that the *Pioneer,* Dowell's paper became suddenly very rich; being well supplied with all kinds of material, and with means to meet
expenses. Journalism in small towns is far from lu-
crative, and people marvelled that the little, red-eyed,
fellow of the Radical sheet should prosper, when it was
well known scarcely anybody ever subscribed for it.
The secret he revealed in 1876, in a long letter to the
Raleigh *Sentinel* from which I extract.

. . . . When I first met Swepson, he had just been
appointed president of the Western North Carolina
railroad, and I believed him to be honest. I was
a republican, and as an editor of a republican organ,
when the Sentinel assailed my party, I defended
it.   And when I assailed the ring in 1870
My Destiny Was Sealed
in North Carolina. I had to leave the state for
I had incurred the displeasure of the magnates of
the republican party who were also the magnates

of the ring. When in Asheville, Littlefield entered the Pioneer office one day and said: "Dowell, you want a power press, a nice job-press, and a new lot of type. Now make out an estimate and send it to me and I will send you material for as fine an office as there is in the state." I replied that I had a good office and didn't wish to incur further liabilities. "Oh, never mind about that, you can have what you want, and pay me back in twenty years if you can; and if you cannot, you need never do so," said the general. Then my eyes were opened, and I began to look with suspicion upon the newly elected president of the W. N. C. R. R. I had no idea, however, that the man was so corrupt as he was afterwards proven to be, yet I am inclined to believe there are in the state to-day worse men than Milton S. Littlefield. There are a number of leaders in the party in the state, who if they had the opportunity, would prove themselves to be as venal and corrupt as Littlefield or Swepson.

Some one will express astonishment that the writer should utter such sentiments. I am free to confess that I never dreamed a few years ago that I should be a democrat. I prefer to-day to stand on independent ground; but I am of the [*line missing*] I was a republican solely from principle, and when I found all principle had left the party, I left it too. It was not because my generous (?) republican friends in North Carolina gave all the offices to newly pledged republicans, carpet-baggers, unprincipled natives and negroes, to the exclusion of honest, original union men, that I became what I am; nor was it because , when I applied to President Grant for a minor foreign consulship I did not get it, while men like Hester, Bergen and others were favored, that I changed my colors. No, for I believed until a few years ago, that Grant was honest and that his advisers were not. But alas! what do we now . . . .

It will be observed, Dowell mentions the offer, but forgets to say he accepted it, though he may consider the "good word" given Littlefield will keep him quiet.

October 2nd. It has been suggested to me that Hearne's assault upon me is due to my connection with the *Sentinel* in times past. He hates Josiah Turner, the present editor with a most inveterate hatred, and I, as a friend of Turner's, come in for a share. I have been thinking of an address to the public stating my connection with the Klan, detailing the outrages put upon me by personal and political enemies under the forms of law, and appealing to all honorable persons to withhold judgment until I am free to vindicate myself. But I have so often appeared in print of late that it will seem as if I am desirous of seeing myself in type. Besides there are hundreds of poor wretches awaiting trial, whose cases may be prejudiced by any publication I might make. Already it is said by the cringing and terrified, that "Shotwell is doing us harm as well as himself by his defiant and outspoken manner. He ought to be more politic for the sake of others if not for himself. What is the use of enraging the Radicals by charging them with their acts? Let the matter rest until after while when we get out of their power," etc., etc.

Is this not sickening, disheartening! Think of *innocent freeborn* men thus cringing under outrageous wrong without daring to so much as declare their innocence in a manly manner! True, such declaration and just resentment, is sure to be punished by increased insolence, insult and abuse but ought an honest man to be deterred by that!

Much as I am pained to reflect upon my fellow citizens and men of my own political party, I must state that from the inception of these troubles many of the most influential citizens have not only "courted" the Mongrels, but have counselled all the accused persons innocent or guilty to "keep quiet, keep easy, don't do, or say anything to offend the Radicals, better tell all you know, pretend to be friendly with the officers and don't try to expose their arbitrary acts. It will do no good, and will keep you in jail much longer."

Such was the advice given by lawyers, (J. L. Carson

B. F. Churchill, G. M. Whitesides, and others) to scores of uneducated and frightened men, who hastened, in accordance therewith, to Mongrel Logan's office, and revealed the names of all whom they knew, or had heard, belonged to the Klan, thereby bringing into trouble hundreds of men whose only crime was a nominal membership, in a secret order like the Knights of the Golden Circle or the Union League. I must cease to think of these things; my heart is already heavy enough.

I forgot to mention that yesterday Robert M. Logan and J. B. Carpenter, editors of the Mongrel organ in Rutherford came to see me, and on entering the room remarked that they heard I wished to see them. I replied interrogatively.

"Who said I wished to see you?"

"Never mind," said Carpenter, "But now that we are here I should like to talk with you about this penitentiary matter. We hate to see you going off up there to stay six years—especially as we know you never made anything by the Klan, and we hate to see you punished and all the big bugs get free, etc., etc., etc. Now the best thing for you is to come out and tell all you know—you see we don't want to convict all these ignorant fellows; we want the big bugs like Jo Turner, Matt. Ransom, Dave Schenck and Durham, and I can tell you from Gov. Caldwell—he'll stand up to what we say—if you'll come out and do what we want you'll not have to go to prison at all."

"Who do you want," said I.

"Well the leaders—the big bugs. We want Jo Turner particularly, such men as him."

"So you want me to puke?" asked I.

"Yes, that is what the boys call it, I believe."

"Well you'd better leave here right quick or I shall puke—and the other way."

Poor Human Nature is sadly weak! The stress of social customs, and hereditary ideas, is too great for the independence of ordinary mortals. It did not much surprise me when the first fruits of the farce of my so-called "trial" proved to be the withdrawal of sundry small attentions and kindnesses of friends, known and

unknown, in the city. I had not many acquaintances in
Raleigh at the time, but there were scores and hundreds
of members of the Order then in attendance upon the
courts, who might have shown me some small manifestations of sympathy and esteem, to relieve, in slight measure, the darkness and bitterness then so heavy with me.
It was easy to see that Public Opinion, judging solely
from surface appearances, had accepted them as con-
clusive against me.   It mattered not that my conviction was pre-determined even before my unlawful arrest;
that the instruments of my ruin were to be the dregs of
the backwoods, men whose own neighbors would not
believe upon oath in the small affairs; that the Judge
was an unscrupulous and ambitious partizan, selected
and assigned for the special purpose of seconding the
deeds of a gang of lawless agents, and a packed jury;
that the partizan Attorney-General, with all the zeal
of a renegade, came to Raleigh, and stood behind the
back of the Judges to cast the whole weight of the government against the prisoners; that the Scalawag governor of the State sat by the side of the prosecuting
attorney, a man whom I had caned; and that from all
the history of my life there was a continued protest
against the concocted lies of my enemies; none of these
things were taken into account; it was enough that there
had been a trial, that twelve men, (*no matter if all were
Republicans,* and *two of them negroes,* naturally embittered against the Klan.) had sat as a jury, had found
a verdict of "Guilty," and that the severest sentence
allowed by law had been imposed!   So the majority, or
at least a large minority of the community in speaking
of the results of the trial, and expressing sympathy
probably said, "Well, I pity Shotwell; I'd like to see
that fellow Bond and Jim Justice tried together, and
horse whipped to Albany; but after all there is no doubt
that Shotwell and his crowd have been acting recklessly, and inexcusably: they deserve some punishment,
though it was easy to see most of those witnesses were
lying" etc.   Perhaps I ought to state, however, that the
public generally were not so much to blame for their
mistaken judgments because at that time the real facts,

and the real designs of the men who manufactured my ruin, were but imperfectly known especially in the middle and eastern sections.

It will be remembered that my trial was the first under the unconstitutional Ku Klux Act, the first Ku Klux trial, in short, and as my case was peculiar in many respects, and as not the least attempt at defence was made, except upon legal grounds, it was natural for many persons to go by the mere surface signs. Moreover I am obliged to state that the cue given out by the Democratic leaders at that time was, "Hush! Hush! Don't say anything harsh against the Radicals! Don't let them identify the Democratic Party with the Klan, else they'll heap all sorts of odium upon us, and it will utterly ruin us up North where they think the Ku Klux are fiends! Do keep quiet! Let everything be as still as possible; Let these young men go to prison for a few months; it won't hurt them, and when all is quiet, we'll get them out. Better seem to denounce the Klan till all gets quiet!" etc., etc.

I do not exaggerate this; it was so and worse! There were men who were far more responsible for the introduction and spread of the Order than was I, who yet turned a cold shoulder to us all, when the danger came, and professed to be "always found on the side of Law and Order," men who said, "I pity those reckless young fellows, but after all they brought it upon themselves; we must stand by the Courts!" There were editors who themselves had been members of the Order, and who only a few months prior to my arrest printed the flag—surmounted—floating world at the head of their columns with the legend " Our Country," the password of the Order, yet who spoke of my conviction as another illustration of the text, "The way of the transgressor is hard."

It was this truckling to our foes that disgusted Captain Plato Durham, and led him to listen to proposals for the rescue of his suffering county men. Several times he repeated to me with indignant bitterness his experience with certain of the Democratic leaders who had enjoyed the fruits of the Klan operations at the only time they ever assumed a general political hue, and who then patted the young men upon the back, bidding them go right on with their good works, but who when the trouble came, withheld, with almost contempt, that open support and countenance which was alone necessary to save the state from ruin. But perhaps I may as well give a portion of Capt. Durham's own language in this connection. Speaking of my reported release in 1873, he writes editorially in the Cleveland *Banner;* "If Capt. Shotwell has the sense we think he has he will not now, or hereafter allow his name and misfortunes to be taken advantage of by a set of spavined worn out, selfish politicians, *who patted on the back the young men of the State ,and encouraged the secret organizations so long as all was flourishing, and political preferment their object; but who, as soon as trouble came, folded their arms in virtuous indignation, and allowed scores of young men to be driven into the Penitentiary, like sheep into the Slaughter-Pen, and the whole country well-nigh broken up and ruined, without contributing a dollar or raising a finger to prevent it."* He further remarks, *"No! Capt. Shotwell is not the man!"*

Capt. Durham frequently talked with me in a similar strain, and certainly gave strong grounds for his indignation; giving me names and incidents of the conduct of certain high officials, and leading personages, which pained me exceedingly, and would probably cause not a little surprise (to use a mild term) if now made public. As for instance, in talking with Capt. D, on the hotel porch at Shelby in ——— (at which time I had gone there to deliver an address upon the Life and Crimes of Jeffreys), I remarked that Genl. D. H. Hill had mentioned to me a curious conversation he had, while traveling on the cars with a distinguished functionary of the State, who if not a member of the White Brotherhood, at least knew of, and profited by, its operations. Said the Honorable State Func. aforesaid, *"All the trouble grows out of that blasted fool, Randolph Shotwell's work, and I should like to see him get ten years in the lock-up for it."* "Why that," said Durham, "was *mild,* in comparison with some remarks about you that

I have heard. I remember resenting just such a sneer
at you a day or two before, or after, you went to Albany;
I now forget which. But it was in the Hall of the Yarborough at Raleigh and ―――― remarked "if Shotwell
and his crowd hadn't kicked up all this rumpus, and
given the Radicals the chance to fill the State with
Yankee troops, there would be some chance to carry it."
Then I turned on him, and the party, and tongue-lashed
them well! I said—"So and So, you know you were
elected through the efforts of the Klan?" And he had
to admit it, for you know those counties were always
manipulated by the Radicals until the White Brotherhood spread there. "And, So and So, you know well
how glad you were to have the efforts of the young men
in your behalf; and now when outrage and persecution
are heaped upon us through no fault of ours, you stand
aloof, nay, you help to deepen the damage and ruin
by sneering at young men like Shotwell, who had no better sense than to spend his best years, and incur legions
of enemies, just to elect such selfish politicians as you,
and, you, and you, (pointing to persons) when he had
nothing to gain, nor to hope for!" "Oh!" said Durham,
with indignant emphasis, "I could hardly restrain myself from really denouncing them; for you know it only
needed a little money to squelch the whole trouble, and
these fellows wouldn't give a penny toward it!"

"How was that? Tell me all about that!" I asked.
I had heard rumors, and knew one or two corroborative
facts; but as a prisoner at the time, of course, could
have no definite knowledge.

Capt. Durham then stated, in effect, (and I made a
note of his remarks before going to bed that night)
that during the progress of my trial, shortly before the
jury were sent out, but after it had become manifest
the Government had everything cut and dried, C. M.
Farris, the then keeper of the Capitol came to one or two
of my counsel, and stated that two of the jury were
open to convincement and would "agree to disagraee,"
as the doctors say, if the sum of four thousand seven
hundred dollars, should be located in cash somewhere
within reach of their fingers! And when subsequently

it was seen that this sum could not be raised, it was said that the round $4,000 in cash would answer the purpose!

Durham made an effort to obtain the money. It is not at all desirable here to give all that he narrated to me. Suffice it that one noble old Roman, (whom I shall hold in honor, though we meet no more) met the issue as promptly as it needed to be met, saying, "Gentlemen, I am a poor man, mainly dependent upon my earnings from year to year; but here is my check for one-tenth the amount." And he drew a check for $400. requesting Capt. Durham to have it cashed.

"Little did I expect ever to engage in the bribing of a jury," said this patriotic citizen, "But I believe in this instance we are justifiable, morally, if not otherwise. It is very plain that the twelve Radicals up yonder in the Capitol are not a just and righteous jury and were not meant to be when drawn. I believe they have been selected to convict those young men regardless of right, reason, or common decency; and it is no less plain that this farce of a trial is to be the opening wedge for the wholesale conviction of our people of every class and condition until this State shall be safely handed over to Grant. It is easy to see that the Government has put forth all its power and money to convict Shotwell and the others. We see Bond and Brooks both on the Bench; we see Lusk, and that fellow Justice assisted by expensive counsel, Sam Phillips, Marcus Erwin, and others, and Attorney-General Ackerman at their elbows; we see Caldwell daily on hand to cast his scowls against the prisoners; and we know that the bribe of pardon has been offered for months, in addition to jingling gold, to any low-born creature who would make up a lie against our clients. Nobody doubts the fitness of the jury to complete the long planned plot. Now, if we fight the Devil with his own weapons, and make a *mis-trial* what will be the result? The whole matter must go over to the next term, and there is no telling, what may turn up meanwhile. My own belief is that the Grant gang, after seeing their carefully pre-arranged schemes so signally fail, after all precautions, and with a picked jury, will give up the attempt to carry out their plan of forcible capture of the state. Whereas if they succeed in this deep-laid plot they will within a few weeks run six thousand to ten thousand of our young men out of the State, and steal our electoral vote by 20,000 majority. Therefore as a well-wisher of North Carolina, and an advocate of justice, I will deny myself Bread rather than allow Grant and Bond to carry out their wicked schemes."

One or two other gentlemen spoke in the same strain, but there were others who not only hung back, but also sought to dampen the ardor of the more patriotic and public-spirited by saying that perhaps it was a trick of the Radicals to implicate our Democratic leaders, etc. Durham replied that he alone would be known in the matter, and he would shoulder the responsibility. Then the prudent (?)-pocketed ones said it were better to wait; that $4000 was a considerable sum; that probably there would be no more trials; that the government possibly merely wished to set an example, and would rest the prosecutions now that all was quiet; and as for Shotwell, it would do the young man good—would learn him a lesson in common-sense and discretion if he were locked up for a year or two, etc., etc. This sort of talk greatly enraged the brave Durham.

"You will see what will follow this trial!" he cried. "You will find it merely the first shot of a roar of guns that will rake and ruin our state! I tell you, you do not dream of the effect that will be produced if our people up in the west get to see that they are to be dragged down here, and convicted in droves, by a packed court, without any effort to save them, by those who have means and influence."

Durham realized the situation more clearly than they; and to use his own language, "When I saw men who had encouraged secret associations so long as all was flourishing and safe, now standing back with folded arms, in virtuous indignation allowing scores of young men to be driven into the Penitentiary like sheep into a slaughter pen, and the whole country well nigh broken up and ruined, without contributing a dollar, or raising a finger to prevent it, I determined to spend all I had in the defense, and care of our friends, and then look out for Number One."

Can any one blame him? I cannot!

So the negotiation failed: the emissary of the jury returned disappointed; and the impending thunderbolt descended upon my devoted head. It is hard to reflect that were I not a poor, comparatively friendless, youth, I might have been walking the streets of Raleigh a free man! That for a pitiful $4,000. I might have escaped six years of ignominious confinement, and the odious epithet of "Penitentiary Convict." Truly, in this land, justice is a merchantable commodity: and Poverty a crime.

In truth the whole conduct of the Democracy, at that critical period was cowardly, or, let us say, over-cautious and ill-judged. No wonder that after a year of time-serving *squirming* to escape the Radical taunts of a paternal interest in the klans, they should cap the climax of subservient truckling to Yankee sentiment by selecting as a leader the old Abolition fossil, Greeley. But to come home to our own state, I will simply reiterate my belief that our own leaders were responsible in great measure for the Mongrel excesses, which would never have occurred had a few prominent men declared themselves ready to see fair play for the persecuted Ku Klux.

My young friend and fellow prisoner Isaac Padgett, and others, desiring to have my photograph as a memento of the long confinement we have undergone together, obtained permission for us to have one taken. A couple of deputy marshals were our escort, and one seemed disposed to be friendly. Said he had a brother, in Madison county who was Chief of the Klan for that county. "Where is he now?" I asked. "Oh! you know better than I; I'd like to know myself." "Would you arrest him, and punish him for crimes he never committed?" I inquired with a meaning look. "Not *much!*" said the Deputy Marshall, and had nothing more to say. In the gallery, (Shelburn's) I met *Deaver,* the Asheville Infernal Revenue sneak, who arrested Addie, and has killed one or two men under pretense of "resisting an officer." He spoke to me and I nodded in recognition, but adding in a *"stage whisper"* to McIntire, *"I'm become humble* enough to speak to a dog." Shelburn seemed a clever man, and took occasion to say in a low tone, "We all sympathise with you, and hope you will not have to suffer much longer." I felt much gratified by this assurance from an utter stranger, and was able to fix up a comparatively cheerful countenance to be counterfeited for the benefit of my friends, should I never return from prison. Padgett was delighted with the picture, and declares that one hundred dollars would not buy it from him, unless he could get another. I should be satisfied with 100th part of that sum.

As the afternoon wore on, we were called down into the prison yard, by jailor Maguire, and found Sheriff Lee, with Marshall Carrow, come to inform us of our departure at five o'clock the next morning for Albany Penitentiary. Carrow nodded to me complacently, but I gave him an answering stare of non-recognition, not being able so soon to forget that this fellow with his own hands tied my arms behind my back in the Senate Chamber, before the assembled multitude, *not* because of any unruliness on my part, but solely to gratify his own spitefulness and that of my enemies!

Thank God! Our stay in this miserable hole, subject to such treatment, was about to terminate. Albany Penitentiary surely could not be any filthier, or more confining than Wake Jail, and the Northern keepers could have no personal spite at us. Gloomy indeed must be the situation that makes a change to a distant Penitentiary a subject for rejoicing!

U. S. Marshall Carrow has some reputation among his neighbors for cleverness; but his whole treatment of me, of our party, was such as rendered my life unceasingly miserable while under his control, and for nearly a year after we went to Albany. He had been *dining* when he came into the prison yard, or at least *drinking* and, in detailing to the men what they should have to do at Albany he laid special stress on the instructions to take nothing with us except the coarsest articles of outer clothing, as we should be stripped of everything,

and given prison garments, "out and out," while, of
course, *"your citizen's clothes will be all rotted to pieces
before* you get out." The latter fact was true, but it
was not true that our needs as to underclothing, stockings, etc. would be supplied; so that throughout all the
long winter in that Arctic climate we were without underclothing, etc., as we could not write for them until
thirty days after our arrival, and no immediate response
could be had.

This last conversation with Carrow is memorable on
other accounts; so memorable that I made immediate
notes of it.   His tongue was "limberer" than usual, and
he talked quite freely with the prisoners in hearing of us
all, though I sat on the stone steps apart from the group
to whom he was declaiming.   In answer to one or two,
who had condescended to ask him to use his influence
in their favor if opportunity came he declared, "Well,
now that depends! I'm not a hard man, but let me tell
you, none of you're going to git out so long as you keep
up this howl about the Federal Courts, and packed
juries, and all that sort of thing.   It's all false any way!
We Union Republicans has been abused till we're tired
of it, and a goin' to strike back.   I'm a close friend of
Judge Bond, and me an' him's together pretty much
all the time he's here, and I can tell you these lies of old
Jo Turner's about "Star Chamber Courts" an' sich like
has got to be stopped, else you'll see a good many more
agoing the way you're agoing!   Mark that!   And I
can tell you all that insinuation in the speeches that
your lawyers made about the Court didn't help your case
a bit. Your lying newspapers and big bug lawyers can't
bluff old Bond. I know him, and how he feels; and he
wouldn't have *been half so heavy on you,* but for *Jo
Turner's lying and Fowle's and Bragg's insinuating
about packed juries."*

The latter part of this tirade was so manifestly aimed
at me that I turned to those who sat near me, and remarked aloud—"Fine specimen of a *Just Judge* who
allows himself to be influenced by political editorials and

wreaks his revenge upon helpless prisoners for the speeches of counsel."

Now what a showing is this!

S. T. Carrow, U. S. Marshal for North Carolina, an intimate associate of Judge Bond, presiding over the trials of scores and hundreds of respectable citizens, says that *he knows* (and doubtless he does know) that the Judge was influenced in his decisions by personal resentment at remarks of outsiders and newspapers! That is, he *felt aggrieved* at the plain speaking of an editor, and to *revenge himself,* he made use of the full extent of his judicial power to punish certain unoffending persons unluckily within his power! Think of a Judge of the Circuit Court of the United States wreaking upon a few helpless prisoners, the petty spite he felt towards a political party, a newspaper or lawyer! Is it surprising that our people have lost confidence in the judiciary, and respect for the officers of the law? Is it strange that sometimes men are stung to take into their own hands the punishment of crimes that should be punished by legal tribunals, if there were any worthy the name?

Though foreseen for many weary weeks the announcement that we shall start for the Penitentiary tomorrow morning causes a shudder, and cuts like the edge of glass! Start for the Penitentiary! It seems incredible! the heart *must* doubt it or break. Great Heavens! can it be true that I, Randolph Shotwell, am a convict about to start for a Northern Penitentiary! At this moment I can fancy the torture of mind that must assail the doomed to death on the morning of his execution. How his form must quiver when first he awakes to consciousness! However he may have steeled himself to contemplate the approach of Death, at this hour, with physical system all relaxed, the iron will temporarily unhinged, and the mind preternaturally clear, he will be overwhelmed by the rush of memories, and magnified love of life that must be far more painful than the actual march to the scaffold, under the eyes of the multitude. Of course, my own case is vastly different; yet when I reflect upon the brief period to pass before our departure for a living grave I can well comprehend the torture in the other case.   To leave all with whom I am acquainted all old associations, and prospects, to leave home and those therein; books, papers, society and all comforts; to give up freedom of limb, action, and speech; to enter upon a life of isolation, drudgery under hard taskmasters to be shut off from all intercourse with one's fellowmen: to drag the lengthening chain of days through six years, forgotten of all, blighted for life, robbed of the fairest years of youth—surely there is enough in the prospect to terrify the stoutest soul.   Well 'tis some consolation to know I can escape it all if I would, but will not under the conditions imposed.   I have advised my companions to make terms for themselves if they can; for I know they know nothing to implicate any one, and if the Mongrels will free them in hopes of getting some clue to others through their confessions, I'll be glad to cheat them. In old man Collins's case especially, I have urged Maguire and Tim Lee to exert themselves to procure pardon.   He will surely die if carried off tomorrow. Poor, desolate, ignorant old man! he sits and cries nearly all the day long!

In the *Sentinel* of this morning there is an account of the villainy of Jeff Downey, the principal tool of the government at our trial.   It seems on his arrival here he engaged boarding at the house of Mrs. Rose, a respectable widow lady near the Yarborough House, for himself *and wife*.   The pretended wife came in the dusk of the evening and passed to her room with her veil down.   After two days the chambermaid happening to enter the room suddenly discovered that the woman was a *mulatto wench—not Downey's wife at all!* Of course both were expelled instantly. But mark the villainy of a government that uses the testimony of foul creatures like Downey and his paramour, to convict respectable and honorable men! Bah! what a free government it is! Downey was the right man for the dirty work on which he was employed.   The first time I heard his name pronounced, he was being denounced for having slipped off to South Carolina, and by means of some picked up signs, procured admittance to the Order, thereby gaining the names of members in Rutherford for the determined purpose of betraying them.

This last evening in Raleigh jail was one never to be forgotten. Picture, if you can, the small dirty room, half its floor covered with drippings from the filthy tub, and the sprinklings of carbolic acid, whose stench was sickening, no light, no air, save that which came through two small windows, lessened by the cross-bars, no fire, or bedding, except a couple of blankets per man, no seats, no food, no books, nothing to occupy either mind or body. For me there was not even the diversion of conversing for my companions were comparatively strangers to me, and their lives were so different that we had nothing whatever in common save suffering. The high spirits in which brother Addison had gone home a previous afternoon, and the few hurried words he had whispered as the result of his inquiries among our friends outside, also tended to make me restless and wretched in this sunset hour. "All the Western men have gone home, or will go up on the train tomorrow," he had mentioned, and was gratified to think of having company homeward. But I read between the lines— 'Yes, gone home, all of them, without a word to me who on the morrow will go far to the cold North perhaps never to return!'

After sunset, after all but a faint tinge of crimson shown upon the western wall of the jail, a few rays penetrating even within the bars of the narrow window on that side, I arose from my blankets, and stood looking out into the falling twilight, my companions were all abed, many of them asleep. There was a strong chill wind, and the night promised to be unusually cool for October in this latitude. There were no street lamps, and few lights in the windows; for the view from that side overlooks a poor locality, mainly shops and negro cabins. The city seemed unusually quiet, no footsteps, or shouts, were audible; and an air of profound desolateness made itself felt; just as when I have stood on some lonely hill side, in Virginia, during the war, seeing not one human being for miles, on miles, and hearing only the melancholy soughing of the breeze

through the myriad feathery leaves of the tall pines!
A saddening similarity extended also to my life; for
while every present surrounding was full of sombre
desolation and solitude, how unbroken was the vista of
lonely future years rolling on and on before me, like
the drear expanse of war-ruined country I have so often
surveyed! How I envied my companions—for whom
Memory held no grevious Realms of Self-Reproach—
who were not tormented by hosts of "*Might-Have-
Beens,*" and "*Why-Did-You's,*" and "*What will Become of You's?*" Or to whom there was no mortification over neglect; because *they* had nothing to expect!
To me it was a grievous thing that I who had once had
quite a number of friends in Raleigh, and had passed
some very merry hours, riding, walking, and visiting
with them, both youths and maidens, had now been
weeks on weeks shut up in the filthy jail, amid negroes
and felons, and strangers, without a call from any of
them, or a sign of sympathy or solace from any. I had
dropped out of their recollection, had become as Dowell
wrote, "too poor for anyone to do him reverence!" If
I went off, if I should be crushed under the privations
and oppressions of the "Convict" life to come, who
would care at all!

Moreover I knew that about this hour, my aged and
heart-broken father, in his lonely study, afar on the
slope of the Blue Ridge, would receive the evening tri-
weekly mail, with accounts of my conviction, sentence,
and transfer to the Penitentiary! Proud old man that
he was, notwithstanding his modest backwardness of
self-seeking, and self-assertion, how would he, how
could he, endure this blow? True, he knew from the
hour I fell into the hands of my enemies they would seek
to crush me; but now that they seemed to have succeeded, would he not sink also?

Ah! it is well this calamity escaped me! The fires
of resentment in my soul needed but *that* breath to make
me devote my life to—*Revenge!* Eternal, unceasing,
uncalculating, pitiless Vengeance!

It was not easy, even as things went, to banish such
thoughts utterly from my soul. Many times wild

thoughts kept me awake through the long silent hours of the night as I reflected how much I had suffered and was yet suffering, and must still suffer, while sleek, selfish schemers, really deserving of some such punishment were free, prosperous, respected, yea, quite ready to sneer at "Shotwell's misconduct," "Shotwell's just deserts," and the like! Darker yet were the thoughts aroused by the memories of the cowardly malice that penned me in cages with murderers and felons, dragged me in handcuffs past the door of my own home, where my venerable father was almost crazed with mingled grief and indignation, harassed me in all possible ways, packed a jury to convict me, bribed a dozen cringing scoundrels to slander me, so that even my own friends were deceived and turned against me by their specious false-swearing; and finally—the Penitentiary! Six of the fairest years of my life to be shorn away, to be buried in a living grave, enveloped in the tainting associations of a convicted felon!

Is it wonderful if the heart grew hard, the feelings wrought up, the moral senses o'er burdened by the lava-tide of resentment now and again?

Thank God, my enemies were too numerous to admit of revenge upon all, and this feeling of inability of redress perhaps saved me from mental and moral ruin.

CHAPTER FOURTEENTH

The Journey—Another Petty Deed

Morning found us, after a few hours of fevered, and dreams-broken slumber, as poorly conditioned for a long journey, even with the pleasant destination of ours, as can be imagined. The mist, which was very heavy, had been drifting through the unsashed windows making our hair, faces, and blankets damp and sticky; there was not a drop of water for morning ablutions, nor lights, nor fire, nor any cheering influence whatever. The close, fetid atmosphere, the sloppy, lime covered floor, the bare, broken walls, covered with vulgar charcoal sketches, and tobacco stains; the gratings of the windows, and heavy, bolted door, together, formed a wretched "background," as it were, for the group of sleepy-looking, shivering, coarsely clad, creatures, who squatted on the rolls of their blankets, around the walls, silently awaiting the call to start. Hour after hour passed, the darkness changed to dawn, of a gloomy, cloudy day, the sounds of awakening life in the city began to be heard, and the time was come! Tramping up the steps outside, came Maguire, jingling his huge bunch of keys right merrily. With him, was "Wash," with "breakfast"—the usual table-spoonful of "cow-peas," a "chunk" of half-baked (the crust burned, but the interior still sticky and unpalatable) sour corn-bread, and a piece of rusty bacon, the size of my finger. Ordinarily I did not more than taste the stuff, but this morning the mere sight was revolting; though I knew we should need all our physical strength for the ordeal before us.

And now a full company of Yankee soldiers with fixed bayonets took position at the outer gate. The officer, in command, Lieut. J. S. McEwan,[1] 4th Artillery, entered together with several scalawag "Deputy-Marshals," and Jailor Maguire, who carried a large

[1] John Steven McEwan of New York, who had served in the Seventh N. Y. Artillery as lieutenant, captain and brevet major during the war, and after discharge had been commissioned lieutenant and assigned to the Fourth Artillery.

bunch of rusty iron handcuffs! Tim Lee, at the same
time bustled in with a bottle or two of Raleigh whiskey—"dead shot at 40 rods." My companions, being
nervous and chilly, drank too much of the vile stuff,
and soon began to joke and jabber in a senseless manner; a circumstance that added to my mortification, as
I knew there would be many watchful eyes on the party.

Rumor had intimated that we should be handcuffed
in couples, just as we had seen a white man and a negro
sent away some time previous; but I could not believe
it until I saw Maguire's grin. Repressing pride, grief,
and indignation, I accosted Lieut. McEwan pleasantly
remarking that I was gratified at the prospect of having
a guard of soldiers instead of a gang of political bum-
mers; and then I stooped to ask a favor of the epaul-
etted young Yankee, viz: "Would he not dispense
with the indignity of chaining and shackling us, upon
condition of our giving our solumn pledge not to attempt to escape, nor give any trouble whatever en route
to Albany? If he would grant this never-to-be-for-
gotten favor I would give a special *parole d'honneur*
neither to escape, nor allow any of my companions to
do so," etc.

The officer seemed embarrassed, and courteously assured me he would escort us to the Penitentiary without
any guard, under our pledges, "or, at least *yours,* I
should not hesitate to accept. But my orders are imperative, and *especially as to yourself.* I have no discretion. My orders require me to put you in irons and,
you know, a soldier must obey orders." "Very well,"
said I, "Since you are so instructed there is nothing
for us but to submit to this *needless indignity.* But
you must admit, Sir, it is altogether *unnecessary* on any
ground of our safe-keeping and therefore is a *piece of
petty, purposeless, persecution!*" The officer shrugged
his shoulders with a significant smile: whereupon I added, *"No, not precisely 'purposeless'; the purpose is to
humiliate us to the very lowest degree, by marching
us through the streets of Raleigh, chained together like
slaves!"*

The lieutenant hesitated a moment; then said in a whisper, "My orders only require me to 'take' you in handcuffs; so, keep your men quiet, and as soon as we reach the boundary line at the other side of Weldon, I'll relieve you of your shackles on my own responsibility."

It was a small favor, but "small favors" should be "thankfully received."

Ordered down into the prison enclosure, we found other "deputy marshals," (sent I imagine, by "Fat" Carrow to see that no gentleness was showed to us) who made themselves busy in fastening the shackles on our wrists.   There is something repulsive in even the appearance of a lot of handcuffs, due to the association of ideas; and these were the oldest, roughest, greasiest I ever beheld; they having been used for coupling slaves for the mart in ante-bellum times, it may be, or more recently the larcenous freedman.   The Scalawags, perfectly familiar with them, seemed to enjoy handling them.   "Here's your cast-iron, Ku Klux bracelets!" chuckled one of the low fellows as he snapped the bolt around Adolphus DePriest's wrist, saying also, that it was "a perfect fit," and "must have been made for him!"

It is a small matter, but torture can be made of gnat-bites.   All the little gnats, and other vermin, were abroad in the shape of scalawag officers during this same year of our Lord, eighteen hundred and seventy-one, and together they made much misery for multitudes of decent people.   The following is a specimen of their spitefulness.   All of my companions were virtually strangers to me, as I had never known them prior to my arrest, and had only nominal intimacy with them since.   But, on seeing we were to be handcuffed in pairs, I asked to be paired with old Mr. Collins, the South Carolina miller.   He was nearer my size than the others, and he, being in his 64th year, was more quiet and dignified than most of the others.   Besides he looked to me in the conduct of his case, the writing of his letters, etc.

Surely it was a slight thing to ask to be coupled with him!   But the Mongrels, divining my motive, not only refused to allow it, but paired me with Bill Teal, a tall raw-boned, uncouth, back-woodsmen, the hardest looking man in the party—and so fuddled by Tim Lee's whiskey, that he giggled and pranced like a baboon, who was specially objectionable to me, because he, after being one of the most violent and irrestrainable of the Klansmen, (he it was, as I have been assured by several persons who heard him boast of it, who tried to shoot James Justice on the night of the Rutherfordton Rumpus his arm having been knocked aside just as he would have fired his pistol) was one of the first who yielded to commingled fear and greed, and became a "swift witness" against his neighbors.

After using him until he could neither remember, nor invent, anything more, the Mongrels re-arrested him, tried, and convicted him on another charge, sentencing him to three years in the same Penitentiary with his victims. He knew nothing of me, and therefore, my dislike to him was based solely on his abstract character; (I afterwards nursed him during his last hours of life); but he was so rough and ungainly I could not but shrink from being manacled with him for a travelling com-companion during the long journey northward. And knowing this, the Mongrels forced it upon me.

"It is strange to observe," says Sir James Macintosh, in one of his superb Constitutional Essays, *"how uniformly, when Oppression rules the hour, the tyrant, be he who he may, on the throne, or the lowest turnkey of a prison, contrives, and seems to study to contrive, how to add insult to injury; how to make cruelty more cruel; and inflict new torments and annoyances on those who must necessarily be already wretched."*

How many incidents of our prison experience verify this remark! The deserter-convict, at Fort Delaware during the war, could often be seen cruelly beating with his club the miserable "Rebels," who were forced to draw the heavy cart-loads of unhewn granite; and our negro cook, "Wash," himself a (supposed) prisoner serving out his sentence, but treated as an equal and associate by the Mongrels, delights to come into the jail at meal time, wearing a huge revolver buckled around his waist, and carrying himself in an impudent, bullying swagger towards the Klan prisoners, occasionally insulting those whom he fancied would submit to it.

PARADED THROUGH RALEIGH

The prison gates swing open, and we march out in couples, between double rows of blue-coated soldiers, who close around us with an hollow square of bayonets. Sheriff Tim Lee's wife, nee Miss Venitia Harris, daughter of "Cebe," and niece of George W. Logan, was at one of the windows of the Sheriff's residence, at the front of the jail, and seeing me thus hand-cuffed, surrounded by Yankees, and negroes, marching away to a distant penitentiary, her southern womanly feelings must have temporarily overmastered her Radical training and associations, as she bowed, and made a little gesture of sympathy, whereat I raised my hat in acknowledgment; raising also Teal's hand, (which was attached to my own), much to his amazement.

And this woman, daughter of one of my enemies, niece of the "Donkey" Judge of Rutherford, and leader of the Red String Leagues; also, wife of a Radical Sheriff, an Ex-Yankee soldier, born in Ireland, and reared in Boston, also, sister of J. C. Logan Harris, editor of the Radical organ, and solicitor of the negro district; this lady, I say, though I had never spoken to her more than once or twice, half a dozen years before, was the solitary person to say "Farewell." Hers was the sole parting word, nod, look, or gesture, that was given me by man or woman of this great city, wherein were hundreds who had known me personally and many more who knew that I was being punished for my zealous advocacy of Southern rights and conservative principles and that I was going to a far northern prison because I refused to lend myself to the designs of the Radicals who wished to manufacture capital to defeat our party. Was it strange that my heart lay cold and sick in my breast as I realized this utter abandoment? Nothwithstanding that I knew how great a dread existed of being contaminated, if not harassed, by suspicions of being too intimate with the accused Ku Klux, yet it was hard to believe that not one soul would dare to call upon me to receive any last message I might wish to leave, or to accompany me to the cars, as I would have done any friend similarly situated and persecuted. But I walked alone. Even "Bold Josiah Turner" stood at his office door, but came no nearer to say, "Be of good cheer." A few days before he sent a message to me by Senator Whitesides, "Tell Shotwell I would call to see him but the Radicals would make fuss of it, and say I was attentive to brother Ku Klux." Thus it was with many of my so-called friends; a *dread of what the Radicals might say or charge them with!* This in a *free* country by *Freemen!* No wonder the Mongrels were emboldened to any stretch of power!

It may be I expected more than was reasonable of my friends in this matter, but certainly *I* would have stood by *my friends* in trouble.

Outside of the jail-yard an immense mob of negroes of all colors, sexes, and ages were congregated to see *"Dem Kluxes g'wine ter Pentionary."* The Blue-Coats kept open an avenue for us to march through; the multitude crowded thick as there was room on both sides of the line and many of them, particularly women, were very noisy and abusive. Poor creatures! they were taught by their party associations to look upon all Democrats, and especially "dem Kluxes," as their enemies, whereas there was not a man among all their so-called "friends," who wished the race more solid benefit, and true freedom than myself. And many a night, months after their wild yells of abuse of us, I went up into a cold room to teach the lowest of their fellows; and many a night sat up till nearly worn out, to watch with, and give medicine to, poor degraded members of their race; though I might easily have shirked the miserable duty, and rested at ease while the shadow of death fell upon them! Yet, after all, 'tis not these ignorant, unreasoning creatures we should so much blame as the abominable Mongrels who for base partizan purposes instill the worst of feelings, beliefs, and prejudices into their minds.

As we entered the street Lieut. McEwan came to me and began to pull down my coat sleeve to cover the handcuffs. "It is not necessary to hide them," said I, "I am not ashamed of them, not half as much as those who ordered them put on me." Yet my feelings were sorely tried: for the drunken creature with whom I was shackled became so excited by the shouts and running of the mob of negroes, and others, that I could not check him in his half-prance, half-trot, dragging me by the wrist, as if we were ashamed, hurrying to get out of sight and giggling hysterically despite my efforts to repress him. The bright uniforms of the soldiers, of course, attracted a large crowd.

However as there was no help for it, I calmly and quietly awaited the order to march; and proceeded to the train in the same manner.

For some reason, perhaps to bring us more directly in front of the Yarborough Hotel, where many of my acquaintance were stopping, the procession was made to march through the passage of the Court House instead of going round to the right of it, as any one else would do.

Out in the middle of Fayetteville Street, and slowly down it—until at the place of all places—the procession halts for a full ten minutes nearly in front of the residence of *Mrs. Wm. H. Haywood,* wherein I happened to know were a number of gentle folk to whom I had been known in happier circumstances. Was it not natural that I thought less at that moment of being in handcuffs than of my apparent association with———?

The soldiers were formed in hollow square around us; the mob of negroes swarmed on the side walks; here and there I can see an acquaintance watching, with casual curiosity, our party—but none coming to speak to me—to say, "Be of Good Cheer, my friend; we shall be true to you!"—No!—not one; and so we take leave of Raleigh. There are some other most melancholy circumstances connected with this cruel pause in the main street of the Capital, but they belong to the past— let them go down with the dead, and be forgotten.

The mob followed closely, but were kept back by the "hollow square" of soldiers surrounding us. At the depot, Lieut. McEwan ordered a sergeant to take a

platoon and drive back the crowd at the point of bayo-
net a movement performed with much alacrity by the
"Regulars" whose dislike of the darkey is noticeable on
all occasions. We were placed in the cars of the Raleigh & Gaston R. R. While awaiting the locomotive
Sheriff Lee came in, and asked me if I had any money.
"Very little," I replied, "but enough for my purposes,
I suppose." He hurried out of the car, and I saw him
no more till we were getting under way, when he ran
in to hand me a note. It contained a $10 bill. Instant-
ly I called to him from the window, but he merely answered, "It's all right; from a lady!" and disappeared.
I felt annoyed, yet cheered. It was annoying to accept
charity from the enemy, yet cheering to be assured
there was some one whose sympathy was strong and
generous, even though to me unknown.

Meanwhile, several citizens of the town, young men,
came in, and introduced themselves to me; but I did not
catch their names—as I now regret.

As the train rolled slowly away through the suburbs,
I looked from the window, seeing localities I had visited
with lady friends, buggy-riding in all the jollity of
youth, and high spirits, only two years before, (it now
seemed as if it had been many, many years agone!) and
as the town vanished it awakened some such sentiment
as the traveller feels on sailing away from a port where
he has many acquaintance with whom he had enjoyed
pleasant socialities, but whom now he expects nevermore to see again! However these sentimental reflections must be crushed out of sight, yea, and out of heart,
for a life and death struggle is now begun wherein the
least weakness, or surrender to sentimental brooding,
will destroy soul and body! And so, I get out a roll
of New York papers, purchased especially for their
soporific qualities, and seek to forget thought by thinking—after somebody else.

The company of 'Regulars' did not come with us, but,
after seeing the train safely started, were marched back
to camp, leaving us under the charge of Lieut. McEwan,
with a sergeant and four soldiers as military escort,
together with a squad of "special deputy marshals,"

ostensibly sent along to assist in convoying us to Albany, but in reality appointed by Carrow and Bond as a nice arrangement whereby they might *make a summer tour to the North at the expense of the Federal government!* There was hardly any attempt to conceal this. For example, Young Johnny Bailey, son of a Republican lawyer of considerable prominence, was "deputized" to accompany the party as assistant commissioner, or some such excuse. He laughingly remarked to me, after offering me his shawl to sit upon (i.e. take care of, while he strolled about), that he didn't see that he was of any particular use to the Party, but he had never seen Albany and it was a pleasant trip, at no expense, (i. e.—no cost to himself, and who cares for expenses when the "Best government the world ever saw" is to foot the bills!) On a similar footing with young Bailey was Theo Josephs, a Raleigh liquor saloonist; and also, if I mistake not, Phil Thiem, of the same place. They had business in New York, and expected to transact it, while the soldiers carried us up the Hudson to Albany. The question may be asked why any one beside the military should accompany us? But a little reflection will show the absurdity of the inquiry! If pot-house politicians were not to be allowed to make a purse now and then from the great and good and glorious government wherefore should any of them join the Republican Party and yell for Grant?

Lieut. John S. McEwan, of the 4th United States Artillery, was a young officer, not long hatched from West Point, though married and parentally experienced. He had sought command of our escort because he wished to visit his people at Albany, of which city he is a native. As he, when in Raleigh, of course, associated chiefly with Radicals and office-holders, carpetbaggers etc., his views of the Ku Klux troubles were one-sided, inaccurate, and prejudiced; but being a man of kind hearted disposition and pleasing manners, we got on together quite cordially.

He manifested a kindly disposition towards us, and after we had proceeded some distance, came to occupy the seat adjoining mine to converse with me, offering me his newspapers, etc. He assured me in answer to my inquiries as to our probable life at Albany, that Genl. Pilsbury was a most excellent and humane gentleman, the very model of a Prison-Keeper. All of which I accepted *cum grano salis,* or with a whole handful of "salt," so to speak, simply remarking that unfortunately the "model-keeper" viewed from the *interior* of his model cage was apt to bear quite a *transmogrified* aspect! And this I was to ascertain by personal view.

A DAY OF SYMPATHETIC SUNSHINE

Among those who boarded the train at Raleigh was Mr. T. B. Kingsbury, associate Editor of the *Daily Sentinel* (at the time), and well known as perhaps the most cultivated of our literary writers, and critics. He had recently acted as correspondent of the Baltimore *Gazette,* and had done a very great good to the cause of historic truth by exposing the malicious motives and wicked conspiring whereby the Grantizaries were subjugating our people. I greatly regret not being able to give some extracts from "Tuscarora's" letters.

I had no personal acquaintance with Mr. Kingsbury, but he came to me with so manifest feelings of kindness I derived the first genuine sense of encouragement and sympathy I had met with—notwithstanding that it came from a stranger. How quickly one recognizes a real friend! Many of my so-called friends have been dumb as oysters whereas Mr. K. sought me out. Mr. Kingsbury, also, informed me that he intended writing a full statement of my case for the Baltimore papers. Unfortunately he knows not one half the truth; for all the avenues of information have been unreliable or utterly silent, through intimidation.

As the train checked at Kittrell's Springs station— the celebrated watering place, a number of well-dressed ladies were seen on the platform; and they presently ventured to the windows. Thinking they were looking for friends I turned to my newspaper; when they rapped on the pane to call my attention. It was necessary to drag Teal with me to the other side of the car, as we were handcuffed together; but I raised the window and spoke to the fair ones who said they desired to express sympathy for us, etc.

I was much embarrassed, thus talking with my head out of the window and the other passengers also craning their necks to see who were these brave young ladies who could thus brave public remark to manifest their womanly kindness; though I sought to thank them with somewhat of the sincere gratitude I felt for their sympathy.

"Do you know the ladies you have been talking to?" asked Mr. K., as the cars rolled on. "The Misses L— are among the wealthiest and first ladies of H—," he continued, "they and the others are visiting the Springs I suppose." Whatever their fortune they should have a better one if I might be the arbiter; for the few kind words spoken by them to one an utter stranger were destined to afford me many a strengthening and solacing thought amid the long dark days before me.

About a mile farther on, Dr. Kingsbury took leave of me; with a warm "God bless you!"—and when the cars rolled away from the station I saw him standing in his doorway waving a farewell salute with his newspaper. "This is hard"—I murmured almost involuntarily, forgetful of the presence of the officer. "Yes it is hard—I am sorry for you. Yet, let me tell you, it was well you were not tried by army court martial. We should certainly have *hanged* you."

"Not if you were honorable men."

"Yes, because you were the best informed, you had held positions of prominence in your community, and you were one of the leaders."

"No, you are vastly mistaken. I should rejoice to be tried before a court of intelligent army officers. They at least would have no petty, private, and malignant motives for manufacturing evidence against me."

Upon my return home I found that he had written an article concerning me; of which the following appears to be an extract:

A correspondent of the Weldon *News,* in a letter dated Oxford, October 7th, thus writes of Captain Shotwell, who was recently sentenced by the Ku-

Klux court at Raleigh to six years' imprisonment in the penitentiary and to pay a fine of $5,000:

"On the morning I left Raleigh I saw this brave man and seven others marched through the streets hand-cuffed and guarded by some fifteen Yankee soldiers, armed with loaded muskets and fixed bayonets. On the cars I had an interview with Captain Shotwell, and was glad to find him in such good spirits. He bears up bravely under his misfortunes. He says: 'Tell my friends I go to my doom with cheerful spirits.' I gave him some recent papers, and my address, promising to send him papers regularly, if the authorities will allow it. He is to write me as soon as he can, giving necessary directions. At Kittrell's several young ladies expressed to him their sympathy. To this he replied, that he could bear all his misfortunes bravely, if the ladies of North Carolina sympathised with him. When my destination had been reached, I bade Capt. (Shotwell) farewell and left the car with a heavy heart. He is a remarkably fine looking man, some six feet high, very erect, with a bright, frank open handsome face. He is, I suppose, about thirty years of age, and is the son of a well known Presbyterian minister. He is well educated."

At another station—I regret that I failed to catch the name—a gentleman rushed into the car with an armful of tobacco, which he distributed to the prisoners, giving three plugs to each one of the eight, except to myself, I not using the weed. It was a thoughtful, generous, gift, and I am sorry I cannot here give him credit therefor by name.

It was a little after dusk when the train rolled under the big shed at Weldon, where an immense throng was speedily around the car windows, and supper was brought to us in the car. It had been ordered by Lieut. McEwan at his own expense: else we should have gone from Raleigh to Portsmouth without a morsel, so little care had our captors for our comfort.

Among those who called on me in the car was Capt. H. E. T. Manning of the *Roanoke News*, (now of the

Baltimore *Medical Journal*) who was the last North Carolinian to bid me farewell.

On passing out of the state, the Lieutenant relieved us of the handcuffs in accordance with his promise to me in the morning.

BY BAY BOAT

Four hours run through the darkness over the Seaboard and Roanoke—during which I had a good nap—and we reached the deck of the steamer *Louisiana,* bound up the Chesapeake. After supper quite a crowd of passengers followed us into the lower cabin, to whom I declaimed at considerable length and vehemence, denouncing the outrage of which we were being made the victims. Generally the sympathies of the bystanders were with us, and one of the officers of the ship also seemed to take great interest in my statements.

DISHONORING PROPOSALS

On our return to our appointed place in the lower cabin, after taking supper in the ordinary dining-room of the steamer, I was approached by one of the so-called deputies, who with the introductory remark that Hon. Clinton L. Cobb of the 1st N. C. Congressional District, was on board, and had expressed a wish to converse with me, began to urge me to take advantage of Mr. C's interest in me to secure a pardon, as the latter had great influence at Washington. As may be supposed I did not permit this conversation to proceed. Subsequently, after I had retired to one of the open berths around the sides of the cabin, Lieut. McEwan came to the side of the berth, and, telling me that Mr. Cobb had made many inquiries about me, strongly counseled me to make peace with the government through him by revealing all I knew of the Klan, and soliciting pardon. I discarded all such suggestions but expressed my gratefulness for his personal interest in my unhappy fate, and assured him if he or Mr. C. could do anything to facilitate my release upon honorable terms I should be eternally their debtor. The Lieutenant went off with the remark that before I had been six months in the Penitentiary I would be willing to get out on any terms, and would regret my folly in throwing away a good offer. "If I retain health and reason, I shall not," said I: though as I lay in my bunk and heard the splashing of the waves outside, as the vessel ploughed her way onward towards the far North, leaving all that earth possessed of happiness, and affection behind me, I could not but feel an involuntary dread that sooner or later I must succumb against my will.

THIRD TIME TEMPTED

At an early hour next morning, one of the guards escorted me to the barber's saloon to have my hair dressed as my head was throbbing furiously and I hoped it would have some relieving effect. Returning we passed through the general saloon where Lieut. McEwan, and Col. Cobb happened to be playing cards, after "a night of it." The former sent the soldier below, and introduced me to Col. Cobb, who insisted on my taking a seat with them. I hesitated, explained that I was without my coat, and rather unwell; but finally sat down at their table.

Clinton L. Cobb, of Elizabeth City, is a native of North Carolina, and so far as I have ever heard, is among the better specimens of the Radical party in the state. On the present occasion he demeaned himself with proper courtesy, and seemed a frank, agreeable person. A little man, of average education, good natured, and of better reputation both as to private and public character than most of the Southern Scalawags; he was, of course, involved in all the wickedness of his party, and party measures. He could not have held his post, or any influence whatever had he not acquiesced, if not actually participating therein.

After some conversational skirmishing, manifestory of his cordial interest in me, and desire to relieve me from the fearful fate, already over-hanging me, he advanced his outposts, and remarked that he had recently come from the National Capital, where some people were pleased to intimate that he had considerable influence, and he had had a good deal of conversation about me, and really he felt sorry, exceedingly sorry, to see me going off in this way! It was *too* bad! He had been quite surprised that so little had been done for me.

"We all knew well enough that you are not anything like as much to blame as the real leaders, the men that started this thing and secretly influenced it though all the time keeping in the background, out of danger themselves, while perfectly willing to be elected to office by the operations of the Klans."

At this I smiled—recollecting a case or two that might be so construed; for the fellows were elected to office by the Klan, and yet had made such remarks as that all the trouble was due to *"Confounded fools like Randolph Shotwell and others."*

"Well," continued Col. Cobb, "as you were the most prominent of the prisoners the government had to make an example of you, and, of course, your chance of pardon is less than any of the rest, because of that fact; and then you know you've been very hard on Republicans in your papers, and they'll do all they can to keep you till your six years are up, if you stand it so long! But my friend, it is downright folly and madness for you to go to Albany Penitentiary when you can readily save yourself, and do a good work for the country in the bargain! If you will only make a full statement of all you know of the Klan, I can assure you of immediate pardon," he urged. "Would you have me betray my fellow-citizens into trouble, and violate a solemn obligation?" "Oh, the organization is entirely broken up: the oath is no longer binding," cried both men, in a breath. "For that matter," said I, "I never was sworn into the Klan; never was actually a member of any secret organization whatever; but I was supposed by my comrades, and friends to have been sworn in, and, having allowed them to confide in me upon that supposition, I deem myself firmly and eternally bound not to forfeit their confidence." I added that there was much in the Klan I did not like, or approve of; but that I felt that some such association of white men in favor of honesty, morality, and the suppression of negro brutality to women and helpless ones, was indispensable at that period; hence had lent my name as a member of the Order, though I had never been an active member.

"You see the Government doesn't want to convict the poor countrymen, like those we've got down stairs going with you. They are not the real leaders, or controllers, or gainers by, the Ku Klux movement. I am intimate with the Administration, and I can tell you— all that Grant wants is to get hold of the real wire-pullers, the men who hold the reins and use the Klan as a means of manipulating the Democratic party, and the State. So, don't you see your chance? You know a good many of these big-bugs and you know enough about them to give us clues that will open up the whole business, and do more good than you can imagine. Why I tell you it will be the *making of you!* We'll guarantee that all the plain countrymen shall be let go, and the prosecutions be stopped; then they'll owe their deliverance to you and you can lead them just as you wish. In fact, I don't see how you can refuse to save these poor men, whose joining the Klan was no doubt through your influence."

"There you are wrong," said I, "I do not now recollect having ever asked a single person to join the Order unless it be a few personal friends who have never been arrested, and are not likely to be; for I alone can furnish proof against them, and when I prove untrue to my friends may I—lose them!"

"You seem to have already lost them." he murmured; whereupon Lieut. McEwan joined in, saying, "Yes, I don't want to hurt your feelings, but it was a common remark at Raleigh among the Republicans, that you seemed almost abandoned by everybody. I was leaning against one of the big pillars in the Capital and I heard one of your party leaders telling ,another that you looked *guilty*, and *were* guilty, and if you got ten years at hard labor it would do you good, and all that sort of talk. Why they couldn't even raise three thousand dollars bail for you to be released until Court met!" "That isn't so!" said I, interrupting, "for I never attempted to get bail after being brought to Raleigh, and they wouldn't allow it while I was at Rutherford." "Well," he replied, "One or two of your friends tried to make up bail; for it was common talk on the streets."

"Yes," quoth Cobb, "All the leading Democrats, Senator Ransom and the rest have been working to save Plato Durham, and they've succeeded in getting his trial staved off for six months, or longer. But as for *you* you can go off and rot at Albany, so far as anybody cares. And now will you put up with that sort of thing? Do you suppose that if Durham, McAfee, H. C. Jones, David Schenk, Strudwick, or any of those men who *we* know well enough that you can implicate, would go to Albany Penitentiary, at such a time as this—right in the beginning of winter—and stay there six years when they could get out by just making a statement of all they know about you, and your connection with the Klan?"

I hung my head for a moment, reflecting how utterly improbable that I had any living friend who would thus suffer for my sake—no, not one!—but I replied, "Perhaps not: perhaps they would! I should not ask it of them, I'm sure. But this is not the consideration for me. Candidly, I feel rather hurt at some things; but"—

"If you did *not*, if you mean to allow those men to use the Klan when it suited them, and now cast you off, you will be a queer person! Why do you know what will come of your six years' imprisonment? You will have lost the best of life, you will become prematurely old and broken, you will be forgotten by everybody, you may lose your health, etc.; whereas if you were to do the square thing and help the government to break up this Klan, I'm very sure you could get a nice position in the Departments, and live comfortably."

"It's not worth while to say anything more," said I, very sadly, for it was like signing my own warrant, "I see as clearly as you, or any man, the dark future that is before me, and I much doubt if I shall get through it all; but be assured of one thing, gentlemen, I shall never purchase my liberty at the price of treachery to my comrades and dishonor to myself!"

My interlocutors instantly perceived that I had had no thought of entertaining their suggestions, and both arose, Lieut. McEwan shrugging his shoulders with the remark: *"I like your pluck, but damn your discretion!"*

Col. Cobb courteously invited me to take breakfast with them; and at first I consented, going down to the dining room with them; but as I did so a queer revulsion of feeling made me turn and go down below, among my companions *du voyage*. Need anyone be told the secret of this emotion? It was not the suffering behind, nor the years of torture before: it was the sense of abandonment, desertion, faithlessness; the realization refreshed by the communications of these outsiders, that, after all, my sacrifices, and silence, and suffering was not even appreciated by those, who had the benefit of it; and that shortly, I should be quite forgotten by them. Useless to speak of what I felt. Strange to say the remarks let fall by Lieut. McEwan as to the blame put upon me, by public sentiment, and the failure to obtain a paltry $3,000 bail-bond for me, at Raleigh, (though I could not believe any such attempt would have been made without my knowledge) disheartened and mortified me more than all that had gone before, or was yet to come!

Such moods are dangerous indeed! they make men *desperate*, and Folly is twin sister to Desperation. If any man wonder that I should so lay to heart the casual utterances of casual acquaintance, let him recall a passage of "Old Curiosity Shop's" rare gems of genius and Truth: 'The world," quoth Charles Dickens, "the world being in constant commission of vast quantities of injustice, is a little apt to comfort itself with the idea that if the victim of its falsehood and malice have a *clear conscience*, he cannot fail to be sustained under his trials, and *somehow* or other, to come out right at last, *'in which case,'* say those who have hunted him down, *'nobody will be better pleased than we!'* Whereas the world would do well to reflect that *injustice* is itself, to every generous and properly constituted mind, an *injury of all others the most insufferable,* the most *torturing,* and *the most hard to bear;* and that many *clear consciences have gone to their final account,* and many *sound hearts have broken* because of this very reason; the knowledge of their own deserts only *aggravating*

their sufferings and rendering them all the more unendurable."

True, too true! oh gifted child of Genius, and wonderful Seer of the Human Soul! Physical persecutions
slip from the shoulders like "dewdrops from the lion's
mane," but slander, and false-accusations, when accepted for the truth by those whom one has trusted and
esteemed as friends and fellow country men, acquire the
poisonous properties of pervading the whole frame,
stirring the blood in the veins to wild torture and resentment, but searing the spirit with death-wounds, it
may be!

Landing at Baltimore, and proceeding by rail northward, a little after mid-day we passed through Phila,
and went whirling away to New York. During the
whole route from Wilmington, Del., to Newark, N. J.,
I pretended to sleep, resting my head on my arms on
the back of the desk in our front, with a handkerchief
over my head, silent and thoughtful. I did not wish to
look upon these places, where I had spent my school
days, and whence I had gone ten years before, full of
boyish pride and ambition, whereas instead of the anticipated triumphs of life, I was returning with man-
acles on my wrists and a guard of those same Yankees,
I had gone to fight, and had fought so long as my
country was free, escorting to a Yankee Penitentiary
for six years torture! Surely a most melancholy out-
come of all my proud hopes! Little matter that I was
the victim of horrible outrage and wrong; who would
believe?

We began to approach New York City at 4 on the
afternoon of the 6th, whereupon Lieut. McEwan again
clasped the handcuffs upon our wrists. About sunset the
cars rolled to the Desbrosses Street Ferry in Jersey City
and without delay we boarded the ferry-boat, bound for
New York. The spectacle of eight men, handcuffed in
couples, and guarded by soldiers in full uniform (the
artillery uniform, with its red trimmings and brass
epaulets is gorgeous enough to attract attention even
in New York), speedily gathered a large crowd of
by-standers, who began to ply us with questions. Some

of the men made such timid and modest replies that I came to the front as spokesman for the party, though very nervous from lack of the stimulants of which we had all imbibed freely in the early portion of the day.

Turning to the spectators I said, "I shall not ask you gentlemen to believe anything I may say of myself; but look at this old man, David Collins of South Carolina; does he look like a desperado, or midnight marauder? He was an humble miller, 'tending his mill, as he had done for a generation. One night a gang of Federal deputy marshals went to his home, made him feed them and their horses, deceived him into showing them the way over the North Carolina line, and then arrested him, dragging him to Rutherford jail, 20 miles away, leaving his poor old wife, sick in bed, without a nurse or servant, and worried nearly to death about the old man's disapparance. Then they dragged their kidnapped victim 250 miles to Raleigh, held him for weeks, friendless, penniless, without witnesses, nor any knowledge of what were the charges against him, (for he was innocent as a babe of any real wrong-doing, though I believe nominally a member of the Klan as was every other decent man in his county) finally tried [him] before a packed jury (ten low whites and two negroes), and sentenced—well, what do you think is the sentence of that grey-haired, simple hearted old man, whose homely respectability is written on his face, and of whom the Judge himself admitted there was no specific charge except that he belonged to the *Union League* [*sic*] (otherwise called the Klan). What do you think? *Four years at hard labor, and one thousand dollars fine!*

"Then there are others. Here is this little man, Scruggs. If there is anything desperate or cruel in him, I fail to judge physiognomy! He says, and his neighbors say, he had no hand in any law-breaking and was like Collins merely a nominal member of the Klan. But in a few hours he will enter Albany Penitentiary for two years hard labor.

"Then here are Adolphus DePriest, and Geo. H. Holland; neither of whom were participants in the vigilance committee operations for which they are going

to Albany under two years' sentences. They may have
been members of the White Brotherhood; but it was
not a treasonable organization any more than is the
Union League, or the Grand Army of the Republic to
which I dare say many of you belong."

Etc., etc., etc.

My harangue had some effect. Several spectators declared it was a shame to treat men in this style; but
other's said "Oh damn 'em; that's *their* tale!" There was
one practical result, not to have been expected. The
Raleigh Jew who had heard my remarks slipped around
behind Collins, nudged him, and handed him $3, so
secretly that few saw the deed.

Reflecting that this was generosity pure and simple,
for there could be no return, my opinion of the children
of Abraham raised about half a mile.

UP THE HUDSON

Landing for a moment on Manhattan Island, we
marched a short distance up the dock and passed aboard
the superb steamer *Dean Richmond*, destined for Albany. I should have been glad to see the magnificent
scenery of the far-famed Hudson especially the Pali-
sades, within sight of which my cousin, rector of Engle-
wood Episcopal church resides; but we were marched
straight into the lower cabin, and cooped into one corner
of the extra dining-room, only used on occasion of great
excursions, etc.

As soon as the lamps were lighted a large concourse
of passengers poured down into the cabin, and surged
around us with curious eyes, just as people wander
from cage to cage in a circus menagerie, and their questions to each other had very much the sound of: "Which
is the giraffe?" "Is that the Man-Eater?" "This beast
looks tame enough!" "Be careful, don't agitate the
monkeys!", etc., etc.

Presently a sweet faced, small footed, little woman
in mourning dress, leaning on the arm of a stout old
gentleman with paternal ponderosity of bread basket,
came half way down the stairs and leaned over the
balustrades, watching us very much as women watch
wild beasts, i.e. ready to run at a moment's warning!

My companions were very weary and crouched together on the carpet tamely enough, but I, though equally tired, and almost dead from nausea and nervousness, the effect of continuous travel, in my bilious condition, could not rest, and walked to and fro within the guard-limits very much like a bear chained to a stake, or a village constable conning his election speech. The little lady seemed so interested, I several times was upon the point of making a profound *salaam*, and assuring her that at present we were quite harmless, having eaten up one or two able-bodied citizens just before we started Northward! Then I reflected that perhaps this little-footed lassie was a Southern girl, or a Southern sympathizer, and was really interested in us, not simply idly curious.

About 10 P. M. Lieut. McEwan came down with two well-dressed gentlemen, one of whom he introduced as "Colonel" (of Blank Regiment in the Next War, I suspect, as he declared himself, "disabled" by a boil on his arm, which he carried in a sling, much like a real veteran), and the other a white-bearded old citizen of Albany. They both professed to be Democrats,and kindly disposed towards the South, but were too patronizing to suit me. The civilian amused me a good deal by slipping back after the others had gone, to bid me be very careful how I talked as there were several of Grant's spies on board ready to report anything I might say. Great was his surprise to hear me declare that I would rather talk my views to U. S. Grant himself than to any of his truckling, thieving, and unscrupulous followers; that I had nothing whatever to conceal; that I was a member of the Klan, and should be again if the same condition of things should render it necessary, and as for my sentiments no one could doubt them a moment who ever knew me; though, of course, I felt the kindness of his intentions, and did not at all doubt the presence of the spies; since the whole country was being flooded with them. He no doubt thought me a desperado, indeed; as the army officers hold that Grant can do no wrong, as strongly as any *jure divino* monarchist.

FIVE MINUTES OF FREEDOM

After the crowd had pretty much dispersed to bed, I asked one of the guards to escort me in search of Lieut. McEwan, and when we had gotten upon the upper deck, where a large number of bales of cotton were standing on end, I explained to him how nervous I was, and how terribly weak and prostrate I should be in the morning at the very time I should need all my strength and composure; and in short, I urged him to give me his gun, and let me hide among the cotton bales while he should go, and get a flask of liquor for me; promising all the change from a pretty big note if he would oblige me. "But what's ter hinder your runnin' away while I'm gone?" he hesitated. "My word of honor, which I give you to stay right here! Besides did you ever hear of anybody running away from a dram of liquor? Don't wait! Give me your gun, and take this flask!" He hesitated the nineteenth part of a half of a quarter of a second; then said, "Well, I'll trust you!" and left me for fully five minutes, sitting among the cotton bales, guarding myself! Could I have broken faith with him, it would not have been difficult to escape as there [were] scores of life-preservers hanging within reach, and the steamer was within almost stone-throw of the shore, and the night too dark for the guards to have found me after the few minutes start I should have had. And it would have been glorious news at home, and all over the South to hear that I had escaped almost within sight of Albany! But I had given my word and that settled it.

It is very sad and mortifying to mention these makeshifts to sustain the ordeal of entering the Radical Bastile, to be enrolled as a felon; but it should be kept in mind that I was really very ill, and had been for several weeks, only keeping upon my feet at all, by strenuous exertion of pride, and a determination of depriving my enemies of the exultation of seeing me "break down"; supported by the fictitious strength of stimulants.

Consequently as soon as we began our long journey, and especially after spending a day and night on the tossing boat, my condition became even physically most pitiable, aside from all the mental mortification and harassment. Gladly would I bury the recollections of those days beyond even a casual thought if it were possible; but it is not possible; nor if it were, would it be right, for in sheer justice to myself and my actions both before and after, they must be told, and recorded.

Alas, after all, my prize did me scarcely any good. The soldier no doubt helped himself from the flask, in addition to keeping the "change;" so that it was only partly full. Old Mr. Collins and I occupied the same stateroom, and during the night, as I lay on the upper bunk, too nervous and sick to sleep, I heard him crying and moaning in heart-broken manner. Poor old man! He had never been out of his neighborhood in his life, and this terrible trip of nearly a thousand miles with four years of hard labor awaiting him at the Penitentiary, his destination, was too much for him; particularly as he had left his aged wife sick in bed at home! To soothe his hysterical emotions, I surprised him (for he knew nothing of my upper-deck adventure) by handing him down my flask of stimulants, bidding him drink in welcome. He did so, and though not addicted to drink, quite emptied the bottle in two swallows! It was a *calamity to me*, for which no words can fully convey meaning! Good, pious, phlegmatic folk, whose steady souls, and cool blood never crave any stimulant, or excitement, or sedative, or anodyne, cannot even conjecture my feelings. I needed the liquor, which Collins unwittingly drank, as much as a man in last stages of fever needs the physician's medicine and treatment.

It is the wretched mistake of many Temperance lecturers and most ministers to underestimate the physical torture, and real illness, resulting from cessation from stimulants; Frequently the good Parson is heard lecturing the young Inebriate to "abandon his suicidal course," "Be a *man!*" "Exert your will!" "Throw off the 'thrall'!" "Dash Down the cup!" etc., etc., when perhaps the youth has many times vainly exerted much more will in endeavors to abstain, than he himself ever possessed! Yea, and that same good old man will tell you, when asked if he approves of smoking or chewing, "No! It's a bad habit, a beastly habit. But I've gotten so used to my pipe, or cigarette, that I really cannot dispense with it. I've tried several times to break off, and *did* break off a few weeks, but it made me so miserable and nervous I took it up again."

He, however, would never recognize how many thousand times more trying is the sudden cessation of the stronger stimulants.

Sleep was now out of the question, and I could only summon what was left of my resolution, and prop myself in my bunk to watch for day through the small round port-holes which afford light in the narrow cabins; the door being locked on outside. It was a most miserable night-watch!

Gradually the river became narrower and the outlines of the shore arose from the expanse of black water, which itself became glazed by the greyish light of approaching dawn. Very cold and dismal it all appeared. Soon the sound of the waves flapping among the reeds and cavelets on the banks, began to echo the steady churning of the steamer's screw paddles. Yellow lights began to twinkle in the windows of farm-houses along the shore, speedily these lights became very numerous, indicating the suburbs of a city. The outlines of tall factories and foundries began to be visible through the fog. Several vessels at anchor. A long row of wharves, the waves dashing up under them, and splashing around the barnacled posts. Surely this is the city! And now a long, loud, deafening screech from the steamer's whistles arouses the hundreds of passengers, who have slept throughout the whole night, as sweetly as if at home in bed, though meanwhile the *Richmond* has traversed the one hundred and fifty miles from New York to Albany.

Now the engines are "slowing up," the churning ceases, the bells ring with occasional clangor, the huge vessel glides in among a forest of masts, and the sound of heavy ropes thrown upon the wharf, tell us that—
WE HAVE ARRIVED!

CHAPTER FIFTEENTH

Albany Penitentiary

The handcuffs once more click around our wrists, we march out upon the slippery wharf, eyed curiously by the disembarking passengers, and start for the Penitentiary which is more than a mile distant. A steady drizzle of rain is not strong enough to dissipate the heavy fog; and the aspect of the dilapidated warehouses, dripping awnings, muddy streets, and sloppy sidewalks, as seen in the cold grey light of this October morning, is cheerless and dispiriting beyond description. It is a great change of climate from Raleigh to Albany, at best: but coming out of warm cabins into this chilling rain, we could but shiver *physically* without considering the still more dismal fact that through this desolate suburbs we were proceeding to the Bastile whence some of us should never return! Yet at that moment I recollect having some strange fancies. Have not you at times heard echoes of old-time bells, whose chimes may have long since been silenced? Well, the deep roaring of the steam-blowing off from the *Richmond's* funnels seemed precisely the same throbbing sonorous monotone I heard in childhood as one "Fourth of July" I stood upon the grassy dome of the mammoth "Indian Mound" at Grave-Creek, on the Ohio, and listened to the bells of the steamboats passing amid the dense fog, while a great excursion steamer exhausted her cylinders at the wharf!

How wide and dismal the difference between the epochs of the twin echoes!

Lieut. McEwan at first missed the street leading to the Penitentiary, but at length found the great gate of the Park surrounding the institution. This park embraces some twenty or thirty acres in the South Western suburbs of Albany, high and rolling, and kept in continual good trim by a professional gardener. A broad gravelled carriage drive winds among the shade trees, down into a little valley, over a rustic bridge, and up in front of the main entrance of the Prison, which in the summer time when the lawn is green, the foliage luxuriant, and the numerous flower beds in full bloom, might be supposed some wealthy private asylum, or perhaps a Female Seminary. It is a school, but one with a weary, rigid course of studies, and a God-forsaken alumni.

But on this chill October morning the trees were leafless and desolate, the grass withered, the flowers slain by many a fierce North Blast; *and the Prison,—! !*

The Penitentiary Buildings occupy six acres of a level plateau or ridge at the western end of the grounds. The main building is a long, two-story brick structure, consisting of a square central block, (a story and a half higher than the remainder of the edifice) and two wings, one of which is longer than the other. The middle block, and each of the extreme sections of the wings, are covered by mansard roofs, giving something of the outline of the three domes [*sic*] of the National Capitol. At all the eight corners are battlemented towers, which with the heavy cornices, and small round windows in the towers suggest the general idea of an arsenal or citadel.

On the middle division are four minarets, or spires. This block contains the main entrance, with a handsome office on the left of the hall way, and the Superintendent's parlor, and library on the right. Back of the "office" is the "Guard Room" which is also the "Visitor's Reception Room." All of the second floor is devoted to the Superintendent's residence and is so isolated from the remainder of the building that any one brought in blindfolded might live for months without knowing he was in prison. The third floor, including the interior of the high mansard roof is the Chapel. Its capacity may be judged from the fact that it seats 800 persons, on the floor; besides 100 or more females in the gallery.

The wings are known as the "North Wing" (for females) and the "South Wing" which is also called the "Main Hall" or "Male Hall," which, indeed, is the main body of the prison, as here the bulk of the convicts are confined.

Back of each wing is a square yard, (that devoted to males having about six acres) enclosed by a thick wall, thirty feet high, with a sentry walk on top, whereon the guards promenade all day, armed with double barrel shot-guns, and repeating rifles, watching the interior of the square, and ready to shoot down any convict giving the least trouble.

In the Square in rear of the Female Department are the laundries, bakery, and other small offices. In the "Male Square" are the shoe and chair shops. The roofs of these buildings rise above the walls, but as there are no windows on the exterior side the inmates cannot see out.

Anyone standing on an adjacent hill, and viewing all the white washed walls, windowless, and deserted might imagine it some old fortress in time of peace; or perhaps he might fancy a resemblance to the picture of the ancient Greek Acropolis, where tier upon tier of lovely white walls arise. Yet within that quiet exterior is a *small city of* 1000 *inhabitants*, all busy as the united population of no town or city ever was.

ENROLLED AMONG FELONS

Never had Albany Penitentiary looked more gloomy and forbidding than on this 7th day of October, 1871, as our weary party first caught the sight of its dull-hued towers, massive walls, white and cheerless, and its strongly barred windows, within which all was dark and motionless as if eternal silence reigned in this melancholy abode. The rain pattered unceasingly from the gaunt and leafless trees while the dense fog and mist imparted an unwonted severity to the general aspect of the pile of buildings looming on the hill before us.

From the point of our approach not a creature was visible, but as we reached the great iron door, it swung open noiselessly, as if by machinery, and when all were entered swung shut with a sullen *"slam!"* that seemed to echo the words—Gone! Done! And truly it would have been in keeping with the place to see written in deep black characters over that iron arch the legend from Dante's Inferno:—

"Abandon Hope ye who enter here!"

God and the records only can tell how many wretched souls entering here have found it so! To my own heart the sullen bang of the shutting gate was a pang whose vividness portrayed it to be the death-knell of a last secret hope I must have cherished despite all probability, that something would yet turn up to save me from this fate. Henceforth there remained but to— *Endure!*

REMAINDER OF LIFE

Six Years
Hard Labor

Patience
Philosophy
Truth

PRIDE

And thus great were the odds; a heavy burden truly for the pedestal of Pride, Patience, and Philosophy, even though joined with Truth! It was a fearful future, and the reality was destined to prove even more miserable than my gloomiest apprehensions. But to the facts!

As the outer gates swung open to admit us a loud-sounding bell, above it, clanged the announcement of our arrival, which had been telegraphed in advance. We are marched to a door in rear of the Main Building, through which we pass into the Guard Room, which is also the Visitors Waiting, or Reception Room. It is a long apartment, with windows overlooking the prison yards. The floor is covered with oil-cloth, there are several desks, and large tables, pictures on the walls, and two or three dozen cane-seated chairs. The ceiling is high and airy; the whole apartment wears a neat, clean, and cheerful look. Visitors remark, "This isn't very prison-like," and go away admiring the admirable order and neatness of the Institution!

One thing may have been overlooked—a long rack, against the walls for guns and pistols; also, the windows are heavily barred! True, the bars are only about the size of a broom-handle, and are nicely painted, yet you couldn't cut them in a day! The sleek-looking glove covers every feature of the Prison in similar style; visitors see only the glove and are quite enraptured over it, prisoners feel the iron beneath the glove, and many, after a brief effort to endure it, turn their faces to the wall—*and die!*

How strange is fate, how wonderful the followings of misfortune! One thought I had frequently reverted in mind, while suffering the malicious persecutions of the North Carolina Radicals, was that when finally taken to Albany I should at least escape seeing any of the aforesaid tribe, and should be relieved of their spiteful malice which had added a thousand needless tortures to my imprisonment. Yet the first face I saw within the Guard Room was that of a North Carolina Radical, E. Hubbs, post master of Newbern, editor of the Radical organ there, and holder of other offices to which the negroes of that unfortunate region have overwhelming mastery. Why should Hubbs be here at this unusual hour, on this rainy morning? I can only suppose he was visiting his home (he came to Newbern with the Yankee army during the War) at some point in, or near Albany, and hearing I should be enrolled among felons on this morning came with a party of friends to witness the spectacle! What he said to the prison official I have never learned, but it could hardly be otherwise than in disparagement of me, since I had not been sparing of the Mongrels and Carpet-baggers when I published the *Journal of Commerce* in New Bern. Thus would the first impression received by my keepers, especially the "overseers" and "guards," several of whom were standing with Hubbs when he bowed to me, be an unfavorable and prejudiced one! But I had gotten to expect all sorts of "arrows of misfortune," and really had not long to wonder at this untimely visit of one of the enemy; because the march of mortification was still—onward!

THE LIVING GRAVE

Passing through the Guard Room, wherein every sound, even that of conversation, is suppressed nearly to the tone of a whisper, we are taken in charge by a sullen looking keeper, whose thick-cloth slippers enable him to tread noiselessly as a cat; and are escorted through two (double) doors, lined with green baize to exclude every sound of the prison and down a flight of

steps into the "Main Hall," or convicts quarters, a vast
hall high and broad as a city church, and containing
features which at even the first sweeping glance has
struck a chill to the heart of many a casual visitor, much
more to him who comes to pass years upon years—perchance all of life—within it! It is the Convict's Living
Grave! It is the innermost *Inferno,* the *hopeless* hell!

The prisoner, once securely within its iron jaws becomes an hundred times more abjectly subject to
autocratic rule than the French "galley-slave," or the
Siberian "exile." His very senses, and faculties of sight,
speech, hearing, gesticulation, motion of arms and legs,
clothing, food, hours of sleep—all are controlled, dom-
inated, fitted to iron rules until the man is merged into
a machine, an automaton workman, always engaged in
silent, solemn, sombre execution of a round of prescribed toil, dictated by the master!

To myself, never having so much as seen anything
of the kind, the repulsive features of this abode of ignominy and crime were horribly oppressive. The simple
aspect of the interior struck me with a chill shiver, as
if it had been my grave!

Conceive, if you can, a vast hall, fifty feet in height,
as many feet broad, and two, or more, hundred feet long,
with a floor of stone flagging, and tall, barred windows
too high from the floor to admit of any one looking out.

In the middle of this long shell of brick is an oblong
block of masonry eighteen feet thick, and running
nearly the whole length of the building. In this central
block are the *cells,* honey-combed in regular rows, like
the port-holes of a fort, or the palings on a garden fence.
Half of the cells face towards the east, and at their
backs the other half face towards the west.

The central block of masonry extends from the floor
to the ceiling, and the honey-comb of cells are in four
rows or tiers, one above another; the upper tier being
fully 20 feet from the floor. Iron balconies, two feet
wide, with hand rail, supported upon iron brackets and
stanchions, run the entire length of each of the three
upper tiers, to give means of access to the cells. Stair-
ways at each end ascend to these narrow galleries.

Each tier has 86 cells; so that there are 344 cells opening into the "East" corridor and into the "West". But there are a number of detached cells elsewhere. Between 800 and 1000 convicts have been confined in the Prison at one time. Each cell is three feet wide, six and one half feet long, and the same in height. The door is a frame of parallel iron rods, like a cellar grating, or a grid-iron. The rods have a little more than one inch of interval between them; and through these interstices must come all the air, the light, the heat, the sound, that the inmates receive, summer or winter. Two stoves in each corridor are supposed to furnish warmth, and it is possible the upper tiers of cells are comfortable but the ground floor rarely gets the chill off of its damp and cavernous interior even in ordinary wintry weather of that latitude. Of this more hereafter. As for light, the the lower tiers scarcely know what it is, even by day. The windows do not come down nearer the floor level than about nine feet, and are some fifteen feet distant from the cell doors. In cold weather the glass becomes heavily frosted by the steam from so many breaths, greatly obscuring the light. At dusk several gas jets are lighted at the side of the lateral wall, but are extinguished at 8 P. M. in summer, and 9 P. M. in winter. Except in cells directly opposite the jet the light is insufficient to read without straining the eyes.

The interior of the cell shows four bare walls, whitewashed, (no pictures or other ornamentation, are allowed), a wooden slop-bucket, an iron rack, on hinges, like a shelf, a straw mattress, (or canvas bag, filled with coarse straw) and two blankets; "Only this, and nothing more!" The walls, floor, and ceiling are all of stone.

Viewed on a cold raw day, when but little light penetrates the murky windows, this vast human hive—the cells vacant, the iron doors thrown back, disclosing the cold, damp, cheerless interior, like so many caves in the side of a massive rock—is indiscribably gloomy. Gloomier still is the aspect of the block, when the inmates are within, so that each hole in the wall shows its haggard face either crouching at the door-bars, seeking light and heat, or pacing to and fro within the narrow limits, like wild-beasts in the circus cages!

Speaking of these cheerless hives, (the living grave of many a life susceptible to noble endeavor, and usefulness were an opportunity not denied), the Right Reverend F. D. Huntingdon, Episcopal Bishop of the Diocese of Central New York, last year wrote as follows:—

In our fickle fortunes, in the fierce assaults of sin and dissolving barriers between class and class, no one knows whether one of his own kindred may not be dragged in there. *Think of living in a big box, of which three sides are shut*—a dismal, half-darkened window, more than fourteen feet away from you and perhaps above you, with no southern sunshine even—*in a cell not much larger than an old fashioned oven with only* a grated opening two feet by seven, a box within a box, and wooden balustrades to deepen the darkness, in storms, in fogs, in the heat of summer, with *sweltering human forms all around you and ventilation impossible.* Why, it would make the blood of the toughest Supervisor boil, and he would go mad.

Almost the first glance around the vast hall was arrested by a spectacle surpassing anything I have yet portrayed. Crouching upon their knees, or crawling upon all-fours, to scrub and mop the dark stone pavement, were a dozen or so of sallow-faced, squalid fellows, dressed in ill-fitting and dirty suits of coarse lindsey-woolsey, half of each garment being the natural grey, and the other half dyed black, or tobacco color. Dirt, and the wetting of their clothes by the swabbing rendered them still more revolting. Not one dared to raise his head to view the party of newcomers, but each man managed to cast frequent furtive glances from under his sunken eyebrows with an expression of half-idiotic curiosity suppressed by spaniel-like cringing before the overseer, (who yelled at them to *"Keep your eyes down! Go on with that scrubbing! Mind what you are about!"*) that struck me first as an awful revelation, then as a pang of horrow! as a knife to the heart! Great

Heavens! were these the fruits of prison-life! Were we *all* doomed to sink into the counterparts of these cowering, sneaking, and hopeless Soul-Dwarfs? Far better to die at once! All that ever I read of noble intellects shrivelling into idiocy under the wear and want of iron subjection and drudgery seemed verified in the persons of these creatures! Suddenly my spell-bound gaze was startled by a sharp metallic voice at my shoulder, giving command, *"Fold your arms! Turn your face to the wall! Keep your eyes on the floor! Stop looking around! Stand till you're called for!"*

The merciless grip of Albany Penitentiary discipline had closed upon us! It was the Deputy Superintendent, or Head Keeper, and his harsh, despotic tone had a grating sound, a rasping intonation, such as never before had been addressed to my Southern ears, even when I carried a musket as a private in the ranks of Lee's army, and I *almost* involuntarily resented it by a look and a momentary hesitation turning my face to the wall that probably cost me dearly.

The entire party were made to stand close at the wall, heads bowed, eyes on the floor, arms folded, silent, motionless, weary, sorrowful! Young Bailey and one or two of the "deputies" who had come with the escort passed in rear of us and, while ascending the staircase, Bailey called to me to say, "Good-Bye!" With an infraction of orders, I turned slightly, bowed, and said "Farewell, Sir!"

Luckily the Wardens were not immediately present, and no reproof was given us.

The waiting was long and tiresome. None of us had had any breakfast. I, myself, had eaten nothing for the 48 hours previous; being too sick and nauseated to endure the sight of food; though for lack of it I was now extremely weakened, and could scarcely stand without pressing my head against the wall. Yet, so strong is pride, I stood as erect as possible, and, perfectly motionless while every nerve and sinew seemed snapping with fiery fever!

Behind us were the many new and sickening sounds of the Prison, the clanging of the iron doors, the rapid footsteps of the "Hall-Men," running along the upper galleries collecting the breakfast pans from the cells, the distant rumble of the machinery and ponderous driving-wheels of the engines, and the harsh voices of the overseers ordering the "Hall-Men" (a special class of crippled convicts, and those imprisoned for 30 days— too brief to learn a trade), or reproving some man for negligence, a strange, but suggestive, medley of sounds; amid which the lazy "slush," "slush," "slush," "Swash-slush," "Swash-slush," of the floor-moppers was a constant reminder of the horrible degradation here dwelling!

Meanwhile the wind had risen, and was driving clouds of icy mist down upon our bare heads, from the open window, through the latticed bars of which came the keen whistling of the outer storm, telling that we had arrived just at the beginning of winter, not such winter as we had known in Carolina's temperate clime, but Arctic iciness!

"BOOKED!"

A cat-like step behind us, a tap on the shoulder, a slight nod, and we are one by one marched to a desk, under the stairway leading to the upper balconies, whereon is a ponderous folio, half a foot thick, containing the names of thousands of miserable creatures that have been dragged, justly or unjustly, within the shadow! The "Deputy-Keeper" rasps the formal questions like a talking machine:—

"What is your name in full?" Answer: *Randolph Abbott Shotwell!"*

"What is your native State?" Answer: *"Virginia!"*

"What State do you come from?" Answer: *"North Carolina!"*

"What is your age? Height? Complexion? Color of Eyes? Occupation?"

"Read and write?" Answer: *"Tolerably!"*

"Use tobacco?" Answer: *"In no shape, or quantity!"*

"Temperate or intemperate?—At this question I was slightly puzzled. No man could charge me with being a public drunkard, a frequenter of bar-rooms or anything of that sort; and until after the war I scarcely knew the taste of liquor. But as the sequence (though

far from excused thereby) of my long suffering from fever and ague (or 'the chills,' in common parlance) in 1866, at Newbern, I had learned to drink altogether too freely at times, and as already stated in these pages, had suffered the torments of *Tartarus,* both physically and mentally, from this fatal habit, during the past half-dozen months.   Therefore, when he repeated the question I made answer, sorrowingly as here:—

"Temperate or intemperate?"—"Not habitually temperate, Sir"

"Married or single?"—"Unmarried, and so to remain!"

"I did not ask you that!   Answer what you're asked! No more, no less!   "Now go back to the wall! fold your arms, and keep your eyes down!   Do you hear me? Keep your eyes on the floor; and stand there till you're wanted!"

As I return to the wall, I catch a glimpse of this watchful and wonderful piece of human machinery tip-toeing, in his thick-soled (listing bottom) slippers, a-cross the hall to pounce on a slovenly rascal who is down on his hands and knees in the slops of the floor—scouring, pretending to scrub, but making signs to one of his fellows!   The deputy really seemed to have eyes in the back of his head.

Each member of our party is asked the same questions, the answers recorded, and thus, in a brief space, we, eight Southern citizens, as free from crime or criminal taint as any of our fellow citizens (I speak for myself, at all events) after having been dragged a thousand miles from our Highland homes, and made to undergo all manner of mortification, calumny, cruelty, and persecution, were finally registered as eight convicts, subject to the severest sentences!   Can you realize what this means?   Can you conceive what it is to find yourself in a strange land; among strangers, in a Penitentiary, in the most terrible harsh Penitentiary in America, sentenced to six years of hard labor, afar from every relative and friend, among the vilest of mankind, and really enrolled and uniformed on a footing of equality, with these felons!   Can you even imagine what it is

to stand thus in the shadow of a Penitentiary and upon
the threshold of "six years at hard labor!"   Great God!
the very recollection recalls a fearful shudder such as
few men have known, I hope!

IN CONVICT GARB!

Enrolled as felons on the Prison Register, we next
must be clothed with the felon uniform.   It is the cul-
mination of mortifications, relieved by solely   one
thought, namely that the clothes, no more than the classification, as convicts cannot taint the soul of him who
knows he endures both through injustice and wrong
of powerful enemies.

"Go to the barber's chair," quoth the Warden.   In
one corner of the hall was a large chair, a shelf, and a
negro convict, denominated the "Barber," whose time
was occupied in shaving the heads and beards of the
prisoners.   He was a spiteful, malicious rascal, and
made himself truly *Barba-rous* to many.

Forgetting my situation I foolishly remarked to the
turnkey, *"I shaved last night, and"*—The sentence was
never finished!   *"Sit down!"* roared the keeper.   *"Do
as you are told, and no talk about it!"*   The tone of absolute command made my ears burn, and my heart ache,
during all the time my hair and beard were being
shorn, barbarously.   And yet, so near are tears and
laughter, I came near bursting into a laugh, at the
comical expression of my comrades when their heads
were shaved.   Few men have any idea how much they
owe to hair and whiskers.   The hirsute appendage
constitutes all the difference between a passable looking man and a very ugly looking monkey.

Next we are marched, one by one to the bath-tub, a
big iron pan or tub in a niche of the wall. The cold,
October blasts are driving down through the open case-
ments, and the damp flags are not pleasant for bare feet,
yet we are forced to strip *in puris naturalibus* and
make a pretense of "washing" though, in my case, the
overseer was pleased to remark that—*"Your skin is
mighty white, for such a hairy man!   I reckon you
don't need washin'.* (Is it possible! How kind! Thanks!
—I *thought,* but took precise care not to think out

loud)—*"Come! git out, and put on this here jacket, an'
breeches!"*

This "Ordeal of the Bath" was excessively disagreeable to me, not only on account of the extreme cold, but
because any well-bred gentleman of delicacy, and decency, naturally revolts at such exposure amid such a
gang. But I suppose there are not many inmates of
the place who care in the least, and it would make no
difference to the prison officials if they should care; the
bath is really an excuse to strip and inspect the new
convict to see if he may not have letters, or money, or
weapons, etc., concealed about his person. For the same
reason his underclothing is all taken away, and thoroughly examined, lest these articles (especially money,
wherewith to bribe the guard) should be quilted in the
linings.

As for our outer clothing, including our linen shirts,
collars, cravats, cuffs, etc., all was rolled into a bundle,
tied with a bit of twine, to which a wooden label is
attached, the name written, and the bundle tossed into
the "clothes vault," there to remain until the prisoner is
freed, either by death, pardon, or limitation. This surely is a needless piece of severity, as it would do no harm
to allow the prisoner to have his own shirts, and to wear
a cravat and collar.

"Git into them duds!" repeated the turnkey, impatiently. But the "gittin' in" was not so easy as neither
article was large enough. The shirt was a plain canvas
sack, precisely like a coffee sack with short sleeves sewed
at the sides. It had neither bosom, collar, nor cuffs,
and was so coarse the sensation was very much like
"Sackcloth," or the use of a flesh-towel!

*"Them draw-yers and sock-ses you kin git nex' week
when they is marked, and 'xamin'd!"* vouchsafed the
turnkey in answer to my look of surprise at being left
without underclothing in such climate.

The prison garb consists of a short jacket, a waistcoat, and a pair of pantaloons, all made of coarse,
greyish linsey-woolsey, part of jacket being of a light
grey, the other half very dark, almost making a contrast.
Both jacket and pantaloons were many sizes too small

and too short for me.   Indeed there were features of this uniform that annoyed more than I shall attempt to tell here.

The head covering was a "sailor's tarpaulin," or round, rimless, cloth cap, of a light blue color, and without any stiffening whatever.   These blue caps were originally made for the United States navy, but were not accepted.   They give an "uniform appearance" to the convicts, but are very unfit for such a climate as they have no rim to shield from sun, rain, sleet, or icy blasts.

LOCKED IN "CELL NO. NINE"

I have tried to speak lightly of these details, though when taken together, and under the circumstances, they constituted a most harassing ordeal.   Bravely as I sought to bear them I was almost broken down, and finally the warden, who was not a cruel man at heart, remarked my paleness and tremors, for the stripping entirely nude in the cold damp atmosphere (the 7th of October at Albany—150 miles due North from New York—is much more wintry than the 7th of *December* at Raleigh) had given me a thorough chill, whereupon he gruffly asked "Hello! What's the matter with you?"

"I am very weak, and seem to be getting a chill!" I responded.

"Oh pshaw! that aint it!   You're only a bit nervous. Most fellers feels it fust time they comes here .   You'll git over it purty soon!   Howsomedever, you kin go in that cell, Number Nine, an' wrap up till you gits warm."

And he took me by the arm, for I was ready to fall headlong on the flagging.   Prisoners alone know the meaning of the word *grateful!*   The little touch of friendliness by the Hall-Warden (who soon afterwards was discharged for not enforcing the regulations rigidly) made me forget instantly all his rough and uncouth utterances; and thank him as if he had done me great favor.

For furniture there is a wooden bucket, a small vessel for drinking water, and an iron bedstead fastened to the wall on hinges, like a leaf of a dining table, or a shelf. It is, in fact, simply a shelf attached to the wall at the height of two feet from the floor, and designed to be turned up against the wall, when not used as a bed.   A straw mattress, a straw pillow, round and rigid as a log of wood, with three blankets, constitute the only bedding; which must all be hung upon the wall when not in use. A common Bible, and small box for salt, complete the list of furniture. "Only this, and nothing more"—in the words of the song—is allowed in the cells; except it be a few small articles of toilet service, such as brushes, combs, and mirror, that may be secreted behind the bedding. No pictures, or any other ornaments, are allowed to be exhibited; the object being to have the walls of the cells clean, bare, and glistening with white wash. As may be supposed, the effect is to render them cold, cheerless, and depressing in the highest degree; vastly different from the cells of most State's prisons, which are enlivened by many a trinket, cromo, mirror, or other "home-like" contrivance, according to the prisoners taste.

Turning down the iron-bed rack, I hurriedly stretched the dirty blankets thereon, and myself on the blankets. The Warden slammed the iron door, locked it, and went after another of the Klansmen.

It is impossible to describe the sensation of *oppressiveness* on being first locked into these narrow cells. Bishop Huntington described them as boxes of stone with an iron-grating at one end. To me it seemed more like entering a damp and mouldy vault; for each cell is about as wide, as long, and as deep as a well-dug grave!

Alas! they are in truth a grave for many a man; a tomb wherein have withered and perished, not only many a bright reputation and youthful ambition, but also many a soul for which there might have been—Redemption.

TAKE OFF THEM SHOES

As advised by the Hall-Warden I had lain down on the blankets but did not cover myself with them, because they were very dirty and odorous the cell having been just vacated by some filthy fellow—possibly a negro—and I shrank from touching them more than was absolutely necessary. I did not take off my shoes, because my stockings were taken from me, and I needed the warmth of the shoe; which, moreover, was much cleaner than the blankets. Indeed I was too miserable to think much of it one way or another.

But suddenly I found myself "warmed up" disagreeably. A dark shadow had crept to the cell door, and the rasping voice of the deputy-keeper bade me, "Get up there! Get up and take off them shoes! Don't you know enough to take off your shoes when you go to bed!"

The tone was so stern, yet contemptuous, it struck me like a blow in the face! For I was powerless to resent it, or even worse! I was as helpless as a dog that one might spit upon, and kick brutally without any danger!

Half stupified, and wholly stupid, I returned some answer about my shoes being cleaner than the musty blankets, but he cut me short with a loud "Shut your mouth! Not a word! Not a word out o' you! You take off them shoes. What's the matter with them blankets? They're good enough for you!" etc., etc.

I had not yet learned the full rigor of the discipline, and did not know how grievously I had sinned in thus "answering back." Ah! how bitterly I was learning my lessons! For some time after this occurrence I sat on the iron rack mentally as well as physically. Anger was at first the predominating feeling, for it seemed outrageously unjust to censure me where it was evident I meant no wrong. Then gloom and despondency fell round me like the blackness of a fearful storm; for in these few hours I realized the hopelessness of escaping maltreatment even among these strangers. Thought seemed to wander in a circle, beginning with the agonizing interrogation, "Can it really be? Is it not all a dream that I—that I—am really in a Penitentiary?"—and coming round again to the same question, "Surely this is not *real!* 'Tis some hideous dream!"

But the "Deputy" had just put all 'dreaming' out of my head for many a long day!

A PETTY PRISON NERO

As the Deputy-Superintendent is more feared than the Superintendent himself, and is an hundred times more hated, by the prisoners, because he is never absent from them, and is in direct and pitiless mastery over them; and as he is to appear very often in my journal, it may be proper to glance briefly at his general character.

If it be true that some men are born already shaped and equipped for certain walks of life, Deputy Scripture must have been born in a prison, and molded to become its keeper. If ever there was a born prison keeper this was the man. His habits were regular and stolid as a machine's; and his character was that of a martinet, unrelieved by the vicissitudes and interruptions of circumstance that often prevent the military martinet from developing fully. Albany Penitentiary system is *human-clock work,* without the slightest change or deviation during the 365 days of the year; so that the deputy had full opportunity to make himself, as he was, the arbitrary, unbending, uncaring, unceasing, "Lord and Master" of the miserable men committed to his power. Neither Roman Nero, nor Spanish Philip, nor Turkish Sultan, nor Russian Czar, was ever invested with, or at least ever exercised, the despot's supremacy over his basest serfs that this man, or the Superintendent, of whom he was the executive agent and representative, daily, hourly, momentarily exerted over the inmates of this prison. The Autocrat of all the Russias may cut off a prisoner's head, or send him to snowy Siberia; but the Deputy, is absolute master of my sight, speech, food, clothing, occupation, medicines, posture, and every action of my daily life! When I speak to him I must fold my arms, and assume an attitude of humble supplication. If I am sent for from the workshops, I must fold my arms across my breast, fix my eyes on the floor, and thus cross the square (open and bleak though it is) and enter his presence, or go to meet my father, looking—in this style!

The Deputy is a medium-size, square-shouldered man, compactly built, and standing habitually with feet (which are large and flat as two red bricks) very wide apart, planted as if he meant to stand like the Colossus of Rhodes with a foot on each side the harbor. His neck is short, and stocky; hands large. His hair, and a full beard, are black as jet, as are also his eyes, giving him a rather handsome visage, when his features are relaxed from the expression of cat-like watchfulness fast becoming habitual. The short, firm upper lip are those of a tyrant; his keen, vigilant eyes are those of a detective, and they have a really wonderful faculty of seeing an hundred minute details at a single glance, so swift and disguised that I myself could have seen nothing whatever in it.

His power over the under-officers of the Prison is almost as rigorous as over us. Like the Roman Centurion, he has but to "Come hither," "Go hither," "Do this," and they do it! For this reason he is much disliked, perhaps hated, but *feared,* and obeyed. . . .[1]

MARCHING IN

At the time we arrived the cells were open, the iron doors thrown back; and the men nearly all out in the shops at work. So that after the breakfast pans had been gathered, and the cells brushed out, and the floor of the corridors mopped with sand, and the windows all lowered, the great compartment became almost quiet. Now and then the shadow of a turnkey passed in front of my door, as he peered between the bars, watching to see what I had in hand: but as they all wore cloth-slippers, the sound was scarcely perceptible.

In this quietness I must have fallen into a doze, being thoroughly exhausted, for suddenly I sprang up, with a nervous start, at hearing an incomprehensible loud roaring sound, as if one had awakened to find all the doors and windows slamming amid a hurricane! It was bewildering for a moment. Then I caught the *slapping* of hundreds of feet on the pavement, the roar of hundreds more feet passing along the iron balconies, over-head, and then a successive shower of sounds made by slamming the iron doors of the cells, as column after column ascended to the three upper tiers, and into their cells. The meaning of this roaring-banging noise sound

---

1 A quotation from an article in Appleton's of March, 1874, on New York prisons, is here omitted.

then was the return of the convicts from the work shops to eat their frugal meal.

The first row, or ground tier, was last to come in, and my heart stood still as I heard the regular tramp-stamp! —tramp-stamp!—tramp-stamp! coming along the corridor, each foot striking the pavement at the same moment. Presently the line passed my cell, and it was with a shudder I noted it. Oh! that I had skill to picture these scenes—those men!

The men were in a single file, back and breast touching, each man with his hand on the right shoulder of the man in front of him; the leader having his arms folded on his breast, and his whole body thrown back to resist the forward pressure of the long line behind him.

Each convict carries on his left arm a red bucket for slops: it has a thick wooden cover and serves for a seat in the cell.

Each convict wore the same greyish suit, jacket, pantaloons cut in the old fashioned style (with front flap), and the round blue-cloth sailor's cap. Every man put down his foot at the same moment making a stamping sound; and all were required to face towards the overseer who walked at the side of the line, keenly watching the men's eyes to see that none are raised from the floor, not any convict whispering to another.

The effect of the long line of men, all moving like machines, all with faces fixed and expressionless, and every eye downcast is not a pleasant one.

When the line arrives in front of its tier, each man separates from the rest, hastens into his cell, pulls the door shut, and holds it until it has been locked by the overseer who passes quickly from door to door locking it.

The lower tier, embracing 66 cells, have but a single inmate per cell, as was intended for all, (and surely a room 3 feet wide, by 6½ long, and the same in height is but narrow limits, for even *one* grown person!) but owing to the over-crowding of the institution by the Federal Courts nearly all the second and third tiers, and a portion of the fourth, have two men in each!

A SECOND SLAP

Some time before the convicts came in, a tin pan (capable of holding half a gallon) was placed on the pavement, just outside my cell door, containing my dinner; viz—a slice of loaf bread, a piece of gristle of some kind of dark meat, and 4 small potatoes. It was now two full days since I had eaten a mouthful, but I had no relish for such diet as this, especially as it had become entirely cold, and the pan *greasy!* However I was about to learn that my likes or dislikes were of not the least consequence.

After the convicts were all locked in, the overseer, a reddish-haired, irascible rascal, named Ross (if I am rightly informed), who delights to pull his whiskers on each side of his chin, *a la* Dundreary—and is very overbearing, suddenly appeared in front of my cell, and curtly demanded—

"Why aint you up, an' a-holdin' the door?"

"Sir?" said I, getting up, and coming to the door.

"Take hold of it!" he cried, in sharper tone.

I hesitated; not having the slightest idea as to his meaning; whereupon he roared:—

"Take-hold-of-that-door! *Take them bars, in your lef' han'!*"

Still ignorant of his wishes, and confused by his abusive manner, I stupidly grasped the door with my *right* hand, not knowing that in this case the right was wrong.

"Confound you! Blockhead! Take-hold-of this door with your left!" he roared, in a passion.

"Yes, but I did not understand what you"—

"Shut your gab!" he interrupted, "and pick up that pan!"

At last I had caught an idea of what was wanted. It is the rule of the prison for each man to stand at his door, holding it with his left hand so that the moment the turnkey inserts his key and unlocks the door the man may push it open, seize his dinner pan with his right hand, and hastily spring backward into the cell, drawing the door shut after him, and holding it tightly until the turnkey re-locks it. By this means 300 cells are locked in a few minutes. A simple thing enough when explained, (and half dozen words would have told me precisely what I should do) but as unintelligible from the overseer's abrupt commands, as if he had yelled at me to—"Flip-flop crosswise!"

As may be supposed there was little pleasure in a meal obtained through such an ordeal. Instead of eating it my impulses all prompted me to trample the stuff under feet, and hurl the pan at the head of the low fellow who had so unreasonably insulted me.

A BITTER STRUGGLE

This third rebuff within the *three first hours* of my incarceration was bitter indeed! It fell upon me with staggering effect, as if one who had been wounded and weakened so that he could scarcely keep upon his feet, were struck a tremendous blow in the face!

For a long time I sat on the narrow cot (which serves for a seat as well as a bed), brooding over the astonishing fact that I had been thus hectored and abused by men whom I should not have thought of treating as my equals in any respect, morally, mentally, socially, or physically. Yet whom I had not dared to reply to, or resent! The very fact that my indignation must be concealed, and the brow-beating received in stolid silence, made the aggravation many times stronger. The resentment of a sour, moody, disposition is far deadlier than your passionate person who explodes with dreadful wrath then forgets in an hour! and the reason, I imagine, is that anger, like steam, is safest when unconfined.

Twenty minutes after the men were locked in their cells, a large gong sounded, the overseers hastened to their respective tiers, and at a second tap of the gong the noise I have described was repeated as the six or seven hundred convicts tramped along the iron galleries, down the stairs and out into the work shops: all moving in the same single file, lock-step, silence, and down cast eyes.

It was a sickening spectacle—the long line of lanky forms, and haggard faces, as they passed my cell door, going out for five hours more of drudgery. Truly, as a writer has said, *"There is no melancholy so impressive as that of a convict. There are no faces that so fix them-*

selves on the memory, so some that may be seen in these gatherings of the worst and lowest of mankind! The principal reason is that they have been shaven perfectly bare. They have been robbed of those veils of hair that have kept so many secrets of the physiognomy, and their tell-tale lips stand revealed!"

Sitting back in the twilight of the cell, and watching the procession filing past the narrow door, was like witnessing a panorama of Portraits from Pandemonium; a succession of sullen, sallow, soulless faces! or sharp, sneaking suspicious faces! or silly, snickering, shameless faces! or sad, solemn, suffering faces! nearly all indicating ignominious idiocy, in greater or less degree. And no wonder! For they rarely see or hear anything to suggest new ideas or divert the tendency of gloomy introspection.

"Great God!" I murmured, as the echoes of the heavy tramp! tramp! tramp! tramp! died away into the outer yard. *"Can it be that I, too, must become as these! Shall I, too, acquire that hideous expression and stamp of degradation? Never! Never! Sooner, let me die! Yea! a thousand times sooner let me die, and be thrown into the Potter's field!"*

Yet there seemed no other alternative. How vividly arose upon my memory all that ever I had read of the wreck of mind and body wrought by long imprisonment and abuse! How the victims of Venice were reduced to mere gibbering idiots! How the Huguenots in the French galleys preferred drowning to mental death! How Tasso's reason tottered, and Bunyan became the "Crazy Tinker."

And how much to be envied were these illustrious prisoners, since they were simply *confined,* not subjected to daily drudgery, unceasing watching and above all, surrounded by the associations and attributes of Felony!

Ten years, a dozen years, merely shut up in a room, but supplied with books, writing material, and ordinary prison treatment, would have been a great boon in exchange for only *six* years of life in this fearful treadmill where the body is made to drudge continually, while the

mind is left to sicken and wither, while the soul is warped
to basest emotions!

Already I had seen that no wish of mine to obey the
requirements of the institution, and thereby escape insulting usages would be of any avail. Thrice already
had my ears been made to burn, and my soul to grow
hot with passion at unsparing rebukes for offences arising from ignorance!

THE LAST FAMILIAR FACE

During the afternoon, as I sat on the bed-rack,
wrapped in blankets, and almost unable to hold my
head from against the dirty wall, the doorway suddenly
became darkened, and Lieut. McEwan appeared, under vigilant convoy of the Deputy. Seeing me in convict garb, barefooted, and miserable, he looked shocked,
and thrust his hand between the bars of the door to grasp
mine, saying in a tone of sympathy—"*This will never
do! I must get you out!*" His friendliness led me to
throw off reserve, and speak to him as if a friend, reply-
ing that I heartily hoped he could do something, as I
felt that a long period of this life would kill me. Instantly the Deputy interjected himself with the demand: "What's the reason o' that? What's to hinder
you from standin' it? All you got to do is ter make up
your mind to grin an' bear it!" Probably he had no
idea that this kind of hectoring was one of the tortures
of the life!

I made no direct response, but said that while I had
no hope of release—I should feel grateful for anything
he (Lieut. McEwan) might do towards affecting it.
"Well you can count on me, I am going to see Judge
Bond in Baltimore in behalf of Collins and Scruggs as
I promised while we were coming here; and I mean
to talk to him about your case." Of course I could not
forbid these kindly intentions: though I saw nothing to
be gained thereby. Lieut. McEwan seemed really desirous of extricating me from the position in which my
enemies had forced me. And as his was the last friendly face I should probably see in years, this farewell visit
affected me more than I should have supposed possible
from a blue-coated Yankee officer; one, also, who had

just lent his services as a soldier to support, and carry out, the political persecutions of our Radical oppressors.

Ah! how dreadful the situation that makes even the humiliated victim ready to shed tears of gratitude for common courtesies!

The remainder of the day was gloomiest of my life. Too weak to sit upright, and too nervous to rest a moment in one position I tossed on the narrow iron rack that serves for a bed, until it threatened to fall with me; as, indeed, it afterwards oftentimes did. The afternoon was cold, dark, and rainy, the half congealed drops rattling against the great windows across the corridor with a keen suggestion of the dreary winter so fast approaching. The bare greyish-walls, stone floor and roof, of the cell, on this damp day were to my unaccustomed eyes the very *fac simile* of a burial vault, and the unaired, unclean blankets had much of the musty odor of the dismal tomb. The dense, murky clouds drifted so low as almost to obscure the outer windows so that even the halls were shrouded in gloom; while the little light . . . .

CHAPTER SIXTEENTH

The Early Days—The First Sunday—Chapel Service

"Ugh!" What does this mean! Clang! Clang! Clang! the peal of the great gong at the end of the hall warns every one to spring up, and get ready to go out to work. But, No! this must be Sabbath morning, and there is no work, save for a portion of the inmates. But each man must get up, roll up his blankets, hang his mattress against the wall, and stand by the door, with hand on the bar, ready to stoop and pick up his breakfast-dish when the turnkey unlocks the door.

To awaken from a restless, unsatisfying sleep, amid the chilly twilight of a cloudy October morning, and find oneself an inmate of the narrow cell of a Penitentiary, on the *first* of a succession of *more than two thousand* similar awakenings to the same spot; to find no water for washing, no comb, brushes, glass, or other toilet articles; to hear near by the muffled sounds of five hundred fellow prisoners, shuffling on their coarse garments, or pacing to and fro on the hard pavement within the cramped space allotted each for a home; to feel oneself utterly relaxed, chilly, damp, forlorn and oppressed—What situation more deplorable! And if to all this be added *mortification,* just self reproach, and utter despair of recovering from thrown away opportunities—if this *could* be imagined by the reader he would understand — much! Happily there was no great leisure for brooding.

The morning is dark, damp, and chilly, and I am more nervous, tremulous, and unrested than yesterday, for the sustaining effect of excitement and desperation is wearing off. Gladly would I stake a full year of my life—however short it may be—for some relief, something to quiet my quivering nerves, and aching body which seems in a condition of collapse, from head to foot! But neither liquor, tobacco, nor sedatives can be had in prison, and I could not even see the surgeon until some time near mid-day. What then? Mental resolution must stand for physical strength until help come. I drag on my ill-fitting convict garb, and stagger to the door; take in the breakfast pan and almost gag at the sour smell of the *"corned-beef" hash* (merely chopped corned-beef, and the crumbs and crusts of bread left from yesterday (no potatoes, onions, or seasoning) all of which has been stewing in the immense kettles ever since mid-night; and however palatable while fresh and hot, is now in that luke-warm state, (the pans for all the convicts are filled and set in front of the cells, before a single door is opened; hence those first filled, as was mine—cell No. 9—become perfectly cool before eaten) that may be compared to "dish-slops." With the hash, there is given a slice of bread, and a pint-cup, two-thirds full of a dark-looking fluid, with occasional specimen of parched wheat and rye, bits of burnt bread crusts, and perhaps once in a year a stray coffee-bean, amid the sediment to show that the stuff is issued as "coffee." Exactly what the chief ingredient is I never ascertained, but I subsequently learned that it is known as "Prison Coffee," and sells at about twenty per cent less than ordinary bean-coffee. I give these particulars thus minutely because the same breakfast and dinner are issued throughout the year, and the same system of daily coming-and-going is carried on without an instant's variation.

On this first Sabbath morning in a felon's cell it matters little to me what food is offered; I drink a portion of the "coffee," nibble at the crust of the bread, and then slide the pan under the bed, out of sight. One cannot quickly forget old habits; and it is not appetizing to sit on a roll of musty blankets, to fish chunks of reddish beef out of a greasy, not overly clean pan, before one has performed his ablutions. But here is neither washpan, mirror, towel, comb, brush, or soap. True there is no need for brush or comb—the barber's weapons have provided for that—but a basin, soap, and towel, I long for. I shall learn presently that the convicts wash their faces and hands but once a day, and, as with every thing else, do it at set hours under the regulating tap of the bell.

Even as I am thinking of it, the front of the door is darkened by the Deputy, who, with the same arbitrary emphasis, notifies me to *"Get ready to go out, and wash!"* Only this and not one word more. *Clang! Clang!* goes the gong; footsteps rattle down the guard-room stairway; the jingling of keys is heard, and each overseer, beginning at the head of his row passes from cell to cell, unlocking the doors, at a rate of speed surprising to a stranger. Within three minutes all the three hundred cells are thrown open and the men out. The marching line is instantly formed in the following order; the man in cell number 1 steps out about three feet in front of his door, folds his arms, and faces towards the big door that opens into the yard. The man in cell No. 2, steps out in the same way, walks up behind No. 1, and lays his right hand on No. 1's shoulder. The inmate of Cell No. 3 steps up behind No. 2, and lays his right hand on No. 2's shoulder. No. 4 does likewise, and so do all the rest until a line of 30 or more men are thus formed; each with a long red slop-buckct on his left arm, and his right arm grasping the shoulder of the man before him. All must cast their eyes in the same direction, at the feet of the overseer, who marches on the side of the line, 10 steps distant from it. When all are ready, the Deputy taps with his heavy cane on the flag-stones, and each overseer gives the word *"Forward!"* All step off together, stamping heavily with the left foot like soldiers marking time. Filing through the main door, along a narrow flag pavement, around three sides of the four-acre yard, until the first man of the long line is at the door of the work shop. "Halt!" is then the order; "Set down your buckets!" (at this all the slop buckets are deposited on a line with the outer edge of the side walk; then "Forward!" again, and into the work shops, where every man hastens to his bench, takes off his cap, and jacket, which he hangs under the bench, rolls up his sleeves above the elbow, folds his arms and stands mute and motionless, with eyes fixed upon the bench before him!

Up to the point of reaching the desk, and rolling up the sleeves, the same routine is observed every day in the year, without variation. But on Sundays, instead of going to work, the convict folds his arms, as just stated, and stands like a statue until his turn to go and wash. When all are at their benches, the overseer mounts his raised dais (whence he can look into every convict's eye, if for an instant raised,) and leaning over the front of the desk watches the motionless figures before him, while with one finger he sounds the hand bell;—

Ting! (No 1 goes, and washes). Ting! (No. 2 goes) Ting! (No. 3 goes), and so on. About sixteen seconds are allowed each man to perform his ablutions. The "wash-tank" stands a few paces from the overseer's desk, and is supplied with dirty river water (I never saw it really clear) from faucets directly over the basins. The towel is merely a long band of coarse material, (similar to the bagging towels so common in the cabins of the South) on rollers; the one towel serving more than a score of filthy faces, one third of whom are black as soot.

It was a severe "pill," when my turn came, to follow to the "wash-tank," a big, greasy, odorous negro, whom all the soap in Albany could not have washed to a decent cleanliness! It had happened, (let us *imagine* it accidental, whether or not) that I was placed at a bench whereat there was a negro on my right hand; consequently when the men were called one after another from the benches, the negro came directly before me as above stated. However I went forward without hesitancy; though taking care to simply dabble in the basin with my fingers, (I had already refreshed my face, in my cell by pouring water from one hand to the other, over my slop-bucket).

When all were washed, the signal to re-form the long line was given, and again the thundering *tramp! tramp! tramp! tramp! tramp! tramp!* echoed within the high-walled court-yard, as the convicts were marched back into the main hall, and then each man to his cell. The overseer rapidly glides along the front relocking the cell-doors, which are held in position by the inmates, (as when taking in breakfast) so that there is no pos-

sible chance for slipping outside, because if not held
shut by the prisoner within, the door would swing open,
and the overseer could not fail to observe it.   Soon
after our return to the cells, one of the turnkeys appears
with a tray of books from the Library, one of which he
thrusts between the bars of the door, and passes on.   I
pick up the book and find it to be one of a Sunday school
series, about as interesting as a primer.   Yet how soon
I learned to look for the coming of that book tray as *the
one* agreeable thing in all my weekly round of life!   For
there were *some* books worth reading and when I chanced to draw one it was a real "prize," for it kept my
thoughts diverted and permitted me to exercise my mind
by trying to remember during the week what I had read
on Sabbath.

On this first Sunday, (and second day) in the Penitentiary there was little room in my mind for anything
of that kind.   I obeyed every order, and awaited the
passing hours in a state of stupefaction—moving me-
chanically like an automation.   There was a mental,
and bodily cause therefor.

IN THE CHAPEL

At 9 A. M. the hall-gong clangs, *"One! Two! Three!
Four!"* "Prepare to go out to Chapel!"   Instantly the
rattle of unlocking the cells is heard and the centipede
lines are formed as when going out to the shops.   But
the "head of the column" does not lead the way out of
the great door. "All Ready!" he calls from the top of
the first flight of a narrow (2 feet wide) staircase which
winds, and ascends from one short platform to another
until the level of the top of the hall-room" is reached,
40 feet above the flag-pavement.   Here a double door
opens, and another flight of fifteen steps ushers the
climbers upon the floor of the Chapel, on the third story
of the central block of the main building.

Of course the ascent is made in single file, by divisions
closely watched by guards stationed at each stair-land-
ing.   Every convict walks with down cast eyes and
folded arms, doubtless presenting a novel sight to the
stranger privileged to stand at the wicket in the guard
room door, and survey the multitude of gray-clad con-

victs, of all colors, ages, and sizes, drawn up in single lines, waiting for the turn of each to step forward and follow his "next door (cell) neighbor" up the winding staircase which fairly creaks under the weight of so many climbers.

To me, the tiresome waiting, in the stern hallway, surrounded by all the evidences and attributes of ignominious punishment and long pending confinement, while the subdued sound of scores of city church bells came over the high walls, was indescribably maddening. One of the convicts near me tried surreptitiously to nudge me, and ask where I came from, whispering *"I'm 'up' for five for burglary; what's your term?"* This familiarity, and apparent assumption that I belonged to their class, etc., had a most distressing effect upon me; though it is proper to remember that I was in the weakest and most debilitated condition physically, scarcely able to stand.

On entering the chapel, I found it already nearly filled; a broad sea of shaved heads stretching from wall to wall, around which at regular intervals of ten paces, sat the guard and overseers on high revolving stools that permitted them to overlook each and every prisoner on the benches.   On each side of the pulpit ran a six-feet platform, painted orange color, with green wicker settees for the guests of the Superintendent, and the city visitors, who were present.   The chapel surprised me at its commodiousness and neat appointments; the benches and gallery having a seating capacity of 1000 persons, or more, the ceiling lofty, filling the mansard roof, and ventilated by three large rosette-wheels in the dome.   The windows were high, Gothic, and faced with stained wood resembling grained oak; the walls were grained to resemble marble masonry; the floors were painted a dull yellow, or lemon color, with matting near the pulpit. The benches were narrow, plain, and painted a dull brown to hide the dirt of the convicts' clothes. Costly gilt chandeliers, and wall-brackets, added to the appearance of the chamber but were of no particular benefit, as there was only one service.   The pulpit is a plain desk with large crimson cushion, and gilt Bible.

On the right of the platform is a good sized cabinet organ, which a neat young man from the city voluntarily manipulates every Sabbath. He is the son of the master machinist connected with the institution, but in no wise resembles his phlegmatic Dutch father; his face is beardless, his hands small and white, and his hair being parted in the middle, gives him the necessary completeness of a woman in male attire. Still he is a good performer, and a good Christian, active in good works, it is said. In front of the organ are half a dozen benches, for "the choir." These are convicts, but selected because of their acquaintance with music, to lead their fellows in the sacred service. Their leader, an old Frenchman, under twelve years sentence, is permitted to talk to them (on the single subject of music) and train them for half an hour in the chapel after service on Sabbath, with an officer standing guard. The musicians are allowed an extra ration of food for their salaries. In the gallery, behind a tall front-screen, which barely permits them to see the preacher, and the backs of the heads of some of the convicts in the front seats, sit the female felons, watched as closely as the males, and dressed in loose checked gingham dresses, or uniforms, all alike. They are entirely invisible to the male inmates, and but for their shrill piping voices, and incessant hacking coughs (suggestive of worn out frames, sickness, disease, liquor, vice, and exposure!) we should not have known of their presence within the chapel. Nearly half an hour is occupied in marching the men from the cells to their seats in chapel. When all are seated, the Supt. and Deputy Supt. walk slowly up the two aisles, surveying each row, and seeing that every prisoner sits mute, motionless, arms folded, head bent, eyes on the floor! If a man whispers to his fellow, or passes a note, or snickers, or looks around, the Deputy taps on the floor with his stick, an officer steps forward, and the offender goes down to the dungeon, far below us all! Silence now rests upon all this large assemblage awaiting the tardy pastor. Strange sorrowful spectacle! Almost a thousand law-breakers, offenders against the community, outcasts from society, under the ban, and

under lock and key, are here assembled to—actually!—
Worship God! or, as one of the vilest of them once
whispered, to "go through motions!" No such collec-
tions of human beings could be found anywhere else.
The simple [shape?] of the heads was   . . .[?];
old grizzled heads, young white-skinned heads, battered
heads, round bullet-heads, heads that seemed to belong
to animals rather than man, monkey shaped, dog shaped,
hog shaped, thick bull necks, long goose necks; weazen-
ed, foxy visages, low foreheads, carbuncled noses, weak
watery eyes, pale bilious-looking skins; sodden, idiotic
expressions, keen, vigilant, watchful eyes; ugly scars,
small pox pitted features—yea, these and worse were
the distinguishing marks of that rare collection of de-
formed, degraded, debased and almost demoniac humanity! What chapers of vice and crime were displayed, in the plainest of print upon the simple head-
pieces of these world's waifs! Yet all were not of this
class. And perhaps the most affecting sight in all the
throng, were the youthful, shapely heads, here and there
amid the brutalized majority, of convicts whose crime
had been that of weakness under strong temptation or
sudden over mastering of violent passion, or (in a small
number of cases) unjust conviction under unexpected
circumstances. In the greater number of such instances,
the convict was taken in his first offense; taken perhaps because too honestly clumsy to provide for his own
safety, as a worse man would. I shall allude to some
of these unhappy youths hereafter. At present they
are mingled and herded with the gnarled ruffian multitude, and it is hard to disassociate them from the rest.
Imagine the thoughts working within all these warped
and distorted brains during the utter quietude of this
waiting moment in church. Up from the great city,
stretching afar to the eastward, arose the clangor of
countless church bells, pealing the hour for prayer, and
filling the morning breeze, as it drifted in between the
bars of the great windows, with an indescribable sweet-
ness; especially when the jangling chimes of the St.
Peter's Cathedral mingled with the ceaseless echoes of
the deeper-toned reverberations. As the Chapel is on

the topmost story of the Prison, which itself overlooks
the city, the entire volume of sound came freshly to us,
and must have awakened Sabbath Day recollections in
every heart that had known a Christian childhood. To
me they were distressing. There were particular bells
whose echoes were surprisingly familiar to me—bells
that I had not heard in years, but whose melody now
struck pain to my soul! They annihilated time and
space; rolled back the years; transformed situations;
and seemed to show me the streets of far-off Southern
towns with well-known, friendly forms, winding their
way to their accustomed churches, recognising and ac-
costing each other pleasantly, and exhibiting all the
elegancies of refinement and wealth. How great the
contrast! *Here,* in felon's garb, with folded arms, and
downcast eyes, sat the listener, pale, nervous, shivering,
desolate, smarting under a sense of shameful outrage
and injustice done in forcing him into so shameful a
situation, bleeding at heart, from a bitter knowledge that
many—very many—of those who should be his friends
were quietly accepting the slanders of his foes; and
desponding at the thought of all the similar Sunday
trials that must ensue during the six years yet to come!
I may never tell what thoughts coursed through my
mind at that hour. It was perhaps the saddest of all
my prison life. I fear I must have broken down had
not Genl. Pilsbury deliberately arose from his seat
near the Pulpit, and walking down the aisle handed me
a little book of sacred songs used by the choir. Why
he did this very unusual thing I cannot conjecture; for
a similar copy was habitually kept in each cell for the
use of the inmate. Perhaps he read my feelings—being
skilled by a lifetime of watching prisoners—and kindly
wished to turn my thoughts by this little act of attention,
which I daresay was more surprising to the guards than
to me.

THE PRISON PREACHER

After five minutes' waiting, the organist strikes up
a rapid voluntary, and the Chaplain, descending through
a narrow postern opening from the Superintendent's
quarters into the Chapel trips lightly up the aisle, shakes

hands with Mr. Pilsbury, kneels a moment, hops up, pulls off his gloves, unrolls his sermon, and is ready. Meanwhile the old Frenchman is leading his choir through well-known stanzas, "Sweet Hour of Prayer!" Then all rise, and the "Lord's Prayer" is chanted— mainly by the choir. A hymn is sung from the small "Collection of Songs for Union Sunday Schools," a copy of which is kept in each cell.

Up to this point, the convicts all keep their eyes lowered, but as the preacher repeats the words of the text, every eye is raised and fixed upon him; not the least deviation to left, or right, or aloft, being permitted, and as all the overseers, and guards, are "on duty" during chapel hours, the slightest infraction of the rules brings swift detection.

Strange to say, this rigidity of constrained attention, in my mind at any rate, prevents my hearing any portion of the sermon. With my eyes fixed upon the pulpit cushion, and every feature utterly mute, I could not prevent my thoughts from wandering many many leagues, o'er land and sea, while the preacher's unmusical voice, rolled through my ears like the sound of a scarcely audible waterfall! I think, too, this constraint had its effect upon the singing. The two hymns in the chapel on Sabbath, were the only sounds any convict was permitted to make except occasionally to answer the question of his angry keeper. So long as the prisoner obeyed the discipline there was, in many instances, no occasion for uttering a word from year's end to end. But all were allowed, and *expected,* to sing on Sabbath if they knew how. And after the hour of rigid silence, there was a feeling of relief, I suppose, (I cannot speak of experience) in loudly joining the choir. At all events it was surprising to hear the mighty outburst of sound as the seven or eight hundred throats rehearsed the old familiar tunes with "Rock of Ages," "Jesus Lover of my Soul," or similar sacred airs. Indeed, the convict "congregational singing" has a reputation in the exterior world, and a number of visitors come every Sabbath to hear it. Many of the negro convicts sing as lustily as if at an "old-field" camp-meeting.

Perhaps nothing could more strongly illustrate the lasting effect or impressions, of early Christian training than the ease and *gusto* with which these rough, hardened, distorted, utterly degraded *habitues* of the slums, whom we may suppose have not seen the interior of a church in years, now recalled both the words and tunes of those household hymns, which almost every pious mother croons to her children, and which they remembered through all their vicious and wandering careers. It was a queer sight to see some of these old, hoary-headed, battered, one-eyed, broken-nosed reprobates singing without the book, and in very good tune, *"Come, Sinner, Come all Needy, Weak and Wounded, Sick and Sore!"* etc.

I, of course, did not sing, nor feel any disposition so to do. There was enough for me to do in watching myself, curbing and controlling the passionate inclination to spring up and behave as one bereft of reason.

BACK INTO CELLS

The sermon over, the preacher and visitors pass out, the officers rise, the "deputy" stands on the platform, and with his cane strikes two taps on the floor. Instantly the two front benches rise, fold their arms, and file down the aisle, down the long winding stairway and back into their cells. *Tap! Tap!* two more benches follow in the same order. *Tap! Tap! Tap! Tap!,* with each tap a benchful start; thus keeping a continuous string of men until all are back in their cells. Officers stand at intervals along the line, watching that all shall go promptly, silently, and properly to their cells; while each man stands at his door, holding it closed until the turnkey comes to lock it. These proceedings occupy nearly all of the morning, and at twelve the dinner is brought. It consists of a pan of rice broth, with a small piece of mutton, and a slice of bread. Then there is "rest" until 3 P. M. when the prisoner must stand at his door to set out the dinner pan. Once more at 5 P. M., he must "hold the door" while it is unlocked to hand him the single slice of bread which constitutes his only supper. After this, he can undress and lie down without keeping one ear open for the coming of the turnkey. No one but a man doomed to spend years in a cell can imagine the degree of annoyance and discomfort caused by these frequent openings of the cells; because in each instance the inmate must hop up and stand with his hand on the iron bar from the moment he hears the jingle of the keys, and thus a considerable portion of his leisure is wasted.   It is invariably with a sigh of relief that I close the door for the day—what is left of it—at 5 P. M. on Sundays, and go to bed for the night.

SAD COGITATIONS

On the first Sabbath evening I cannot retire, being in ignorance at to what moment I may be called up, for some new annoyance; so I sit on the side of the shelf-like iron bed, and wait, praying for night!   The sun descending through banks of mist casts a reddish haze through the great windows that tinges even the walls of my cell, though I can not see the window; nor indeed, anything except the blank wall across the ten-foot wide corridor.   How long the twilight seems!   An hour ago the shadows began to deepen within the narrow cells; but still the gas is unlighted in the halls, and those who can see the window may perceive a faint flush on the western sky that reminds them of Sunday summer evenings, long ago, when the family gathered on the vine trellised verandah, and sang together.   Suddenly a distant church bell in the city rings slowly peal on peal, for evening service!   Others join in the mellow chimes, which are softened by the distance, and the many walls, and windows through which the sound comes to us! Oh! the melancholy of those sunset echoes!   It strikes home to more than one heart. This is shown by the spirit of unrest that sweeps over the Prison. The convicts must be mute, noiseless, voiceless; but they are at liberty within their cells.   So all this great hive of statutory offenders starts into restless rustling, each convict pacing the floor of his cell!   Above, beside, all around me, is the sound of lonely men walking to and fro—to and fro—to and fro—backward, forward—backward, forward—backward, forward—each footfall distinctly heard upon the smooth flag-stones; while the shortness of the walk-and-turn (about 6 feet) gives one the idea of caged bears, always in motion. Alas! the occasional sigh or subdued groan reveals that these wild beasts have the feelings of men, no matter how dark their crimes.

My own sorrowful musings on that slow-passing October Sabbath even may not be told. Naturally the newness of the situation, and the vividness of my own sufferings rendered the surroundings intolerably lonely and oppressive. I knew that at this hour, afar in the Southland, my friends and acquaintance would be enjoying the evening air, or wending their way to church; and I knew that of them all few if any would remember even my existence. . . .

THIRD DAY: GOING TO WORK

About 8 A. M. on Monday, when I was half dozing, having slept scarcely any the previous night, an officer unlocked my cell door, saying "Put on your cap! fold your arms! Eyes on the floor! Follow me!" In the hall I found my seven companions from Dixie drawn up in line, awaiting their assignment to "work." The poor fellows looked so distressed that I was tempted to whisper, to the nearest, to "keep up courage"; but the Warden, as if divining my intention, said, *"keep your eyes down!"* in a curt tone of command that made me tingle with resentment. At the next moment, however, I resolved to set my poor comrades an example of patient "acquiescence in the situation"; therefore, quietly took my place in the line by the side of the wall, and stood perfectly motionless.

Presently the man termed "the Boss of the Shops" made his appearance. He is not an official of the prison, but is the manager, and supervisor, of the shoe-making business conducted within the Prison yard by the "Eastern New York Shoe Company," to which corporation the labors of the convicts are hired at the price of forty cents a day per able-bodied prisoner. The company furnishes the steam engine, tools, etc.; and the skilled workmen, known as "Instructors," to teach the new-comers (and the prisoners are daily coming and

going) how to make their several portions of a shoe.
The Penitentiary authorities furnish the overseers, and
guards; and of course, have full control over the convicts.

"Boss" ―――― is a little, dandyish man; quick in his
motions and gesticulations; full of self-conceit, vain,
petulant, and fussy, the fussiest man I ever knew.   He
is said to be a good manager, or "driver" but his incessant worrying, and irritableness must ruin the good will
of all his men.

He came bustling in, and said, "where are those Ku
Klux?   Oh! here you are!   What can you do?" (then
seeing my look of bewilderment, he continued) "What
is your trade?   What do you follow?"   "My profession has been that of   a   journalist," I   responded.
"Have you ever done any manual labor?"   "No, Sir!
unless you count some days work at fort-building during
the war."   "Oh, then you were in the Rebellion!"   "I
fought for the South, Sir, and so did every other man
in our section who was able, and of any account."   "Well,
now you can learn to make shoes; nice trade when you
get used to it.   Shop No. 4: Trimmer," then turning
to Collins, "Well, old man, what's your following?"
And thus he passed down the line, examining each of
the eight, and ticketing him for some class of work, in
one or other of the four shoe shops.   Usually the as-
signments are made according to length of sentence;
convicts likely to remain three years or more, being assigned to the most difficult duties; while those who come
for only six months or a year, are put at the light work
which requires no special training, or experience, such
as "sand papering" blacking, labeling, etc.   Unfortunately for me, *Sir Fussybuss* (as I mentally styled the
Boss) prides himself on his skill as a physiognomist,
and boasts that he can tell at a glance of his eye, the
capacity of a new comer, and whether he will make an
apt learner, and good workman.   So in addition to my
six years' sentence, I was under the disadvantage of
looking more *teachable* than most of my fellow sufferers; consequently he ticketed me for the most difficult,
careful, never-ending, and (to me) disagreeable por-

tion of the work; viz, to cut, trim, plane, and neatly round the soles of ladies fancy gaiters—sixty pairs per day! One hundred and twenty single shoes! Sir Fussy's boasted discernment too, was more woefully at fault in assuming that I could learn rapidly the delicate process, for of all capabilities I have the least of mechanical sort; so little, indeed, that I cannot this day whittle a straight edge to a stick, or make a willow whistle, or point a quill pen. And as for keeping my tools sharp (as is absolutely necessary for a "Trimmer") I cannot strop my own razor, or whet a Barlow-knife!

However, it does not matter in the least what I think or wish; my own opinions are no more to be considered than are those of the fly whose *severe* bite furnishes to Sir Fussybus an excuse to rub his nose with his big finger ring before our admiring eyes for quite sixty seconds.

After we have been labeled for our several places of toil, the "Boss" darts away, and a different inspection takes place as we stand by the wall. Old General Pilsbury, the Superintendent, for some reason takes upon himself to come down, and give us a lecture, a thing unheard of, before. Possibly he had some curiosity to see the much talked of, (more abused! and slandered!) Ku Klux; perhaps he wished merely to impress upon us a knowledge of the fact that we were in a Penitentiary, on the footing of its inmates.

A BORN PRISON-KEEPER

While the general inspected us, I inspected him. Standing before us, he asked, "Which is Shotwell?" The Deputy in quite another tone said, "Step forward Shotwell!" I did so, and raising my eyes, quietly stood before them with folded arms, and an assumption of all dignity that could go with an ill-fitting, dirty, prison garb, and the condition of utter submission to the will and pleasure of these men for half a dozen years to come.

General Pilsbury unmistakeably possessed the quality of a born prison keeper, or, let us say, prison manager as distinctive from the mere jailor. He was about 60 years of age, a little above medium size, very portly and corpulent; with an aspect of singular firmness and mild-

ness, dignity and pomposity, yet suavity and consider-
ateness, sterness and severity accompanied by natural blandness and complacency.   It was the face of an
elderly man, of strong will, *who for forty successive
years,* had ruled with absolute arbitrary power over a
small empire of desperate, but helpless, men, who were
worse than serfs, because the serf is regarded as an
hereditary family appanage whereas the convict slave
is held only by bonds and gyves, and ceaseless watching,
and is stained with crime and suspected of treachery.
But it was also the face of a man of Christian character,
and humane instincts, who had learned from long experience and study of human nature that many men
whom the law consigns to his custody are more sinned
against than sinning—victims of circumstance, inheritors of vice, ignorance, and crime, trained from youth
and encouraged by the facility with which smarter, and
wealthier offenders violate the law, and escape its pen-
alties.

In addressing us Genl. Pilsbury spoke in a low, easy
tone, but with all the absoluteness of an autocrat, whose
nod is Destiny to his subjects; an arbitrary dictation
that made me chafe almost to the insanity of open rebellion, while he was slowly haranguing us as follows:—

ONLY DO AS I SAY—AND BE HAPPY

"Now, men, you are to be taken to the Shops to do the
work that will be assigned to you.   You will find the
shops much pleasanter than staying in your cells, because you will have work to do, and it will keep you
busy! (coughs)   Everybody gets along smoothly if
they obey the Rules, but if they don't there is *serious
trouble* till they do.   Now, go to your shops, and remember—the Rules!"

All this was said in the bland tone of one stating a
cheerful piece of instruction to his slaves in the old
days, as if the considerate master addressed them: "Now
men, go and pile rock all night; it is not pleasant; in fact
it is very hard service so hard that I am *sorry*—but
you've got it to do! Go and do it faithfully and according to instructions, and all will be right."

I think the old General meant his remarks for kindness; but his forty years of autocratic rule over men, his one hundred thousand dollars in the bank, and his wide reputation as the only successful, and money-making Penitentiary manager in America, all seemed to be represented in his dictatorial expressions.

TRAINED IN THE LOCK-STEP; SYMPATHIES

And now we were formed in line, single file, each man with hand on his predecessor, as heretofore described, and were marched up and down the hall way to train us to this method of marching.   I caught it easily enough, but old Mr. Collins, and one or two of the others were slow and clumsy; throwing the whole line out by their mis-steps; whereupon the Warden roughly reproved them.   I was ready to cry with rage and indignation.   Indeed I from our first arrival had felt the sincerest pity for my unfortunate companions, because I knew they were uneducated, unaccustomed to isolation, or mental communings; in short were without any resources of intellect to solace their weary prison hours, and without intelligent friends to correspond with, and keep them cheered and comforted.   Alas! as it came to pass, they received *half a dozen letters apiece for each one of mine!*   I reflected, moreover that most of them had wives, mothers, sisters, families either of their own, or of their father's homes, whereas I was not only without wife or child, mother or sister, but also, lacking even a sweetheart.   *Per Contra,* also, they had an advantage in caring nothing for books, papers, writing material, toilet articles, and an hundred other minor luxuries, whose deprivation was almost too grievous to be borne, by one accustomed to them.   I think, too, they cared less for the confinement than I; being less harassed mentally, and not so much mortified at the treatment we so often received from coarse and bullying officials.   There can be no doubt that education and gentle rearing add greatly to the griefs, and sufferings of those who are called upon to suffer, and to endure illusage.   Barrels of ink, and many (paper) tears, were wasted by sentimental people the world over, in sympathy with the "miseries," the "crushed lives," and "gasping anguish," so-called, of the Southern slaves, when in point of fact, forty-nine out of fifty of the latter were more jolly, light-hearted, and happy than their own masters and mistresses.   This is *proven* by the further fact that since the war thousands of ex-slaves preferred to remain with their former "cruel masters," and would fight for them and are proud to bear their family names!   Who ever heard a negro complain of ill-treatment while a slave?   Who does not know that if the slaves had been "mal-treated" and "outraged," as the Abolitionists succeeded in making the whole world believe they were, the South would have been filled by assassinations, retaliations and horrible acts of revenge, when in 1865-6-7-8-9-'70 and '72 the freedmen were not only in political supremacy, in many states both as a race, and as a party, but were continually incited and inflamed by vile carpet-baggers, to attack, rob, and outrage their former masters and mistresses.   The truth was, the Freedmen knew they had been well treated and their simple minds often hungered for the "flesh pots of Egypt"—the freedom from care, or want, or any other necessities of free-life.

Capt. Pilsbury (as will hereafter appear) once remarked that he would rather have fifty burglars, murderers, etc., sent to the Penitentiary than one genteely reared and educated person; for it was painful to see the latter crushed, and sorely tried under punishment that the more brutish and common culprits accepted without a thought and perhaps found no more confining and arduous than their daily work.

SHOP NUMBER 4

"Sir Fussybus" having assigned me to Shoe-Shop, No. 4, I was escorted thither, and made to stand for several hours at one end of the room close to the wall, with my arms folded, and my eyes fixed on the wall. Behind me for more than one hundred and fifty feet stretched a large room containing four "divisions," or shoe-making gangs.   I could not, as yet, see what was going on; but there was a mighty rumbling of machinery, buzzing of wheels, and ceaseless thumping of hammers, and all the clatter of 150 workmen busily plying their tools.   It was a strange, almost incredible, thing that among all these noises,—in all this scene of busy toil—not the sound of a single human voice could be heard; the whirl of the human machinery was muffled and mute! Not one of those one hundred and fifty workmen dare to *speak,* or *laugh,* or *sing,* or *whistle,* or *look about,* or *glance at his fellows,* or even raise his eyes from his work! Yea, he must not even move his lips, lest the overseer's eye accuse him of *muttering,* or *whispering to his neighbor!* No, not even go for a drink of water (at the bucket, directly under the overseer's nose) without raising one hand, like boys in a country school, until the permission is granted. During all the long days, (days without a single variation in dozens of years, or a moments relaxation) each, and every one, of all this toiling company has not opened his lips to speak, has not conveyed an idea, nor received one! Could the power of penal training further go?. . .[1]

This writer merely recorded the effect produced on his mind by a passing observation of the men at work: he had little conception of the reality; nor can any one have, who is not doomed to remain years on years, under this surveillance. A single day, or a week, or even a month, might be borne with some equanimity, because of the supporting consciousness that it was a mere experiment soon to be over! Alas how different to him, as I, who foresee six years, six times three hundred and sixty-five days, to be passed in the vice-like grip of this fearful system! No wonder the old offenders who have been in nearly every State's prison in the land *often* beg the Judges to give them *ten* years in Sing-Sing, or Blackwell's Island, rather than *three* in Albany Penitentiary!

The workshops are, as I have said, long apartments, about 30 feet wide, with a double row of windows on the side open looking into the Prison yard, and only a blank wall on the other side. Each shop is entered at the end and has a six-foot aisle running its full length. On both sides of this central aisle are the work benches, arranged in the same order as the pews in a church, or the desks in a school-room; except that there are no

---

1 Another extract from the article in Appleton's is omitted.

seats, and the space between the benches is just wide
enough for four men to stand and work.   The benches
are about as high and as wide as a store-"counter," or
say three feet high, and 2 feet wide.   Each has its top
divided into four square sections, in the middle of each
of which is an oblong block, six inches tall with its
centre cut out leaving an horse-shoe shaped notch, or
cavity, for holding the shoe while the workman manipulates it.   There are also quite a number of machines, for
various purposes, such as cutting the heel-taps after
they are put on; punching holes, putting in eyelets,
besides a great many wheels for polishing, etc., all of
which are driven by a powerful engine in one corner of
the yard.

PUT AT WORK, TRIMMING SHOES

The overseer beckons to me to follow him, points to an
empty space at one of the benches, directly in front of
his desk, whereat two negroes and a filthy looking white
man. are working.   "Take off your jacket," he growls.
"Hang your jacket and cap, on the nail under your
bench, roll up your sleeves, fold your arms, and stand
until the Instructor gives you your work!   *Put down
your eyes!"* (this in the shortest of tones, because I was
looking him in the eye as he spoke)   "Understand, that
you are to keep your eyes down right on this bench, on
your work!   You are not to look about, nor talk, nor
have any communication with these men!   You've nothing to do with them nor they with you, understand that!
You are to obey the Rules, mind you do it!   You—"

But what "you" was next to hear is forever lost because at that instant the overseer's cat-like watchfulness
caught some piece of trickery across the room, and I
was not yet sufficiently "disciplined" to prevent my
looking after him as he seized the offender, and roughly
hustled him against the wall, choked him an instant,
then dragged him by the collar, out into the aisle, and up
to his own desk, there to await transfer to the dungeon!
This sight of this rough usage threw me into a perspiration, of agony; for I reflected, "if this is common, and
all the prisoners are thus treated I shall never leave
these prison walls, I shall certainly kill that fellow the

moment he takes *me* by the collar or strikes me, and then I will never be released! Happily I learned ere long that it was not common for the overseer to strike the prisoners, except in the case of certain negroes and incorrigible rascals whose conduct was utterly exhausting to human patience. One or two of the overseers were very rough with the men, but the usual course was to scold and browbeat in the most aggravating manner for slight offences, and report to the "Deputy" in more serious derelictions.

Whether it was designedly or not that I was placed by the side of a filthy, lousy *negro,* sentenced for housebreaking, I cannot say; at the time I believed it a deliberate attempt to annoy and humiliate me: but possibly my feelings were unduly wrought up by all the petty persecutions put upon me. Certain it was that I was given the most arduous, and unceasing labor in the shops, and was located between this black burglar, and a Canadian scavenger little less slovenly and disgusting than the negro; while several other stinking blackguards (I apologize for the language, though nothing less strong would express the truth) were in front and rear of me within touch of my arm, had I dared extend it! Oh! the horror of the thought that for six years I must be herded, ranked, classed (in the estimation of the Prison officials, if not of other people) on a footing with all this vile assemblage of murderers, ravishers, burglars, thieves, vagabonds, and every species of social and legal outcast; think of it! I do not wonder that there are three or four lunatics in the hospital continually; though at the end of three months, the patient is sent to an asylum. The number is kept up by continually recurring cases.

As I have already stated the convicts are hired to the "Eastern New York Shoe Company," to manufacture ladies' and children's shoes. There are some forty, or fifty, "short-term" men, (sentenced for 30, 60, or 90 days, and men too badly crippled to make shoes, who work in the "chair-shops," cane-seating chairs for another company. But the large majority are employed by the shoe company which furnishes the material, tools, and skilled workmen, called "Instructors" to teach the new-coming convicts how to work. The working hours are from dawn till sunset, except an hour at noon, for dinner. In the long days of midsummer, the convicts work five hours before dinner, and five afterwards. Let any one try the experiment of standing in one spot, with downcast eyes, neither saying, seeing, or hearing anything to entertain his thoughts, let him try this for a *single one* of the long, sultry, summer days—*and record his feelings!*

Presently the "Instructor" came to set me at work. He was a small size, dark-skinned English Crispin, wearing sickly side-whiskers, smutches of grease paint over his face, a very greasy apron, covered with lamp-blacking stains, and a pitiable hacking cough that quite won my sympathy, as it showed he needed nursing rather than *twelve and thirteen hours'* work, in this dusky shop. He subsequently informed me that he was almost at death's door, and needed to go South, or somewhere else than this crowded, fetid shop, whose atmosphere being filled with minute particles of leather-dust, was particularly distressing to his throat and lungs, but "Need's *must* when the Devil drives," he said sadly, "and wife is sick, I have no support but this, and so I must go on for a while, though I am mighty tired of coming here before day, and leaving after midnight, sometimes." It was in the winter-time when he told me this, (whispering one day while pretending to show me how to round the toes of a new style of shoes; and after he had gotten the idea that I would be released soon, and might help him to come South). He seemed to take an interest in me from the start, or say after the first few weeks, when he learned that I was *"sent up"* (in Penitentiary parlance) for "Ku Kluxing," and not for throat-cutting, house-burning, or similar "mild mannered" offences!

He instructed me that my "work" was to "trim" the soles of the ladies' kid gaiters. Taking up one of a great pile on the bench before me that the "Last" (block of wood shaped like a foot) was still in the shoe, and though the "sole" was sewed on, it was still rough, considerably larger than the bottom of the shoe, and was without proper shape at the "toe" and in the neat curves of the "shank." The sole as it stood was a mere rough, oblong piece of leather sewed upon the bottom of the shoe. My task was to use a very sharp knife, of peculiar shape, in cutting down this sole to about the size of the shoe-bottom. Then, use a narrow plane, just the width of the thick sole, and smooth the edges of the sole all around so that they can be waxed, and blackened, as are all new shoe soles on the edges. Then, use another implement to "cut out the welt." Then, use another kind of knife to cut out neatly the beveled curves on each side of the "shank" or "instep" sole. Then cut down the perpendicular (inside) of the high heel. Then, wipe off the shoe, and pass it to the next man to have the bottom sand papered then to another man to have the edges waxed and blacked, etc. It is conceded, I believe, that this "trimming" is one of the most difficult and laborious parts of the manufacture of shoes, if it be not *the most!* And when I state that our "task" was *sixty pairs,*—one hundred and twenty shoes—per day, the "hard labor" is apparent. It is, also, a work demanding the closest, and undeviating attention. The slip of the keen blade only 1-6 of an inch means distruction for the soft, pliable kid, which under the extension of the last, seems to open and tear at the very *breath* of the knife! Of this fact I received painful knowledge within a few hours after I began. My clumsy attempts at shoe-making, my sick, nervous, and unhinged condition of Saturday and Sunday was scarcely improved on Monday and even before I took my first shoe in hand, I foresaw that I should *bungle* the work, if I did not utterly ruin it. Perhaps there is no man living who has less mechanical genius, or readiness in handling mechanical implements than I, and certainly no one has so little aptitude in learning how to do so. Much of this is due to early training. I was reared with an older brother who attended to everything of a constructive character for me; besides I had no occasion for acquiring mechanical knowledge. It happened, therefore, that I was the poorest possible of persons to

assign to the "trimming block," which requires a ready
turn for handling edged tools, rapidity in sharpening
them, a firm wrist, steady muscles (able to shove and
draw without wavering the slightest) and a quick, correct, comparative eye, able to take the measurement
of a tenth part of an inch, and to shape the curves of
half-a-dozen different sizes of shoes, and finish one hundred and twenty of them every ten hours! The consequences were as might have been expected! My knife
was dull, my nerves unsteady, my hands awkward!
As the long day wore off, I foresaw a scolding for I
had "mangled" (so the Overseer said) only five shoes!
The Instructor looked worried, and finally said, "You
must try to get on faster than this," then turning to the
Overseer, he said "This man don't know a thing about
tools. My team never *will* catch up with such slow
draggers!" The overseer came just opposite me and
growled at me until my face flamed hot as fire, and
perspiration dripped from my forehead, partly due to
mortification over my own awkwardness and tremul-
ousness and partly to the fierce resentment that half
choked me as the low-born fellow lectured me, "See
here! you want" (Yankee brogue—meaning you ought,
or must!) "You want to do better than this here! I aint
going for to have you loafin' round mangl'n shoes, this
here way! You've got to do better'n this, tomorrow.
You want to pay attention to your work, and walk it
right a-long! Not stand'n here foolin'!" etc., etc.

The effect of this "talking to," by a man whom I
know to be physically my master, although one whom
I should not think of recognizing socially, or intellectu-
ally, in any way, can scarcely be imagined by the casual
reader; because it is not easy to conceive of the torturing
situation, in which I was placed. As I write these
lines—even mine own self—can hardly comprehend the
deep dejection and bitterness of the notes I made in my
secret journal—more than a month after this first day's
essay at "hard labor." Thus strangely doth circumstance affect one's judgment and feelings!

Possibly the harshness of my first day's experience
"in the shops," was beneficial in the general result. It

dispelled every lingering hope, foolishly cherished in the recesses of my heart, that I should be treated as a *political,* rather than a *felonious* inmate, or receive any special consideration from the authorities.   Several persons had intimated previously to my arrival, that I would certainly be treated kindly, and given some lighter employment than the general herd, and, while I invariably declared it was silly to suppose any such consideration would be shown me, I must have hoped they were right. For it was a severe realization to find myself actually posted among a knot of filthy negroes, and set at work upon the footing of the vilest of them!   But it is always well to get rid of all self-delusions in such a case.   I now more clearly realized the seriousness of my situation, and how serious would be the strain upon my mind and character.

SORROWFUL RESOLUTIONS

It was a very gloomy evening this Monday evening, as I was the third time locked in Cell Number Nine for the night.   The hour was sunset, but hazy clouds obscured all save an half-disk of blood-red like Indian Summer at the South.   The effect of this ruddy glow outside was to render more than usually sombre the windowless interior of my cell, which was below the line of the windows across the corridors.   I am very susceptible to atmospheric influences, and for years have not enjoyed the sunset hours.   Need I speak of this one? The prison supper, a single pan of boiled corn meal, without butter or sweetening, was by the side of the door; but I was too weary to eat such stuff, notwithstanding that I was hungry having scarcely touched either breakfast, or dinner.   I preferred to rest.   Pulling out the iron shelf-rack which answered for both bed and seat, I took my Bible, and with a pin made certain shorthand, or stenographic, signs to record these resolutions, which I determined to carry out;

1st.   To "Obey the Rules," so closely that none but a devilish delight in torturing by my captors, should cause me abuse, and hectoring: to make myself deaf, dumb, and blind when out of my cell, and to seek to force [?] every possible occasion for being spoken to, even by the overseers and guards since the very tone of voice in mere mention of some duty made me wretched.

2nd. To endeavor to maintain my physical health by careful attention to cleanliness of person and cell, (so far as possible) and by as much cheerfulness as at all possible, ever remembering that the lack of these two characteristics—or habits—have wrecked more lives among prisoners than all other causes combined.

3rd. To hold myself superior to my situation; always superior to those surrounding me, officers and convicts alike; never forgetting that malice, not crime, sent me here, and that my keepers cannot make me that which I am not; always superior to circumstances, free and uncontaminated, though shackled, and watched, and herded with the off-scourings of the Earth; always remembering that while my enemies have the power to call me a "Penitentiary Convict" and force me to drudge for years in ignominious servitude, they cannot attaint my character, my soul, my gentility, if I say nay!

4th. To watch myself as closely as the overseer watches my body, lest my character and disposition be warped, and distorted to utter ruin by the fearful ordeal through which I am passing. 1st. "I must not give way to fits of anger, nor worry over the slights and annoyances with which I am surrounded. (N. B. to ask the Deputy if he will not give me cover, and more comfortable suit, for this one is *too* bad!) 2nd. I must not give way to useless repinings and heart burnings; I have often been silly, have made mistakes, and sometimes acted shamefully; but who has not? Wisdom is a plant of late growth in man's life; and if I have acted unwisely in the past there is the greater need to avoid foolish regrets now, when I need cheerfulness above all else save moral strength. 3rd. To drive from my mind, and lock the door against their return, all the revengeful and embittered thoughts that arise in troops—aye, legions!—at every recollection of the foul wrong, outrage, and insult, heaped upon me during these four months past! This is one of the greatest perils I have before

me.   Assuredly if I allow myself to brood over all the
events of the past month even—Oh! name them not!—I
shall go from these walls, a gibbering lunatic!   I shudder as I think of the faces of many of my fellow-prisoners!*   Yet how much more have I to apprehend than
these rude, low-born wretches, many of whom are as
well situated here as outside except in liberty!   Alas!
even as I resolve my thoughts rush on in wild resentment!   But it must be done!   Else all will be lost.

5th.   I must seek to strengthen my *mental* and *intellectual powers*.   This will be hard; for I have neither
leisure, nor books for study.   But I can take a daily
task of *memorization* of the chapters in the Bible, and
also the hymns; and can study the construction of sentences in the book I get on Sunday, and which I shall
endeavor to get permission to select from the tray when
it is brought around.   Oh! for the poor boon of plenty
of reading material, how many other comforts would
I forego.   Thank God! the shackling of the body cannot cripple the soul.   Yet how sadly are the mind and
soul affected by the sufferings and persecutions which
afflict the person!   How hard it is for me to forget
where I am; or divert my thoughts from all that I have
undergone!   And I dread the monotony of labor—the
daily undeviating round of drudgery—with nothing to
suggest new thought, and obliterate the vivid recollections of—But this will never, never do!"

MAKING SHOES

In accordance with my resolve to avoid all "cause of
offence" (and other accompanying brow-beating, from
the overseers) I labored daily with great diligence, and
an earnest effort to master the art of trimming shoe soles.
My assiduity, indeed, provoked the rascal who worked
at my elbow, who watched his chance, and whispered,
*"Don't be a fool and learn before you want to; I was
six months learning."*   On another occasion, he whis-

---

*The writer in Appleton's Journal alluding to this feature of convict life, says,
"There is no melancholy so impressive as that of a convict.   There are no faces,
that so fix themselves in the memory as the faces of some that may be seen in
these gatherings of the worst and lowest of mankind. The principal reason is
that they are bare and shaven. They have been robbed of their veils of hair
that have kept so many secrets of the physiognomy and their tell tale lips stand
revealed."

pered, *"Go slow! They'll pile on the work just as fast as you learn!"* I paid no attention either to his whispering, or his advice; being determined not to be led into any infractions of the rules, though, had I been willing to "put up with" frequent scoldings and abuse for little work, I should have taken much more time in learning since as he said the amount put upon me increased with my skill. If it be wondered how the Canadian could speak unobserved it must be remembered that almost every hour the overseer caught some fellow talking, or trying to pass a note to his neighbor, and as he (the overseer) darted to capture the offender, the tricky scamp at my side, would mutter in low tones which could not reach the overseer's ears, owing to the rattle of the machinery, but was perfectly audible to me. I learned eventually that numbers of the convicts trained themselves to mutter without moving their lips, so that if the officer were watching their very faces he would not detect the conversation at six paces from them. Of course this *sotto voce* intercourse could only take place between the two men working at the same desk. I never answered my talkative neighbor, and he took great offence thereat; intimating that I was trying to curry favor with the officials.

However, notwithstanding all my industry to escape repeated hectorings for my alleged "slowness and bungling" "Sir Fussibus," whom I have already alluded to as an inveterate driver, daily passed down the shops, picking up shoes, looking them over, and tossing them down contemptuously; generally calling the "instructor," and "overseer," to whom he would pour out a stream of fault-finding, threats, and expletives; his shrill voice rising even above the uproar of the machines and hammers. The explanation of this "driving" lies in the fact that the convicts are hired at a fixed price per day: hence the "Boss" tries to get as much work as possible, and the best possible quality of work, out of each and every man in the shop. And he succeeds! The "Eastern New York Shoe Company" which organized ten years ago (1861) with a cash capital of only $10,000, now (1871) has above $300,000 invested in the business, besides fully $50,000 worth of horses, wagons, machinery, etc.   The office of the Company down in Albany is fitted up at almost as great cost as the original capital.   The ceiling of the reception room is composed of strips of all the different kinds of wood in America, closely joined together, and varnished, at a cost of $3,000!   This will give an idea of the profits of the concern. The advantages of having steady workmen, doing a fixed quantity of work every week, and completely under control, so that there need by no "botch-work," or irregularity, are so great, and recognised, that the company is constantly crowded with orders; consequently crowd the poor devils who are forced to drudge for them, without thanks or recompense.

It would be interesting to describe the various processes through which each shoe passes on its way to the packing box: but I am not able to speak otherwise than in general terms.   Each shoe passes through the hands of 37 men, from the beginning; the man who cuts out the upper leathers, (using sheet-iron patterns), to the man who pastes the ornamental labels on the bottom, and packs the cases, 60 pairs in a case.   Thus, there are men who sew the "uppers" and "linings;" men to put in the "lasts;" men to drive the heel pegs; men to "trim;" men to "bind;" to "sand-paper;" to "blacken and polish;" to "punch the eyelets" and clamp the nickel-plated linings; to varnish the exteriors; to "whiten the shanks;" to string the pairs together, to "number and label;" etc. Several large sewing machines are used; several clamping machines; a large "heel-cutter" to each "team" (37 men), and other valuable machinery which so accelerates the work, that, although thirty-seven men handle each shoe, the aggregate daily work of 100 men is above 600 pairs, equivalent to *twelve shoes a day* for all!   Country Crispins who would require two full days to make a pair of shoes of as fine finish as these, can realize the surprising advantage derived from the use of this improved machinery.   The quality of the work is generally above that of outside private factories, as the convicts can be beaten and bullied into extreme carefulness of execution, and they are not supplied with paste, and

other means for concealing a careless cut, which ruins
the shoe.   The shoes made are almost entirely for ladies
and children: and are of all sizes and qualities.   Any
one not accustomed to the shoe business would probably
be amazed at the sight of a dozen different streams—yes,
actual streams—of shoes, moving rapidly from bench
to bench until neatly bunched in pairs, and strung on
poles to be carried to the packroom.   I do not know
how many minutes are occupied in making a single shoe,
but to the onlooker it must appear a very brief period.
Perhaps a better idea may be gotten from the fact that
the *daily* product of the four shops must be above *three
thousand pairs! Eighteen thousand pairs each week*
the whole year round!   Where do they go?   What becomes of the "old shoes" that step aside every month for
these *seventy-five thousands* of pairs of "new shoes?"
Yet this is but the yield of a single institution, and all
for women and children.   I often wonder if the fastidious dame who purchases a pair of fancy, silk or satin-
lined gaiters for herself, and a little chubby pair for her
baby's "footsy-tootsy" would ever dream that they had
been cut out into shape by a forger, "lasted" by a negro
burglar, who transferred them to a sneak-thief, who
passed them to a ravisher, who handed them to the murderer, under "life-sentence," at the sewing board, who
passed them on down a line composed of a villainous-
looking gang of villainous-acting men, from all the
slums of the land! Hardly! Indeed I suppose there are
very few persons, even of the men who sell retail the handsome products of felon-labor who have any idea whence
they came, or how they were manufactured.   A complete revolution in shoe-making has occurred by gradual
stages within the past twenty years or so.   The cobbler
and his lap-stone, have long ago given place to machinery and "piece work."   Large manufacturers have
found that twenty men selected according to their capacity for particular work, and put at work, each upon
his "specialty," will make a dozen times more shoes than
if each were set at work to make the whole shoe himself.
This is the result of ingenious machinery.   Probably
from 75 to 80 per cent of all the work now done in mak-

ing a pair of shoes, is by machines, which not only far
surpass manual labor in speed, but also in the excellence
and regularity of the work.   The "uppers" of the shoe
are cut by hand because of the variableness of the leather
in the skin; and the "lasts" are inserted by hand.   But
there are machines to do the binding, pasting, closing,
crimping, stitching, heeling, and polishing, all without
help of the hand.   By the use of all these machines ten
men can make between five and six hundred pairs of
shoes every twelve working hours. Many New England factories turn out 2500 pairs a day, when trade
is flush.   The annual product of the shoe business in
the United States according to the Census of 1870 was
$18,644,090; being the fourth largest industry in the
country.   Flour, iron and lumber, were somewhat greater.   Considerably over *one hundred million* of pairs
of shoes are annually manufactured in the Northern
States alone; not to speak of the cobblers, of whom there
are from two to ten in every village and hamlet in the
land.   The Massachusetts manufacturers become millionaires in a few years.   A single factory turns out
200 different varieties of shoes.   Millions of shoe "lasts"
are turned out every year.

  *   *   *   *   *   *[1]

Respecting the system of discipline enforced in Albany Penitentiary I hesitate to speak, because it is not
easy for one in my situation to form a correct estimate
of the difficulties and necessities of the case.   To form
a just judgment of such matters, one needs to have
some acquaintance with the persons to be affected by
them.   Thus many things which seem unnecessarily
rigorous and severe to me, may be actually indispensable as curbs to the ungovernable characters, which
compose the bulk of the inmates.   This illustrates the
great lack of something like classification.   During the
first eight or nine months of my imprisonment I was
frequently spoken to by the overseer in a rough and
domineering tone in reply to questions I had asked,
or to reprove me for some minor infraction of the rules,

---

1 A discussion of the profits of the factory and the weaknesses of the system is
here omitted.

committed through ignorance, or *perhaps momentary forgetfulness.* I have mentioned the instance when I smiled; the overseer told me he would make me "laugh on the other side of your mouth if you try that game again," etc. Another time he abused me outrageously for not doing enough work, when I had never been idle a moment during the day. Another overseer almost cursed me for cutting a shoe, although I was a green hand, and having never worked an hour in my life, was naturally awkward with tools. Again I asked an officer (white) what *"that cannonading meant;"* he replied, "Mind your business," etc., instead of merely saying "Prisoners must not ask such questions," in a firm, but not *insulting* tone.

I must admit, however, that from the majority of the officers I have received respectful treatment; and after the two overseers mentioned above, had perceived that the Supt. was favorably disposed towards me, they altered their manner, and I had no more trouble. Furthermore, I know that it is contrary to the wishes and instructions of the Supt. for any subordinate officer to use violent and abusive language to the men. General Pilsbury, (whose system is continued by his son, the present Supt.) took an advanced and enlightened view of the objects for which Penitentiaries should be built. He thought they should be something more than mere barracks, where a few hundreds of misguided men might be collected and tortured until they paid for their crimes with the Shylock-pound of flesh; but on the contrary, he would have them act as *Reformatories,* in which the offender must undergo a salutary punishment, but still preserve his manhood, and some measure of self-respect. Men, he considered, must be made to see that their sufferings were the natural results of their faults, but at the same time, be encouraged to hope that both the fault and its consequence might be avoided in future. In this spirit, he enjoined upon his officers that they should be stern and firm, but *calm;* be prompt and vigilant, but *just* and impartial; be severe when necessary, but exercise discipline without showing passion, or personal resentment, etc. Such I believe, were his sentiments, and the policy he desired to carry out. But unfortunately *all men are not so liberal;* and the class of men, who commonly fill the subordinate offices, is not the one in which wise and enlightened views most fully abound. And the subordinates—the *Overseers, Guards, Watchmen,* etc.—have it in their power to nullify more or less, *if not actually to defeat,* the policy of the Supt. For they, being in constant contact with the prisoners, may if they choose, irritate, and provoke even the mildest of men into some breach of discipline which will afford them an excuse for severity to him. Thus in my own case, I was resolved to obey the rules and demand the respect of my custodians; yet there were occasions when I felt that I had been roughly and unjustly used, and very little would have goaded me into some act or speech that would have been turned very much to my disadvantage. The only remedy for this, that I now think of, would be to give an higher salary to the subordinates, and thereby obtain a more intelligent class of men.

Upon the whole I must admit that so far as I can see Albany Penitentiary is admirably appointed, and conducted. I am satisfied that if the inmates shall faithfully obey the rules they will sustain no ill treatment, nor other hardships than is the *object of the institution,* i. e., hard labor, close restraint, coarse food and clothing, together with the deprivation of all comforts not actually indispensible to existence.

I have never seen any act of violence and brutality, such as is apt to be suggested in the popular mind by the mention of a Penitentiary.

I have seen an insolent and insubordinate darkey or still meaner white man, cuffed or kicked occasionally, but always the wretches were so provoking that I did not blame the overseer, and I doubt if the offender cared for it in the least. I know, also, that great complaints are made by some of the prisoners that they were kept in the dungeon with their hands and feet chained in such a manner that they could neither stand, sit, not lie, for weeks at a stretch. But I daresay they richly merited all they received, and very likely they did not receive what they say they did, for there is very little truth to be got from the majority of them.

I must mention to the credit of Capt. Pilsbury that, instead of wishing to throw obstacles in the way of men applying for pardon, he is always ready to assist any of the prisoners whose conduct has been exemplary; and to my knowledge he has of his own motion, written for, and obtained the pardon of men whose ill-health made them objects of pity. And I am satisfied that any man who shall behave properly can in time obtain his recommendation for pardon.

ANOTHER OFFER OF FREEDOM!

The first half dozen days of my confinement in Albany Penitentiary have no parallel in the recollections of my life time, either in length of duration, or physical, or mental misery. Grasp the idea, if you can, of suddenly realizing yourself on the footing of a convict, (it matters not how wrongfully so) surrounded by convicts, and undergoing all the drudgery of ignominious labor; working with automatic regularity from dawn till after sunset; standing, mute, motionless, speechless, voiceless, eyeless in a measure, without change of posture, of employment, or of thought, for there is naught to suggest new ideas or divert the mind from the bitter recollections of the recent trial, the abuse of the Judge and Radical lawyers, the misconstruction of friends, the falsity of suborned witnesses, the brutality of the officers,—the whole sad story! Herein is the terrible difference between Albany Penitentiary and all other prisons in existence! Instead of being merely confined, and forced to labor the specified terms, with the privilege of working for himself at odd hours, or employing his little leisure in reading, writing, or other harmless occupations, the poor wretch who enters Albany Penitentiary, whether for a week, a month, or a lifetime, instantly learns that all volition, all opportunities for self-culture, all exercise of his natural powers, except those of eating, sleeping, and laboring, have passed from him, leaving him in the aimless condition of the blind horse turning the treadmill; nay worse, a mere human machine, for the animal is as well pleased in his treadmill round, as when otherwise employed, and if badly treated will resent the abuse with his heels. Is my statement too strongly colored? Let me call an intelligent witness who visited the Penitentiary during the same year I passed within its walls. He was kindly disposed, his predilections were in favor of the Superintendent, (who to his *friends* is one of the cleverest gentlemen) and he was given every facility for forming his judgment. Here is his report as published—an extract from—a few days after his visit to Albany. It is much less than the actual truth and no one could judge the reality without being turned over to the "tender mercies" (!) of the prison "understrappers" for a season. He writes as follows: "*It is a principle with the Rules at this Penitentiary to so enclose the prisoner with restrictions that for him to take the least liberty whatever, indicates Revolt! In other words he is enveloped in the meshes of the rules that should he step aside from his rank, or turn his head, or stumble, or drop his hand from its appointed place, or whisper, or nod,—the Keepers put their hands on their revolvers and in due time the man is punished. He is not like a man manacled at the wrists, and at the ankles, who may speak, crawl, bite, turn, and move as far as his irons will permit him, but he is like a man thrown upon his back, and bound with cords, gagged, blinded, and ear-battened. He is helpless, almost breathless. He is down; he is under a weight and cannot resist.*"

These, however, were but physical ills—scarcely noticeable by me, in comparison with the mental torture of being herded with the outcasts and outlaws of half the continent; being looked upon and rated as a "pal" by them, and so considered by the prison authorities; being isolated from all companionship; deprived of instructive books, papers, etc.; and cut off even from a knowledge of passing transactions in the world, as well as among my acquaintance. A man may isolate himself for a time, from all his former friends and associations, but to keep it up long he must have some engrossing mental occupation, or he must have first had his

mind soured by disappointment, failure, or other mis-
anthropic cause. Ordinarily your Hermit is half-crazy to
begin with, and soon wholly so. Although even the hermit in his cell was shut out from human sympathy and
congenial diversions less than was I; because upon him
rested no sense of constraint; no hostile, ever-present
eye played spy upon his movements; and so long as he
possessed his pipe, his pictures, his pen, and his pet pro-
duction, whether in the realms of science, religion, or
poesy, he was measurably armed against solitude.

I have said that the first week of my Penitentiary
experience surpassed in misery anything I had ever
before known, or ever can again. It is thus with all
the genteel class of prisoners, I am told; the first fortnight reveals all the harsher phases of the condemnation, unrelieved by habit, or the dulled acceptance
which comes in the course of time through the consciousness of necessity; while also aggravated by the distress of
mind attending the conviction. To me, each feature
and incident of the prison system was a fresh mortification, and every day seemed longer, and more unbearable than its predecessor. It was startling enough
to my equanimity when put at work among a gang of
filthy creatures, without having them use the same wash-
basin, towel, and drinking cup, (whites and blacks alike)
that I must use if I did any! It was quite as trying to
have the coarse coffee-sack shirt which replaced my
linen, and my underclothing, changed only once a week,
and having been thrown into a pile with the vermin-
covered, nasty shells of the other prisoners (white and
black) and washed together, returning to me often
much blacker than when sent out (because boiled in
the same boilers with the lamp-blackened shirts of the
polishers and varnishers) and often so infested with
vile vermin as to take all my leisure for several days in
cleansing it! Worse still, was the constant [torn] at
night with the bed-bugs and chinches, which infested
the crevices in the bricks, and swarmed in search of
"meat or blood" almost before the sun had retired to *his*
couch among the fleecy clouds upon the blue level of the
Western horizon. But of this more anon. Most annoying

of all things was the inevitable weekly "shave" by the mulatto barber. He had been a tenth-rate "hacker" in some half-dime barber shop, and being quite as reckless with his razor outside of his shop as within it, came hither on a long term sentence, and was assigned to repeat his barba-rous operations upon the helpless prisoners. It was no light job to shave *600 stubbly faces*, and he slashed his way through them with no light hand, or apparent care whether he chopped the nose, eyebrows, and an inch of the chin of his victims, or only a small portion of their ears. Having so many to dock, he usually began on Friday morning and went from shop to shop in regular order. He carried with him a rough barber's chair, two small washpans, two ordinary paint brushes, and a couple of razors. When he appeared in the shop, the overseer thereof sounded his hand-gong, and two of the convicts stepped up to the overseer's desk, by the side of which they ranged themselves, and each taking one of the big paint brushes hastened to swab his face all over with white lather from the soft-soap stuff in the basins. As soon as one of these was seated in the barber's chair, to be shaved, the overseer tapped his bell for another man to come forward and daub his face. Thus the stream of going and coming men was kept up until all were shaved. Here was another ordeal for me, viz., to use the brush and lather just laid down by a filthy negro, or equally revolting white vagabond and after enduring this, to undergo the whacking of the mulatto's razors, which if even sharpened at the start were dull as a wedge long before my turn came! My skin is very tender and often, almost always, indeed, the blood was oozing from various portions of my face for half an hour after the operation. These things may seem of small moment to the general reader. But ah! the bitterness, the humiliation of having to submit to them. And just after my first week's experience thereof there came to me the sorest temptation and self-abnegation of my life. Every hour of my confinement had revealed new evidence of the fact that I was virtually in a living grave, and that if I remained the full extent of my sentence I must make up my mind not only to lose the six best years of my youth but also give up health, energy, and mental power, for no man reared as I had been, and naturally sensitive and shrinking, could undergo such a term of years in the daily treadmill of the shoe-shops without losing heart, hope, and health.   It was not so much the confinement as the discipline, the rigidity of monotonous routine, and the absence of all food for thought, and diversion for the mind. . . .

Having now reached the date at which my private diary begins, I cease to generalize, and henceforth shall give only such notes as I have made from day to day.

I know not whether any apology is necessary for the keeping of a record of one's personal experience; although it may appear to be dictated by egotism.   But for my part, I have a deliberate purpose in view, and every little light or shade of my present life I desire to remember, to grave it indelibly upon my memory that I may resent where resentment is due, and appreciate where gratitude is due, and draw lessons for future guidance from all.   Moreover, having no opportunities for social converse, no congenial companions, nothing diverting for the mind, I find it an agreeable interlude to my studies to take my quill and scribble the vagaries of the hour; not doubting either that one day I shall derive pleasure from the reperusal of these scrawls. For, like most persons who have been bred upon books,

> I love to linger on the track
> Wherever I have dwelt;
> In after years to . . . [?] back
> And feel as once I felt.

I must explain, however, that for 8 months or more after I came here I was without a pencil or writing material; nothing of that kind being allowed the prisoners.   All my notes, therefore, were made clandestinely on scraps of waste paper; with an home-made pencil, consisting of a piece of lamp black fastened in a pine handle.   Nearly every convict here has one of these, and, although the authorities do their best to break it up, an active correspondence is kept up between the

men of each shop. Notes are tossed and passed about
with astonishing dexterity directly under the overseer's
eyes, or at the moment his back is turned. Fortunately,
I had no desire for any intercourse with my fellow prisoners; and in time, Capt. Pilsbury saw fit to make an
exception in my favor, allowing me pencil, book, etc.
The following entry is taken *litteratim* from the notes
made on the evening of the day of Lieut. McEwan's
visit, and I copy it in full, because subsequent transactions are somewhat connected with it; i. e., I have
been *misrepresented* with respect to my language etc.,
at that interview. Capt. P. will confirm my report of it.

CHAPTER SEVENTEENTH

The Diary, 1871-1873—A Tantalizing, But Shameful Offer of Freedom

Albany Penitentiary, Oct. 16, 1871.

For eight days I had walked from dawn till dusk in the monotonous and depressing tread-mill-round of the Prison requirements. Eight days! and without the deviation of a hair's breadth in time, in labor, or in the enforced rigidity of our movements! It was almost impossible to realize that *only a week* had elapsed; only a week! when I could make oath it had been a full month or more! On the morning of October 16th, the overseer startled me by a silent punch upon the shoulder, with a beckoning gesture, to follow him. "You are wanted at the Hall; brush your clothes," he muttered in low tone. I was still very nervous, and this mysterious summons affected me so that as I crossed the broad court yard towards the main building I staggered like a drunken man. Furthermore I forgot to fold my arms, and was still farther unbalanced by a cross command from the "Deputy" whom I chanced to meet on the walk. *"Fold them arms! Keep your arms folded when you are not at work; And don't be gawking all over this yard! Keep your eyes on the ground! That's the place for them!"* were his surly utterances and no language can convey the arbitrary despotic intonation with which they were half-hissed into my ears! My face burned as he spoke, but instantly a feeling of sickening helplessness, and hopelessness took possession of me, and I walked on as in a dream. A turnkey led the way up the steps through a double-door (padded to exclude every sound of the prison) into the guard-room, or Visitors' Reception Room; a broad, handsome apartment carpeted with oil-cloth, ornamented with pictures, and so bright, light, and comfortable as to form a vivid contrast with the prison hall just left. The only sign of the proximity of the latter, are the rows of racks along the walls with the double barreled guns, carbines, and pistols of the Guards. But we do not stop here. Passing into, and along a broad hall, the main entrance to the Superintendent's residence, or middle block of the edifice, we enter the "Office" of Genl. Pilsbury. When in the hall, we discover that all traces of the prison have given place to the ornaments, the comforts, and elegancies of a wealthy private residence. The office is like the drawing room of a cottage. Engravings and statuettes adorn the walls, flowers in vases fill the windows, a large oleander occupies one corner, large crimson-plush easy chairs and sofas, a library of books, a splendid safe, etc., fill the room. Flowering vines are trellised on the outside of the windows, and there are fancy cages suspended in the arches. Seen through these windows the front grounds of the Prison are those of a magnificent private mansion, with not the slightest suggestion of the gloomy sepulchre of human lives a few feet distant. On each side of the broad graveled walk, or carriage drive, are well-trained beds of flowers, carefully selected to show delicious contrasts of color almost all the year round; a smooth cut grassy lawn slopes down to a little rivulet, (over which are several rustic suspension bridges), and rises again to the distant road, and the high iron enclosing fence. Shade trees over-spread the lawn, and have painted seats at their base. The broad streak of morning sunlight enlivens the curving carriage-sweep in front of the main door; and the merry prattle of Genl. Pilsbury's three grandchildren, two girls and a boy, gaily dressed and playing "hide-go-seek" among the shrubbery, joins with the chirp of the canaries, and the odor of large bouquets of bright gladiolas, chrysanthemums and dahlias, or other cut flowers in the great centre-table vase, do impart an air of charming cheerfulness, culture, and refinement that seems a perfect Paradise to me, after my experience in the solitary, gloomy cell, and the sullen, joyless workshops. Even the air seems of a different quality—brighter, sweeter, free from the faint, irradicable, prison odor which no condition of cleanliness will altogether prevent in a crowded prison. It is hardly necessary to

state that all these details were taken with a few glances
of the eye, in much less time than herein described;
though in after visits I had opportunity to verify my
first observations, and accompanying impressions.
Trembling and nervous I paused on the threshold, until
a familiar voice said, "Is that you, *Shotwell?*" It was
Lieut. McEwan, who at once came and offered me his
hand; remarking to Genl. Pilsbury that he scarcely
recognised me: did not think the prison "uniform," and
a few days confinement would make so great a change
in any one's appearance, etc. "But," he continued,
addressing me, *"It's all right now, Shotwell. I've come
to fix things to set you free!"* I muttered my doubts
and, in my agitation, seated myself with him at the
large centre table. *"You may take a seat,"* said Genl. P.
in lordly tone, which told me very plainly I was presum-
ing on good nature, and the omnipresent "Rules;"
though I knew it not. (N.B.—At this time, of course,
the old General knew nothing of me except what the
lying correspondents, and Radical U. S. marshal's deputies, had told him).

"Yes," quoth McEwan, "I have had a long and tiresome jaunt of it, but I promised you I would get you
out; so I went right to Baltimore and talked it over with
Judge Bond, and he directed me to go and see President
Grant. But I thought the safest way would be to go
back to Raleigh, and see Govr. Caldwell, Phillips, and
the rest; so then I came to Washington and saw Grant,
and its all right—I knew I could fix it easy enough.
*Now all you have to do is to sit right here, and give me
a full statement of all you know about the Klan,"* (Here
he ceased sharpening his lead pencil, and unrolled a
large roll of "legal cap" paper which he had brought
with him, under his arm, to receive the important revelations I was expected to make in exchange for the sweet
hour of liberty!) *"and here is Capt. P. who is a Notary
Public: he will attest your affidavit as soon as I write
it out."*

Instantly I saw that McEwan was laboring under the
mistaken idea that I was crushed and outdone: willing
to do anything whatever to escape from the hardships

of the Penitentiary; and I also realized how his action had complicated matters and thrown an additional coil of the chain around me; for after an officer of the United States Army had arranged with the Government to release me on certain conditions, and had caused the Grant-Ackerman-Bond (and local lights) conspirators to believe I was humbled, and anxious to "play into their hands," and effect the ruin of a great many prominent Democrats—after all this, for me flatly to refuse to accept freedom on such terms was to extinguish the last spark of hope of release until Death or the end of my six years' sentence should come! The thought was agonizing! However I responded in general terms that I was sorry to disappoint him after the interest he had shown in my behalf, but that I had no knowledge of any *crimes* committed by the so-called Klans, and— here the Lieutenant burst in—"Oh! Come, now; all we want is to know the facts, about this organization, who are the leaders, who are the chiefs, and the prominent members; Come! Be reasonable, make a clean breast of it! You know you told me to do all I could for you, and that you would do anything I wanted, and all that sort of thing; and here I been to great trouble and expense (this trip cost me over two hundred dollars!) and now you hang back!" Here I myself interrupted to repudiate any such idea as that I had promised to "make a clean breast," or become a witness against my fellow members of the White Brotherhood. As for "confessing," said I, "there is nothing in my connection with the Order that I would hesitate to tell you, if I could do so without implicating scores and hundreds of respectable citizens who are no more guilty of any crime than am I myself, but who would doubtless be subjected to all the maltreatment, and wrong that I have received were their names known. I cannot bring them into difficulty to get myself out." He then changed his tone from "high-horse" key to that of persuasion. *"Do you suppose,"* he asked, *"your friends would go to prison to keep you comfortable at home? "Name one who would come here for a week, or remain here one hour to shield you from annoyance? You can't do it!* Why, it's the common talk

in Raleigh that nobody stuck up to you, except Plato
Durham and he is coming here to keep you company, if
you play the fool and sacrifice yourself to save a lot of
fellows who did nothing for you, wouldn't visit you,
wouldn't go your bail, and are now abusing you in the
papers as if they hadn't encouraged this whole business.
Why Maguire, the jailor, says as soon as you were sentenced all your friends kept away from the jail, and
stopped sending anything; and *I can tell you there are
plenty of leading Democrats, such as* Col ——, and Dr.
——, and old —— and Major ——, who say *openly on
the streets that you deserved all you got, and they are
glad you were sent here,"* etc., etc.

I listened to these declarations with the feeling of one
who stands upon a lonely sand bar, cut off from escape
by the rising tide and watches the steady encroachments
of the hungry waves, as they eat away the pebbles from
beneath his feet, and steadily narrow his standing place,
his hopes, and his life! Every day seemed to discover
some new circumstance affecting my present situation,
and my future prospects! All of this I cannot here explain. While these were my secret sensations, however,
I endeavored to answer as calmly as possible, that this
was a portion of the grievous wrong done to me in
"lumping" my case with dozens of others, all strangers
to me previous to my arrest, and in bribing a few ignorant, knavish fellows from the wilds of the mountain district to manufacture falsehoods concerning me, so that
even my friends in other parts of the State, not knowing the low character of my accusers, were deceived, and
astounded, thereby. "Yet," I continued, "you who profess to be my well wisher and friend, would persuade me
to descend to the level of these infamous "Pukes" who
have perjured themselves twice; once when they broke
their solemn oath of secrecy and again when they swore
falsely on the witness stand."

"Ah! but you stand differently. They have exposed
and disrupted the Klan. You admit it no longer has
any existence. All its oaths, signs and passwords are
known, so you are released from your oath of secrecy.

You can now state all you know about the Order without doing violence to your oath, or your feelings."

In reply I asked him if he was a Mason; also whether, in the event of the disruption and exposure of his Lodge by a hostile force during the war, even if the Lodge should never re-organize, he would consider himself absolved from his oath of secrecy. He laughed and shrugged his shoulders as if to say there was no parallel in the comparison; and the reader will be apt to think the same. But I cut short the argument by stating that I never had taken any oath whatever in connection with the Klan, or its secrets; the tacit confidence which one honorable gentleman reposes in another being the only obligation I had ever incurred. This sense of honor, and confidence, must, however, close my lips much tighter, if anything, than the strongest oath so long as my fellow citizens were imperiled. Thereupon, Genl. Pilsbury who had been sitting by the window apparently engrossed in his newspaper, suddenly spoke, (having been asked to do so, before I came in, perhaps), "Shotwell you had better tell what you know and get out of here! I have no interest in the matter; I don't know you, or anything about you. But as between man and man, I advise you to take this chance, and get out of here. It's a hard place; that's what it's made for! You'll have to obey the Rules, and they're not easy for a man that has been decently reared. But we can't make any distinctions here. It's nothing to me, but I advise you to get out of here if the government will let you! You won't get many chances, I can tell you that!"

"No, this is the last chance," added McEwan. "You've got lots of strong enemies, and they are swearing they mean to make you stay here every minute of your term; I had hard work to get this order from Grant to offer you."

Saddened and disheartened, I arose and prepared to return to my cell, only answering Gen. P. "I thank you, Sir, for your friendly wishes, and I feel already that I am undergoing a living death; but as I told Lieut. McEwan on the Bay Line Steamer, I must spend my best years here if I can only purchase liberty at the price of treachery."

"Hold!" cried the officer, "you are nervous and troubled now; think the matter over! Study your own interests! You needn't betray your friends; just give us the names of the leading Democrats who are members of the Klan, and all you know about them. Go back to your work and think the matter over; I am going down town to see my family; I'll come again at 4 o'clock, and send for you."

I have omitted to state that he renewed the suggestion of Congressman Cobb, that if I preferred not to return to North Carolina, they had no doubt a paying office in one of the Departments at Washington could be gotten for me, etc., etc., etc.

"Though you needn't shrink from returning home," quoth he, "Because you will deserve, and receive the thankful gratitude of thousands of the bone and sinew of the State, who will owe their escape from prosecution to you. The government only wants the Leaders; well known, prominent men like Gov. Bragg, Jo Turner, Jones, Durham, Schenck, Col. McAfee, and others. You know who I mean. Give us all you know about them, and you can assure your friends that they are safe," etc., etc.

I silently shook my head, and turned away, feeling that if the interview were prolonged, I must break down in unmanly tears. The Hall-Master (who was the same officer that spoke to me gently on the day I entered the prison, and while in a chill) had been posted at the guard door, listening to all the conversation, escorted me back into the "Main-Hall," and as he banged the great prison doors which divided light from darkness, gloom from happiness, the prison from the parlor, whispered in my ear, *"Get yourself out o' here ef they'll be lett'n ye! I'm agoing to quit me-sef afore long. The ole man"* (Genl. P) *"says it's a hard place, but he don't begin to know how things is worked! You get out'n here ef you kin!"*

Can the reader imagine the effect of this two-hours' interview, coupled with Gen. Pilsbury's own warnings that I should regret it, if I did not take advantage of this last opportunity for affecting my release. No! no!

no! no! He cannot even conjecture the physical effect thereof. Here was 1st Excitement; My nerves strung up in wild anticipation and anxiety! 2nd, Pleased surprise! 3rd Painful perplexity! 4th Deepening depression, and despondency at the prospective results of my refusal of this offer sent me by special messenger so great a distance, and with assurances that it was the ultimatum. To the foregoing must be added the reaction from the enjoyment *of a conversation* after so long a silence; the enjoyment of seeing the interior of the private mansion, the fine pictures, books and flowers, and above all the sight of the green fields, the beautiful landscape, the waving grove, the chirping birds, and the pretty children at play! How cold, cheerless, lonesome, stifling, after all this, seemed my two-and-a-half-feet-wide cell with its blank, whitewashed walls, its hewn stone floor, its grated door, and sullen silence, save for the occasional rattle of a dinner pan, as the weary inmates finished their scanty meal! I ate no dinner: food would have choked me! Besides, I had obtained permission of Capt. P. to have the use of a pencil during the half hour in the cells at noon, and I wished to make a note of my interview with Lieut. McEwan. I wrote it in stenographic characters on the margin of my extra copy of the "Union songs" which Genl. P. had handed me on Sabbath in the chapel. Mention is made of this insignificant circumstance, that the reader may understand how I managed to keep a journal without pen, ink, or paper. The little book had very broad margins, and by learning to condense my writing (as the recent MSS shows) I managed to put a great deal on every page whenever I obtained leave to have a pencil for half an hour to write a letter, etc., etc.

I must make a confession. I was afraid of myself all that long afternoon. It was a steady battle hour after hour. If the original and Historic Father of all Tempters knows his business he takes care to set his [torn] afts in motion at a time when his selected victim is *alone* and forced to perform manual labor. It is well known that many women enjoy knitting and churning, and similar monotonous hard-labor because it facilitates reveries of a personal, pleasant, or aggrieved, [torn] all this melancholy afternoon, I stood at my desk, surrounded by the odorous outcasts of every hue, nationality, and grade of crime, working as hard as ever I did in my life, seeking thereby to divert my thoughts from the shameful things told me by McEwan with regard to the remarks of men who, if not my most intimate friends, were acquaintances, and all aware that I was suffering for the same cause they professed to uphold and advocate; seeking to forget all my wrongs so vividly called by this conversation; yea, and fighting the wild suggestions that swarmed in my mind with every picture of the fearful future, to wit, for example, "Why remain here, drudging like a slave, until a breakdown in health and in mind, and are turned loose to seek some out-of-the-way corner, and die, with a stigma on your name, and not even the sympathies of the very men whom your silence has saved! 'Dead, or in Prison; soon forgotten!' says the old adage, and what made it an adage but the experience of thousands in every generation! McEwan says my forbearance will do no good, because the Government has hundreds of trained detectives all over the South, and will soon know all, and there is no doubt, as he declares, that GRANT means to keep up his Ku Klux war until after the election in November of next year, and it would be idle to expect the release of any one until the prosecutions cease; they will hardly turn loose us who are already here so long as others are daily being sent here. So I must accept this offer, or surrender all hope."

Happily pride strengthened principle just as it often strengthens courage when on the bloody battlefield; for in answer to these temptations arose the "Better-Thought:" "Were you silent in former trials merely for the approbation of your acquaintance? And will you now, after suffering the most shameful assaults that ever were heaped upon a man and mainly in revenge for your outspoken denunciations of renegades, scalawags, shirkers, and sneaks, will you surrender your side of the question, and actually join their ranks thus tacitly sanctioning all the wrongs that have been done to you! Perish the thought! Rather let me die, and go out among the vagabonds that are tumbled into the Potter's field!"

Thus the hours wore on, and off; Then came my first scolding from him. Again the overseer appeared in front of me; I supposed he wanted me and looked. Instead of summoning me to the Hall, as I, naturally enough expected, he said gruffly, *"Go on with your work! I didn't tell you to stop, and look at me! Let's see that shoe! What botchwork!* (examining my clumsy attempt at trimming) *You mar more than you make! Stop! Take your plane off! What's this? You've slashed this shoe! Now that's a piece of pure carelessness! Do you see this? That shoe is spoiled, and by your confounded carelessness! I'll have no more of this. You've been shown to do your work, and you've got to do it right or I'll know the reason! Instructor!—look at that shoe! Gashed and slashed all around the welt! Next time this fellow does that sort of work let me know! There's no need of it! And I'll not have it!"*

Ah! that scolding—memory must fade ere I lose any part of its fierce anguish! I know not whether the overseer was "set upon" me purposely by a hint from the authorities, or whether it was purely accidental. For a long time I believed the former; but it may have been that the "fellow" was angered by my having been kept out of the shops a couple of hours, or there may have been other reasons. Certain it is that his abuse was entirely disproportionate to the offense, as I had only 'creased' the shoe, a thing of daily occurrence with new beginners, and easily remedied with a little black paste; though of course somewhat injurious to the shoe. The wonder is considering the brief period I had been at work that I did not "slash and gash" every shoe I attempted to trim. Furthermore this "crease" was as nothing compared with some accidental slips I made, in after days, burying half the knife blade (which was sharp enough to shave with) in the soft kid.

When the overseer ceased his tirade and withdrew, though still keeping his eye upon me, (as I could very plainly *feel,!*) watching me like a hawk for some sign of a mutinous spirit, so that he might return and "bully"

me again, I found my forehead dripping with perspiration resulting from the enforced subjection of my nerves
and feelings while the "fellow" hectored me as above.
I think the fact that I had been talking so long with
McEwan had made me temporarily oblivious to my situation, hence the stinging bitterness of this uncalled for
reproof. Never did a rebuke happen more inoppor-
tunely. My mind was too full of other matters to grasp
anything but the rugged fact that I was being abused
and calumniated outside the prison, and abused and
outraged undeservedly within; while the effect was to
tempt me to secure my freedom at any cost, and then
"run-a-muck" against mankind; like Ishmael whose
hand was against all men, and every man's hand against
him. Happily these desperate thoughts were not lasting:
though they had not entirely subsided when I was sent
for at 5 P. M. to go again to the "office" to meet Lieut.
McEwan.

He declared that my conduct seemed unwise to the
extent of folly; that I was sacrificing half-dozen of my
best years to a mere boyish sentiment; that instead of
shrinking from lending my aid to the government, I
ought to be ready and zealous to do all I could, especially as it would relieve the masses of the expense of
the scheming few who deserved no consideration from
any one, etc., etc. I replied that I had no idea to whom he
alluded. He then asked me if I knew Plato Durham,
Col. McAfee, Maj. Lee, Maj. A. C. Avery, David
Schenk, Senator H. C. Jones, F. N. Strudwick, G. M.
Whitesides, and perhaps others. He had a number of
names on a sheet of paper. As he called each name, he
asked me if I knew them. Some I knew; others I did not.
The page of "legal cap" was almost entirely filled with
names of leading North Carolinians. The design fixed
upon at Raleigh when he returned thither, was, I suppose, to get me started, and when my affidavit was prepared, to add as many of these names as I would swear
against. Lieut. McEwan being a Federal officer and
only partially acquainted in the State was given this
list to guide him in case I proved pliable. I ran my eye
down one page of the names, and saw dozens that I

knew. Finally to get rid of the, to me, distressing interview, I said, "Lieutenant it is not worth while saying any more: I shall give you no statement implicating any one, because I know nothing to incriminate any one." "Don't you know that Messrs. Durham, McAfee, Schenk, Whitesides, and others, are members of the Klan?" he asked. "Well, I suppose they are: Capt Durham says so in his Washington testimony: and I suppose none of those gentlemen *will deny it.*" He then changed his tone, and began to counsel me as a friend to *"make a clean breast"* I replied that I supposed I could implicate a number of persons, but, as they were equally innocent as myself, I could not be so base as to get them in trouble to get myself *out.* McE.—"Do you suppose your friends would do as much for you? They did not stand by you; they allowed you to lie in jail among the negroes and vagabonds rather than go your bail; they were afraid to show you any sympathy; and they would 'puke' on you in an instant if they could get out of this scrape by so doing." "I have no doubt"—said I—"that much of what you say is true: but as for bail—I never tried to obtain security." McE.—"But somebody did, for you, and he could not get even $3000." "Be that as it may, (I never knew of it before) the conduct of those of whom I expected better things does not relieve me from the oath of the Order." McE—"The Klan has been broken up, disorganized, dissolved; you need not be restrained by an oath to a thing which has ceased to exist." "But we were sworn never to reveal the secrets, etc., and although the body to which I belonged may be scattered, the Order still exists. I wish it did not, the day of its usefulness is over; and reckless men may now make worse, what is already bad enough." Genl. Pilsbury—"Shotwell, I have no interest in this matter except as between man and man; but I'd advise you to confess all, and get yourself free from here; for you will find it an hard life." "I am aware, Sir," answered I, "that I am and shall suffer almost a living death as long as I remain here; but I shall never purchase liberty at the price of treachery and dishonor."

I assured him there was no use pressing me, I should

sign no affidavit, nor make any statement. I told him his best plan was to have me summoned, or put upon the witness stand. Of course this could not be done without setting me free; and if done would afford me the eagerly longed for opportunity to tell my own story before all the world, showing the villainy of which I was the victim, and setting forth the truth about the Klan.

"Will you tell all you know?" "I will tell nothing until I am *put on the witness stand.*" "Will you put in writing that you will do this?" "Yes, I will write just what I have told you."

He then handed me a sheet of paper, and I prepared the following note: "Capt. J. S. McEwan, Sir:—You will please represent to the proper authorities that I am willing to appear against certain persons named in a memoranda now in your possession and that if put upon the stand, I may make other disclosures. Very Respflly. R.A.S."

McE. said this was not very explicit, and wished me to promise to tell all I knew. "No," said I, "put me on the *witness stand,* and you will see how I act."

I must confess I was acting with some duplicity in this matter; but it was my only method to avoid giving offence to the Government; and I desire nothing so much as to get on the witness stand. There I can explain my connection with the Klan and show how I have been wronged and slandered; in short, can vindicate myself from the false appearances which may have deceived even my friends.

Now would there be any harm to my friends in my disclosures for I know nothing about any one of them to implicate him in the least, and what I do know has been published time and again by others, etc.

I, of course, did not tell all this to McE., but he suspected it, I fear; although he promised to neglect no means to aid me.

He doubtless saw what I had in mind, and did not take kindly to the proposal. Indeed he had become quite angry at my obstinacy, as he was pleased to term it; and made much complaint of being "surprised" at me, as he believed from my remarks that I would do anything he suggested, and now he had been at $200. expense all for nothing.

McEwan then asked me if I would advise all the other men, who came with me, to confess. "Certainly," said I, "if it will get them out of here." I knew of course that nothing they could tell would implicate any one, as we had conversed on the subject previously.

He also advised me to write at once to the Attorney-Genl. etc., etc. Capt. P. promises to give me paper next Sunday. I feel ashamed of myself for bending in the least to the pressure: but one thing I swear that if I succeed, and get on the stand, I will make these infernal Mongrels rue the day they placed me there!

Lieut. McEwan then had the other Klan prisoners sent for, and interrogated them briefly as to what they knew of the Order etc. Meanwhile I slowly walked back to my work bench in the shops; walked with folded arms and down cast eyes, and trembling footsteps, for all the excitement of the day was giving place to depression at the closing of the door of all hope. The sun was just sinking in the west, great clouds were piled high above the dead horizon of the prison wall,—and the deepening shade of the court-yard seemed gloomier than ever by contrast with the crimson flush of all the cloud-peaks and towers. Glad, indeed, was I to meet the head of the "centipede" marching in from the workshops. In my cell it was lonelier than can be imagined: but, at least there were the comforts of rest, and of being alone,—no longer watched by hateful, fault-finding eyes.

Sunday Morning, October 22nd. Shortly after dawn a shadow flitted past my cell door, and something white fluttered through the bars upon the flags at my feet. It was the Deputy gliding from cell to cell distributing the Sunday morning mail which had accumulated during the week. My hands trembled until they could scarcely pick up the white missive, whose superscription was in the well known handwriting of my dear old Father—now I feared on the verge of distraction. Happily he had sustaining influences of which I took no account, and this letter, while indescribably sad, and saddening, was less incoherent, and perturbed, than I dreaded. Doubtless he sought to write cheerfully and hopefully with intent to encourage me. Yet no words could dissipate the effect of this messenger from the South, breathing love and sympathy, and distilling the odors of "Home" amid the barren solitude of the grave-like cell.

An overwhelming flood of miserable memories rushed upon my mind—and this day has been the blackest of my life. Yet I replied to father's letter in a cheerful tone, and he, I dare say, will think me as careless and trifling as ever.

Wrote to Attorney Gen Akerman, sending the letter to McEwan to be forwarded. I told Akerman that I had expressed to McE. a willingness to appear against certain members of the Klan, in N. C., but that on reflection, I thought I could be useful to the Govt. in S. C. where I had many acquaintances. I would therefore advise that I be sent to Columbia, etc., etc. My object is to get down there where a *few courageous friends* may be of service to me, especially as the authorities will suppose me resolved to *puke*. I told McE. to do all he could to get me brought down there—where he is at present.

October 30, '71. Coming in to our cells on Sunday evening we find a "clean" (God save the mark!) shirt, stuck between the bars of the door. I generally try to keep my person somewhat neat; but here, all such things as clean linen, collars, and cravats *are prohibited*. I have no mirror, no hair, no beard; and, Great Heavens! what an object I must be! Nobody could guess how much I am annoyed, and mortified by such trifles as these. I fear I shall lose the habits and very tastes of a gentleman. Surely no man can stand this life for six years, without showing it on his features, face, and general appearance. Being obliged to keep your eyes on the ground, day after day, it will be hard to keep from acquiring bent shoulders, and a *downcast, sheepish* look! But not if I can help it!

On the following Sabbath (Nov 1st) my anxiety to hear from home, and the outside world, was so great that after tossing restlessly nearly all night I arose at the first peep of dawn and sat on the bed-shelf, awaiting the coming of the Deputy with the prisoners' mail. He arranges the letters in the order of the cells so that there is not an instant's hesitation in the delivery as he passes down the long corridor. Presently there was the least sound of a foot fall, the doorway became darkened, and through the bars fell four letters! Instantly the dark vault seemed flooded with beautiful sunlight! All the sorrow, the hardships, the petty tortures of the past night vanished, and were for the moment wiped out of existence. No one who has not had experience of close confinement, under trying circumstances, can form even a conception of the effect of these letters. It was as if one, who had been lying helpless in a dismal dungeon, devoid of a single ray of light, should suddenly find himself free, and under the broad glare of noonday sunshine! Not that the letters were from kith or kin, or long attached friends; they were all from lady friends (Miss M. W. F., Miss R. L. D., Miss Alice H., and Mrs. H.). whom I had visited in a social way, and who had shown womanly sympathy while I was caged with the thieves and murderers in Rutherfordton jail. And it was this expression or remembrance and sympathy, and the "news from mine own people" that stirred my long desponding and much suffering spirit. All the letters were written from the fullness of womanly kindness and pity, mixed with a good deal of Southern indignity at the outrages of the Mongrels.

It is hardly worth while to say I forgot all about breakfast in the perusal of these welcome but altogether unexpected messages from absent friends. Indeed it was the happiest hour I have spent since my arrest all the letters were full of kindness and sympathy; and must have showed the officers here that their prisoner is not esteemed a criminal by the good people of this country, whatever the mongrels may do or say to the contrary. Noble women! I thank you heartily for your sympathy and cheering words. Truly "words fitly spoken are like apples of gold in pictures of silver."

It seems that the young ladies of Rutherfordton have

agreed to write so that I shall have one letter, at least, every week; than which arrangement, nothing could be more acceptable to me. But will they do it, will they continue this plan for any length of time? I confess I have many doubts, the very biggest kind of doubts. Nothing was ever kept up for many days in Rutherfordton, and if this notion does not "play out" during the first month I shall be greatly surprised. Nevertheless, ladies, I thank you for your generous intentions. Laura, writes an excellent letter, and assures me that my conduct receives the approbation of all the decent people of R. If this be so, I can say, like Daniel Webster, "I still live."

Nov. 5th.   It is very annoying to have to work in the shops by the side of filthy negroes; and much more so, to *wash,* and *wipe,* and drink after them! We have no basin in our cells; consequently cannot wash until we go out to the shops after breakfast! All drink out of the same bucket, and all wipe on the same towel unless they have one of their own, (which I have not, although I have applied to the officer to purchase one, or two for me) and very little time is allowed for attention to the toilet. Those dirty wretches don't need much for *their* ablutions. But I have known "better days."

Nov. 13th, 1871.   Genl. Pilsbury came down to my cell, bringing me the *Charlotte Democrat* sent by the Editor, W. J. Yates, containing the legislative proceedings in the case of Judge Logan, who to my delight, has gotten into hot water at last. By cunning and base intrigue, and depravity beyond description, he has acquired the title of "Judge" but 'tis the title only! And he may be stripped of *that.* The Committee of the House of Representatives pronounced him *ignorant, arrogant, unworthy of the ermine,* and *worthy of impeachment!*

"Grown old in villainy; and dead to grace
Hell in his heart, and *Tyburn in his face!"*

Eo die— Casually glancing over the advertisements in the *Democrat,* I discovered among the marriage notices, —"Miss M M W to Frank Cameron, etc.—Nov. 7th '71"!! and Oh! How sad has this day been to me! Not that I regret that my amiable and elegant friend is happily married to the man of her choice; but the announcement recalls many a moonlight promenade, many an hour, passed on an ocean shore, listening *perhaps,* to what the "wild waves were saying," and drawing pictures of the beautiful future! Bah! One of the parties is married—the other in the Penitentiary! And thus the world goes round—round—round; and thus the world goes round.

> "Leaf by leaf, the roses fall—drop by drop the
>   Springs run dry
>   One by one, beyond recall—Summer fancies
>   fade and die!"—Selah!

Nov. 30th. Have just had the gratification of receiving a kind note from Genl. C. Leventhorpe who is now with his lady at Patterson, Caldwell Co. N. C. He assures me of his kind interest, and earnestly prays for my speedy liberation and restoration to my home and friends. Sympathy from such a source is doubly comforting, since the Genl. is not a man to favor an undeserving object. Oh, that I could show him in return some sense of the appreciation I feel for his straightforward, genial letter. Let me preserve the respect and esteem of the intelligent and honorable class of our people and to care not how much the Mongrels may abuse and slander me. Leventhorpe is one of Nature's noblemen, a knight *sans peur, sans reproche* if ever there was one. Strange that I should never have more intimately cultivated his acquaintance. But this is one of the lessons of my recent sad experience that by my carelessness, levity, and intemperate habits, I have lost the society of more than one truly noble friend; and have lost opportunities for attaching to me the personal esteem of others, whose support would have been invaluable, to me under present circumstances. But these regrets belong to the category of spilled milk!—let us do better in future!

December 13th. This day twenty-seven years ago, a very unlucky event happened to me—*I was born!* I celebrated the occasion by doing 15 pairs of shoes which

is considered a fair day's work, for so green a hand as
I. But for all I worked hard, I could not fatigue the
little demon of Thought, which from morning till night
racked my heart with bitter memories, of gloomy forebodings. This day nine years ago I was celebrating my
birthday by killing Yankees, on the plain near Fredericksburg, and today I am making shoes for the sur-
vivors! And with six similar, sorrowful anniversaries to
pass within these walls. What a Prospect! What a Present! I feel sick—tired—cynical. Why was not *infanticide
more popular twenty-seven years ago?* Oh, that some
second Herod had played havoc among the infants of
West Virginia, a double dozen or so years ago! Better
had one died young, like those whom the Gods love, than
toil painfully up the hill of life, until one has gathered a
back-load of sorrows, which finally tumbles us into the
grave! And yet how wonderfully do we cling to our foul
breath. Sometimes I agree with the Frenchman, whose
philosophy ran thus—if the house is not full of smoke,
let us try to put up with it; but if it becomes unendurable, we *know the way to the door!* But, perhaps, a wiser
philosophy is that taught by Tennyson in his *"Two
Voices"*—

"Thou art so full of misery
Were not it better *not to be?"*
Then the bright answer,—
"The little whisper—silver clear
The murmur,—Be of better cheer!"

Twenty seven years ago, today, happened the greatest of all the misfortunes of my life!—*My Birth!*
Twenty seven Birth-Days stand like memoric milestones across the plain of life, showing the strange vicissitudes of the wanderer! Scarcely any two of those anniversaries are alike. The first five passed in the old Virginia Homestead under a mother's loving care. Half a
dozen of them succeed in the same place, but under the
rigid discipline of a maiden aunt, who for some reason
never liked me, and whom I suppose I gave no reason to
change her opinion of me. Then came four years in Central Pennsylvania, in two of the loveliest valleys on

Earth's surface, *and my school days!* Sugar and salt mixed!

December 13 1860, I spent visiting my school mate's family in Phila., where I frequently met the widow and daughter of the lamented Iturbide of Mexico. So this, my sixteenth birthday, was chiefly notable from the circumstance that I played several games of chess with the Princess, daughter of a murdered Emperor.

December 13th 1861, I stood all the day on a lonely hillside almost within sight of the rotunda of the Federal Capitol; stood on picket post in snow above my ankles, and without any shelter except a very thin, wet blanket, wrapped loosely (so that I could handle my musket instantly if shot at) and a small sapling, not as thick as my body.

December 13th 1862, found me exposed from dawn till dusk to the deadly fire of two guns, and the terrific successive charges of Burnside's columns near the foot of Marye's Hill in the Valley of Fredericksburg. "Strange if I should fall on the very day of my birth," I thought, after seeing man after man of my comrades close their career.

December 13th 1864, I lay shivering under a single blanket in the flimsy barracks of Fort Delaware Prison Pen. For food we had three small crackers ("hard tack") and a bit (bite) of rusty bacon, which only a famished stomach could hold. For bedding only a single blanket per man—though the single stove in the center of the long "barn" gave no perceptible warmth ten feet from it. All the barracks contained small pox cases, and one poor fellow died with the loathsome disease directly over me, he occupying the "top bunk," and I the "middle" one! No pleasure in that birthday, surely! *December 13th 1865-'6* were passed in Newbern.

Dec. 25. My fingers are almost too numb with cold to make this note (which I do with my new *plumbage* pencil) but when I think that all over the South my friends are making a holiday of this day, I feel that I am entitled to chronicle the fact that I have worked hard, trimming fifty pairs of shoes, and instantly choking down every incipient thought of repining or bitterness, resolved since I am cruelly forced to drudge like a slave (yea worse than a slave, for he has numerous holidays) and among the brutal outcasts of creation, I at least, shall not permit myself to be still further injured and lowered by yielding to vain regrets and moodiness.

Christmas!—without the gift. I had somehow formed the idea that people did not work on an holyday; but I discovered my mistake when called upon to trudge out to the shops, and make shoes on this eighteen hundred, and seventy first birthday of our Lord. Truly it is an hard experience! Santa Claus! Santa Claus! when thou was distributing gifts, why gavest thou not liberty to me! Perhaps my stockings were too dirty, but they were the only ones I have, and one cant go barefooted in these polar regions.

I have already suffered intensely from the cold, and I am full of dread of sickness arising from cold. We turn out in the frosty air three times a day; and, leaving the heated shops, with no covering for our hands or ears, are chilled through in the brief period during which we are exposed.

Naturally at such a season one's thoughts recur to happier scenes—the festive occasions of the past. It would be strange if sadness and depression were not ever present to one in my situation. And yet I am more cheerful than I have been for many days. The crisp, sharp atmosphere has something to do with it I suppose.

January 1st. 1872. The New Year opens with the thermometer 5000 ft below zero! It is so cold there is no use of talking about it. I am crammed with cold, ears frozen, nose like an icicle, and hands covered with chillblains; of which I never so much as heard before I came here. I wonder if there are any Esquimaux hereabouts? It is a shame to send Southern men to this abominable climate.

Today we worked all day as usual. What an miserable holiday is this!

Jan. 2nd—1872. Genl. P. having wished me to take a class in the Night School he has opened for the benefit

of the prisoners, I went up to the school room last evening and was given a class in mathematics. The school is
held on Monday and Thursday evenings, and all who
desire it, and whose conduct is exemplary, are permitted
to attend. The Chaplain acts as superintendent, and intelligent convicts are the teachers; reading, writing, and
arithmetic, comprising the present course. The room is
a large one in the attic, or French roof of the Male
Wing, and is neatly furnished with desks, seats, etc., of
the best pattern, with numerous gas jets to give light.
All the guards and overseers occupy armed chairs
around the walls to see that the prisoners have no intercourse, except with their teachers, who are supposed to
be reliable men. The session durates about one and an
half hour. *Teachers receive a biscuit and a slice of ham
on School nights as their salary!*

Wonder what my friends would think if they saw me
teaching a class of convicts, several of them vicious looking negroes? I believe it is the Radical theory that the
Ku Klux prefer to kill a darkey than to eat. What a
poor Ku Klux I must be!

The establishment of this school for the improvement
of the wretched creatures brought here from year to
year, marks an advanced stage in the march of Prison
Reform; and reflects credit on the philanthropic and
enlightened views of the Superintendent, who permits,
if he does not expect much from the school.

Coming into my cell at 6 P. M., I found to my surprise and delight a good size box from home! Christmas
had come at last! But better still was it to find that more
than one friendly heart had remembered me; and sent
tokens of esteem and sympathy to cheer me in my distant prison. Mrs. Capt. Clark sends a *mammoth* frosted
Fruit-Cake, Mrs. Young a fine jar of peaches. Jennie,
my sweet sister, a variety of little useful articles for the
toilet; and Miss Mattie R. Miller, a pair of beautiful
slipper patterns in crimson velvet, and white tippet, and
a neat needle book, with scissors, thread, thimble, buttons, etc. Moreover she sends a pair of gloves, which are
more useful to me than anything else just at present.
Altogether, 'tis a rich treat, and I am sure I appreciate

the kindness of the donors. I wish they were aware of my thoughts this night. It is cold and dreary beyond description, outside; but the good cheer in my heart lights up my bleak cell with a pleasant look, and the fragrance of "good things" from home makes me forget that there is sitting at my door a pan of cold mush, which I intended to have eaten for supper. Mine friends, one and all, I wish ye an abundance of happiness! Father writes that he has sent a number of newspapers as wrappers in the box; but I was not permitted to have them, which was very provoking, for it would have afforded me many an hour's pleasure to peruse these papers, no matter how stale they might be. Nothing can be old to a man who never sees *anything new*. No one can tell how much I long for the news of the day—intelligence of how the world wags. But when one is in Rome he must do as the Romans—wish him to do.

January 4th 1872. The Captain fetched me a letter from father, containing the following paragraphs from the Era, the Radical Organ at Raleigh.

"We learn from reliable authority that Randolph A. Shotwell *confessed* before he entered the walls of Albany Penitentiary, and intimated that he could make revelations which would startle the public as there are (or were) men belonging to the Klan, not now, even suspicioned. We look at no distant day for this young man Shotwell to 'puke,' and 'make a clean breast.'"—*Era* Oct. 31st.

Again

"We understand that R. A. Shotwell will be here during the sessions of the U. S. Court to make startling revelations. Somebody will be hurt"—Nov. 28th.

The phrase "make a clean breast" shows the author of these lies; McEwan constantly urged me to make a clean breast; and he was the only man who knew of my proposal to appear as a witness. I now see the folly of my attempt to get on the stand! The Mongrels know me too well to believe me willing to fall into their designs; therefore they take advantage of my offer to McEwan, to misrepresent me and damage my reputation among my friends. I confess I expected this from the hour I consented to appear as a witness; but it seemed the only chance to get into a position where I could publicly vindicate myself, and confound my enemies, and for this reason, I parleyed with conscience so far as to pretend a willingness to serve the wicked persecutors. It was a fault, and I am sorry for it.

Fortunately my friends give me credit for too much honor to turn traitor, and the Shelby *Banner,* of Dec. 2d. boldly crushes the floating lie.

> We are authorized to state that the report that Capt. Shotwell has *confessed* and implicated his friends in crime, or will do so, is without the shadow of foundation. All the gold and allurements of Radicalism cannot tempt this brave man to perjure himself, and swear against his friends. We had rather be Capt. R. A. Shotwell in the Albany Prison, than Todd R. Caldwell, George Logan, or Bait Carpenter, in the positions they occupy. Well may his friends be proud of him. The report that the other prisoners sent to Albany with Capt. Shotwell have joined the Regular Army is also false.

Much obliged, Friend of the *Banner,* for your defence of my reputation! Nor is your confidence in me unfounded. Under no circumstance would I break my plighted faith with even the least of my acquaintance. The above sounds like Durham's *hand writing;* there is one man who is not afraid to avow his principles. But men of that class are rare nowadays. The *Vindicator,* also notices the *Era's* remarks, and with more than usual spirit, replies:—

> The above extracts have no foundation in fact, and only exhibit the meanness of striking a defenceless man. Capt. Shotwell was offered his liberty on condition of his making revelations, but he treated the proposition with merited scorn, saying he would spend his last moment in prison before he would perjure himself or swear against his friends. It is bad enough to seek the injury of a free man, but to strike a defenceless one is despicable.

This don't sound like Maj. Erwin, and I am at a loss

to think who could have written it. By the way it is
curious that, while I have *started no less than three of
the newspapers now published in N. C.,* I have not had
a word in my defense from any of them before this article; although other newspapers have spoken freely in
my favor. How different would have been my conduct if
I had been in charge of either of them, when such persecutions were going on as that from which I suffer! But
the times are given over to selfishness and meanness.

The Charlotte *Democrat* also has a fling at the *Era:*

> In regard to the *Era's* allusions to Mr. Shot-
> well we will say that it was reported some time
> ago that he would be pardoned if he would make
> revelations of men connected with the Klan, or who
> participated in its depredations. We do not believe
> Mr. Shotwell would do anything of that sort even
> to obtain his release from the Penitentiary.

Perfectly correct, friend Yates! I might have escaped
from coming here by acting in that style; but I said then,
and I stick to it, that I shall stay in prison until I grew
gray before I would dishonor myself in such manner.
I have read somewhere a letter written by Count De-
Beauharnais, while in the Bastile, a few days before his
execution, in which he says, (language to that effect)
"When we are unable to make a successful resistance to
Despotism, there is but one possibility of resistance,
namely, to receive its inflictions with a virtue which
shall cover it with dishonor. Those who come after us
will at least profit by our example, and the legacy of
the proscribed will not be lost to humanity."

> Let *honor* be the spring of all my actions,
> Not *interest,* nor gain. Let no selfish views
> Reach safety at the price of truth and justice!

Jan. 5th.   Called to the office, where I found brother
Mel. in good health, spirits, and clothes. He greeted me
so affectionately that I could not but wonder at it, seeing that we have been so long separated, and so rarely
agreed when together. Yet his heart can be no warmer
than my own; and now that he has come and gone, I
feel indescribably gloomy. But something of this is due
to the brief glimpse of the outside world, I had while

talking with him. Indeed it is quite an event to be called out to the office; for, after going for month after month without a word to any one, and scarcely a look except at the sloppy walks, or the everlasting piles of shoes on your bench, it is a wonderful change to enter the office, where all is clean, warm, and comfortable, soft carpets, cushioned chairs, neat furniture, flowers, paintings, and every convenience for elegant leisure, as well as the transaction of business! And then to meet some familiar friend, to talk of familiar matters, to hear of startling events, and imbibe some of the cheerfulness which, (in Bro. M's. presence) is often contagious; all this is like coming up out of some noxious pit to get a breath of fresh air, and catch a glimpse of the beauty of the world! But how dark the hour when one returns into the pit! M. brought me a number of little articles for which I thank him much. Capt. P. passed him my letters without looking at them, which shows he can be a gentleman as well as a keeper of a Penitentiary.

M. says my Yankee kindred are horrified at—"as they consider it"—my disgrace. Bah! nobody hurt! I care very little for their good or bad opinion, notwithstanding their wealth. And I should be terribly bored if it were necessary to write and explain to them the wrongs, and unjust persecution I have received.

January 21, 1872. Lucky again! I have just had another substantial box from home sent by my thoughtful and generous little friend Miss M. R. M., assisted by her sisters Miss Mary, and Miss Carrie, and Mrs. Capt. Camp. These noble women have constantly sought to contribute to my comfort from the hour on which I fell into the hands of the Philistines; and I must be ungrateful indeed, if I ever cease to hold them in grateful remembrance. By all the sweet saints in Mahomet's Paradise, I swear there is no danger of it! My little friend *guesses* at *my wants* like a *prophetess,* and is as liberal in supplying them as if I were a brother. She has sent me several articles for which I had *particular need,* and which will relieve me of some pain. May she ever find friends to brighten and cheer her life!

January 27th. Still they come! Twenty-four citizens of S. C., charged with Ku Kluxing, were brought

in today. They are as a general thing all miserably
poor and illiterate—small farmers, field hands, hired
laborers, etc. S. G. Brown, Esq., a magistrate of his
county and Dr. Thos. Whiteside, both of York Dist.,
are the principal persons among them. Hays Mitchell
was the first man tried in S. C.; and his lawyers (Hon.
A. H. Stanbury and Hon. Reverdy Johnson, late Minister to England) received $15,000 to defend him.
Capt. John W. Mitchell, chief of Klan is also here.
Many of these men are entirely innocent! Thus the
war goes on!

January 31, 72. The last day of Jany. is marked
with an "white stone" in the prisoners' calendar, because
on that day they get an extra dinner! The originator
of this feast is a Mr. H. C. L. Dorsey of Connecticut,
who was at one time confined here, and who sends a certain sum every year to buy turkeys or ham and vegetables for a Jubilee dinner for the prisoners. Today
the bill of fare is: one pound boiled ham, do. cabbage,
do. Irish potatoes, do. crackers and light bread; a royal
repast for poor devils who dine from one years end to
another on a pan of cold beef soup, thickened with the
sour hash left from breakfast; or a piece of "salt horse"
and three or four half boiled, and often "frosted" Irish
potatoes!

I do not exaggerate this matter, in the least. It is
a fact that for months I have not eaten a single meal
with relish; and commonly I do not eat more than one
meal per day, although at hard labor for 10 hours.

Undoubtedly if I were to complain to the Supt. about
our intolerable fare he would blow up the cooks; but I
should certainly gain the ill will of the officers, and be
exposed to every sort of petty persecution and insult.
Wherefore it is better to bear the ills we have, than risk
a perpetual annoyance. And so I too, am glad that
Dorsey opens his pockets, *am glad to eat a 'charity
dinner'!*

Colder than Iceland!—Monstrously windy—bleak—
and disagreeable!

February. 10th. By an accidental slipping of a keen-
edged knife, I whittled off the end of my first finger on

my left hand. It bled profusely, and I went to the over-seer, Rose, for some sticking plaster. He took an half hour to get it, although he had only to raise the lid of his desk, and then insinuated that it would be a good excuse for me to stop work, or something to that effect. I felt blind and angry enough to take my knife and give him an excuse for stopping work! I have never yet missed a day since I came here; although often sick; whereas there is not another man in the place who does not stay in his cell once or twice a month.

But these overseers know that I regard them as my inferiors in every respect, and like all small-souled peo-ple, they take a delight in trying to humiliate me. I only replied to Rose with a look, but I did not stop work.

I told the instructor, however, that he ought not to count me a "full hand" for I had only nine fingers.

February 11th. I am pained to hear of the death of Ex-Gov. Thomas Bragg of N. C. I had been looking for an answer to a letter I sent him several weeks ago; but today I learned the reason of his silence!

Gov. Bragg was no ordinary man; nay, he had few equals among men. It is his highest eulogium that al-though his whole life has been spent in public station, not even his enemies can pick a flaw in his character. As a lawyer, legislator, statesman, U. S. Senator, Gov-ernor of his State, and Cabinet Officer of the Confeder-ate States, he invariably won golden opinions and tow-ered unassailable, in his private character. He stood always among the first, as a man, as a citizen, as an official, as a philanthropist, and as an advocate of in-dividual and civic rights. In this last attitude, he won my lasting esteem during the recent K. K. trials. Al-though suffering untold torture from physical infirmi-ties, he sat for days in the Capitol, watching the devel-opment of the Mongrel schemes to deprive us of our liberty and reputation, and then arose to denounce the injustice and wrong which was being perpetrated under the forms of law. Indeed I believe this was his last effort—a dying protest against Despotism, and the Pollution of the Judicial Bench to Political Ends!

Noble old man! Well may one of his admirers pronounce him a piece of moral statuary without a blemish. His decease has been mourned throughout North Carolina. In Raleigh business was suspended—flags at half mast—and both houses of the General Assembly acted as his funeral escort.

"Why weep ye then for him who having won
The bounds of man's appointed years—at last
Life's blessings all enjoyed—Life's labors done
Serenely to his final rest has passed—
While the soft memory of his virtues yet
Lingers like twilight hues when the sun is set."

From Bryant's "Old Man."

February 22nd. Washington's Birthday—and also brother Hamilton's. Of him I have been thinking all day—the last scene of his life; when he lay in my arms, talking of home, of his lovely wife, of his brave men, of the future, etc.—a most sorrowful reverie. Strange how a certain train of thought sometimes will fasten itself on the mind, and refuse to be shaken off; perhaps, though, it is the result of long brooding, and monotonous confinement. Often a disagreeable recollection has haunted me for days, and let me dismiss it an hundred times, 'twould be in vain. Thus I fell a-thinking of my last evening and day in Asheville, and, despite my efforts, was rendered miserable for days by it. Am I becoming a monomaniac? Or is it 'bile' on the liver? At all events I must try, and be more cheerful, or I shall not endure six years here.

February 23rd. Work! Work! Work! Nothing but work from dawn till dusk, like the unhappy milliner in Hood's "Song of the Shirt." "Work! Work! Work! my labor never flags. And what are its wages? A bed of straw, a crust of bread, and rags. That stony roof, this naked floor, a bucket, an iron chair, and a wall so blank, my shadow I thank, for something falling there."

By the way, it was an excellent fore-thought of Hood's in not naming his verses "The Tale of a Shirt"— which in reality it is—for such an suggestive title would have *shifted* every bit of pathos out of the piece.

But it is no joking matter the way we have to work nowadays. I get so tired that at 6 o'clock, when I enter my cell, I prefer to lie down and rest than to eat. Right before me in the shops is a small wheel, which revolves with great rapidity and is always at it. This wheel has whirled so incessantly before my eyes that I can see it plainly as I write these lines in my cell. Will it *ever, ever, ever,* stop!

March 4th. The weather is intolerably cold. Men say 'tis the coldest winter they have ever known, even in this latitude; and surely it must be the truth. The thermometer, I understand, is a mile and a half below zero, and still falling! A few whiffs of the exterior air would make a frozen mummy of me; although these Yankees don't seem to mind it much.

I have suffered outrageously from cold all winter; but today it is indescribable.

March 5th—72. Genl. Pilsbury paused at my door and ejaculated, "Coldest I have known in twenty years!" and was gone before I could thaw my tongue to reply. The instructor told me that in the morning the mercury stood at 22 degrees below zero! Ugh! it gives one a chill to think of it! When Irving got up that story about Rip Van Winkle snoozing for 20 years among the Catskills he ought to have appended the plausable explanation; to-wit, that old Rip, who was full of mean whiskey, was frozen, and lay torpid, as snakes and toads are known to lie, for months or longer. I have not yet seen any weather warm enough (in this region) to thaw a frozen man. That was a wise remark of the "Autocrat of the Breakfast Table," viz: "A good deal, which in colder regions is ascribed to mean dispositions, belongs really to mean temperature." I confess the extreme cold makes me cross.

I have no doubt that the climate has a good deal to do with the Unionism and centralizing tendencies of the North. Here men are obliged to make costly defences against the cold; not only for themselves, but for their stock; and for the housing of their crops. The farmer needs a warm and substantial dwelling, a costly barn, out houses, etc., and the mechanic labors to surround himself with similar comforts.   In fact the inclement climate compels these people to be more domestic, and pay more attention to the petty matters of the household than Southerners who are not under any necessity of providing costly shelters for themselves, and their cattle. Now the Yankee, having two thirds of his fortune in houses, barns, and other perishable property, is loth to disturb the existing order of things, lest riots, disorders, etc., shall endanger his goods.   He knows that a mob, or the torch of an incendiary, can almost beggar him in an hour.   He sees that a strong and established government is the best for him, no matter if it is tyrannical.   He therefore, shouts for the Union, and permits himself to be led on to an inevitable monarchy in America.

Not so with the Southerner whose wealth lies in the *land,* not in the buildings on it.   He is not much hurt, if you burn and plunder every thing that he has under roof; in a week he will have up a new log house, and his cattle are not supposed to know the luxury of any sort of shelter.

Furthermore, the Southerner being less occupied with domestic cares, has more leisure to give to politics, is more independent, more zealous of his individual, and local rights.   He cares very little for the Union, except as a defensive arrangement against foreign enemies. MORAL: The Yankees are Unionists because it is to their advantage to be so.   The Southerners are State's Rights men because they think themselves better than the Yankees and are anxious to show, by State lines that they are not a common part of the country, and on the same footing as the latter.

N. B. and my fingers are so cold I'll be hanged if I've anything more to say on the subject.

March 9th, 1872.   Greatly to my surprise, I this morning received the following notification:

"Shelby, N. C., Feb. 23, 1872, R. A. Shotwell, Esq., U. S. Prison, Albany, N. Y.—My dear sir;— I have the honor to inform you that you were elected an Honorary member of the Philologian Society in Shelby. The Society begs to be remem-

bered to you. With kindest regards, Very truly
your Obedt. Sevt. A. C. Miller, corresponding
Sec'y Society."

These Shelby people are not afraid to show that they
are men, and *free* men! They act as if they possessed
some of the blood that whipped Pat Ferguson at King's
Mountain.   There are a few at least whom Loyal
Leagues, and Loyal Legions cannot bribe, purchase,
nor terrify. This unexpected honor is peculiarly grateful to me as an intimation that though absent I am not
forgotten; that although confined in a penitentiary and
surrounded by all the marks of a felony, I am not lowered in the opinion of those whose respect and esteem is
worth having.[1]

The Cleveland *Banner* says:
The statement so industriously circulated by the
enemies of Capt. R. A. Shotwell that he had turned
State's evidence, and made confessions of his guilt
as a Ku Klux is positively contradicted by letter
from that gentleman of recent date. Having
wronged and attempted to ruin the character of
Capt. Shotwell the villains thought by these statements to lower him in the estimation of respectable
people. The thing is past gentlemen. Capt. Shotwell in the Albany Penitentiary has the respect of
all honest respectable people. They know that he
has been grossly wronged for the basest political

---

1. Shotwell sent the following letter in reply:
Albany Penitentiary,
March 31st, 1872.
My dear sir:—Your favor of the 23rd of February apprizing me of my election
to Honorary membership in the Philologian Society of Shelby, was duly received,
but owing to the regulations of the Institution it was out of my power to give it
earlier attention.
I now beg that you will be so good as to make my acknowledgments to the
gentlemen of your society for the unexpected honor they have been pleased to
bestow upon me. Under any circumstances I should have esteemed it a compliment to have been chosen a member of so intelligent an Association, but in my
present peculiar position, such a mark of respect is the more acceptable to me as
an intimation that the persecution and ignominious wrong of which I have been
a victim, because of my political opinions, are properly understood by the public,
and that I am not forgotten—although in a distant prison, nor bereft of friendly
sympathy, although environed with the attributes of Felony. I hail it, moreover,
as a token that there is life in the Old Land yet; that there are some whom
Loyal Leagues and Loyal Legions can neither bribe, purchase, nor terrify.
Brave old Cleveland! Armed Despotism may indeed hold her in its grasp, dis-
turbing her tranquillity and paralyzing her industry, but it shall seek in vain to
make slaves of her sons, or to check the patriotic sympathies of her noble daughters! Methinks the spirit of 1780—the spirit that animated the bold yeomen, who,
mounted two on a horse, with rusty rifle and pockets full of bullets, galloped
night and day in the wake of old Isaac Shelby to hurl Pat Ferguson and his
renegades from the brow of King's Mountain, still lives to defy a similar and
no less unworthy combination of Foreign and Domestic Treason in our day. Let
us hope—let all good men see to it, that the result be as decisive and auspicious

purposes. His persecutors from Judge Logan down are vile contemptible low-bred people, and have the respect of none but the ignorant, the corrupt and the vile. This is the difference, and all that these people can do, or cause to be done, cannot change it.—*Banner,* Feb. 24th, 1872.

The writer of the above—whom I take to be P. D.— tells nothing but the truth. I have not the slightest idea of "confessing"—(having nothing to confess), and I am sure I shall never be guilty of perjury and bad faith with my late friends.

I cannot but feel deeply stirred, and grateful, for these expressions of sympathy and respect; and I begin to hope, with brother and others, that I may be able to turn the very persecutions of my enemies to some good end, when at liberty to push my fortune in the world. Thus, it would seem that, [*Several lines are inked out.*]

March 16th. Have just had a letter from Gov. Z. B. Vance, as follows:

R. A. Shotwell, Dr. Sir:
I received your letter. I wrote to your father about you, although I suppose he hears from you regularly. You need feel no anxiety in regard to the reports circulating from time to time about you here. If they gain a moments credence when first told, time soon upsets them. You are not *degraded*

---

for the whole country. I am not unaware that these, or any allusions to our political and local trouble may be considered something inappropriate in a letter addressed to a purely literary society. But I think I do not err by assuming that the young men of Shelby in organizing for the benefit of self-culture, have likewise had in view certain responsibilities devolving upon them as inheritors of a glorious personal and civil liberty, namely, the duty of upholding and maintaining those time honored principles upon which the fabric of their freedom is founded. In other words, young gentlemen, while it is your aim to attain excellence and skill in the forensic arts, you have already dedicated that skill to the defence of the institutions of your forefathers, now assailed on every side.

If such be your motives, you have not been unmindful of events transpiring around you; nor have I given offence by alluding to them. Grave responsibilities do, indeed, devolve upon you, for it is to her youth that the South looks for political health and material prosperity. It is yours to draw lessons of experience from the past wherewith to inaugurate a new and radiant era for the future. But chiefly it is yours, and yours only, to demand and obtain for your long-suffering people that measure of just equality in the family, in the nation, without which there can be neither lasting peace nor fraternity of feeling between its members.

Allow me, therefore, gentlemen, to express the hope that the Philologian Society may flourish, and exert a wide influence for good, and not only in a moral and educational sense, but also as a medium for the dissemination of honest political principles.

It has been said that the American people are upon the point of demanding an honest government. Such a cause deserves your hearty support. May the right prevail.

With sentiments of respect and esteem, I am, gentlemen,
Your obedient servant,
R. A. Shotwell.

among your acquaintance for whatever may be the crime of which you are accused, it is lost sight of in the crowning infamy of your trial and conviction. The disgraceful and indecent spectacle of an United States Judge, Attorney, and Marshal uniting to pack a jury to convict a political opponent, presents a crime for the contemplation of mankind, so black and damning that the trespass of which you are accused appears like angels raiment beside it.

But regrets and denunciations will avail nothing now. I can only advise you to a ready submission to all the requirements of prison authorities, and a willing submission to all the requirements of your unpleasant situation as to the will of God. Meantime the content to believe that the good people of N. C. will do your reputation full justice, and will appreciate exactly the measure of your guilt, your temptation and your punishment. Rest assured, too, that the precise amount of censure which is yours will be visited upon you in spite of your misfortunes which pervert our judgments, and the same measure of sympathy which is your due, you will receive although you were forty times in the Penitentiary, and forty governments surrounded you with the attributes of felony. In short your reputation depends upon yourself.

Very Truly your friend,
Z. B. Vance.

This letter disappoints and saddens me exceedingly. It shows that popular belief has not been able to resist the persistent reiteration of slanders against me, and that while people may consider me a greatly wronged man; they still think me more or less guilty. How absurd is it for Gov. V. to say that I shall receive full justice from the public when his own letter shows that he and others of the public have accepted the Radical lies against me for full truth, therefore laying me liable to censure!

What is the use of telling me I had a shameful and indecent trial, and in the next breath intimate that I am more or less guilty.

Now I ask no man's sympathy for my *misfortunes;* I want no *pity.* If any one thinks I have yielded to *"temptation,"* or committed "crime," he had better bestow his commiseration upon somebody that needs it worse, and will appreciate it higher than I. No doubt the Governor meant to write kindly, but he feared to say something that might get into the papers, and so he mounts the stilts of dignity, and moralizes over my injuries as if he were giving counsel to a murderer on the scaffold. Of course I resent any such tone when addressed to me. Yet this letter confirms some of my saddest forebodings, and no day of my prison life has been more gloomy than this.

March 21st. Rec'd a long and affectionate letter from Father containing an extract from the *Cincinnati Enquirer,* calling upon the people of the North to call mass meetings, and denounce the wicked persecutions of the Government under the head of enforcing the Ku Klux Klan. It also states that martial [law] has been declared in 9 counties of S. C. and that over 4000 Southern citizens are lying in jail awaiting trial! This shows how the political crusade, of which I was the first victim, is gaining ground.

Father says he thinks better of me now—in prison— than ever he did! How curiously tenacious is the affection of a noble hearted man. The simile of the oak, growing stronger, and reaching farther, the more it is shaken by the storm, is the aptest comparison that can be devised to illustrate it.

April 2nd. Kind letter from Genl. Leventhorpe, who assures me of the best wishes of many friends in the Valley, and gives me more news than any letter I have had in some time.

April 3rd. Whosoever has never felt the weariness and disgust which a long and monotonous occupation at physical labor is apt to create in an intelligent mind, can form no idea of the pleasure to be derived from books, the delights of *reading.* Suppose that all day you have been engaged in mechanical pursuits, in which the mind takes no part, waging a war of muscle against blind forces—wood, iron, leather, and the like—which yield only a passive resistance. You consider yourself tired out, you have been chopping wood without seeing any chips fly. But now you take up a book, and how charmingly your mind runs over the pages! The weariness of the body is forgotten in the sprightliness of the intellect. You read with a freshness and zest which the man of sedentary habits, never knows.

* * * * * *[1]

April 18th. This afternoon brother Mel. I was delighted to see him, although I am in very low spirits, and was rendered more so, by the trouble in which he evidently is involved. He, however, was very cheerful, as indeed he always is. I was very glad to get some reading matter; a blankbook which he had been thoughtful enough to bring me. Best of all, I am now permitted to keep a pencil, and need no longer steal opportunities to make an hurried note of my experience. During the interview with brother Mel, I had occasion to use his pencil, and with singular forgetfulness, put it into my pocket. Afterwards came the Deputy, and asked me for it, but as I promptly produced it he said, "Well you may keep it; but see that you make good use of it."

This privilege I cannot estimate too highly; for I have constant demand for a pencil, and it was hard to use one clandestinely, starting every time an officer passed the cell, as if I had been about to steal something.

As for making an improper use of it, that I should not do if I had a gross of pencils. I have no desire in the world to correspond with my fellow prisoners, unless it be to hear occasionally from one or two of the more respectable of the Ku Klux, to learn what news from the South they have.

Bro. M. went up to Troy to call upon some friends. I am preparing a note or two to send my lady friends.

April 19th. Mel returned, came up this afternoon. He had an agreeable visit in Troy, and is in high spirits,

---

1 A brief discussion of the value of reading is omitted.

as usual. Sent by him notes to Miss R. L. D., Miss
M. F., Miss M. R. M., Annie P., L. P., Erwin, and
father, also T. B. K., Richmd. Va. When he was gone,
I went back to the shops—back to my position between
two filthy negroes—back to be hectored by the overseer
—back to hard work, rendered inconceivably irksome by
the brief glimpse I had of the outside world.

The drudgery of penal labor is (for one in my situation) as bad as a treadmill. It is dull, soulless, spiritless,
interestless, toil without thought, without object, without the least return! But 'tis folly to repine. "Are these
things necessities? Then let us meet them like necessities."

April 21st. Kind letter from my amiable friends,
Miss M. F. and Miss Alice H. The former speaks of
sending a box soon. I wish I could prevent it by going
after it. Both these are full of kindness and sympathy.
Alice H. as usual gives the more news than any one else.
Unhappy Rutherford! The Mongrels still wage war on
all decent people. W. S. Guthrie has been arrested,
forced to give $3,000 bond, upon the evidence of John
Harrel, and others—all false. Perhaps after while the
public will begin to understand the kind of testimony
on which I was convicted. It is generally the way with
perjured informers; they carry their abominable false-
swearing a step too far, and break down all they have
accomplished by attacking the reputation of men whose
conduct has not made them so vulnerable as the first
victims. Thus Titus Oates, after *having hung some dozens* of good citizens of England at last became so bold
that even the false hearted Judges were obliged to pronounce him unworthy of belief. So the witnesses in the
negro plot in New York City, after having caused the
death of more than a dozen innocent persons, at length
attacked some members of the family of the Chief Justice, when the whole thing fell to the ground. So in the
Salem trials for witchcraft, the witnesses were perfectly
reliable so long as they only hung or burned poor helpless creatures but when they began to accuse men of
wealth and influence their testimony was too apparent
to go down even with the blind populace. So during the

French Revolution. And so it will ever be. And I am glad of it; for when the John Harrellites have been proved to be, what I know them to be—perjured foul-souled liars—people must see the full farce of my trial and conviction.

W. G. Edgerton has been re-arrested and held in additional bond of $4,000, charged with being one of the party which released the seven K. K. from Marion jail. If the indictment had named him the leader of it, it would have been nearer the truth. He is a good fellow, and more of a man than many bipeds. We will make these things all right—in the morning.

April 23rd. I am very blue in mind and not well in body. Day in and day out I suffer from the greatest depression of spirit.

April 27th. Another Saturday night. Blessed Saturday night! No one appreciates this hour as does the mechanical laborer. In other employments there is usually something to divert the mind, and give exercise to the body; but the poor shoemaker, weaver, or factory hand, has worked during the whole week like a mere machine. His hands and arms perform their duty by sheer force of habit, and the man himself is little better than an automaton, going through with certain motions by clockwork. But on Saturday night, when he lays aside his tools, the *machine* is abandoned and the *man* appears. He is now free to attend to any little matters of his own, while before him is the prospect of a day's rest on the morrow.

All these feelings are intensified with the prisoner working at penal labor. For him there is not even the consolation of knowing that he is earning something by the sweat of his brow. There is nothing whatever to direct his mind. No wonder that so many men go crazy. No wonder that when the whistle blows on Saturday evening, I fold my arms with a sigh of relief!

Beside on Saturday night, we are almost at Sunday morning, and who knows but I may get a batch of cheering letters.

April 28th. Disappointed again! No letters. The Deputy passed my cell with a handful of letters but not any for me! It is positively shameful the way I am treated by those who profess to be my friends. Very well gentlemen, I will try not to forget you. Someday we may get even!

April 29th. Capt. Pilsbury, having fetched me a letter from father, called attention to its having been opened by cutting off one end, and re-sealing with gum-arabic. This is not the first instance of the kind lately. Of course the Mongrels in our Southern post offices are the authors of it. They can do anything, no matter how lawless, or felonious in the purview of the law, with utter impunity. Even if detected in breaking open a letter, they have only to plead that they were doing a good service for the government by ascertaining what information my friends were sending me. But who would listen to the complaints of a convicted Ku Klux in the Penitentiary even if I could prove that the villains had pilfered my letters. The Govt. needs the political support of the Mongrels and the negroes, and to retain their votes, they are permitted to do just as they choose with the liberty and property of their unfortunate but less obsequious neighbors. *But we live in "the land of the free,"* etc.

May 1st. The following is my *Programme* for daily division of the little leisure I have. Rise at or before day-light—10 minutes for washing my eyes (pouring water out of a cup), hanging up my blankets, getting ready to go out etc., etc. Read a few pages in Butler's "Analogy," and Kerney's "Compendium of History." Breakfast 5½-6:15. Study "Harrison on English Language," or Mathematics, until 7 o'clock. Work in shops till 12 M. Eat dinner hastily, and read Library book until 1. Work till sunset. Read 20 verses in Bible, History 30 minutes, and whatever light reading I have, until it is too dark to see—this last in order that I may go to sleep with agreeable images in my mind.

I have followed this course for some time, and find that I make some gains; although the twilight is so short in this latitude that it grows dark almost as soon as the sun is down. It will be seen that the shops get an unfair portion of my time. But the shops are "run" by "Yankees," and Yankees "carnt" see any use in allowing "convicts" to study, etc.

May 2nd.

May 3rd, 1872. Genl. Pilsbury came into the shops and calling me to the overseer's desk, asked how I was getting on, whether he could do anything for me, etc. Said I must keep cheerful, and try to make the best of circumstances. That he would be glad to show me any kindness in his power.

I thanked him, and assured him I was "accepting the situation" with as good grace, as human nature would permit of any man's doing.

Strange power of a civil word! After this little chat I returned to my work bench cheered and invigorated almost as if I had a promise of release, because I felt that here was an utter stranger, and one who from long experience in the management of criminals must be disposed to distrust all who are placed in his charge, this gentleman, I say, I felt to be both interested in me, and satisfied of my innocence. And *less than this* might comfort me in my present distressed and broken condition.

In truth none are so grateful for small favors as prisoners. Many men have found sincere attachment for their jailors merely in return for trifling benefits, although there may have been great disparity in rank, breeding, morals, and every other particular between the parties. I recollect a remark of Casanova, who when shut up in the dungeons of the Inquisition at Venice, received a present of one or two articles of clothing, a pencil, some paper, etc., from a nobleman in the city. *"in the fulness of my heart," said he, "I pardoned my oppressors; indeed I was nearly induced to give up all thoughts of escaping; so pliant is man after misery has bowed him down, and degraded him."*

My experience corroborates his; I have been astonished at the cheerfulness created, perchance when I was in the gloomiest mood, by a friendly letter, or a courteous word from those whom fraud, violence and injustice have made my custodians.

This day should be regarded as one of the brightest and saddest in Southern history. For on this day nine years ago was fought the battle of Chancellorsville—the acme of Southern triumph—the turning point in the fortunes of the Confederacy. The blaze of this victory died out under the funeral pall of Stonewall Jackson, slain by the untimely vigilance of his own men, and from that hour a sombre shadow spread over our Southern land, each day darker and darker until finally came night—ruin—and Appomatox. It was not that Jackson was an irreparable loss to the army, since his *forte* lay in the *execution,* not in the *conception* of great maneuvers, and Lee still lived to direct the campaign while many trained soldiers were ready to take up Stonewall's sword. But the country, and the army, loved Jackson, and when he fell, all minds received a cruel shock, resulting in more serious foreboding. People began to talk in this wise:

"Well Sir; We've whipped them again: we drove them back to their holes, Sir; we always do it. But what good does it do? They have all Europe, Asia, and Africa; besides the Indians, and our slaves, to fill up their armies—and so they get up, and come again. Whereas we, why, the fact is we have nobody to draft. We have already robbed the cradle and the grave, and there is scarcely a man in the country to make crops for the support of our women and children, to say nothing of the soldiers. Now in such a state of affairs every victory we gain is as bad for us as the defeat is for the enemy; and worse, for the Yankees care very little for a defeat, provided it prolongs the war, and makes sure of robbing us of our negroes, and other property. They have all the world to supply them with recruits—food for powder; whereas we have put forth our full strength; we are dry at the fountain head."

Thus people talked; and though the popular pulse gained a feverish strength during the abortive invasion of Pennsylvania, every sagacious observer, in the army and out of it, could very well see that sooner or later the forward movement must be changed to a retrograde one; and when Lee should begin to fall back, where could he stop? The result justified the gloomiest forebodings, and the 3rd of May 1863, may be considered the last bright day in the calendar of the Confederacy. True, our arms were covered with glory on more than one subsequent occasion, but they were the small gains of a ruined gamester—the tide of fortune ran steadily against us.

Singularly enough I chanced to have received from the Library a Federal account of the Battle of Chancellorsville, or the Wilderness, by one Rev. Alonzo Quint, an army Chaplain of one of the Massachusetts Regiments, and correspondent of a Boston Religious newspaper. And still more singularly, this man, who is the most inveterate liar I have lately read, gives a tolerably fair narrative of that battle. I quote his summary of events:

> History records that this army numbering according to the official and published reports of the medical director, 160,000 men—of which 120,000 must have been effective—magnificently equipped —taking its own time for its movement—evidently surprising the enemy—with confidence in its commanding general—with splendid fighting qualities —was *baffled*—not routed—only baffled.

He should have added—"by less than half our number of men, and they badly armed—some barefooted— and all on short allowance of food." What he *did* say is, however, sufficient to the genius of Lee, and the bravery of his troops. And had not Jackson fallen, their whole army would have been routed, for he was reconnoitering to make an attack, which Schmucker (Federal) in his History of the War, says must have completed the panic which already prevailed on that wing of the army.

I have called this Reverend Quint (he ought to be called *Squint,* for all his judgments are formed *squint-eyed*) an inveterate liar; it may be well to prove it by a few more extracts from his Book, entitled the *"Potomac and the Rapidan."* Hear him:

"There is no reason to qualify any statement of Rebel barbarity." "Southerners steal negroes whenever they have a chance to steal them to make them slaves." "I have ceased to feel any wonder at the brutality of a slave holding people." "The women of Winchester shot from

the windows and threw hand grenades on our poor
wounded helpless boys." "The black drivers of ambu-
lances under flag of truce at Manassas were seized and
carried away to slavery." etc., etc., etc.—These specimens are taken at random. But hear him inculcating the
gospel doctrine of forgiveness of enemies:

"That the Rebels must be *conquered, subjugated,* or
what you please to call it, admits of no question. That
our armies will eventually triumph is sure from the fact
*that Southerners never dare to meet an equal force of
Northerners* in the field." "But when the South is conquered it must be *held*—not a mere emancipation of
slaves, *but a change* in the *owners of property."* "The
simplest way is for Congress to pass a confiscation act
by which every man committing a *single act* of Rebellion
shall forfeit his *entire* property. *For this the Army
aches."* (Rally round the Flag boys! Be Patriotic—Save
the Union and fill your purses with the property of the
Southerners!) "If you confiscate you have the means
to pour in a new population." "At the end of the war
there will be thousands of young men ready to *take* and
hold, with an arm used to the rifle, (sweet Disciple of
the Blessed Prince of Peace!) these properties" etc.,
etc., etc. "Strike then for a confiscation act!" "Do not
divide the North, and weaken our armies by impracti-
cable proposition of *un-constitutional* measures," ("The
War is to protect the Constitution"—A Lincoln)
"From an active Rebel you need not expect honor, truth,
nor principle." "Southern chivalry is a myth." etc., etc.
Ad nauseam; ex uno disce!

Now this man was exceedingly popular as an army
correspondent, and his views were those of nine-tenths
of the population of New England; and are still, for
Squint, after publishing his letters, finds them so popular that he throws them on the world in book form. And
I learn, that he is considered a shining light of his church
in Massachusetts! Like people like priest; like priest
like people. But this liar tells the truth without meaning
to; he pulls down the mask, and shows that it was not
veneration for the Union and the Constitution that actuated the boasting patriots of Yankeedom; but solely

and simply their *hatred for Southerners,* and their *avaricious hopes of growing rich in confiscated property,* as their fathers grew rich by stealing negroes from Africa, and selling them to Southerners. It was only a trifling number in the North that went in for coercion on principle, and even they were soon swept away by the current of greed and prejudice. But we shall see— perchance the story is not yet fully told.

May 5th. Again disappointed about receiving letters. How much would I give for one warm-hearted intelligent friend, accustomed to keeping up with current events, and willing to write weekly, and thus relieve me from utter mental stagnation! But of all those who profess an interest in me, not one seems to have any conception of my wants, or else they are too timid to gratify me. Left a prey of suspense, I suffer daily, more from many causes, which it is quite unnecessary that I should state, than from the actual hardships of my case. One thing certain; I must cease to expect news from home or elsewhere. For these Sunday morning disappointments are destructive of my peace, and also my temper. Yet while philosophy and experience cry—*nil admirari!*—look for nothing—expect nothing—wonder at nothing, I find myself breaking wise resolutions in this respect, regularly as the Sabbath comes.

May 9th. "To the Deuce with all Barbers!" quoth a certain shoemaker when called up this afternoon to have his head shaved. Seriously I am exceedingly annoyed by this quarterly head shearing. A decent person dislikes to have his hair cut close to the skin as if he were a prize fighter, or wished to wear a wig; to say nothing of a suspicion that one has had lice in his head. Still I have to put up with it; and as my hair is naturally "cross-grained," my head looks like what the ladies call "an object." Indeed like the antiquated Uncle Edward (familiarly termed, Uncle Ned) I have no (wool) capillary substance on the summit of my cranium, in the place where the capillary substance ought to vegetate. Of course the regulation is perfectly proper for the mass of the prisoners, who rarely comb their heads, and for other reasons are better off with close-clipped heads.

But I think an exception might be made in favor of well bred men. At least it shows another advantage to be derived from the classification of prisoners. Respectable men might thus have privileges in such small matters.

May 12th.   Addie writes that "Every young man of your acquaintance in the county—in fact nearly every young man of any sort except the "Pukes" have fled to parts unknown." Unhappy Rutherford! For ten years you have been distracted and torn by vile wretches born and reared on your own soil. These dogs—nay! let me not insult the canine race by the comparison—are now guarding at the very best of your people, and frightening others into exile! When you, some day, come to realize the folly into which you have been betrayed by George Logan, with his imps, Justice, Scoggins, Carpenter, *et al,* you will arise and cast out these devils, as the whale threw out Jonah! "May I be there to see." I never advocated, nor approved of violent methods of redressing public or private wrongs; yet some diseases require desperate remedies; and nothing would give me greater pleasure than to hear that summary vengeance, or *justice* rather, had been meted to about one dozen of the leading incendiaries in Rutherford. Not that I am vindictive, and actuated entirely by resentment, although of course I have my feelings, as any honorable man must. But I am satisfied that there can be no rest, nor peace, for the decent people of Rutherford until a few scoundrels are hung or ejected.

May 13th.   An Irish whelp, named Costello, who has charge of my division in the Shops, insulted me today, so grossly that I could think of nothing else during the entire afternoon. I have not yet learned to trim shoes very neatly, and probably I never shall learn, as I have no mechanical turn whatever; but today I thought I would ask the instructor (who is put there to show us how to trim, etc.) to give me a little instruction in cutting out the shank. *"No! Attend to your own business! I've got no time to fool with you. If you haven't got sense enough to learn how to trim a shoe in all the time you have been here you'd better quit."* This contemptuous reply, coming from a mere Yankee-Irish mechanic, whom I should not think of asking to the table in my father's house if he were there at meal time, made my blood boil; and had he not went [*sic*] hastily away I should have gotten into trouble. Indeed, I am always afraid of getting into an altercation with some of these fellows, who seem to have a dislike to me—political perhaps—and may sometime provoke me beyond endurance. Still I shall try to avoid it; and, as I endeavor to obey the rules and do my full duty I shall take whatever comes with as much composure, as any high spirited and nervous person can retain under daily experience of what Shakespeare calls the "insolence of petty office."

May 17h. Called out to see Dr. F. C. Curtis (135 Washington Av. Albany) who had rec'd a letter from father, written at the suggestion of Rev. R. E. Johnson of Mecklenburg Co., asking him to visit me, and supply my wants as far as practicable etc. I am exceedingly mortified that father should have written such a letter. I would rather go without anything than be supplied by a stranger. Really father must have been deranged when he wrote that letter.

Dr. C. is a young man, son of Dr. Curtis (not he of Limestone) who used to preach in South Carolina, somewhere; and he seems to sympathize with the South. But his fears that I should ask him for something were quite apparent. I soon relieved them, however by thanking him, and declining his offer, except that he might send me an Harper's Magazine if he wished. This he promised to do, and we parted to meet no more, I verily believe. His visit was nevertheless an agreeable interruption of the monotony of past days; and I should be pleased to see more of him.

May 18th. My situation in the workshops at present is to say the least a novel one for a Southern gentleman. The tables on which we trim shoes are in parallel rows, and each table has four men, who stand and work at a "knee," or block upon which the shoe is held by one hand, while the other drives the trimming tools. Now by some *chance or other* it happens that the men on each side of me are negroes—big, greasy, stinking fellows, whose favorite amusement is to pick lice off their bodies, and crack them on the bench in such a way that I cannot avoid seeing them. Beside these two at my elbows there is another darkey immediately in front of me; so that I am like the bread in a sandwich—*between Ham!* But the worst of it is the stench, the odor *de Afrique,* which, when the weather is warm, quite overpowers me. A gale from Ceylon, or a tornado in the Spice Islands might sweep the shops without purifying the atmosphere in the least; at all events not in my neighborhood.

When I am jostled by these blackguards, I often think of a parody on the charge of the Light Horse at Balaklava.

> Niggers on the right of him
> Niggers on the left of him
> Niggers in front of him
> Volleyed and—stank!

Negroes and polecats, as everybody knows, have a strange eccentricity of smell. Yet after all I pay very little attention to such matters. The darkeys are not placed along side of me purposely, I presume; and if they had been designedly placed there I should have only felt a supreme contempt for those who could seek to annoy a prisoner by any such treatment. The Mongrels tried it, but did not succeed. And as for the negroes, they are not allowed to interfere with, or speak to, or even look at me; therefore I have no trouble from them.

Nevertheless as I said it is a novel spectacle—or would be to my Southern friends—to see me in my shirt sleeves, bare arms, close-cropped head, beardless face, working in the middle of a group of darkeys. True, our Southern farmers often work in the fields with negroes; but the circumstances are different, the negroes being slaves, or hired servants as humble as slaves.

May 19, 1872. To my intense delight, I last evening discovered a fine box in my cell when I came in from the shops. No one who has never been shut up in prison for many wearisome months, can comprehend the importance which even the most trivial gift from outside friends assumes in the eyes of a prisoner. I have before mentioned the paroxysm of gratitude into which Casanova was thrown by the simple present of a new gown, and some writing material, by one of the Patricians of the Council board; *"In the fullness of my heart,"* he says, *"I pardoned even my oppressors."* How then, *Mademoiselle, ma chere amie,* way down South in Dixie, how shall I thank Thee for the elegant feast which I am having and shall have for days to come! "Sweets from the sweet," isn't that the language of the song, or is it only from my heart? Certainly I am fortunate in having a few friends who cling to me, through evil, as well as good, report. And blessed indeed, is a friend in need.

The box is from Miss M. F., and contains two mammoth frosted cakes, 2 jars of pickles, a large ham, several lbs crackers, pecans, etc., etc., besides some warm stockings, books, etc. It could not have come in better time; for I am in wretched condition, not being able to eat the sour hash, or "salt horse;" and as for the "mush," it nauseates me; hence I have been going down hill for many days.

May 20th. Genl. Pilsbury, passing by my cell, asked if I had gotten the Blackstone Commentaries, about which I had written father. As I had not, he said he would endeavor to borrow a copy from some one of his legal friends. I shall be much gratified if he succeeds, although my leisure for study is wonderfully little. The weather is improving, and the South wind finding its way between the bars of my cell as I write this whispers to me of pleasanter scenes, where the South wind came from.

May 25th. Our contemptible "Instructor" reported me to the overseer for not doing as much work as he wished me to do, to wit: 50 pair of shoes per day. The overseer came and told me I must work faster. I replied that I had been doing between 35 and 40 pairs daily, and that I could do no more; that I was an awkward workman at the best, never having worked before I came here. He said I ought to do as much as the negro working on my left hand, and that I must do more than I had been doing. I answered that I should do as many as I could, but as for doing 50 pair; that was beyond my power at present. He then left me.

It is terrible to be exposed to this sort of humiliation and hectoring from day to day. Sometimes I think I would rather die than remain here for six years, which is the only prospect before me now. Of course I know, that I am in a *Penitentiary* where rigorous treatment is to be expected; nor can I look for much distinction in my favor, since I am a stranger, unknown to the officers, and sent here on the footing of a felon. Yet, while my reason tells me that these things are all to be expected, I cannot forget that I am an innocent man, that I am a gentleman, and that very likely some of these follows hate me because I am from the South. Still I must say for the overseer (Francis) that he always speaks to me more courteously than he does to any other prisoner; and today he seemed disposed to be friendly.

May 26th. After waiting and hoping another week, I am disappointed! I am full of disgust on the subject. Someday; if I live and my hopes prosper, I shall try not to forget those false friends who now forget me, leaving me here to languish in a distant prison without a line, without even an answer to my inquiries, although had I (like them) consulted my own ease and interest, I should never have come here. But 'tis idle to complain now; 'twas ever thus."

May 30th. Genl. Pilsbury came into my cell at noon, bringing 4 vols. of Blackstone (an old London edition) which he said had been sent me by Messrs. Gould & Son, Law Book Publishers, 68 State St. Albany, to whom he had gone to buy a copy. Upon his explaining what he wished to do with it, they gave him this old set of Blackstone, and offered to let me have the loan of any law books I might need. I assured the Genl. that I was much indebted to them as well as to him for the interest he had shown in providing for my wants. Indeed the acquisition of these books permits me to take to study in real earnest, and I shall try to manage it so that I

shall get an half hour or so for study while out in the
workshops.

I told Genl. Pilsbury that through his kindness I
should no doubt become a first rate lawyer if I stayed
here six months longer "Yes and as you may be here an
year or two, I'd advise you to give your whole attention to it," said he. This was quite a dash of cold water
on my budding promises; although he has no more idea
than I when my liberation shall take place.

June 2nd. No letters! Disgusted again!

Eo die—Genl. P. asked me if I would like to go out
to the office and acknowledge the receipt of the books
from Messrs. Gould and Son. I went and wrote as follows—

> Gentlemen
>
> I have the honor to acknowledge the receipt, by
> the courtesy of Genl. Pilsbury of a set of Black-
> stone's Commentaries; for which and also for your
> kind offer to let me have the loan of other law books
> as I may need them, I beg you to accept my grate-
> ful thanks.
>
> It was a pleasant coincidence that the volumes sent
> by you were once the property of an acquaintance
> of mine (Hon. W. B. Meares of Wilmington) and
> it will be a still more pleasant circumstance for me
> to relate to my friend upon my return to North
> Carolina, that I was indebted to Messrs. Gould &
> Sons, for the means of perusing my studies while
> confined in a distant penitentiary. With renewed
> thanks, I am, Gentlemen
>
> Your obt. Sevt.,
R. A. Shotwell.

While I was writing this note, the Genl. stepped out
of the room, and presently returned with a bundle of
cake and crackers, "from Mrs. Pilsbury." I had a good
laugh over this last when I got back to my cell, as it
shows they think me quite a young man, and doubtless
fond of "sweet things." Still it shows equally plainly
that the Genl. and his lady take a friendly interest in
me, and that is not a little consolation. The General has

always treated me better than I could have looked for, considering that I came here unknown and friendless.

June 8th. Genl. P. and lady sailed for Europe today to attend the International Congress to discuss the question of Prison Reform. The Trustees generously voted him $5,000 for his expenses during the trip; a very handsome present I should say. They can afford to be liberal; for he is doing what no other Superintendent in the States has succeeded in doing, i. e., making the Institution not only pay its debts, but actually return a fine balance to its credit. This year, or the last rather, he cleared $27,000, besides making considerable improvement in the fare, etc. These gains are the result of good management and no *stealage.* There are four other Penitentiaries in the State; but they are managed by politicians, and each superintendent knowing that he is liable to displacement by the fluctuation of politics, takes good care to feather his own nest while feathers are flying.

June 9th. Sadly out of heart when the Deputy passed my cell with his hands full of letters but not one for me. But since he has brought me a brief note from my noble friend, M. M. F. and which [is] dated May 25—*fifteen days ago!* Those rascally post masters no doubt can tell where it lay during the extra *ten* days. She says, "I wrote you a long, long letter by last mail giving all the news; but somehow I think you do not receive all the letters I write." I judge not, *ma chere,* if you write more than one in the year. Of course the long letter *giving the news* never came to hand; the *news* letters never do. I suppose the Mongrels examine all my correspondence and whenever they find anything of interest, they lay that aside to increase its merits, like old wine, by age. But Mary says, "I wish to assure you of our constant remembrance of you. I hope soon to see you face to face," etc. This is pleasant; and would be more so, if I could answer "by word of mouth."

Brother Mel. has won the $100 Thomsonian Prize for Heavy Weights—Gymnastics. He appears to be going it heavy with the Heavy and Light Weights of Princeton Society. To read his epistles is like hearing a youngster boasting of the pigeon wings he had recently cut in the region of some old coquette's heart. Still I am glad he is enjoying himself, and I wish him the best of success in life.

Rev. Carter Burnett, Col. Bryan, and Anderson Harris are the latest arrests in Rutherford. Who next? This is a shameful outrage. These men, excepting perhaps the last, never knew there was such a thing as a Ku Klux in their neighborhood. But the Mongrel Man Hunters only wish to get their fees for the arrests.

June 10th. An intelligent young man named Cook, who had been sent here for 10 years for pilfering $10 from a letter in the post office where he was a clerk, made the prediction, and wrote it in a book that he should not live to see the 9th of June. On Saturday night last he died in the Hospital. His cell mate has the book in which the foreboding entry was made several months ago, when Cook was not in serious ill health. People who believe in presentiments would like to have the particulars of this case. He died of consumption. He was a Virginian, and apparently a decent sort of fellow.

June 22nd, 1872. Another detachment of soldiers arrived today, bringing 20 citizens of South Carolina, convicted for Political Purposes by Judge Bond's Star Chamber Court at Columbia. Their names and sentences are as follows: Pinkney Caldwell, Leander Spencer, and Wm. Smith—each ten (10) years at hard labor, and $1000 fine! David Ramseur, Wm. Ramsay, Walker Dawson, Walker Moore, Jos. Lickie, W. P. Anthony— 8 years and $1000 fine. Julius Howe, Elijah Hardin, Alison Hayes—4 years and $100 fine. J. C. Robinson, Gal Hambright, Jas Saunders, Wm. Lowry, G. S. Wright, Miles McCullock—18 months, and $100. Benj. Strickland—actually 1 year *only!* (he humbled himself).

All these are poor ignorant men—small farmers or tenants, or laborers—and it is safe to conclude that more than half of them are unjustly sent here. Indeed none deserve to be sent to a penitentiary, although it is possible that some of them were engaged in Ku Kluxing. But with a negro population so numerous, and politically opposed to the true interests of the State, as that of South Carolina, the Klan was an indispensable necessity for the suppression of crime and for the protection of the weak and defenceless. But that has nothing to do with the sentence of these poor men; because, as is well known, they were dragged from their families, and shipped here to undergo years of ignominious confinement, not that the laws might be vindicated, but solely to answer the political ends of the Administration party, which hopes to consolidate the negro vote, and intimidate thousands of Conservative voters by its prosecutions. Ah! 'tis shameful! 'tis cruel! 'tis pitiful! It calls to High Heaven for redress, but doubtless it is designed that the American Republic shall be overthrown by the blind and fratricidal hatred of the Yankees, who appear willing to surrender their liberties provided the South shall be ruined. One thing certain, if the Northern people permit the despot utterly to crush their southern brethren they speedily will find the heel upon their own necks also, or the teaching of history is false.

June 14th. "Go to the hall," said the overseer this morning. I went, trembling with agitation, not unmixed with Hope. "Go back to the Shop," said the deputy in his shortest tone, "You are not the man I want; send Chadwick. He is the man I want." I returned to the shops muchly crestfallen and hurt by the tone in which I had been addressed. Happy Chadwick, it was *your friends,* not *mine,* that had come! So I resumed my wearisome planing of shoe-soles.

I mention this trifling incident to preface a remark that a few months of this life is very apt to *shatter the nerves;* and to deprive one of all his composure when anything unusual occurs. I have grown so nervous that when suddenly called to quit the daily routine of my labors, or to go out to meet a friend, I find myself in a tremor of excitement which almost takes away my voice. This arises from physical weakness from lack of proper nourishment, disuse of language (I do not speak at all for weeks at a time), and the perpetual brooding occasioned by utter deprivation of society, and the current intelligence of the day. And the worst of it is that after a sudden agitation of this nature, one is left weak and spiritless for the remainder of the day, if no longer.

June 16th. Rec'd printed copy of a speech on the Civil Rights Bill, opposing admission of negroes to white schools in the South, by Hon. J. C. Harper, M. C. from the 8th Dist. N. C. Mr. H. sent the speech to me *at Rutherfordton,* apparently forgetful of the fact that I have been arrested, wronged, calumniated, and finally sent to the Penitentiary. Yet I *was one of the six* who signed the card announcing him as one candidate for congress! Truly the memory of men in office is short. Harper, however, has done himself credit by his speech, and I wish it could be read by every man and woman in the land. For while he is a moderate, and impartial speaker, he states the case so clearly that he who runneth may read. One fact he mentions that, U. S. deputy marshals are accustomed to scour the country with blank warrants, already signed by the commissioner, in their pockets, and upon these warrants they arrest scores of men, and fill in the names afterwards! But this after all is only a bagatelle in comparison with the graver villainy of judge, jury, marshals and attorneys in hundreds of instances since the beginning of the Mongrel Crusade. I am glad, however, to see that Mr. H. has taken so bold and manly a stand, and I wish him every success.

Nothing from home in two months! My friends—so-called—are too cowardly or indifferent to waste an hour on me. But I shall not forget them!

June 20th. It is reported that more than 60 K. K. were arrested in a single day last week in Union Co., S. C. The infamous Joe Hester has also kidnapped Dr. Rufus Bratton of Yorkville, and brought him back from Canada whither he had fled. Hester or some instrument employed by him, approached Dr. B., and clapped a handkerchief filled with chloroform to his nostrils, and then got him on a train, and carried him quietly into the United States. I trust the Canadian Government will have the pluck to demand his restitution. How glad would be my heart could I learn that the Yankees were fairly embroiled in a foreign war which might afford the South an opportunity to unfold her flag and march to victory once more. Then would it be discovered, happily *too late,* that the men of the South are not all mere *peons* whom it is allowable to abuse, calumniate, and enslave. Then would the most conciliatory, fawning, tone be used towards the "Rebels," and be used in vain. I know that in giving expression to these views I may seem to be actuated by personal resentment for the wrongs I have suffered. But more than that is the conviction that the South can never throw off the yoke of tyranny, and negro-carpet-bag-scallawag-Rag-tag-supremacy until she free herself with her swords. And all this is the result of the deliberate policy of the Yankee leaders. When the war closed, I with every other intelligent person in the South, accepted the situation, and resolved to give the government our hearty support, and contribute as far as we were able, to the growth of friendly relations between the sections. To this end I wrote daily and weekly in my paper, spoke daily and hourly when occasion occurred, and was instrumental in bringing out more than an half dozen Northern men to settle in the South. But all our advances have been repelled by the Administration and Grant, calling out "let us have peace," while he drew the sword, has done every thing that his feeble intellect could devise to cripple, humiliate, and provoke the South, until now there are hundreds of thousands of our best people ready to fight again, and even to put themselves under the protection of a foreign government to escape any connection with those who have won our lasting hatred. The day may never come while I live; but come it will!

June 22nd. Hot! Felt like taking off my jacket for the first time since I came here! Bah! the atmosphere in the shops would sicken a scavenger. The "seventy several stinks" of cologne cannot smell anywhere in comparison with the half dozen darkies in my neighborhood. I dread the long summer days!

June 28. At last another letter from my dear faithful friend Miss Mary Forney, who writes that the K. K. cases have been postponed and are to be transferred to the new (or western) judicial district of N. C., to sit at Statesville in October. Sanguine people regard this as the final postponement of the trials, but not so I. The object aimed at by the Mongrels is, no doubt, to lull apprehension, and create a false Security, in order that many of the refugees may return home (as they are doing) and be taken; as well as to prolong the excitement, and consequent intimidation until the Presidential election, thereby carrying the State for Grant, and deceiving the whole country, which will suppose that from the resumption of the trials the Ku Klux are still rampant in the State. These devices of the Mongrel Managers are perfectly transparent, and no less iniquitous. What can be said of a Judge (Bond) lending his judicial power to advance base party ends? Capt. Pilsbury informs me that a N. Y. City paper, contains an allusion to *"Shotwell the Editor, in Albany Penitentiary, sandwiched between two negroes."* He had mislaid the paper, or some one had carried it off, and he did not recollect the connection, but it was intended as a slur on me, etc. "But," said Capt. P., "as soon as I saw it, the thought occurred to me that your letter, *in which you made use of that expression had been intercepted by your enemies."*

There can be no doubt that this is the case. I have only mentioned the fact about my being *sandwiched between negroes* in two letters, one to Genl. L., who is not a man to give much publicity to private communications, and Miss R. L. D. who, as she has not acknowledged it, I feel certain never received my letter. I suppose the Rutherfordton Mongrels captured, nay stole, it; and the story was too good to keep. They very likely wrote the statement to some of their cronies, and thus it finally reached the correspondent of my paper!

This shows what security there is for my correspondence, which has to pass through the hands of half a dozen of these Mongrel post master-thieves before it is at liberty to reach its final destination, provided they see fit to let it pass. Very well, Messieurs, far more decent, far preferable, is the company of my colored neighbors, to yours! Yet if rogues and mail robbers were convicted of their crimes, you too would be here; and honester men would fill your places. But of course, we cannot expect the Radical Administration to send its chief supporters in the South to the Penitentiary, even though they *do steal.* Beside, in these days, under Radical rule, thieving, corruption, and rascality is too general, too much a matter of course, to receive punishment. Only honest men, of a Democratic turn of mind are liable to prosecution.

Eo die. My cell is utterly in possession of "the plague that walketh in darkness"—*bugs!* Every crevice, nook and cranny swarms with the cannibal foe! They lie in wait during the day, but no sooner do I enter the door at night fall than they rally in groups, battalions, brigades, and pounce upon me, like the African ants on a dead lion. Methinks there is a conspiracy between the chinches, flies, lice, spiders, ear wigs, bed bugs, and every other sort of bugs, to phlebotomize me, and to drain the last drop from my veins.

These *knight-errants* take for their watchword, *E pluribus unum—Many on one!*—and they advance like an Highland Clan, shouting

Fee! Faw! Fum!
I smell the blood of an Englishmun!

I must say, however, that the authorities do all they can to extirpate these pests, and the Deputy has just told me he will have my cell thoroughly cleansed on the morrow. It is curious that vermin and prison quarters should be almost inseparable. When the enemy once gets possession it is next to impossible to dislodge him.

June 24th. The Hall Master says he obtained nearly a *peck* of bugs from my cell. I suppose that accounts for my being so weak lately. I may get a little sleep now, as the cell has been very well cleaned, and all crevices plastered with white lead. I feel much relieved.

These are small matters to mention in one's journal; but they go to show how our time and thoughts are occupied; therefore should not be omitted.

July 1st. A brief note from A. confirms my suspicions concerning the interference with my correspondence, by the Mongrel P. Ms., and U. S. detectives. He mentions the names of a number of persons, who have written to me; although their letters never came to hand. This is provoking; but only what might be expected from the Representatives of the administration, in the South. I presume Judge Logan, and son, Wallace, Carpenter, Justice, Mooney, and the whole brood of Scoggins, read every one of my letters before they reach their destination. Is it any wonder that there are Ku Klux organizations in a country where mail-robbery is systematically carried on by the very leaders of the Government party?

Eo die.

Called out to the Supts. Office, where I was met by Col. Chichester, of the Charleston, (S. C.) *Courier,* who is now visiting the North, the Boston Jubilee, etc., in connection with the members of the "Southern Press Association," (Some 40 or more in numbers) who are returning the visit of the Northern Association. Being delayed in Albany, over the Sabbath Col. Chichester called to see if he could be of any service to the Ku Klux; and said if we desired it, he would remain an additional day, and take down our statements, with a view to publishing a campaign document, etc. I thanked him for his kindness; but thought best that no publicity should be given to our cases, just at present, as the Government still held the rod *in terrorem* over thousands in the South, and possibly an *expose* might call down its wrath on other innocent heads. As for my own individual case, I would gladly proclaim to the world how deeply I have been wronged and maltreated; but as a matter of expediency, i. e., for the preservation of others, I should keep silent for a time at least.

Col. Chichester said we need have no fears of a warm welcome on our return. That the best people of South Carolina regarded us as *martyrs,* not criminals. He also, stated that more than 5000 young men had fled from that State, fearing arrest and annoyance from the Mongrels.

Capt. P. told this gentleman to give my friends a good account of me; that I had not received even a reprimand since I came here. This shows that he is not aware of the hectoring I occasionally receive from the overseer. Sometimes I think I shall tell him; but 'tis best not to complain, for, of course, the officers have the *inside track* in all such races.

July 3rd, 1872. Really it is outrageous! Seven citizens of Alabama charged with Ku Kluxing have just arrived—the second batch from that State. Their names are as follows. Richard S. Grey, Neal Haskins, John D. Young, and Reuben G. Young—each ten (10) years, and $5000 fine! Ringold Young, *seven* years and $2000! Chas. Howard and Jas. Blanks *five* years and $1000!

These men were tried before the notorious "Dick Busteed," and according to newspaper accounts had nothing like a fair trial. All plead not guilty, and prayed for a new trial; but the judicial tool of the Government had neither justice nor clemency to show them. Four of the victims are *old, gray-haired* men; the others *mere boys;* all poor, and more or less illiterate. Thus the Despot begins his work in another State. An Alabama paper complains that these men were not allowed even the beggarly boon of serving their terms in their own State Penitentiary, but must be sent to one in the far North, where even the rigors of the season would be penalty to any Southerners from the Gulf States. But I expect they do not regret this change of location so much as the Editor supposes; for I imagine that they would rather be here, than be exposed to the petty annoyances and malevolence sure to be put upon them in their state penitentiary; if it, like most of our public institutions, is in the hands of scalawags, or carpet baggers.

4th July, 1876. At length we celebrate another spread-eagle day! We've been looking for it, or forward to it, for quite a while; having patriotic appetites, if not sentiments. To explain which remark I must add that on this day we receive annually a feast, consisting of ham, potatoes, cabbage, onions, strawberries, and sugar! besides it is actually observed as an holiday— the only one in the year for Penitentiary Birds.

Today we had exercises in the chapel, which was neatly decorated with the Yankee bunting, flowers, etc. Upon a platform, an amateur glee club of ladies and their beaux from the city, discoursed the northern airs (the ladies put some on) with much spirit. Several divines, and legal fledglings, interluded the music with melancholy attempts to say something new about the "glorious Fourth," and the "best Government the world ever saw." Not one of them seemed to be aware (as I daresay they were not) that more than three score and ten guiltless citizens of the South, were in the audience before them, undergoing an unjust and tyrannical imprisonment! Yet what a commentary was this bare fact upon the flowery panegyrics, with which they decked their fictitious Republic! What monarchy of the Old World can do more this day than is being done by Grant, and his military and civil, and judicial servants!

To me this occasion has been an indescribably sad one. It happens that I occupy one of the front benches in the chapel; consequently am face to face with all visitors, who drop in. Today the platforms were full of ladies and gentlemen, and my feelings may be imagined as I sat with folded arms, and downcast eyes (the rules require this) while they gazed at me with that curiosity, pity and abhorrence, with which women, and pious people, regard criminal outcasts from Society! What matters if I felt innocent, injured, aye, and superior in birth and breeding to many before me, this knowledge could not relieve me from the embarrassment and annoyance of the position.

The thought occured to me during the services: No wonder that the Administration dares to establish a despotism at the South, dares to tamper with the jury box, and the ballot box, dares to carry elections by force, and consign its opponents to a life time imprisonment. When such outrages on law and liberty as that of my trial, and other Ku Klux trials are unable to arouse the public, nay, are hardly heard of by the majority of the Northern people, and while blatant orators bespatter it with obsequious and nauseating praise, such as we have heard this day!

July 7th. To my intense surprise, at last, a letter! Mary having written to say that she has written often! She writes regularly, but the Mongrels are opposed to my receiving letters; hence they stop short of Albany. Well 'tis provoking, irritating! But as the Hard Shells say, what is to be will be. Genl. R. B. Vance is out for Congress in our Dist. He was my choice in 1870, although I was not opposed to Durham. I thought Vance could get his seat without trouble; while Durham had already been once rejected. But the majority of the convention choosing Durham I gave him my hearty support until he ill-advisedly withdrew. I did all I could to prevent his withdrawal, which I regarded as a political dodge of certain aspirants to get him off the track. Time has confirmed this view of the business, and Durham no doubt recognizes the truth of my arguments on the former occasion. But Vance has finally gotten the nomination and will come in with an handsome majority. He is personally very popular, and being an able, moderate, and scrupulously honest man, is sure to make a good representative. Aunt Susie writes from Constantinople, Turkey, under date of June 3d, assuring me of her love and sympathy, and giving me a practical token of it, by enclosing a "bit of gold." Yet with all her affection she cannot withhold a regret that I am *Southern-born!* Wonderful prejudice of the Yankee mind, that can outlive 20 years in a foreign land! Still I know that Auntie never hears but one side of my story.

July 8th, 1872. Having been sent for, I this afternoon, went to the "Office," where I was introduced by Capt. Pilsbury, to an elderly gentleman, of portly bearing, having thick locks of long white hair hanging upon his shoulders, giving him rather a leonine aspect, and who promptly came forward to give me his hand. The Capt. had whispered to me in the guard room, that my visitor was Hon. Gerrit Smith, the famous Abolitionist, and that he had come from High Authority having an order from the President or Sec'y of War to admit him to hold conversation with any of the political prisoners, etc. Mr. Smith was accompanied by his son, a dark featured young man, reputed "fast," and directly opposed to his father in politics, or at least, in his abandonment of Horace Greeley. Indeed it is said that all of Smith's relations are Greeleyites.

Mr. Smith began by informing me that the object of his visit was to ascertain something about the condition, degree of guilt, etc., of the Ku Klux, intimating that his inclinations were on the side of clemency, and that he should be glad to be of service to us. I replied that I should take pleasure in giving him any information at my command. He asked what was the object of the Klan. I explained that the excesses of the Loyal Leagues, the incendiarism of worthless whites, playing with the emotional and excitable nature of the uneducated freedmen, together with the utter corruption, and worthlessness of the legal and civil authorities, obliged the respectable people of the South to enter into some organization or association for the suppression of crime, and to exert a salutary restraint upon the rowdyish propensities of the dissolute darkeys. "Did you fear an insurrection?" "Not in our part of the country, Sir; for with us the whites are equal in numbers to the blacks; but in the thinly settled sections of some other Southern States, such an event is not improbable, so long as mean whites are permitted to lead the negroes by the nose." I then proceeded to give him a frank and truthful statement of the object of the order, its oath, etc., and showed him by many illustrations how grievously we, and indeed the whole South, had been maligned. Told him that hundreds of the disorders attributed to the Ku Klux were private feuds between families or localities while others were actually committed by Radicals, and Loyal Leaguers. Asked him if he had not seen the Adair murder ascribed in the *Herald* to Ku Klux; and assured him the Adairs were the most *violent Radicals* and *Grant men* in Rutherford County! Still their crime is in the North laid on the Ku Klux. I then told him about 'Squire Brown, Scruggs, and DePriest, who to my belief—almost to my knowledge—were as innocent as he was. To old man Collins's case I gave particular attention, Mr. Smith listened with interest, and asked

many questions. Wished to know what I thought of
Holden, Judge Settle, the negro Jim Harris, and others.
I said that we regarded Holden as a disgrace to our
State. Judge Settle is an able man, and I know of no
direct charges against his private character. As for
Harris, he is said to be a smart darkey; I know nothing
about him. "He is a splendid man, one of the best you
have," said he. Settle was his particular friend, and he
should write to him to do something for me. I thanked
him, but considered it would be hardly worth while to do
so. He asked if I knew Genl. Clingman, John Kerr,
and others. I replied that I knew Judge Kerr by reputation, and Mr. Clingman personally, the latter being
from Buncombe where I lately published a newspaper.
"Ah! Yes, Buncombe! I recollect now Thomas Clingman was from Buncombe; but he was a smart man, Sir;
I thought very well of Clingman, Sir." In reply to
other questions I remarked that there were several gentlemen of ability connected with the Republican party
in N. C., (Judge Settle, N. Boyden, Victor Barringer,
W. Bailey, etc.) ; but that they could hardly be called
Radicals, since they were not identified with the violence,
and *stealage* of the party, and were apparently genuine
Federalists on principle. Mr. S. said he was glad to
hear me say so, etc., etc. He then asked me what I
should do if released. "Return home, obey the laws and
endeavor to make a living by my profession." "What
is your profession?" "Well, Sir, I am studying law."
"What! Studying law in penitentiary!" "Most assuredly, Sir." "Well I do assure you I am sorry to see
a young man of your abilities here." "I regret it myself, Sir, but I do not consider that I deserve to be here."
"The worst thing I find against you is your intelligence," said he with a smile; and Capt. P. coming to the
table, he repeated the remark to him. Capt. P. said,
"Shotwell won't tell you, but I will, that he had every
opportunity to get out by betraying some other persons,
but he wouldn't do it; although he told the men who
came with him that he, as their chief, gave them permission to make what terms they could, and get out if
they could." "That was very honorable in him," said

Mr. S., arising and giving me his hand. He said, "I will see what I can do for you." "Ah Sir, I thank you but I have many enemies who will oppose my liberation to the last moment." "Of course, you must have enemies; your talents would make you many enemies in public life," etc., etc. *"Well you will get out in two or three years at all events."* "I shall try to endure whatever falls to my lot, Sir."

He then shook my hand for the third time, and I withdrew. What a funny exhibition must this not have been—the father of Abolitionism, or at least of the incendiary phase of Abolitionism, and a Ku Klux hobnobbing together! Bah! Misery makes strange bed fellows.

Now what does this visit portend? Is Grant becoming alarmed at the noise created by this tyranical usurpation? And is he paving the way, by the *farce of Smith's intercession,* to the liberation of his victims? Or is it only a *blind* to still the *awakening sympathy in our behalf* by an apparent disposition to restore us to freedom? The last I fear, and believe, is the true explanation. Be that as it may there is no hope for me. These wretches will never permit me to escape so long as they know me to be un-humbled. As for Mr. Smith I was favorably impressed by philanthropic countenance and courteous manners. In nothing did he intimate any consciousness of my ignominious situation; and very naturally I felt pleased at this thoughtfulness; although I cannot forget that it was the teaching of this man and his colleagues that brought war and ruin upon my country.

July 10th. Porter, one of the S. C. men died in hospital of spinal diseases. He is the first of us to succumb under long confinement, hardship, and home sickness. It is sad to think of this man dying so far from home and friends, in a prison, alone and uncared for; and last of all, being sent to a felon's grave! He was a poor, ignorant, lowborn fellow, and had little character in his own community, I am told; but it is a crying shame that he should have been sent to die here in a Penitentiary.

July 13th. Capt. P. gave me a pencil and folio to write out my account of the origin, etc., of the Klan for preservation. I wrote about 12 pages, giving a running sketch of the causes which lead to the formation of the order, etc., taking good care to say nothing that I should regret to see in print. This I suppose the Captain will keep in his office to show visitors who may desire to hear the Ku Klux version of the Southern troubles. I showed in it that while the majority of the Klan were Democrats, the Democratic party could not be held responsible for the conduct of the Klan.[1]

July 14th. Depressed and gloomy beyond telling! And, Oh, so sad and out of heart! Another week without a line from home!

July 18th. Saw several nuns this morning among the visitors; queer looking demoiselles in sombre colored garments, and huge bonnets; but very pretty and coquettish withal. One displayed a remarkably neat boot, and wasn't ashamed of it either. How did I see it—*her* I should say? Ah! that would be telling tales out of school, and who knows but the deputy may read this?

---

1 The document referred to was later printed in a New York newspaper and copied in the Charlotte Observer. The original is now in the possession of Judge Harris Dickson of Vicksburg, Mississippi. A typewritten copy is in the possession of the North Carolina Historical Commission. The following letter gives its history.

SIXTEEN WALL STREET
New York City

January 26, 1928.

Judge Harris Dickson,
Players Club,
New York, N. Y.
Dear Judge:

Here is this document about the Ku Klux Klan, which is authoritative, and which possibly you may be able to use some day. At any rate, I think it will interest you. This is the history of it.

I went on the SUN staff just after leaving College, and during the first two or three years while I was on the City Staff, I did a number of special articles for the Sunday SUN on prisons in and around New York and became very much interested in the subject. I wrote a number of special articles about Blackwell Island penitentiary, and in getting the material for them, met Louis D. Pilsbury, who was Warden at that time. Pilsbury's father was Warden of the Albany penitentiary probably in the late 60s or early 70s, at the time when a number of the Ku Klux Klan, who had been convicted, were serving sentences there. Louis Pilsbury was a young man at the time and became well acquainted with Shotwell, who, when his term was finished, gave him this diary. Shotwell was either from Virginia or the Carolinas, where he later served in his State Legislature. I have no doubt, if you are at all interested in running this thing down, it would be comparatively easy to do it. Pilsbury was interested in the stories I had written about the Blackwell Island penitentiary and thought that possibly I might do something with this diary.

Several years later when I became Asst. City Editor of the SUN and did a good deal of magazine work, one of the magazines here in New York asked me to do a special story on the Klan, basing it on this diary. I fully intended to do it, but was so busy with other work that I never got around to it. I haven't re-read it since that time and I am not sure whether there is anything in it that could be used or not. At any rate, it is a curiosity of an interesting period, and as I know that you will value it more than I do, I take pleasure in passing it along to you.

Cordially yours,
GEORGE BARRY MALLON.

Therefore let us be discreet, and if we *must* look at pretty people, let us say, we "seed 'em in our dreams."

By the way, it is noticable, and characteristic of Yankee latitudes that there are more lady visitors during the pleasant weather season, than gentlemen. Indeed I think they are the most numerous the year round. Daily and hourly, in groups, pairs, and singly, young and old, with and without male escorts, they come, and are conducted by an officer to see the cells, yard, shops, chapel, etc., and, of course, to see the convicts at work. Strange and vulgar curiosity this! I cannot imagine how a delicate and refined lady can take any pleasure in looking at a lot of dirty desperadoes in their shirt sleeves! I know many Southern girls would as soon think of coming to kiss me as going without an escort to a Penitentiary to be conducted about by a strange turnkey. Yet it is, I believe, a legitimate natural trait of feminine character to have a curiosity about prisons, and desperate criminals; and of course, visitors know that they are just as safe from insult or indignity here, as if they had an hundred male protectors in their train. It therefore only shows the difference in *custom* between the North and the South in such matters.

July 21st. Anniversary of the battle of Bull Run— when the Yankees run. How varied has been my life since that day eleven years ago. I was then a long-haired, tall, rather dandified, youth, practicing with a pistol in the groves near the beautiful village of Media in Pennsylvania, and "murdering the King's English" daily in my recitations to the paternal Mr. G., who often prayed that the war might be stayed before [we?] were drawn into it. A few weeks later, and I was running the blockade on the upper Potomac, under a heavy fire of musketry.

July 24th. The popular belief about Penitentiaries takes it for granted that they are filled by abandoned reprobates of the most degraded and irredeemable character. The very name of *"convict"* suggests murder, manslaughter and all the more serious crimes; and the man who has once borne it is shunned like a dog under a paroxysm of hydrophobia. I speak whereof I do know, since this was even my own opinion previous to coming here; although I have ever been disposed to look charitably and leniently on the weaknesses of human nature where they were not deliberately wicked, and especially if redeemed by courage and generosity. Experience has better informed me on this subject; and I now see that the public greatly errs by an improper classification, of penitentiary prisoners. A very great distinction should be made in favor of many of these unfortunate persons; for they are neither vagabond, brutal, nor irredeemable; nor are they so deficient, in the moral and intellectual attributes of a respectable character, and good citizen. They may have made a slip; but who is altogether blameless? Many of them are here for a first offence, committed under circumstances which, while they do not excuse, certainly palliate the deed. . . . I suppose there are hundreds of cases within the recollection of every criminal lawyer, in which the offense would have been passed over as a trifling pecadillo if the machinery of the law, often too rigid in small things to the exclusion of exact justice, had permitted any mitigation, or modification of the penalty in those particular cases. Let me illustrate with an instance or two. McN. is a good hearted old man, in a good business, and two years ago was doing well. A friend, wishing his endorsement of an official bond, plied the old man with liquor until he *grew rich in his own estimation,* and was persuaded to certify that he possessed a certain amount of property. Arrested soon afterwards for perjury, he was convicted and sent here for 2 years. He will be a wiser and better man hereafter I'm sure. A young man, clerk in post office, took $7½ from an open letter to pay a pressing board bill. He was sent here for 10 years. Another says, "I went on a picnic, and drank too much, and wanting more liquor arose in the night, and robbed my friend. I am ruined, but I swear I meant to return it." Another, "I was not used to drinking, and when the liquor flew to my head, I fell to fighting, and here I am for assault and battery."

Ah! thou Demon of the Still! What a record is here of thy devilish pranks! Was't thou banished from the world there would be but small need for Penitentiaries!

*   *   *   *   *   *[1]

July 27th. This afternoon I remained in my cell, feeling too ill to work. Biliousness and cold cause it I suppose. It is the second attack of this nature I have had since I came here. The Deputy prescribes pills, of which he always carries a box in his pocket; they are supposed to cure all diseases. Mr. Reynolds, the Chaplain, has just fetched me Russel's Modern Europe, Stephen's Central America, and Dick's Celestial Scenery, a supply of reading matter which I was glad to get, as I had nothing; the overseer taking advantage of my absence from my cell door to slip past and deprive me of my regular book on Sunday. It was a trifling matter to him but it left me without a book all week. Mr. R. however, very opportunely supplies the deficit, and I am grateful to him for this, and other acts of kindness he has shown me.

July 28th. Addie writes that it is strange I complain of not getting letters, as "Some of the family write every week; Miss M. F. every two weeks." *If this be true* (A is apt *to take things for granted,* and suppose that what *once* was still *is*) it is plain I am robbed of scores of letters; for neither the weekly nor semi-monthly correspondence reaches me. It may be, however, that I have blamed my friends for neglecting me when I ought to have laid the fault at the doors of the thievish postmasters. What rascality yet remains unpractised by the Mongrels?

Addie says troubles are considered at an end in Rutherford. The refugees are returning in peace and safety. I doubt if they are wise in doing so. The appearance is delusive and they will find it so I am sure before long. But if it be true that the clouds are dispersing, and calm settling on the troubled waters, how sad is my fate! For how many have been storm tossed I only have been wrecked! If the K. K. prosecutions now stop, those who

---

1 A discussion of the classification and rehabilitation of prisoners is omitted.

have escaped will soon begin to claim that they are in no wise implicated and that we who are sent up are the only really guilty parties. Whereas this is directly contrary to the truth, our misfortune being that we did not run away, but stood our ground, relying on our innocence; and being the most convenient victims whom the Mongrels could find, we were made to bear the full brunt of their malice, and cruelty. Many of the *actual* *"raiders"* are now at home in peace.

Mirabile dictu! L. F. C., who so shamefully inveighed against the Ku Klux, and publicly declared in a speech in the court room that *every Ku Klux ought to be hung,* is now the candidate of the Conservative party in Rutherford and Polk, for the State Senate! Can it be that members of the Order (and one half of the Conservative voters in Rutherford were connected with it) will vote for this man, after all his denunciations?

July 29th. Tired! Tired! Tired! I feel like a man must feel after walking in a treadmill until he can walk not a step farther. It is not that the work I have is so heavy, though among the heaviest branches of the trade; but the exhaustion arises from the daily, constant, unceasing, hopeless, uninteresting *drudgery,* which makes my life, as Sidney Smith would say, "a state of suspended vitality." No one who has not undergone it, can conceive of the mental and physical nervousness, fatigue, and prostration, caused by ten hours' hard labor, in a crowded, foul smelling room, where the dust is almost tangible as it flies, and the noise perfectly distracting; where one is surrounded by whirling machinery and all the senses excited and cramped at the same moment; the head bowed, the eyes fixed on the object in hand, and the mind wandering to a thousand objects in a second! Repeated day after day for weeks, months, years, without hope of delivery, this strain and *ennui* become almost unendurable, often threaten insanity. I mean, of course, in cases of persons of cultivated tastes and mental sensibility. Factory hands, and that sort of people, would no doubt find it not at all annoying. And yet it is without question a similar mental and physical exhaustion that produces the intemperance, and low morality of the laboring classes in all manufacturing towns. Mechanics, and factory men leaving their work benches at the close of the day, feel so wretchedly prostrated that they must have "a drop of something" to brighten their spirits, while in addition to this false appetite is a violent craving for amusement, gaity, "something lively," all of which, *for the men, can* be found at the grog shop. The women, young girls, are driven to a private bottle and the "nice young feller" who brings it. Thus does Nature add to the allurements of Vice to destroy these poor people.

For me there are many causes, aside from the foregoing, to create depression and lassitude; so taken all together the dose is sometimes over heavy, and I come into my cell at night in a mood for mischief. But I soon get over it, and in time I trust shall take every feature of my suffering with decent composure.

Aug. 1st. Phoebus! what a climate! Slept little, shivered much, under two blankets last night. Today it is raining and cold, and I am decidedly *agueish*. In N. C. the State election comes off today; there is much excitement there. I shall await the news with anxiety. Surely if the people are not utterly blind, or basely obsequious, they will testify at the ballot box their scorn of the man, and his party that have established a despotism in the State. True, Grant has been sending hundreds of thousands of dollars to bribe voters, and as several thousand of the best conservatives of the West are in exile, and thousands of others frightened out of their wits, all the odds will be in his favor, to say nothing of his holding the polls in all the negro majority counties, where the boxes may be stuffed at pleasure. Nevertheless, I hope that there is enough true blood in the State to save her from the degradation of endorsing a tyrant who has trampled upon, and robbed her for nearly a decade.

Aug. 2d. Grape Vine Dispatch—"Democrats victorious in N. C. Great rejoicings! 100 guns in N. Y." Noble old North State! If this news be true, I am proud of you.

Aug. 3rd. Democrats reported 12000 ahead in N. C.! Hurrah! for Horace Greely! The Liberals are

firing 100 guns in Albany, and everywhere the news is
received with tremendous enthusiasm. I need not say
how gratifying this intelligence is to me, since I take it
for granted that on Greeley hang my only hopes of liberation.

Aug. 4th. Capt. P. brought me a letter from Genl.
L. and told me there could be little doubt that we have
N. C. by a much smaller majority than was supposed.
Enough is good as a feast; still I am sorry to hear of
this reduction, as it makes the State doubtful for November. Genl. L. writes under date July 28 from Patterson, in the kindest manner. He is the Conservative
candidate for State Auditor, and will make an excellent
one. There is no better man for the position, in the State.
But he is not sanguine of election. Says Boutwell,
Grant's Treasurer [*sic*] has been to Charlotte to make a
speech, and distribute gold. His oratory was an utter
failure, but the eloquence of three hundred thousand
dollars made itself felt; and [with?] bribery, illegal voting, stuffing of the ballot-boxes, and intimidation, the
contest may result in a Radical triumph—not the first
stolen election by any means. Genl. L. says, "My wife
gave your message to Annie Jones and she wrote us a
note full of kindness and sympathy." Mrs. L. says in a
postscript, "I often think and speak of you and *deeply
sympathise with you in your great trials—indeed all
good people do; and all know that it is a shameful cruel
persecution you are suffering from.*"

Considering the high character of my esteemed correspondents, I derive unusual comfort and satisfaction
from their unmistakable assurances of respect and sympathy. It is proper that I should say furthermore that
I do not copy these, or other extracts from my private
correspondence from any feeling of vanity, on account
of remarks in my praise; but solely and simply to preserve them as small marks of the outrage which has been
done to my person and reputation. In after years if the
occasion should arise they will be valuable as evidence
that though confined in a Penitentiary and treated as a
common felon, I was not so regarded by my friends, and
the contemporary society of the South.

As a specimen of the marvelous (in)accuracy of Northern Historians of the war I note in Kerney's Compendium, the following errors concerning the battle of Leesburg, which the author calls "Ball's Bluff," although the battlefield is no part of Mr. Ball's property. "This battle," he says, "was fought on the 21st of September 1861. (wrong—21st October). The Union forces under Gen. Banks (wrong, Banks did not come until after the battle. Genl. Stone, was the Union Commander,) were defeated by the Confederates under Col. Jenifer (wrong—Lieut. Col. Jenifer had about 50 cavalry in the neighborhood but they took no part in the fight. Genl. N. G. Evans was our General, so-called though not on the field, and drunk at the time) *Gen.* Baker was killed at the head of his *Division* (Colonel Baker of 1st Cala. Regt., was killed at the head of his *brigade* of which he had temporary command) etc., etc.

These are but trifling errors to be sure, but they *lie* in a History "prepared especially for schools," and published more than three years after the war, they are amusing if not important. All these Yankee historians assert that Lee had more than an hundred thousand men at Gettysburg, when the truth is he had but little over half that number. No wonder the Government takes so much care that Confederate Archives shall not see the light; they would show, I am fully satisfied that we continually fought against three, four, five times our strength.

Aug. 7th, 1872. Stealthily glancing out the window this morning I noticed many of the Ku Klux prisoners going and returning; and at once my curiosity was excited to the utmost; for while I know none of these men, nor am I identified with them (they being from another State) I took it for granted that something unusual was in progress. Presently I was called, and proceeding to the Hall, met Capt. P. who whispered to me that Col. Whittley, the Chief of the Detective Bureau, or Secret Service Corps was here to interrogate the prisoners— with a view to pardon perhaps. "I thought I would tell you this so that you would know how to act," said Capt. P. Col. Whitley was seated at a table with a clerk to

take notes, and without rising or showing the least courtesy, he began his examination with the question, "Well
what are you here for?" "I can hardly say, Sir; the
charge against me was connection with the Klan, and
being a chief." "Well, were you a chief?" "I believe I
was chosen to such a position, but I never exercised any
authority as such." "Well, what was the object of the
order?" "I suppose you have read the oath, Sir; that
embodys the objects of the order." "No I dont know
anything about it, what did you mean to do?" "To suppress crime and punish such offenders as the lawful
officers neglected to punish." "Well but you had no
right to do that; you were violating the law." "I believe
the laws were made for our protection and when they
fail to perform that duty, we must act on Nature's law
of self-preservation." "So ho! you are for doing just as
you please in a lawless violent manner. You admit that
you are a lawless desperate character." "I admit no such
thing, Sir; I have not given you nor any other man
grounds to form such an opinion of me." "Oh very well,
I haven't time to argue, Mr. Pilsbury, send another
man!" "Good morning Col. Whittley," said I as I left
the room; but he made no acknowledgement. Indeed his
whole bearing is that of a N. C. 20-dollar Lawyer, who
thinks to make up for lack of brains and dignity by an
assumption of *brusqueness* (if there is such a word).
Thus therefore the interview closed; and I suppose
Whittley will take good care to misrepresent me at
Washington, and utterly cut off all hope of release if
Grant is reelected. Well, so be it; if there is no help for
it. I shall rather stay here with honor than go out upon
my knees, for offences which only exist in the foul imagi-
nations of rogues and political demagogues.

Capt. P. tells me that the other K. K. have told everything they ever did or thought of doing, making the most
piteous appeals for pardon, and some of them promising
to do anything the Government wishes them to do, if
only Grant will forgive them this time, etc. The cowardly loons! But of course not all were so low and contemptible as this. Whittley told old Squire Brown he
lied, and repeated the offensive language more than once

because Brown protested that he was innocent and that he did not have a fair trial! In truth he was perfectly insulting to every one of the prisoners who refused to "confess" (i. e. perjure themselves) and humble themselves before him.

The object of this visit is plain enough. Grant finds from the way N. C. went that his military tyranny is beginning to bear some fruit, and he now intends to make a show of clemency to deceive the country. But that his cause be not weakened so much *as a single vote,* he sends his Chief Detective here to *"pump"* us, and see *who will buy their liberty at the expense of their life-long principles.* Besides he will now be able to get out *a new campaign document,* to wit, the *"Horrible Confessions"* of the K. K. at Albany.

Aug. 8th. Again called to the office where I found a reporter of the N. Y. *World,* come, he informed me, to get the statements of the K. K. confined here. Flurried as I was, and unusually nervous from having slept little last night, I was not in a condition to command my ideas readily; consequently I fear I gave him (who took down word for word) anything but an intelligible account of the rise and progress of the Klan. Still what was said cannot be unsaid, and is now, I suppose, in print; therefore I can only regret that I had not time to collect my thoughts, nor any intimation of his coming that I might have arranged a systematic account of transactions in connection with the Ku Klux Krusade.

I have before mentioned how nervous I am growing. This is getting to be a serious matter, and I must try to remedy it, though I know not how to begin.

The *World* man states that the Radicals have cheated us out of N. C., electing Caldwell by near one thousand votes! Great Hercules! What are we coming to? Gold, Office, and Intimidation, have done their perfect work, and the result is another disgrace to the State and the South!

The Radicals are firing 100 guns over the election. The sound is mournful enough for me; since it tells that Greeley's chances are small, and with them my hopes of release. If N. C. goes for Grant, there is slight showing for the other Southern states which have a larger proportion of negroes.

Aug. 11th. Letters from M., Annie and Jennie and Miss M. F. The latter writes regularly. It seems the postmasters must get not a few letters of mine. They well deserve a Ku Klux visit. The Rutherford refugees are returning home, and are expecting me! How foolish! It will be many a long day before I get home!

Aug. 12th. The Columbia *Phoenix* (or *Union*) contains a dispatch from Washington, dated Aug. 3, as follows:

> Gerrit Smith has visited the Ku Klux prisoners at Albany and urges clemency in the case of Saml. G. Brown, aged 60, who plead guilty under bad advice, and Hezekiah Porter, aged 19 who is dying, and David Collins. Mr. Smith says in his letter to the President that Shotwell, one of the N. C. men is defiant, scorns a pardon, and is studying law. He, however, suggests that these pardons be postponed until after the election lest it be thought that the clemency was prompted by interested motives, etc., etc.

Now if Gerrit Smith wrote any such stuff as that to his master he asserted a plain lie. The idea of one in my situation being defiant and scorning a pardon is absurd. To be sure I shall never beg pardon on my knees for crimes of which I am innocent, nor abase myself to propitiate the ill will of those who sent me here; but for all that I am not a desperado, and if a returning sense of justice on the part of my oppressors should open my prison doors, I should even hail the boon as a great gift, although I could feel little gratitude for the restitution of that liberty of which no one has any reason or right to deprive me.

But I think I understand this announcement. Mr. Smith left here—highly pleased with me, (Capt. P. has said as much) but being stuffed with lies and calumnies by some of my enemies, he thought to make a show of severity against me to palliate his recommendation of the others who were more obsequious, tho' not more innocent. Yet how unjust to seek to deprive a man of every chance of liberation merely because he boldly maintains his principles, and endeavors to improve his few hours of leisure in the study of an honorable profession! And consider Smith's second thought: "Keep these poor old ignorant men in prison, absent from their destitute and sorrowing families, until after the election. They deserve to be released, but for the looks of the thing hold 'em a month or two longer!" Now if these men are worthy of clemency—and God knows, and I know they are—they should be released at once; every minute they are unnecessarily detained is a crime. Poor Porter dont need their pardon; he has been released by an higher Power than Grant; but Brown and Collins are grey haired old men, who have no more business here than Judge Bond who sent them.

As for myself I feel satisfied that I may as well accept the situation and settle down for my full term of six years within these walls! My prospects seem clouded in every quarter; nor is there anything cheering in my future. Not a star shines to attract my gaze in the dreary waste which stretches away from my prison doors. But I vowed when I came here not to be broken or subdued by the degradation to which my enemies had reduced me; and I mean to fulfil my vow. And hence forward I shall try to cultivate patience as an *habit* as well as a virtue.

Aug. 14th. N. Y. *Herald* contains a 5-column report of the correspondent's visit to the Ku Klux here. He, however, only saw Brown, Collins, and myself; and while he has given *verbatim et literatim* our statements, he has received an erroneous idea from the remarks of Capt. P. that most of the other prisoners were deplorably ignorant—hardly one remove from brutes. This is hardly just. Many of these men are deplorably ignorant; but they are sensible, honest, respectable, well doing men of the small farmer class in South Carolina. Having none of that *smartness, read-and-write* accomplishments of most Northern men of their station in life they seem to Northern eyes much more illiterate than they really are. Many a Southern man, who can scarcely sign his own name, is nevertheless, a thriving honorable, hospitable, and high-spirited person. Without doubt the majority of the Ku Klux here are poor, ignorant, and certainly not much better than negroes, so far as social position is concerned. But they have feelings, and they have rights, and they are an integral part of the State, and as De Toqueville says—*"No citizen is so obscure that it is not very dangerous to allow him to be oppressed —no private rights are so unimportant that they can be surrendered with impunity to the caprices of government."*

The very fact that these men are poor, ignorant, unimportant persons adds to the ignominy of the tyranical rulers, who sent them here; because men of their class had no means, talents, nor influence to protect themselves with!

I hope my statement will find its way into the papers, but I fear it will not, for although many of N. C. eds. are K. K. themselves they are too much frightened to show any sympathy or even interest in their less fortunate, because less cowardly, comrades. *N'importe!*

Aug. 20th. Whitley's Report has been published, and as I anticipated is a mixture of *false insinuation, and pure lie.* It is as follows—

COL. WHITLEY'S REPORT—HE RECOMMENDS THE PARDON
OF SOME OF THEM.

Col. Whitley, the Chief of the Secret Service Division dates his report to the Attorney-General, New York, Aug. 9, and writes as follows:

Sir: I have the honor to acknowledge the receipt of a communication from your Department under date of the 2d inst., inclosing a copy of a letter from Gerrit Smith, addressed to the President, in relation to those convicts in the Albany Penitentiary who were convicted for violations of the Enforcement Act, and requesting me to go to Albany, make a thorough investigation into the condition of those persons, and report to the Department my views as to the expediency of exercising Executive clemency in regard to any of them. In accordance with your request, I proceeded to Albany on the 7th inst. for the purpose of fulfilling the duty, assigned me. As a means of conducting my inquiries in a manner best adapted to arrive at all the facts in the case, and also to lead the prisoners to express themselves as freely as possible, I deemed it best to see each of the parties separately, without any knowledge on their part as to my official character or the object of my visit. In this I received the fullest aid of Mr. Louis D. Pillsbury, head keeper of the Penitentiary, who brought each prisoner in separately, with the simple remark to each that "this gentleman desires to talk with you."

The prisoners were mainly frank and communicative. Some of them are very poor and unlearned and have left large families behind them, and while acknowledging that they were members of the various orders of the organization known under the general head of Ku Klux Klan, and that they had been justly sentenced as such, plead in extenuation that they had joined the order without a full knowledge of its aims and objects, and had been incited to deeds of violence by their leaders, who had managed to escape from the country leaving them to bear the responsibility and the punishment of their misdeeds. A number of them stated that they had been compelled to join the Order to save themselves and families from a visitation of the Klan. Others had entered into its ranks under the supposition that it was a society organized for mutual protection, but learned subsequently that its real designs were the extirpation of the negro race, and the driving out of such of the whites as were in favor of the political equality and social elevation of the blacks. These severally expressed the heartiest contrition for their misdeeds, stated that the organization was one inimical to the best interests of the society, and that the Government was fully justified in breaking it up.

In further extenuation of having been members of the Order they state that the operations of the Klan were widespread, embracing within its folds men of superior intellect, to whom they had been accustomed to look for advice and counsel, and whom they did not suppose would lead them into any combination that contemplated personal violence and murder if these were necessary for the accomplishment of its ends. They were told that it was a good institution, one to put down meanness in the country, and they accepted the statement implicitly. About forty examinations were made in the manner above indicated, neither prisoner knowing that any one but himself had been called out, and none of them being aware, as before observed, of my official position or the object of my visit. There was a singular unanimity in these statements, and a general expression of regret that they should have been drawn into an organization differing so entirely in the object which they supposed it had in view when they joined it.

In reply to the general question, "What were the objects of the organization?" the answer was almost invariably, "When we joined the order we supposed it to be a society established for mutual protection; but after having been fully initiated, discovered it to be for a political purpose, which purpose was embodied in an oath, in which we swore to oppose the Radical party, in all its forms, and prevent the negroes from voting. It was this great deception that misled us, and which has brought us to our present condition."

The contrition manifested by many of these prisoners, the healthy abhorrence expressed by them for the acts into the commission of which they claim they were betrayed by unscrupulous and designing men, of more enlightened minds, their general want of intelligence and their extreme poverty, all appeal strongly for mercy. My views as to the expediency of restoring any of them to society through the exercise of Executive clemency, are clearly in favor of such a course with some portion of them; and I believe it may be done in some of the cases, not only with great safety, but fully in the interest of the public good.

In those to which I intend respectfully to call your attention, the prisoners appear not only truly repentant but absolutely ashamed of the course which they seem to have unwittingly pursued.

Now it was tolerably certain that Whitley came here for no other purpose than to extract *confession* and information from the poor heart-sick prisoners whom, it was supposed, the prospect of obtaining a pardon would induce to criminate themselves, and make any sort of acknowledgments. The result to some extent justified the expectation although, notwithstanding Whitley's cunning, and shameful sophistry by which he made many of the ignorant men admit more than they meant or were aware of, he was obliged to call to his aid all his powers of lying and false insinuation to make his paper the views of his Radical employers. To explain this remark I must state that the manner in which he framed his questions was that in which lawyers are said to *lead* a witness at the bar; and as nearly all of the prisoners are miserably ignorant and illiterate men, it was not difficult to confuse, browbeat and *"draw them out"* into any sort of "confessions" he desired. For instance he asked me if I did not know certain deeds were contrary to law. I replied that they were perhaps contrary to the "Ku Klux Bill," but that the law of self preservation being the first law of Nature, we were obliged to act, because the regular officers of the law failed to protect us. "Then," said he "you admit that you are a desperate lawless character," and although I vehemently [repudiated] any such forced construction of my language he refused to hear me, and called another man. Doubtless many others were made to appear criminal by just such style of examination, who were far more innocent than himself. However, I suppose that some dozen or two (out of the 75) did actually "confess;" and bleat most piteously for pardon (thus showing that Whitley *lied* when he said we were unaware of his office, and motives) but all who abased themselves in this contemptible manner were men of the very lowest class, and of little more consequence in their communities than the same number of negroes. And so far as I can learn they all are the very

worst criminals who have been tried. But this only verified what I have observed from the beginning of the Ku
Klux War, that those who were most lawless and turbu-
lent as "Raiders" are the very first to "confess" and become persecutors of their innocent comrades.

Aug. 21st. Did not go out to work, being unable to
stand on my ulcerated leg. This is a revival of Lusk's
grudge against me, since it arises from the wounds he
inflicted on me in Asheville at the time I caned him. It
is, by the way, a curious coincidence that I, who became
embroiled in a personal affray, and received more than
one wound, in the cause of the arrested Ku Klux in
Madison County (when I was not even a member of
the order) should afterwards be sent to the Penitentiary,
for complicity in the deeds of the Order (alleged complicity I mean), and be prosecuted by the very man
whom I had caned on the former occasion. And that
while I took up the cause of utter strangers, and did
much to secure their release and vindication, now *I* am
left without a dog to wag his tail in my favor! Was *I*
wrong *then;* or are my *"friends"* (so-called) wrong
now? Exceedingly out of heart all day. The life I am
leading is miserable, the future miserably dark!

Aug. 22nd. Rumored that Collins, Scruggs, Owens,
and Teal have been pardoned. C. and S. are old men—
very ignorant—and to the best of my knowledge and
belief—not guilty in the least degree. Collins' case, I
have alluded to; Scruggs' is pretty much the same. Both
were decoyed out of their State on charitable errands,
then arrested, leaving their families destitute, and overwhelmed with terror, and after being carried 300 miles
away from their acquaintance, where it was impossible
to produce any evidence in their favor, were tried and
sentenced to four and three years (respectively) in a
distant penitentiary, for no other crime than mere connection with the Klan, to which every respectable man
in their county (including their own ministers, lawyers,
doctors etc.) also belonged! And now at last there is a
prospect of their getting back to their wives and children! I am glad of it; although I doubt if be true. As
for Teal, he was among the most active of the "Raiders,"

and one of the first to "puke;" and would have got off if
he had known more than he did. But after debasing himself (if that were possible) he was sent here.

Aug. 23rd. Confined in cell by my sore leg. 'Tis as
unpleasant here as in the shops from various causes.

Aug. 27th. Capt. P. informs me that the pardons
issued to B. C. S. and T. have been rescinded, at the
instance of certain parties (Mongrels of course) in
N. C. and S. C. who wrote letters to Washington stating
that these men were violent and disreputable characters,
who had occasioned great trouble to their neighbors during the war, and would be likely to take revenge for
their imprisonment by acts of murder, arson, etc., etc.
What infernal and malicious lies are these! More peace-
able men than Collins and Scruggs could not be found
in any community; they can hardly be said to have an
opinion of their own; and would never wander out of
their own corn patch if permitted to return to it. But the
basest falsehood coming from a negro or meaner white
man is accepted for truth by the Radical Administration
so long as it coincides with the malignant and tyrannical
policy of their party leaders.

I thought it doubtful whether these men would get
out; and now—I know I was right.

Aug. 31st. For four days have been confined in cell,
suffering not a little from my ankle. The Doctor pro-
nounces it a varicose ulcer, caused by incessant standing
in the shops. It requires much philosophy and more patience to get along in these times. Twice a day the Deputy comes—"Well, what is the matter with *you?*" "I
have a sore leg, Sir." "Put some kerosene oil on it," and
so I rest, until he comes again. This man is an excellent
officer; indeed there could hardly be a better one; but
he has become so accustomed to *ordering* the reprobates,
that he forgets himself when speaking to a gentleman,
and (sometimes) uses a tone that is extremely humiliating for him who has to hear it without remark. I judge
that he is in some measure unconscious that he is giving
pain; for, he generally appears to be friendly disposed
towards me. But such trifles as these make life exceed-

ingly irksome just at present. And when shall I be better off!

Sept. 1st, 1872. Letters from M., M. F., and C. G. Dawson of Atlantic, Cass Co., Iowa. The latter writes to ask if I am the same "R. A. Shotwell of the 8th Va. (Rebel) Regt. who saved my life on the battlefield?" If so, nothing would please me better than to hear from you."

Correct! Charles—tis the very same long haired youth, who, about this time, ten years ago, came *"over the water to Charlie."* How happy were those days— full of hardships and dangers as they were—in comparison with these! I would rejoice to be with you, or even to write to you, Mon ami, but these pleasures are denied me at present. But I judge you have read my statement, which will—must—suffice.

M. is still puzzled about a choice of profession, says he is waiting advice from father but I suppose he has no money to pay his board bill and can't get away from it. Well he does not want to go South at any rate, as he has become infatuated with the P. girls.

Ma chere amie writes sadly, though ever kind and sympathetic. She mentions a long letter, giving "all the news," mailed a few days previous, but which as usual failed to come to hand. Nor had she rec'd my letters to her of May and June 2nd. Those rascally postmasters, how mean they must be, to seek to persecute a man after he has been swallowed up in a distant penitentiary; aye, and to rob him of the only comfort he has—the pleasure of an occasional line from his friends!

But we can expect no better of men (Southerners) who can sell themselves to Grant for the beggarly salary of a country post office in the South; of course I dont mean to include *all* post masters in this category; for some take the office for convenience sake, or at the urgent request of their friends, not because they are Mongrels. But unfortunately none of these reliable men have lately held the offices where my letters are mailed, and delivered. *Hinc illa lachrymae.*

Alas! my friend sends me intelligence—anything but cheering; although I am glad to know the worst. Just as I predicted the apparent peace and tranquillity in Rutherford was delusive, a snare laid to catch gulls. Many of the refugees, supposing that the troubles were finally appeased; that no more victims were wanted; returned home, and began to show themselves. When suddenly the Man Hunters and Yankees flew in every direction to spring the trap, and must have taken much game, as Miss F. states that 30 were bagged in a single day! Rutherford jail is again full, and the Devil holds high carnival in the county. B. F. and others of my acquaintance were spry enough to give "leg bail," and postpone their cases until another time. Well, well, it is not worth while for me to worry any longer about it.

Have been reading a diverting book (Parisian America) by Ed Laboulaye, the well known French author. But I mention it chiefly to quote a passage from it. The author was one of the warmest friends of the North during the late war; he still approves of Radical treatment of the South; the Abolition of slavery being his pet theme, upon which he raves. Yet in this book, he says, (speaking of the French)

> To fling liberty to an enslaved people is to entrust children with a weapon which will explode in their hands, Why? Because respect for one's self and for others, the feeling of right, the love of justice, the essential conditions of Liberty, are not articles of the law; they are not decreed; they are virtues which the citizen acquires by dint of patience and practice. So long as liberty does not live in the soul, it is but as sounding brass, a tinkling cymbal; when once it has entered into our very essence all the artifices and fury of tyrants will not wrest it from us.

All this is very well *per se;* but it sounds somewhat inconsistently coming from an apologist of the subjugation of the Southern people to the supremacy of the ignorant, brutal, and recently manumitted negroes!

But Laboulaye, after all is not so bad; inconsistent, I mean, as that old Radical Abolitionist, Horace Mann of Bost*ing*. Hear him on the same subject!

The human imagination can picture no semblance
of the destructive potency of the ballot-box in the
hands of an ignorant and corrupt people. The
Roman cohorts were terrible, the Turkish Janiza-
ries were incarnate fiends, but each were powerless
as a child for harm compared with universal suffrage without mental illumination and moral principle. The power of casting a vote is far more
formidable than that of casting spear or javelin.
On one of those oft recurring days when the fate
of the state or of the United States is to be decided
at the polls; when all over the land votes are falling
thick as hail, and we seem to hear them rattle like
the clangor of arms, it is enough to make the lover
of his country turn pale to reflect upon the motives
under which they may have been given and the consequence to which they may lead . . . . If they ema-
nate from wise counsels and loyalty to truth, they
will descend like benedictions from Heaven to bless
the land and fill it with songs and gladness, such as
never have been known on earth since the days of
Paradise. But if on the other hand these votes come
from ignorance and crime, the fire that rained on
Sodom and Gomorrah would be more tolerable!

*Can any Southerner draw a stronger argument
against negro suffrage?*

Sept. 2 and 3rd. Off duty on account of my lame
leg, which is exceedingly painful. Genl. P. and lady returned from Europe. I am glad to hear of it. Am less
liable to get into trouble while he is here. Am reading
Russell's *Modern Europe.*

Sept. 4th. Off duty and blue as indigo. It has been
an exceedingly dull day, have nothing to read and little
of an agreeable nature to think about. This sort of day
is becoming monstrously common with me, although I
try to prevent it. It may seem strange that I do not
study; but, indeed, one might as well attempt to write
as he walked in a crowded street. There are almost
momentary interruptions, and many other causes to divert the mind.

But perhaps more than that is the doubt which fills my mind as to my future life, i. e., what profession would be most suitable for me upon my reentrance to society. The Law has ever been my favorite study; yet this may be the most unprofitable and embarrassing line of life I could adopt. The fact that I have been confined in a penitentiary—innocent though I am—will always be a dead weight upon my shoulders in public life, especially were I to aspire to eminence at the Bar. Upon the whole, therefore, I feel that I am not for the law, or rather the law is not for me; and so up comes the question: "To be or not to be?"

Hence I judge that it is best to employ my time in the acquisition of general information that may be of service to me in an editorial career.

Sept. 6th. The Babies-Crop must have been monstrously fruitful in this latitude during the past year or two; for our whole force is now employed in the manufacture of children's shoes; of which we turn off more than 2000 pairs daily. Seeing the never-ceasing stream of chubby toes pouring from bench to bench, one might wonder that there were youngsters enough in the land to need the half of them. But this perhaps is not "talking like a father."

Sept. 8th. Sultriest morning of the season. Suffered all night from feverish condition of my leg. Nothing by the mails from N. C. I am utterly disgusted.

Sept. 15th. Another week without a word from N. C. I shall never forget the neglect I received.

Sept. 19th. Deputy was severely cut in the head by a refractory convict.

Sept. 20th. Genl. Pilsbury came to the shops; and calling me aside, told me he should have come down to see me, but he felt too old and infirm to go about much now. Did I eat my rations? Yes, Sir, I eat *at them.* He advised me to keep cheerful, and promised to allow me an extra letter on Sunday.

Sept. 21. Atmosphere becoming *purer* in my vicinity owing to the release of the darkey on my left and one in front. I wish it had happened earlier in the summer. But after all the negroes are no worse than the whites of the class who are sent here.

The vagabond on my right hand hourly picks off (off himself) the largest kind of lice, which he plays with on the bench in unblushing contempt for decency or manliness. There are hundreds just like him.

Sept. 23. I felt quite unwell yesterday morning, but went out to walk and soon was shaking with a severe chill. Deputy gave me an extra blanket and an opium and camphor pill, and I spent the day in a stupor—dreaming dreams and seeing no end of curious visions. It was the anniversary of the day of my sentence and, as may be supposed my thoughts were by no means pleasant on the subject. The Genl. sent me a double sheet of paper but I was too sick to write.

Sept. 29th. Extracts from father, without a word of comment. No wonder the Genl. should think it strange that envelopes could come, when there was not a written line in them. He was not aware that nothing was sent. Discouraging news about Greeley's chances. Defeat is now tolerably certain, and with his defeat comes certainty that I shall not get out any time short of my full term.

Oct. 2nd. Foreman of the shop offers to put me in an easy position (Examiner of shoes when finished) provided I am likely to remain here an year or longer. Told him I could not answer until after the Penna. and Ohio elections. If they go for Grant, the jig is up—

And I am flung—sky-high—and more than that;
The man whose praise I have sung,
With pen, with pencil, and with tongue
Will go; must go, will go—go—go
Up Salt River, with his "White hat."—*Dog Rell.*

Oct. 3d. The weather is quite cold, and fires not being started, we are quite uncomfortable. My spirits are decidedly at low ebb.

Oct. 5th. Georgia reported for Greeley by 25,000! First encouragement of the season.

Oct. 6th. Two or three uninteresting newspapers sent by F. "Only this and nothing more." 'Tis provoking. No one seems to have any idea that I am interested in political matters; yet they might know I have the deepest interest in every occurrence of the campaign for upon it depends my continuance here. Besides I have been accustomed to keeping up with the news of the day. But 'tis useless to complain—I have tried it.

Oct. 7th. "Just one year ago today

As I remember well"—I passed beneath the portals of Albany Penitentiary. Unhappy Anniversary! The year has been one unremittent round of hardships, trials, and sufferings, physical and mental, such as I could not have conceived possible to be borne. Yet I am alive, comparatively well, and looking forward to other years of the same kind of life! Strange vitality of the soul—strange tenacity of existence—that makes us bear all this, rather than cut loose adrift on an unknown sea! 'Twas a cowardly saying of Shakespeare's "better to bear the ills we have, than fly to those we know not of." All happiness has been discovered by adventurers into the great Unknown, the untried.

One thing comforts me for my long confinement; I have learned a deal of experience, patience, and worldly wisdom that I should not have gathered so soon under any other circumstances. May I not hope to say with Kossuth, "So many years lost, but all my after life gained?" So mote it be!

Oct. 9. An end to hope! Pa., Ohio, and Indiana, casting 76 electoral votes go for Grant by unheard-of majorities! Greeley and Brown may as well haul down their flag. The despot, with his moneyed ring and Radical Clique, is too strong for the honest men of the country. *Hic gloria* etc.—respublicae! Hence forward the march of the monarchy shall not be slow; a third term, and an increase of the army is all that is wanted to prepare the way for the *coup d'etat.*

To me this is a serious blow, since upon Mr. Greeley hung all my hopes. But, as I have so often remarked, 'tis useless to repine.

Oct. 11th. Abominable climate! The mornings unpleasantly cool, hot at noon, and freezing in our cells at night. I have a disagreeable cold in the head and my mental thermometer descends with the caloric—As Stoddard has it—

> I am weary and gray
> And my thoughts fly away
> Like a long flight of cranes
> On a dark autumn day.

> They go till they find
> The warm sunshine and wind
> But my autumn remains
> And my darkness of mind.

Oct. 13th. Penna. gives Grant 35000! Ohio and Indiana similar majorities! A monstrous, inexplicable, ruinous fatuity of the people! No wonder the President dare usurp dictatorial powers, and establish his sham courts and armed cohorts upon the necks of Southern men. Never were fraud, force, bribery, and open desecration of the elective franchise more boldly and thoroughly exposed, than has been done by the Liberal writers and speakers. Yet for all that, Grant sweeps the country with unparalelled success. The key to it can only be the degeneracy, indifference, and corruption of the Nation. Men would not stand by and see a throne erected in their midst if they did not feel satisfied the days of the Republic are numbered. This sort of thing cannot last, thank God. It will continue to grow worse until they whose interest it is to . . . .[1]

Oct. 14th. Capt. P. brought me a letter from father, mailed at Charlotte and conveying some unpleasant news. It appears that another scurrilous article about me has been copied from the N. Y. *Herald* by several of the State papers and has occasioned considerable uneasiness to my "friends" (so-called).

I have just finished a communication for the N. C. papers, which I send with the following, under cover to Gov. Vance at Charlotte.

---

1 There is a break in the manuscript here.

Albany Penitentiary,
Oct. 14th. 1872.

Hon. Z. B. Vance

Charlotte N. C. Dear Sir: A recent letter from
father informs me that he will be in Charlotte about
this time and will likely enjoy your hospitality. He
likewise informs me that my friends have been rendered somewhat uneasy by a new calumny set afloat
by the enemy, and copied by your city papers. I
have therefore prepared a card for publication, but
as I have been a close prisoner for over 12 months,
and have had no intelligence from N. C., since the
first of the year except a note or two from Gen. L,
I am not sure that I shall act judiciously by again
appearing in print. I take the liberty, therefore, to
submit the enclosed communication or card for your
consideration, leaving it altogether discretionary
with you to eject the whole or any part of it. If
deemed advisable please enclose it to the editor of
the Charlotte *Democrat,* the *Sentinel,* or such other
paper as may be most convenient for you, and send
me a copy.

I am the more sensitive on the subject treated of
in my card because now that my prospects for release have been withered along with Mr. Greeley's
by the October blasts from Penna. and Ohio, I feel
an increased desire for the respect and sympathy
of the better classes of our people during the protracted and irksome confinement before me. All I
have left is some little reputation for conduct as a
soldier, and for zeal and firmness as an editor—
both in defence of my State. Let me preserve this,
and please God, I shall greatly better it when once
more restored to liberty. All my leisure time (which
however is but little) I employ in the study of history and the elements of law, seeking to fit myself
to resume the tripod at the earliest opportunity.
I have been fortunate in having had good health,
and although suffering from many privations and
discomforts am usually cheerful and patient. I undergo the same labor and discipline with the felo-

nious class here: But I have, I think, the respect
and confidence of the officers—the superior officers
at least—and I have never received a reprimand
since I came here. I allude to these personal matters
thinking possibly you may meet with some friends
to whom they might be of interest. Hoping to have
your favorable influence, and with warm assurances
of esteem,

I remain, Governor,

Your obedt. Sevt.

R. A. S.

My card for publication will pretty effectually quash
all rumors of the kind or prevent their gaining circulation in future, I think. That at least I wish. As for the
author of the *canard* in question, there can be do doubt
that it originated with either C. L. Cobb, or Lieut. Mc-
Ewan, and is merely a malicious exaggeration of our
interview on the Balt. Steamer. I did indeed admit that
I had been a member of the order; but this I have never
denied. But as for "confessing," "offering to stump for
Grant"—Bah!

Oct. 15th. Genl. P. gave me a slip from the Albany
Argus, detailing the recent attempt to blow up the Raleigh *Sentinel* Office.[1] When the printers were absent on
Saturday night a keg of powder was placed under both
presses and ignited by a slow match. The office was completely wrecked.

The animus of the deed cannot be mistaken; it was
the blind malice of Grant's supporters in N. C., the vile
Mongrels, seeking to injure one of their most persistent
exposers. The *Sentinel* has never shown any quarter to
the Scalawag Carpet-bag Rogues and Ring thieves who
infest the capital and the State; and in the issue preceding this wanton outrage, there had been some hints of
new startling developments. Hence the result.

This is not the first assault on stout old Joe (Turner).
In the height of Holden's military despotism, he was
arrested by the would-be despot, confined in a cell with
a negro felon, drenched with water and subjected to the
grossest indignities. Twice has he been shot at, and once

---

1 The explosion took place shortly after midnight of October 10.

the assassins sought to wound him through the murder
of his wife, who was fired at through the window. Many
times has he been attacked on the street; and Radical
mobs have more than once pursued him for his life;
which, however, he always foiled by his cool courage.
Failing in these dastardly schemes of murder they
sought to destroy his property, and too happily succeeded.

I hope, however, the Democrats of N. C. will make
sure that he is not long in need of a press. He has done
more to break up the "Rings" and run rascals out of the
State, than any three men in it. Such public services
deserve remuneration for all losses he may sustain by
Radical violence. As for the base deed I have mentioned,
there is no call for comment except to say that it is the
fruit of Radical teachings in the South, and shows how
much Ku Klux organizations are wanted about the capital.

Genl. P. alluded to my letter to the press in very kind
terms, giving his opinion that it would do me good
among my Southern friends. "Oh you will get to Congress someday," said he in a jocular tone, and expressed
civil regrets that he could not better my condition,
"which," said he, " I would gladly do if I could consistently with the regulations make any distinction between
prisoners." Said if I had any serious trouble with the
under officers to appeal to him and he would see that I
should be rightly treated.

Altogether he makes me regard him in a warm and
affectionate light, by his repeated assurances of friendly
interest. He is undoubtedly an humane, kind-hearted
old man; although, from long habituation to the control of prisoners (convicts) he has acquired a dictatorial
pompous bearing, which would be apt to repulse a
stranger. To me, however, he has always shown that a
generous and courteous soul lurks under the outward
crust of dignity; and I have not the least complaint to
make of his treatment of me.

Oct. 19th. Confined in cell by my lame leg. The
weather is turning excessively cold. School commenced
tonight; but I shall give up my class, as I find two nights

in the week a great waste of my own time, and I wish to devote every leisure moment to study, and studious reading.

Oct. 12th.   Capt. P. says Wm. Teal, who came with me, is pardoned. He is in the hospital laid up with white swelling in the legs or some similar disease. The Capt. wrote to Whitley stating that T. is likely to die, and suggesting that he be pardoned, and the application is successful. Such an action is very creditable to the Capt. and I'm sure T. ought to feel grateful for the interference in his behalf. Told Capt. P. I would be much gratified if he would intercede for Brown, Collins, Scruggs DePriest, and the other boys. Wrote a long letter to father by today's mail, acknowledging his surprise of the 9th inst. I adopted a gentle and affectionate tone, although I feel much hurt by long neglect. This day is the anniversary of the battle of Leesburg, the first engagement in which I participated. I cannot help having some wicked wishes that I had all my enemies in so close quarters as we had the Yankees on that day, when they sprang down a bluff forty feet high and perished by hundreds in the cold Potomac.

Oct. 22nd.   Much struck with a remark of "Junius:" "*Injuries* may be atoned for and forgiven; but *Insults* admit of no compensation. They degrade the mind in its own esteem, and force it to recover its level by revenge."

True oh Prophet!—most true! But thou shouldst have added that long constrained submission to insult and humiliation actually weakens the mind, and lowers the understanding—almost changes the character of the sufferer. And how dreadful when one has *nothing but his degradation* to *brood over,* while the future offers him no prospect of being able to *resent his injuries, and the insults he has received!* It is such trials that contribute to the filling of our insane asylums.

Oct. 23rd.   Indescribably nervous, depressed, and weary of my existence. Nor could it well be otherwise with one in my situation, standing all day long, with down cast eyes, cold, speechless, and knowing nothing of the current events of the world. Truly it is but a living grave for me!!

Oct. 27th. Worried by an abscess on the jaw, neuralgia, and a foolish letter from brother M. who has been offered the privilege of reading law with Gov. Vance but is indisposed to accept it. Strange that he should be so infatuated with Princeton, although, having become somewhat a popular favorite among the ladies, there is small hopes of him until he either marries, or becomes so insufferably vain as to forfeit the advantages he now receives from youth and high spirits. The offer to study with Vance is one that hundreds of young men in N. C. would pay liberally for; and for my part I would gladly jump at it; and perhaps obtain a magnificent start in life, through it. "But boys will be—boys." And no doubt 'tis the best policy to permit them to follow their own inclination in the choice of professions. Although unfortunately—

"It never is to a baby told
What will become of him when old."

Oct. 28th. Suffering intensely with my jaw—*jaw-gon-it!*

Oct. 29th. Wrote to Aunt Susie, enclosing extracts from Southern papers and begging her to withhold censure of my supposed mis-conduct until she had further particulars. I intended not to trouble myself with the least attempt at vindication to my Yankee kindred; but as Aunt S. has written me so kindly, and seems so desirous to show her affection, it is proper she should see that she is not cherishing a really guilty man.

Oct. 30th. Capt. P. fetched me a copy of the Charlotte *Observer* sent in accordance with my request to Gov. Vance. It contains my "card" on the *Herald's Canard,* as follows. The editorial comments, I give below wishing to send Aunt S. the print.

A Voice from Albany.—A Vile Slander Refuted
—Mr. R. A. Shotwell Vindicated Himself

The subjoined letter was received by us last Saturday from Mr. Randolph A. Shotwell, who is now confined in the Albany Penitentiary.

Albany Penitentiary.
October 14th, 1872.

To the Editor of the Charlotte Observer:

My attention has been called to the following article copied from the *N. Y. Herald,* as I am informed, by a number of the State papers:

"A Ku Klux Prisoner wants to stump for Grant. —It has transpired that *Richard* Shotwell, one of the leaders of the Ku Klux Klan in N. C., and now confined in the Albany Penitentiary, proposed to a prominent member of Congress that if the President would pardon him he would cheerfully take the stump and labor for the success of the Republican candidates and denounce the Ku Klux organization. Finding that he was disposed to plead for pardon it was proposed to ask if he would give evidence against the principal leaders, such as Ransom, Vance and Merrimon. This Shotwell declined with a defiant air, and said he would die rather than betray anybody. Application for the pardon was therefore refused. When Gerrit Smith visited Shotwell two months ago he said he found him defiant and unwilling to accept a pardon on any condition."

I presume that I am the person alluded to in the above, although the writer, having set to fabricate a falsehood, had not thought it worth while to give even the name correctly. The entire statement is without foundation. I scorn to refute the imputation of having offered to barter my principles for a pardon; but for the sake of my friends I will merely say that I have never applied for pardon, nor made any proposals to a prominent member of Congress, nor to any one else. Having been illegally arrested, falsely accused, unfairly tried, and unjustly sentenced to the full severity of an unconstitutional law, I have long hoped (and shall continue to hope) that future devolopments and the subsidence of bitter passions would lead to the restoration of my liberty as an act of justice rather than one of executive clemency.

The last paragraph of the *Herald's morceau*

wrongs me in a two fold degree by imputing to me
a piece of silly and theatrical braggadocio in refusing to accept liberty on any condition, on the one
hand; and again affording the President a fair excuse for declining to hear any future application in
my behalf.

Mr. Gerrit Smith appears to be the originator of
this calumny. It may not be improper therefore to
state briefly the facts in the case. Mr. Smith visited
the Penitentiary on the 8th of July and let it be
known he came from High Authority. In the interview with me he was very courteous and I answered
all his inquiries with courtesy and frankness. After
acknowledging that I had been a Grand Chief of
the Klan, and was well acquainted with its designs,
I assured him that it, and our people generally had
been greatly misrepresented, not only by the Radical press, and irresponsible correspondents, but also
by the circulation of so-called confessions and testimony invented by perjured vagabonds, or exorted
from intimidated witnesses. I emphatically denied
that the Klan was a conspiracy against the Government, or against the negroes, or against any class
of people on account of their political opinions.
Reverting to the Government prosecutions, I
called his attention to the fact that there were several gray-haired old men of 60 years and upwards,
doomed to years of toil in this penitentiary, over a
thousand miles from home for no other offense than
having sought us to preserve order in their communities, and to shield their wives and daughters
from the brutal passions of white and black desperadoes, etc.

Mr. Smith seemed surprised and shocked at my
statements and strongly expressed his intention to
intercede with the President in their behalf. I
learned that he fulfilled his promise, and recommended three out of four whom he saw, as fit subjects for clemency. But he grossly misrepresents
me. Nothing was said of pardon during the interview except a volunteer offer on his part to write

to a certain Republican Judge in my favor, for which I thanked him, but thought it hardly worth while for him to be at that trouble, although I should be glad to have his own personal influence. Great was my astonishment, therefore, to hear of his letter to Grant, and I am forced to conclude that it is a part of a scheme to exclude me from the benefits of amnesty. Hence this statement of facts.

Begging the indulgence of the public for so lengthy an intrusion of my private misfortunes, I am Mr. Editor,

Respectfully,
Randolph A. Shotwell.

Mr. Shotwell's Case. In another column will be found a communication from Mr. Randolph Shotwell who is now serving out his term in Albany Penitentiary. The letter was addressed to us and was intended for publication, Mr. Shotwell deeming proper to refute the base and slanderous imputations of the Radical press of the North, which have been so assiduously circulated South as well as North.

The letter is a calm, dispassionate and well written document. It is a clear exposition of the facts in the case, and a triumphant refutation of the charges against him and will be read with deep interest by those of his friends who may see this.

In relation to the publication of his card, Mr. Shotwell says, in a private letter, 'I am the more sensitive on the subject treated of in my card because now that my prospects for release have been withered, I feel an increased desire for the respect and sympathy of our people during the protracted and irksome confinement before me. All I have left is some little reputation for conduct as a soldier, and for zeal and firmness as an editor—both in defense of my State. Let me preserve this, and please God I shall greatly better it when once more restored to liberty.'

In regard to his confinement, he says—

'I have been fortunate in having had good health,

and although suffering from many privations and discomforts am usually cheerful and patient. I undergo the same labor and discipline with the felonious class here; but I have I think, the respect and confidence of the officers—the superior officers at least—and I have never received a reprimand since I came.'

Whatever may have been Mr. Shotwell's offense against the law, the manner of his conviction was a graver offense; for in his own terse language, he was illegally arrested, falsely accused, unfairly tried, and unjustly sentenced to the full severity of an unconstitutional law. The victim of partisan malice and fury, his severe punishment excites the sympathies of all who can feel for men who have been tried before partial juries, and sentenced by unjust judges.

The present editor of the *Observer* is Johnstone Jones, of whom I know nothing. But the foregoing editorial was written, I suspect, by Gov. V. himself; for the extracts are from my letter to him, and the beginning of the last paragraph but one is almost identically the same as one in a private letter from him to me. All of which gives weight to the remarks; although I am well aware that Gov. Vance highly disapproves of the whole K. K. movement; and I daresay he considers me very censurable for having any connection with it; although many of the best of his townsmen were more deeply implicated than I.

I imagine, too, that Mrs. Dr. Chapman, of Asheville tried a critical pen (for which I am obliged to her) on my letter before it went to the printer; since I find a redundant word omitted, and a missing "a" supplied, and the infinitive mood changed to the present in one instance, all of which I might have noticed myself, had I time for a second reading ere I dispatched it. But the Deputy came for it before the ink was dry. Wherefore I think I came off well.

And now, I think, both my friends and enemies ought to acquit me of any intention to desert to the Radicals, or to save myself at the expense of others. Surely there can be no mistaking my published declarations on the subject. Indeed it is quite certain that I have been far too earnest and explicit for my own future good; for my enemies will be sure to shut the door of pardon (Oh how I hate that word!) against me. But I could not do less. Reputation is of more value to me than personal liberty. Nor do I think I shall ever stoop to solicit clemency of my vile Persecutors! although when I reflect that if kept here my full term I shall have become forgotten by my acquaintance, and be powerless to obtain redress for past wrongs, I feel like undergoing almost any additional humiliation, provided it shall loosen my arms to resent all the outrages done in sending me here, as well as the humiliation in begging out.

But I cannot forget that in asking clemency I place myself in the attitude of a confessed criminal, which I am not, and never shall be. The very term pardon implies guilt; hence, as I remarked before, I hate it, when used in connection with my name. I want no pardon, but only simple *justice*. I have been wronged as few men ever are or were.

I have been wronged by *false accusation* and slander.

I have been robbed of time and liberty by *false imprisonment*.

I have been cruelly wounded, by *false assumptions* on the part of many friends.

I have been foully damaged by the *false verdict* of a packed jury.

I have been shamefully insulted by the *false declamations* of a political judge.

I have undergone every sort of ill treatment and humiliation at the hands of the cowardly and *false hearted* officers of government:—and now to cap the climax of outrage, I must *falsely* forswear myself and seal my ruin by a *false* confession of feigned crimes!

Not much shall I be found in such an hypocritical, false piece of business. Nay, let the command of my tongue be denied me, if ever my heart prompt so false an utterance!

"Smile on, my lords!
I scorn to count what feelings, withered hopes
Strong provocations, bitter, burning wrongs
I have within my heart's hot cells shut up."
"I've had wrongs
To stir a fever in the blood of age,
Or make the infant's sinews strong as steel"
"But here I stand and scoff you; here I fling
Hatred and full defiance in your face!"

Oct. 31. Wretched torture from my swollen face, be-k.ks I can't eat. Tried to get a mouthful of our so-called soup into "the proper channel" for a visit to the interior; but the soup was too weak to crawl over my teeth, and as my puffy lips forbid the entrance of a spoon "the matter was dropt." Tomorrow the dock-ter must punch it with his "gough" (lance) or I cant survive.

Nov. 1st. Du Chaillu the famous traveler mentions that among the African tribes he found many in whose dialect there was no word to describe an *honest man.* They didn't know the meaning of honesty. What a co-incidence that we should have a tribe (called office hold-ers) which is in a precisely similar state of ignorance of honor and honesty? But then it must be admitted that the office holders at present have many traits in common with the negroes, by whose votes most of them were elected.

Apropos of Honor, I have read that the mythological Temple of Honor had no entrance of its own, nor could it be entered except through the temple of Virtue which conveys a beautiful moral, i. e., that man must practice virtue before he can reach Honor. Alas! the aspirant to Honorable Fame does not nowadays commonly enter by the sombre portals of virtue.

Nov. 3rd. Was much disappointed in getting no let-ter from the South. But after breakfast Genl. Pilsbury came to my cell, and handed me the following from Hon. Gerrit Smith.

Peterborough N. Y. Oct. 31st '72.

Dear Sir:—A friend has sent me a newspaper containing your letter of the 14th inst. I am very sorry I misapprehended you. I judged you to be a man of proud, self-gratifying, and defiant spirit. I understood you to say that you had no confessions to make and expected no pardon. You justified all you had done and laid the blame on others. How then could I ask the President to pardon you!

You are young—only 28 you told me—you have talents and education; and I wish you were out of prison, and doing good in the world. But I see not that your term of punishment can be shortened if you feel and express no regrets; for being, as you admit you were, the Ku Klux Chief in your part of the country.

I shall be happy to help you but you must first help yourself. Let me assure you that the President is a kind man, and that you have much to hope for from his kindness if you will but allow him scope for its exercise. The President knew nothing of my visit to the Penitentiary. I was moved, however, from an influential quarter to undertake it.

Your friend
Gerrit Smith.

Mr. Smith's handwriting is crabbed and hieroglyphical beyond anything I ever saw, unless I except that of Gov. D. L. Swain, who once wrote me several letters which I was obliged to answer at a venture, not knowing much of their contents. It is not surprising to read of Mr. S's letter to the President, "that the whole force of experts in the Attorney General's office was necessary to decypher it for the perusal of the President." Such a joke as that ought to send even an octogenarian to writing school. However, I translated my letter; and, in the afternoon, Genl. Pilsbury came to take me out to his office to answer it. Without having an opportunity to arrange my ideas or cull expressions, I wrote as follows; and, as I now think rather too obsequiously; although Genl. P. told me it was just right—couldn't be better" etc.

Albany Penitentiary, Nov. 3d. 1872. Hon Gerrit Smith

Dear Sir.

Through the courtesy of Genl. Pilsbury I am permitted to acknowledge your favor of the 1st inst. in which you state the impressions made upon you by my language and demeanor at the time of your visit and which occasioned your representations to the President. I am glad to be reassured in the opinion I had formed of your kindness and benevolence; an opinion that led me to note in my journal that I had met the great abolitionist Gerrit Smith, and felt the antipathy of a life time melted almost away in the course of a short interview. But it is apparent that I have not made myself understood. When I told you that I had no confessions to make and did not expect a pardon, I simply expressed a sincere conviction. I have no confessions to make because I am conscious of no crime of my own doing, and I know of no criminality on the part of others. I was a chief of the Klan, but the Klan as I understood it, was not a treasonable organization, and I did not, and do not approve of the outrages said to have been committed by it, and I utterly refuse to be criminated by them. At my trial it was elicited from the witnesses—*government witnesses* against me—that I had repeatedly threatened to expose any raiders of whom I could obtain knowledge.

It is true that I might give the names of a large number of persons who have been members of the order, and thus bring them into trouble, although they may not have been guilty of the least infraction of law. But I should be slow to purchase freedom at the price of treachery, and dishonor of this sort. From which you will see that I cannot conscientiously criminate myself or others; hence *I have little hope of pardon.* Yet it would be a consolation to know that I had the friendly influence of one whose claims upon the President and the Republican party are so great as those of Mr. Smith, and in asking this friendly influence I can assure him that if pardoned I shall return home and endeavor to aid all lawful authority in the preservation of order, morality and the Rights and Privileges of all classes of citizens irrespective of color or Party.

With respectful regards, I am, Sir, Your obedt. Sevt. R. A. S.

After directing this letter, Genl. P. invited me into his drawing room, and named me to his wife; with whom, however, I could have no conversation as she is quite deaf. Mrs. P. then went out, and got for me a bundle of cake to take to my cell, and the General finding I was not well provided with underclothing said he should have me supplied. No one will ever know how much mortified I am on these occasions, when my poverty and present ignominious situation, are so forcibly brought to mind by the very kindness of these friends I have found or made in a strange land. But reason tells me 'twould be silly not to do the best I can to gain regard of those who are my custodians in law if not by right; so I endeavor to seem pleased and grateful.

Nov. 6th.   All is over! *The Great Farce,* (*The Presidential Election*) closed yesterday, as had been foreseen for the past month, with a complete triumph for the Bully Butcher, and National Gift Taker. *Grant walked the track.* Telegraphic reports from all quarters leave it doubtful whether Greeley will get a single State. Even New York—the Democratic Old Guard—surrenders to the tune of 3500 majority for the "Coming Man." Twenty five other states are in the same column —marching the Despot gaily to his throne! Selah! It is absolutely amazing, the apathy, the blindness, the infatuation of the people! Is there no longer any patriotism, any conservatism in the land? What do we see this day? A nation yielding its elective franchise to elect a worse than Napoleonic despot! I say the nation yields its franchises because no one believes that Grant is the choice of the people, that he is worthy of the High Authority which is now his for another term and doubtless for life. But corruption, and greed, and avarice, and fear, and Prejudice, and Misrepresentation, every malignant passion, every dishonorable and illegal means have been made to bring about the stupendous result. And now what next?

Historians tell us that every Republic that has fallen, to shake the faith of man in his own capacity for government, has been, preceding its final fall, the scene of just such transactions as these; sectional prejudices, the majority trampling on the minority, the courts corrupted and used for political ends, open corruption in office, bribery of voters, use of the military to intimidate the opposition, great monopolies supporting the most promising candidates, and finally much unanimity in favor of some popular leader, who quietly took the crown and Royal Robes when a suitable opportunity occurred. This is the political panorama now unfolding, slowly but surely, in our own country. The end we may almost see. And then bloodshed, insurrections, turbulence, and anarchy! Now, I do not predict that all this is to occur in a year or two; it may be postponed for a score of years. But one thing is certain it will not be half so long, nor a third of it, if the Government continues to usurp power, and *hold* it, as it has done during the last decade.

Nov. 7th.   Genl. P. came down to my cell to present me with a couple of suits of underclothing of the best quality. They are precisely similar he said, to those he wore himself, and were excellently fitted for me, being large, warm, and strong. Of course I thanked him; and was glad to get the articles, as the weather is now quite cool day and night. It is true I felt somewhat mortified at the necessity which obliged me to accept such a present, which possibly came out of his own pocket (for although the institution occasionally furnishes underclothing to destitute prisoners, the quality is decidedly inferior) and which at all events was not one I ought to have needed. But I have learned to pocket my pride, and be thankful for small favors, and undoubtedly it was both unusual, and an high mark of favor for Genl. P. to suggest and procure them for me. Consequently I feel gratified, grateful that I have found, like Joseph, a friend in the Keeper of my prison.

Nov. 9th.   I think I have said enough about the election; but it is as well to state officially that Grant has carried every Northern State, and all the Southern States, but half a dozen, not worth mentioning.[1] *Ave Caesar!* Now let him but play his cards prudently, and the largest empire on the Globe will be his. No! No! Let me not give up faith in the patriotism, and integrity of my countrymen! That Grant is ambitious to play the King I have no doubt: that he is already virtually a tyrant I need not say, because my own experience is plain evidence of the fact, but that he can succeed in overthrowing Republican Institutions is hardly probable; although, as I have said, if demoralization, degeneracy, and corruption continue to gain in the country as they have done during the past decade, every obstacle to a throne must soon fall.

Nov. 10th.   Kind note from Jennie dearest of sisters, telling me of the arrest of W. T. McE. He has been stationed at Joe Carson's 14 miles from Greenville. He was bound over to Jany. Term of U. S. Circuit Court at Statesville. It seems Court met a few days ago, and "continued" all the K. K. Kases until next term. This is an outrage! The indicted persons to the number of 600 or 1000, with all their witnesses, lawyers, etc., have been obliged to attend court after court, many of them going over 200 miles at great expense and loss of time; and nearly all being poor men, such demands must impoverish them and their families before they obtain a trial—farcical as such trials are known to be! Nothing worse than this can be charged against the corrupted tribunals of Justice (so-called) of the most tyrannical Kingdoms of the Old World; and it is directly in violation of the Constitution which declares that every man is entitled to a *speedy* and *fair trial* by an honest jury of his countrymen.

The weather has grown very cold, making me shudder at thought of spending another winter here. Indeed my situation has become almost unendurable, and I

---

1 Grant carried Georgia, Kentucky, Maryland, Missouri, Tennessee, and Texas.

daily "dont know what to do with myself." Misere, misere, me!

M. writes cross and complaining notes. It is a shame to be misunderstood, neglected and misjudged by one who should be anxious to serve me: but Lord!—the selfishness and stupidity of the present annum mundi!

Nov. 17th. M. writes, "The other day, Genl. Karge, professor of modern languages (in Princeton College) came to me, and told me to give you his respects and to assure you of his high appreciation of your noble bearing towards those Government officers. He had seen your letters to the papers. He was a General in the Federal army during the war; but says, although he had fought us, he knows something of our wrongs since the surrender. He says he thinks he will go to see you in vacation and bids me tell you he would be glad to welcome you to his house when you get out" etc., etc. It is cheering to know that my case is gaining some notoriety, not for notoriety's sake but that my reputation may be cleared.

Nov. 18th. Wrote to father, enclosing my letter to M. H. Justice for greater security.

Nov. 19th. Went up to the school room to get the benefit of the light, and a desk on which to practice Phonography. Last night, however, there were no school exercises, but, instead, a magic lantern exhibition by Chaplain Reynolds, given as a treat to the scholars for good conduct. It was, I judge, casting pearls before swine; as most of the scenes were of statuary, flowers and views of ancient castles etc., in which these poor fellows could take very little interest. Something highly colored, striking, tragic or ludicrous, would have been more to their liking.

For my part I could have enjoyed the exhibition if I had not been half frozen all evening. I got very little sleep all night after being so thoroughly chilled.

Mr. Reynolds fetched me Motley's "Rise of the Dutch Republic" from his private library in the city, which is quite kind of him. The book is equal to fiction in incident and is written in good, and *pleasant* style. I was much amused at the character of Count Hoogstraaten, who vehemently denounces one of his false friends as a man who could "lie twenty four feet down his throat." Some of my enemies beat that.

Nov. 20th. For some weeks past I have been studying law, etc., in the workshops at such odd moments as I could snatch, by keeping ahead of the supply of shoes. In this manner I frequently got two hours a day for study. But our overseer (White) who has ever manifested a disposition to *pick* at me, although he has had few openings for censure or abuse because I obey the rules like clockwork, happened to see me looking on my book, which I had partially under the bench. Such an opportunity could not be lost on so willing a mind; and I was very rudely commanded to "Put up that book and attend to your own business." Of course I "never a word said once." But my views on the constitutionality of the Ku Klux act were *prodigious.* This interruption of my shop studies is a serious loss to me, as we go out so early and come in so late I have no time for study or reading; and the occasional scraps of learning I could pick up in the shops, were useful in diverting my mind during the long hours while at work.

But the overseer is not a lover of learning; and I dare say in this instance hates the student.

Nov. 22nd. First snow of the season, and so cloudy that we were released from the Shops an hour earlier than usual. I was so delighted I could have sung the Yankee *Te deum* (*doodle*) had there not been a tendency among the authorities to repress anything like rowdyism.

Nov. 24th. Note from Miss M. M. F. who says she has written to me very often and is still "one of the best friends you have on earth. May God bless you!"

This is very kind, and I am sure my amiable friend ought not to think me ungrateful although I presume she does. It is strange what a fatality seems to pursue me with respect to my correspondence; my own letters are commonly misjudged, and those of my friends seldom reach me.

Nov. 25th. An envelope from father contains the

following extracts from N. C. papers to which he only adds the ejaculation—"God bless my son!"

From the *Greensboro* Patriot.

"We publish on the outside of the Patriot this week, the manly letter of Capt. Shotwell, who is now confined at Albany N. Y. on the charge of Ku Kluxing! What a splendid contrast the conduct of this brave man makes to the cowardly cringeing of those who were terrified into sacrificing their manhood and their principles to avoid the wrath of an angry administration. Shotwell in his prison is an hero deserving of admiration before whom these cringeing cowards should slink in shame."

The Southern Home—Edited by Genl. D. H. Hill, at Charlotte says:

Capt. Shotwell—This fearless youth publishes a card in the Charlotte *Observer* indignantly denying that he had been trying to make terms with the enemy. We believe he would rot in the Penitentiary before he would do an unmanly or a cowardly thing. The whole story was a low Radical trick. The impression sought to be made was that Shotwell could convict Vance and certain Conservative leaders, but was too honorable to do it. The men who got up the lie, knew that these leaders were no more connected with the Ku Klux organization than Genl. Grant, or Horace Greeley."

I am rejoiced to learn that there are two newspapers at least in North Carolina that dare express their sympathy for men, who have been wronged and injured as I have been. These editors seem to have some back-bone; their pens do not shrink from telling what their conscience dictates. But such courage is very rare in the State I imagine: for, although in the heat of a political campaign, none of the country papers utter one word (that I can hear of) in denunciation of the Radical outrages, military and mock-civil, hourly transpiring around them.

To show how the times are I quote from a letter, re-

ceived by Brown from a respectable citizen of Yorkville, S. C. The writer is 70 years of age, and formerly
was a clergyman I believe. He says:

> And has it come to this at last that our boasted
> model Republic no longer affords protection to her
> best citizens, but has become an engine of persecu-
> tion to her children (through her courts, too) as
> furiously insane as were ever the Inquisitions of
> Portugal or Spain! As yet (thank God!) I have
> my personal liberty, but I feel that I have no coun-
> try, no protector, of my purse, property, or reputa-
> tion, when I hear every day the military bugle,
> drum, and clank of arms, and see every hour be-
> fore my eyes the attired soldiers, cavalry, infantry,
> and artillery crowding our streets, and hunting
> down my neighbors and the best citizens we have;
> and find our jails packed with men charged with
> offenses of grave sort which they did not commit,
> and tried by juries packed for the purpose of a sure
> conviction and witnesses paid in money or other-
> wise to swear to suit the tastes of the prosecutors;
> and a prejudiced judge to impose a fine and pass
> sentence which is equivalent to confiscation of an
> whole estate and confinement for the remainder of
> the term of life! When I see all this, and worse,
> daily occurring I am appalled at the sad and sicken-
> ing spectacle! For we all well know that this is done,
> not for the public good but for the support of a
> political party. I venture to affirm that there has
> not been, nor is now, a single man from this state
> sent to Albany prison who ever was or is now, a
> member of any organization, or single handed, who
> has opposed the Federal laws; and it is only by a
> forced and far fetched construction that even the
> most violent act of Ku Kluxism can be so regarded
> by any Court, etc., etc. I know of no man to whom
> I can compare Judge Bond except it be Jeffreys
> of England.

IN THE HOSPITAL

Nov. 27th, 1872. Capt. P. came out to the shops,
and told me the General wished to have a little talk

with me, in the Office. The latter informed me that he had thought of placing me in charge of the Hospital, to fill the vacancy occasioned by the release of Maj. L. L. Hodge, one of Grant's defaulting paymasters, who was sent here for 10 years, but is now at liberty in less than 12 months. The Genl. then asked me if I would give him a promise to execute the rules and see that everything was rightly attended to precisely as if I were a regular officer. I replied that if he chose to give me so easy a berth I should take care to fill his expectations of me, so far as I should be capable.

Accordingly I am now duly installed; Librarian and Hospital Steward. The advantages of the position for one of my turn of mind can hardly be estimated. The Hospital is a large room, on the second floor, having five windows, from which there is quite a pleasant prospect, taking in the suburbs of the city, and the Catskills in the blue distance. At the upper end of the room is a large book case, containing a thousand volumes, or more; long table; high desk; clock; chest for clothes, etc. This end is my "quarter deck," being the place where I do principally abide.

Along the right wall are the patients' cots, 17 in number, each of which has chair, spoon and cup, for its occupant. There are two stoves and gas jets for light and heat. In the lower end are the sinks, pans, etc., for washing, together with two closets for luggage and the use of the nurses. On the walls are several fine lithographs in walnut frames. The library comprises many standard works of History, Philosophy, Poesy, and the Sciences; but is largely supplied also with "war literature" and trash.

The care of both Library and Hospital devolves on the Steward, who has, however, an assistant to attend to the minor matters, such as giving out rations, cleaning up the floors, etc.

It is impossible to estimate the difference between my old life and this; but I can already realize the advantages in many important particulars; viz, clean beds, clean clothes, use of books, writing material, etc., better food, freedom to converse, walk about, and hold *my head up*—last but not least. But why say more than that I get rid of the shop, with all its dirt, drudgery, down cast eyes, and degrading associations! That of itself is almost like being set at liberty, so great is the relief.

To Genl. Pilsbury, who kindly rescues me from the many hardships and sufferings that I have faintly alluded to in the foregoing pages, I am very much indebted, and, of course, shall endeavor to merit his confidence.

Nov. 28th. "Thanksgiving day!" (so-called) This is observed as an holiday in the Institution and is celebrated like "4th July," by exercises in the chapel.

Genl. P. came up in the morning, and giving me a small black book, desired me to draw up a notice of the performances for one of the city papers, whose editor had requested it. I complied as well as I could after being so long out of practice in matters of that sort. Services were opened with the reading of the Proclamation after which an amateur quartette of ladies and gentlemen discoursed patriotic airs and a half dozen amateur orators spouted eloquence, "and sich-like" for the edification of the Inmates.

When all was over the men were marched to their cells, where they found a big dinner consisting of roast beef, ham, cabbage, potatoes, onions, cheese, crackers, and apples. This dinner is the chief feature of the day for the prisoners and is looked forward to for months. Fortunately I need no longer await the "Annual Dinner" with so much impatience; as my fare is decidedly improved in quantity and somewhat in quality.

As for my duties I find they are by no means onerous; being merely to issue medicine, preserve order, see that the patients and convalescents are properly provided, and look after the Library. I have, therefore, more than half the day to myself, and may read, *write, or amuse myself as best I can.*

At present we have ten men in hospital but several of them are old chronic cases, useless in the shops; and sent up here to get rid of them I suppose. One is Teal, who was sentenced when I was, and who is fairly *shrivelling* with some disease unknown to me which has eaten up all the flesh and muscle of his legs, and arms, leaving his skin flapping around his bones, like a wet sail against a mast. His days are not many on this, or any other land, I apprehend. Another patient Lynch will die of consumption in a few days. He called me to him, and expressed pleasure that I had got the stewardship, although I know not how he gained any knowledge of me previously, and if he is aware of his own condition I should think such matters would have very little interest for him. Tonight I shall sit up with him a part of the night; as most of the other men are weary with watching. It is a new business for me to have anything to do with sick people, but I intend to make myself thoroughly acquainted with it. Who knows but I may turn out to be a "doctor" after all? At all events I shall learn something about drugs.

Nov. 30th. This evening Teal's wife came to carry him home (his pardon has been here for several weeks). Wonderful strength of women's love! This poor wife, who I venture to say was never 20 miles from home in her life, and knew no more about traveling than flying, actually contrived to collect means to bear her expenses, and (having obtained an order for transportation for her husband) inquiring her way from city to city finally reached Albany, and came here today, in an old "sun-bonnet," half frozen, timid, and looking like a scarecrow; but cheerful and full of affection for her ghost of a man, whom she has undertaken to carry home with her. What heroine of romance could do more?

Teal is a miserable wreck; his legs and arms are wasted away until they are not much larger than pipe stems; and he must be lifted about like an infant. If he lives to get home (which I very much doubt) it will be a miracle, the miraculous influence of a woman's loving care. True this little "ministering angel" uses snuff, and *leaned over the spittoon to discharge a gill of tobacco juice in the corner of our white floored hospital!* But these little accidents come from lack of knowledge; the heart is better tutored; and most bravely has hers sustained her. We fixed Teal as comfortably as possible, the Dept. giving him a new suit of clothes, a blanket,

and a bottle of liquor; to which I added a comforter for
the neck, and some other matters, together with a letter,
recommending him to the "aid and assistance" of all
friends, and the public generally on the route homeward.

Sunday Dec. 1st.   Shortly after I had retired (if you
can be said to retire when you turn in to bed in a room
where a dozen others are spectators) last night I was
called up to superintend the "laying out" of *Lynch,* who
had just closed a day of delirium and a life of shame
and crime by falling alseep—that last sleep which knows
no waking. Poor youth! his dying request was that his
sister, a prostitute of Binghamton, should be telegraphed for. It had already been done; but she neglected
to come, I suppose.

It was not a pleasant duty to disrobe, and handle a
corpse; but I desired to conquer my aversion to such
matters; and therefore, I took my first lesson then and
there. Few are the attentions however, that are given to
convict corpses. With no other shroud than an old shirt
—the one they had on—they are laid on a sheet on the
floor, until a coffin is fetched. It is only a rough pine box,
and contains a few shavings, or a little straw, upon which
the body is quickly placed, a nail or two driven, and the
whole carried away to a felon's grave or the dissecting
table, as the case may be. Our surgeon is also professor
in the medical college of this city; and has a good opportunity to select fine subjects for his knife.

Apropos of corpses I must mention that we have here
a large Thomas cat who is in the room with the bodies
all night long, but never makes the least attempt to disturb them; thus contradicting the old crony theory that
cats will attack the dead. But perhaps our Tom is an
educated cat. He is well trained in some things (self
trained too) I could mention; for he does not give us
the slightest trouble although in the room day and night.
Usually he sleeps under the blankets with some of the
men. Salt meat he wont touch; tea is a favorite drink;
and he will not *bite* his own food; it must be cut for him.
And so no more about Thomas, except that he eats
fresh straw like an ox.

Dec. 4.   Capt. P. fetched me a note from father,

open as usual. I trust the Mongrels enjoy my correspondence.

The Columbia S. C. papers say that the Governor, and Governor-elect, and many State Officials (Radical) have signed an appeal to the President for the pardon of the Ku Klux here. The Grand Juries of York and Chester counties have sent up a similar petition. This looks like earnest work; and ought to silence some of the Radical papers that still harangue the public in denunciation of us. But they know that they have been apologising for an infamous crime committed by the government under the forms of law, and now they fear that a returning sense of justice may lead public opinion to re-act on them. For instance, hear the Raleigh *Era,* edited, I presume, by Lewis Hanes of Salisbury who was once my friend, and a staunch conservative; but basely went over to the Mongrels for the contemptible bribe of the Editorship of the *"Era."* I thought better of the man; but it is impossible to "touch pitch without being defiled," and Hanes has long been too *"moderate"* for a good and true Southern man.

> That Captain Shotwell and his associates will all be released and returned home long before their terms of imprisonment expire, we have not a doubt, notwithstanding the imprudence of their friends who seem to have sympathetically determined the prejudice of their cases; but such release will not be obtained on any promises of political support to the Republican party.
>
> But whenever the President and the country is satisfied that the spirit of Ku Kluxism is dead in this State, all who have participated therein will be forgiven, and the punishment of those under conviction promptly remitted. We confidently look to such consummation, and we earnestly appeal to every citizen of North Carolina to join in bringing about an end and a state of affairs so devoutly to be wished for.

Hanes knows perfectly well that there are no disturbances to warrant our retention here, even if there were legitimate excuse for the original sentence. But it was necessary for him to make some reply to the popular cry against our being held, and here we have it.

Dec. 6th.   Have just had the surprise and gratification of a visit from Bro. M. who ran up from Princeton to bring me some needed articles, viz: Hair and tooth brush, soap, sugar, coffee, spice, gloves, neckties (which, however, I am not permitted to wear), blank book, etc. He says he saw Gen Karge before starting who desired him to tell me to draw up a full statement of my case and send him, as he expects ere long to visit Washington and shall make it his business to work for me, etc.

Poor brother! He looks badly and is in much pecuniary perplexity. I wish I could help him. But I can't. Our interview was short and unsatisfactory, owing to the presence of Genl. P. who was in bad health and seemed anxious to get out of the cold room. Indeed the result of the visit is only to make me very sad. I shall not see him again soon I think.

Dec. 7th.   Sat up till past midnight with Light who is literally *rotting* to death; the natural result of a life of vicious sensuality and intemperance.

Dec. 8th.   Up half of last night with Light.

Dec. 9th.   Light went out at 4½ P. M. yesterday. This fellow's real name is said to be Fuel, Joe Fuel of Ohio, but he assumed the name of Light, which is quite appropriate, as I dare say he is serving for light and fuel both, in His Satanic Majesty's Big Kitchen at the present moment. Pious people might reprove me for jesting on so serious a subject, and to be sure it is a *lapsus pennae;* but a little flippancy seems indispensable to existence amid so many depressing influences. N. B. Here am I spending the bloom of youth within prison walls, and occupying my time watching by the bedside of sick ruffians, and "laying out" filthy creatures in whom no man could take the slightest interest.

Dec. 11th.   The Supervisors of the Institution, several hundred in number, have just passed through on a tour of inspection; a mere matter of form of course. Most of them were laughing, talking and paying no attention whatever to the condition of the building. Yet I must admit that there is no necessity for much examination as one may see at a glance that the establishment is well kept, and in the best of order. Still if the supervisors were on an official tour they ought to have examined things in detail.

Capt. P. called me down to caution me against C. a plausible fellow, formerly a colonel in the Yankee Army, who was once Hospital Steward himself, but lost his position by making love to a silly matron, whom he persuaded that he was immensely rich, and should certainly marry her when he got out. This seems to have been quite a *Platonic* affair; as they could not get within 30 feet of each other—she being on the ground and he on the 2nd floor behind a barred window. But they kept up a daily correspondence by means of a piece of string which the lover let down to receive the *billet doux* of his mistress. Finally, however, a false friend revealed the intrigue to the officers, and Clark was sent to the workshops to make shoes. The matron (who was one of the paid attaches of the institution) was discharged. It only remains to add that the gay Lothario is 62 years old! He is now brought up to the Hospital with something like the *jaundice*.

Capt. P. also gave me some disheartening news from the seat of war. The Attorney Genl. of the U. S. replies to the S. C. petitioners that there will be no "General Jail Delivery" of K. K. prisoners; but that each case will be considered separately and pardon be meted to the most deserving. This is the substance. The motive and the object are plain as daylight. Motives: 1st. to prevent further application by influential Radicals, or any general expression of sympathy by our friends. 2nd. to afford an excuse for delaying action as long as possible. 3rd. to fill the pockets of the creatures about the courts, who will of course demand full fees for the necessary transcript of judgment, etc.

Finally by this plan every prisoner can be made to humble himself, to promise to support the Radical party, and to bring his friends under some apparent obligation to the government by granting pardon in response to their petition. Bah! 'twas a most contemptible piece of chicanery.

Capt. P. consoles me with his opinion that we shall all be out in *6 or 8 months or so!* Which is like telling an hungry man he shall get his dinner tomorrow or next day, or some time soon! Still I am obliged to agree with him; although I presume there is a lurking *imp of Hope* somewhere in my soul or I could not be so cheerful in the face of such a future. Goldsmith says—

"Hope like the glimmering tapers light
Illumes and cheers our way
And still as darker grows the night
Emits a brighter ray."

Dec. 12th. Kind and sympathetic letter from Mrs. J. B. M., who writes as if she knew something about corresponding with a prisoner. She also cheers me by the assurance that all the good people of Rutherford know (none better than herself) how much I have been wronged, and injured by our vile enemies. Perhaps they do, Aunt Muff, but not all of them have the courage to say so, like you.

Dec. 15th. Becket, a negro, died. Strange how quickly we become accustomed to death! Two hours ago I assisted to stretch this fellow on the floor, and had actually forgotten him, when just now I glanced around and saw the corpse. Yet I sat up with him for several nights, and tended him as patiently as if he had not been a black cut throat. Becket stabbed a man in the streets of Washington, for accidentally running afoul of him in a violent storm. He never gave the slightest sign of remorse; but pretended to die a Christian. A letter from his mother, breathing the most affectionate sentiments and in a style superior to most letters from colored people, came today just in time to be too late.

Dec. 16th. A kind but not very palatable letter from Aunt Susie; who as I expected is thoroughly prejudiced by the misrepresentations of the South and the K. K. which have been poured into her ears from the hour she landed in America. I have written the following letter, which I here copy because it will show my views on the question of my imprisonment, etc., in a concise form for future reference. Yet I do not hope to change her opinion; for ladies of her age do not easily surrender their

opinions—especially if there is a family or local prejudice involved in them. Still I think she ought to know
what my complaints are; and therefore I write as follows.

Albany Penitentiary, Dec. 16th, 1872. Dear
Aunt. Perhaps it is not worth while to trouble you
with another letter, but you ask me to write, & it
seems to be due my own reputation to attempt to
disabuse your mind of an erroneous impression,
i. e. that I have been *"breaking the laws," "acting in
defiance of the laws of my country"* &c. I do assure
you that I have done nothing of the sort and the
assumption does me great injustice. I have violated
no law, state nor national, except that piece of partizan, sectional legislation, known as the Ku Klux
Bill, which the Supreme Court (as I am credibly
informed) has already declared unconstitutional.
But my liability under even that act, arises from its
ex post facto effect, because I had become a member
of the Klan long before its enactment.

My motives for connecting myself with that organization were entirely conscientious. I believed
that it was necessary—and if rightly conducted
would be beneficial to the country—our Southern
Country I mean. Its objects were good and patriotic: To maintain order, to check loose morality,
to assist the needy and protect the helpless, and to
counteract the pernicious teachings of base and unscrupulous men, most of them vagabonds from the
North, who were fast deceiving, misleading, coax-
ing, and driving the credulous and excitable negroes
into a course of flagitous crime and outrage that
bid fair to repeat the horrors of St Domingo on our
soil. These I say were the objects of the order. And
I think you will admit there is nothing objectionable in them.

It is entirely untrue that we had any disloyal or
treasonable intent. The very first clause of a most
solemn Oath, bound us to support the Constitution
of the United States as handed down to us by our
forefathers—aye to support and defend it too! And

among our members were scores of men who were
obliged to live in caves, and lonely forests all
through the war because of the *Union Sentiments*.
Would these men now engage in a treasonable conspiracy?

It is true that the Order had a political coloring,
was for the most part composed of Democrats; but
this should not be held to attaint it with disloyalty,
and lay liable its members to trial for conspiracy,
so long as the whole country is covered with Radical secret societies of a similar character that are
not counted treasonable. Many of my Northern
cousins I daresay are connected with the *"Union
League,"* or the *"Grand Army of the Republic,"*
both of which are secret organizations with signs,
grips, and passwords precisely like the Klan and
yet I have no idea that they (my cousins) will be
arrested, thrown into jail without privilege of
bail, dragged from place to place in handcuffs, tried
before a packed jury, and finally sentenced to the
Penitentiary for a large part of an ordinary life
time. No they run no risk of this because they live
in the North and are in accord with the sentiments
of the administration. But let them go to N. C. and
give offense to the petty powers that be under
Grant in that State and they shall do well if they
escape my experience. However, you may say that
other secret political associations do not seek to
carry their purposes by violence, whipping, hanging,
and shooting their opponents. To which I reply,
nor did the Klan. We have been outrageously misrepresented on this head. I have made diligent inquiry into the so-called "Ku Klux Outrages" and
I can hear of no case in which the sufferer was molested merely on account of his political opinions;
some piece of aggravated misconduct invariably induced the attack. Yet let any thief, robber, barn
burner, ravisher, or other desperado be lynched by
the Klan, and mighty quickly would he put up a
piteous howl about "Rebel Barbarity," "political
persecution," and the like, and forthwith the whole

North would blaze with indignation, and the Radical press teem with accounts and denunciations of "outrages" on "Union men," or "respectable colored men" by Rebel Ku Klux. By such falsehoods, persistently retailed, the Northern people have been miserably deceived and prejudiced.

Now please do not misunderstand me. I have no apology for any act of violence actually committed by the Klan (unless necessity compelled it) but I merely wish to show you, first, that there was nothing in the nature of the order to make my connection with it, an indictable offense; and second, that I neither approve of nor participated in any of these alleged "Outrages." At my trial it was elicited from the government witnesses—perjured wretches though they were—that I had always discountenanced such proceedings in my part of the country and that I had actually threatened to expose any raiders of whom I could obtain information.

There is little of the rowdy in my disposition, I think, and I trust I have too much of my sainted Mother's high tone of character, to disguise myself like a mountebank, and go prowling about the country in company with a lot of low felons, such as were the perpetrators of these "outrages." I never wore a disguise in my life, either for my face or my sentiments.

But why say more? I have assured you already that I am an innocent and cruelly wronged man. And I think my conduct during the past 18 months' confinement ought to add some weight to my protestations. Has not liberty been offered to me repeatedly, merely upon condition of my confessing, of my making some penitence? And is it likely that I, unaccustomed as I was to any sort of manual labor, and naturally of a fastidious and sensitive temperament, would continue to undergo year after year of drudgery, of indescribable discomfort, of ignominious confinement, of mental stagnation (as far as the exterior world is concerned), all for *nothing,* or for a *lie,* out of sheer obstinacy? No, Auntie, I think not; I am not of the stuff of which martyrs are made; I could not long hold out against the temptation of fresh free air, and green fields, and sweet society, and Nature's Kitchen bounties, if I did not feel that it would be a crime to blacken my character with my own tongue. No, I am here in a Penitentiary; sent here by the foul injustice of our oppressors, but I shall never confess that I am worthy to be here.

You saw my published letter. Since it appeared Mr. Smith has written me to regret his misapprehension of me and to say that he would be glad to be of service to me, although the first step on my part must be *confession!* To whom I replied that I had nothing to confess; and even if I knew anything of importance I should never purchase freedom at the price of treachery and dishonor of that sort. I consider, therefore, that there is small chance of my release short of my full term, which is a matter of five years or so longer.

I have now given you, my dear Aunt, a frank and candid view of my views and you will see how much I was pained by your censure, even though veiled as it was, in civil language and accompanied by a practical token of your affection. We will now if you please dismiss the subject once for all. Any further allusion to it will be distasteful to me; unless at any time you shall come to agree with me that I have been the victim of shameful tyranny and injustice on the part of the government. . . ."

Dec. 20th. Genl. P. who read my letter to Aunt Susie, tells me that the Supreme Court has pronounced the decision in the K. K. case; and that I am in error about it. In proof of which he sent me the following.

The South Carolina Ku Klux Case.
Washington, Dec. 16th.—The South Carolina Ku Klux case was disposed of in the Supreme Court today as follows:

Ex Parte.—T. Jefferson Greer on *habeas corpus* to the Marshal of the District of South Carolina.

In this case Greer was held under a bench warrant, issued by the Circuit Court upon indictment charging him with a felony under the Enforcement act of 1870. The question was whether this Court had jurisdiction to discharge the prisoner on *habeas corpus*. The Court are divided in opinion, and the writ is denied in consequence. A decision of the case would have involved also a decision upon the question of the constitutionality of the Enforcement act. The case was argued last spring.

But I dont think this is the leading K. K. case which is that of Hays Mitchell, whose attorneys, Hon Reverdy Johnson and A. H. Stanbery were given $15,000 to argue his case, and they appealed to the Supreme Court of the United States. Still it does not make much difference; because the Supreme Court is now only a mock-tribunal used by the Radical leaders in Congress to sanction their violence by the appearance of legality.

Dec. 21. Heavy fall of snow. Cold as at Spitzbergen! How I wish I was in Dixie.

Dec. 24th. Roan, another darkey, died. Getting rather too much practice in the "Obsequies" line. These miserable creatures are generally half putrid when they die; consequently the preparation of their bodies for the coffin, small though it be, is anything but agreeable to me—*even to superintend.*

Dec. 25th. This day is called Christmas by most people, and is supposed to usher in a season of songs, gladness, and good cheer. Not so here. Santa Claus positively "cuts" the establishment. He brings gifts, mirth, nor music, nor even rest, for the convicts labor all day, and all the ensuing week without any "variation or shadow of turning." Christmas avaunt! Begone! Appear to me no longer, even in memory! What happiness we might have if we could but *forget* at pleasure! The gift of memory is a blessing but the gift of Forgetfulness would be a greater one to nine-tenths of the world.

Dec. 26th, 1872. Well I thought it would be queer if I should have no Christmas—and so at last it has come! The gong sounded an hour or two ago, and on my going down, I found the Deputy with a large box

from home! It was a most charming surprise, for I had
no knowledge that one was on the road or even in preparation. Contents: large fruit cake, bottle wine, gallon of
brandied peaches, grape preserves, chow-chow, pepper
sauce, walnuts, etc., tippet for the neck, wrist cuffs, neck
ties, etc., all of the nicest sort. Therefore, I poured out
a libation to the muse, naming my kind, thoughtful and
generous little friend, the donor, in a poetical toast,
whereof the refrain was:

> Let your summer friends go by
> With the summer weather
> Hearts there are that will not fly
> When the storm clouds gather.

And to you, Mademoiselle Mignon ma belle, I wish
joy, contentment, and all the happiness that can attend
the young and pure-hearted!

Dec. 28th. A little after midnight I was awakened
by the now familiar sound of the death rattle; it was
another darkey, Moore, bidding us good bye. He was so
full of scrofula it is surprising he did not go sooner.
These Northern negroes, living in the large cities become so shattered by vice that the least cold, or indisposition generally results fatally. Besides a darkey gives
up as soon as he is flat of his back, and disease has only
to draw his last breath for him. A very nasty breath it
is, too.

Dec. 29. Letter from father via Charlotte, whither
it was sent to escape the Mongrel Post Office thieves.
Gov. Vance (to whom it had been sent under cover)
added his kind regards, and compliments of the Season.
Dear father does not write cheerfully—it is saddening
to see how depressed, and unhappy he is—although he
tries to encourage *me*. Alas! he has little rest or enjoyment in these winters of his life. I can only hope he may
survive all to welcome me home, and learn my solicitude
to contribute whatever is in my power, to his happiness.

Dec. 30th. Ten citizens of South Carolina were
brought here on the night of the 28th. One is Rev. Jno.
S. Ezell, an old man, and a preacher of some fame
among the Baptists of upper S. C. Nearly all are middle aged men. Alfred Le Masters, H. C. Mathias and

Jno Whitlock are from Union Co; Robt Moore, W. C. Whitesides, Marion Fowler, Jas. A. Donald from York District.

This batch arrived about 10 o'clock at night and I (who was sitting up at the time) really pitied them for the aspect of the place is dreary enough in its best looks to say nothing of being ushered to one's cell in the darkness, and awaking to find what they found. I know nothing about these men; but I have heard that Mr. Ezell is only charged with simple connection with the Klan! How great the outrage to send a gray haired minister of the Gospel to the Penitentiary for no other offense than connection with a Society organized to preserve order and a semblance, if no more, of morality, in the community.

These arrivals are no very promising indication of my own liberation, because it is not probable the Administration would continue its persecutions if there was any intention to do justice to those already doomed.

Still this is only as I expected; I have never been sanguine of getting out before the termination of my unjust sentence. Patience! Patience! Patience! That is the only motto I need trouble myself to obtain.

"May better days soon be our lot
Or better courage—if we have them not."

Dec. 31st. Peterson (negro) died at 1½ A. M., the sixth man in five weeks. This is going off pretty fast; although the percentage is not large (there are 600 inmates) considering the character of the majority of the convicts, whose constitutions are worn out before they come here.

Jan. 1st, 1873. The gloomiest day of the year, I fancy. Had some trouble with refractory patients, which kept me in an ill-humor half the day.

Jan. 2nd. Having laid down a rule to do as much as I can for my fellowman, no matter what my own situation may be, I sometime ago began to teach old man Scruggs his letters. Already he is making some advance, and I shall try to teach him to write, telling him as an incentive the gratification it would give his wife to have

a letter from him in his own hand writing. Thus I hope
to do a little good even in a Penitentiary.

Chaplain R. came in and chatted pleasantly with me
for an hour or more. Asked me if I expected to enter
public life when released. I replied that I believed it to
be due myself, my family, and my friends to obtain all
possible elevation in life that my reputation might be
cleared by the testimony of after years, etc., etc. He
wished me success and seemed to think I might obtain
it by proper conduct. This gentleman is quite popular
as Chaplain, and is peculiarly qualified for the post,
having been rather wild himself in his youth, as he frequently tells us.

Jan. 5th.   Kind letter from A. P., but *so* feminine! I
begged her to send me some newspaper extracts giving
me *news,* but lo! an whole column of twaddle about the
sleighing in N. Y. City! As if I cared a picayune for all
the sleighing parties in Yankeedom. Few of my correspondents, however, do much better. It seems impossible
to make them understand that I am not a fool, that I am
not interested in mere idle gossip, that I am anxious for
the general and political intelligence of the day. Mel.
sent me *leaves from the almanac,* until I sent him word
that I had a perfect almanac in the letters I received
weekly; and I should be glad to have a page from the
dictionary as a *change.* Poor M. felt hurt about it, as he
thought I would be at a loss to count the flight of time,
hence the Almanac. But I could tell him Time has no
flight within these walls. He is a slow coach, a rheumatic
on stilts. Instead of flying he creeps. I'm sick of him!
We take no note of Time—and not many notes of anybody else.

> "Day chases night, and night the day,
> But no Relief to me convey."

Deputy has just brought me a note from father, dated
Dec. 23rd, but post marked at Rutherfordton, Jan. 1st;
having been a full week in the hands of the Mongrels.
Father says, "I intend between this date and 1st of April
1873 (only 3 months!) to make an earnest, well considered movement for your release—on the ground of justice if possible, but release at all events. . . . The Supreme

Court has not declared its decision, nor does the present administration wish it. The President would rather pardon all the Ku Klux than have this decision made public. If it can be suppressed in any way it will be .... I shall make haste slowly, but *certainly* and in reliance on the aid of my covenant keeping God, I now think you can calculate on release by the *first of April, without doubt.*" I doubt!

Poor father! your expectations are illusory, your efforts will be fruitless. The 1st of April will come—and May—and June—and April again; but the "whirligig of Time," though ever changing will bring no change for me, until the last moment of my unjust sentence shall expire. Nothing short of a revolution, or a general jail delivery such as Napoleon made when he turned loose the miserable victims of the Inquisition in Italy, is likely to liberate me before that limit. Yet, while I can but know the futility of all hope, I cannot cease to hope. And doubtless it is well that the mind can thus cling to a shadow; for otherwise the Reason must totter. It is a well known fact that there is not one man in ten of the prisoners here, who does not expect pardon, or release in a short period.

Jan. 6th. I have now a patient who throws up over a quart of blood every day! Strange vitality that can endure such depletion of the vital forces daily. This fellow is superstitious, ignorant and debased, yet I pity him; he has twelve years yet to serve. But he will not serve them. He called me this evening to ask if I thought they would dissect him when he died, and seemed so agitated about it that I took pains to assure him there is not the least likelihood of it, as his disease is too common to make his case at all interesting to the surgeons. Rather a poor consolation I should think, to know that one wont be cut up when he dies. For my part when I am done with my physical apparatus, the Doctors are welcome to it.

Jan. 9th, 1873. I am glad to know that David Collins is on his way home at last! The wrongs and sufferings of this innocent and ignorant old man, I have often alluded to in these pages. He lives in S. C. but was en-

ticed over the State line into N. C. by one Leander
Jolly, acting deputy United States Marshal, who came
to Collins's humble dwelling to get supper, and pretending not to know the road, begged his host to act as his
guide, and then when in Rutherford, arrested him! His
aged wife was left sick in bed! The old man was then
carried 300 miles to Raleigh, where he had neither
money, friends, nor witnesses; and being tried before
a packed jury, was sentenced to four years at hard labor
here. Judge Bond admitted that the only evidence
against him was to the effect that he had loaned his mule
and gun to a party of raiders who demanded them; but
nothing could save him before such a Judge. When
brought here he was placed in a cell by himself, which
was kindly meant, but, as he could neither read nor
write, was very bad for him.

How often have I pitied the poor old man, as I saw
him going out to the shops through all sorts of inclement weather, bent in body—sorrowful in countenance,
toiling his way down to the grave!

But he is free at last, thanks to Gerrit Smith, and his
own pitiful humility; and as I said, it gives me real
pleasure to hear it; although I knew him not before my
arrest, and am not desirous of seeing him again.

Now if a few more innocent men could get out the
public would begin to learn something about the wrongs
that lie almost hidden by these walls.

Jan. 12th.   Letter from Bro. M. who says father is
certain of having me out *soon.* Ah! yes *Soon!* How I dislike that word! Every letter I receive promises me freedom *"soon."* All my friends are going to write *"soon."*
Or I am to receive something *"soon."* Or this or that
will be done *"soon."* And after weeks and months of in-
terminable length I am still fed up with promises of
what shall occur *"soon."* Bah! There is no meaning to
the word for one in my situation. No brevity of Time is
soon to the weary occupant of a tread mill.

Now I do not mean to reflect on the earnestness, affection, nor watchful care of my welfare of my father,
nor my friends. That they will do all they can for me as
speedily as possible I know. But I wish I were not

treated so much like a child, who must be encouraged by unmeaning assurances, such as, "Be still, baby, it will quit hurting *soon.*"

Jan. 13th. It is a familiar saying that "crime is never young"; and, judging from the looks of the large majority of hard cases confined here, the remark is perfectly true. Among the 600 convicts who pass before my eyes daily I see few that appear to have known youth, although perhaps the majority are in their 'teens.' All have the crime-hardened, prematurely-old look that distinguishes the denizens of Five Points or Rotten Row. All have cocoanut shaped heads, furtive eyes, and, usually, a bristling shock of hair, which is, in most cases, dark brown, or gray.

Eo die.

To my surprise and gratification I had a letter today from the South; and better still from my noble-hearted friend Genl. C. L. He at least, is true as steel, and uninfluenced by the machinations, calumnies, and threats of our oppressors. "I see an occasional article," says he, "which leads us to hope that a policy of clemency (*justice, mon ami*) may be adopted and that those who have so much affection for you; ourselves, I need not say, among the number, may have the happiness to welcome you as a free man once more. I must think that this will be the case ere long. I can scarcely imagine any circumstance that I should hail with more heartfelt delight."

How kind, how thoughtful, how comforting this!

The condition of things in our unhappy section he alluded to as follows: "The fact is the South with its lazy thieving negro population, supported in almost every atrocity, as the negroes are, by those in power, is anything but a pleasant residence. I try to hope for the best and that the future may be more bright, but I do not see at present any grounds for feeling sanguine in this respect."

I have drawn up a note, to send in reply, if I can obtain permission, in which I say, "I have to solace myself with all sorts of small hopes, since my Great Expectations have turned out to be broken reeds. The last stay snapped the other day when the Supreme Court agreed to disagree in the S. C. K. K. Case. I trusted that tribunal would set aside the piece of partisan sectional legislation under which I was falsely accused and unjustly sentenced; but it seems that Grant has the court well in his pocket. As for pardon, I have not yet applied for it, and I find it hard to bring my mind to consent to do so. The very term 'pardon' implies guilt and in asking for clemency I place myself in the attitude of a confessed criminal. I have been sufficiently wronged and humiliated without going down on my knees to the vile wretches who have injured me. I am not one of those who believe in turning the other cheek to be buffeted; I should be slow to kiss the rod which had lacerated my own back.

"Yet as there is no prospect of a General Jail Delivery of prisoners it may be wise—certainly is necessary—for me to beg for my *rights*. F. intimates that he intends to do something between now and 1st of April, but does not state his plan of procedure. I presume, however, he will get up a petition although I see not how one could be drawn without admitting more than I am willing to admit," etc.

This is no more than the truth. I shall remain here six years, or as long as they see fit to hold me—if I can obtain justice in no easier way than self-abasement, perjury and dishonor.

"The fate of Regulus is changed, not Regulus
I am the same in laurels or in chains
Tis the same principle; the same fixed soul,
Unmoved itself though circumstances change."

I regret to learn that Genl. Pilsbury is in so low health that there is little prospect of his recovery; a consultation of eminent physicians giving no hopes of successful treatment of his peculiar disorder. I should feel his loss as a personal affliction; not only because he is some guarantee of respectable usage while I remain here but also, because in gratitude for his invariable kindness and courtesy I am very much his friend. He has few equals as a Superintendent of Prisoners, as indeed he may well be, having been in charge of this Institution more than 27 years!

1873 January 18th. By rising at dawn I am now enabled to get nearly ten hours for reading and study. At this rate I may be making more mental "headway" than if I were at perfect liberty. My order of the day is as follows: Rise a few minutes after 5 A. M., make my bed, ablutions, etc. Read couple of chapters in the Bible and a page or two of some other religious work. Then my studies. Breakfast at 8 o'clock, at my own table, which is supplied with "extra rations." Afterwards I attend to any little duties, as shaving, marking clothes, etc., etc., until 10, when I take hold of books again, and so on until 8 P. M. when lights must be extinguished, and all hands to bed. This is repeated day after day for weeks, months, years perhaps. 'Tis dreadfully monotonous, but try not to yawn. Indeed I give less thought to "my troubles," than almost any prisoner here I expect; although it was not easy to conquer a natural tendency to brood over them. But I fortify myself with many aphorisms; as, "Sorrow is the lot of all human," and "Tis better to laugh than be sighing," and

"Care to our coffin adds a nail, no doubt

While every burst of laughter draws one out."

20th. Sick.

21st. Bilious.

22nd. Feel like a wet dishrag looks.

23rd. Crazy men are getting rather numerous in this establishment. We have three in the Hospital now; and there are one or two in the cells. One of my patients is an Irishman, guilty of epileptic fits. I was obliged to sit up with him half the night; although I gave him heavy doses of chloral. He is of opinion that I am a priest; calls me "Your Reverence" in deepest humility of tone and with many genuflections of body. His "confession" apprized me that he had not been altogether faithful to Mrs. Murphy, but "indeed your Reverence, *she caught me at it, so 'tis no matter;* that don't be much of a sin does it, your reverence?" I absolved him.

Another of my patients is precisely on the other tack; for he fancies himself a preacher. He sang and prayed with such ardor that the Deputy sent him up here to get rid of him. He is a tall, gaunt, mean looking rascal, who was sent here from Tennessee for robbing the mail.

I am glad to put this on record as one instance of a Southern scalawag being tried and convicted for robbing the mail! His name is Wilcox.

My other lunatic is a Dutchman, who seems to be the victim of circumstances and of some trickery on the part of the Government detectives. He was at the time of his arrest keeping an eating shop in N. Y., but being ignorant and inexperienced was induced to take some counterfeit money from a false friend, who then turned upon him, and gave him up to Col. Whitley who, knowing that Myers was likely to come off if he stood a trial actually frightened the poor Dutchman into pleading "guilty." Then he was sentenced to three years at hard labor. The disappointment affected his brain, and he seem unlikely ever to recover full reason although he is now, harmless, and decent in habits.

It might to some people, be no very agreeable situation to occupy a room in which three demented convicts are, day and night, but 'tis nothing when you're used to it."

Just now looking from the window I saw a couple of well dressed women, without a male escort, trotting around the court yard behind a blue-nosed turnkey—for what?—to see the prison! And the wind blowing a tornado! And the air fairly crackling with cold! *"Ah! ter duyvel vot a peoples!"*

Jan. 24th. Deputy kindly fetches me a letter two days in advance of the regular Sunday mail. It is from Genl. Leventhorpe, who thus counsels me.

"I am clearly of opinion with your other friends, that the time has now come to make as strong an effort as possible in your behalf. Any sacrifice of honor on your part of course no thinking friend would counsel; but there is no doubt I think that if your release is granted some concessions will be exacted (not certainly in the revelation—the very idea is infamous, even if you had anything to reveal which could implicate others, and which I am sure you have not) of yourself personally, and which

I should decidedly advise you to make, and which may take the form of a personal petition, etc. . . .

The thought of your long confinement, my dear Randolph, is so intolerable to me that you may well distrust my discretion where there is a question of your release. Still, reversing positions and placing myself under your circumstances, I should feel that there had been no sacrifice of honor or principle in writing myself 'Your humble petitioner,' when I had to do with people who had got hold of me contrary to law, and would assuredly keep me contrary to law until a hard sentence was completed, and therein according to their own good will and pleasure" etc.

Ah! *mon cher ami,* this is writing as if you knew my wrongs, and felt them too! How few of my acquaintance in the same honorable grade of society would dare to express themselves so freely! Even Govr. Vance in denouncing my persecutors must qualify his sympathy for me by allusions to the "trespass," "the temptation," the "crime of which you are accused." But Genl. L. is not much of a politician; and is a firmer, nobler friend. He is, however, somewhat too sanguine as to the success which he anticipates from Mr. Harper's and Senator Ransom's intercession at Washington in my behalf. If the whole Southern delegation should solicit my release, it could effect [nothing] in the face of a secret remonstrance from Caldwell, Sam Phillips, Logan, Lusk, or other leading Mongrels of North Carolina; and I well know that the malicious spirit necessary to induce such remonstrance burns in every one of their bosoms against me. *Nous verrons.*

Genl. L. says, "There was a time when I thought there could be no prison life with books for one's companions; but a few months experience in "lang syne" (during the war) in Fort McHenry, Pt. Lookout, and other hospitals and places of refuge for used up Confederates served to convince me that the mind is little fitted for study when the green fields are debarred from us, and the blue sky is seen only between iron gratings."

True, Genl. the mind's eye is not to be hoodwinked

concerning one's situation, and is ever craving something new and novel, something to make the nerves beat, and especially something giving promise of active life. 'Tis useless to attempt to pursue any study requiring earnest mental application unless you can utterly lose yourself in the pursuit. Kossuth said he found perfect oblivion for his sorrows in the study of mathematics, during the three years of his imprisonment. On the other hand Bishop Wren could not even read while a prisoner in the tower of London, and is said to have walked around the Earth during his confinement.

I both read and study—but not to advantage.

Jan. 26th.   Sunday's disappointment, etc., etc.

Jan. 27th.   One of the Rutherford prisoners has had a letter telling him that *"Shotwell is pardoned."* What a country that is for false rumors!

Eo die—

Deputy has just fetched me a letter from father, containing the very singular intelligence that George M. Arnold of Greensboro, a negro, who was, I believe, a member of the Legislature,[1] and reported the Holden Impeachment trial for the Washington *Chronicle,* offers to go to Gerrit Smith (who is his friend) and get his endorsement of a petition, which he will then present to the President, asking my release.

Father writes: "Arnold says that he and Smith are on intimate and confidential terms and he knows he can secure the pardon. He has other Radical friends at Washington. He is aware that there may be objections to him on account of his color and has written to Whitesides and gotten Jas. Gilmer, President of the Senate to write also. My views are that Smith . . . has suggested it to Arnold, and would bring you under obligations to the Radical Party and stop your mouth by always being able to refer to the negro's interposition in your behalf, and that a Radical negro too; although Gilmer says of him that he got the enmity of both parties in the Legislature by not being willing to do their dirty work. Further he wants $100 to pay R. R. expenses to Petersboro, and back via Washington where he may want to

---

1 Arnold was never a member of the Legislature.

go to get office. Still I think he would be successful and that is all we care about. Another consideration to be regarded is that Judge Fowle, Gov. Vance, G. V. Strong, T. S. Fuller, signified (I understand from Gov. Bragg) that they would make a united effort for your release as soon as the opportune moment should arrive; and to favor Arnold's movement now might seem to set a slight estimate on their past services and kind proffer of aid in time to come," etc., etc.

The last paragraph is rather "sarkasstikull," I judge. Not much do either of the persons named, care about my release or intend to interest themselves to obtain it. It is strange that father, with his knowledge of the world should count on the casual remark, or even the promise of a lot of politicians; made, too, in the height of the public excitement over the Ku Klux trials. Gov. Bragg might have done something but he is dead. As for Arnold, there is not much doubt of his motives; although the proposal is very good evidence that the injustice of my sentence is known and appreciated even by my enemies; else why should this negro, a leader of the League, come forward to offer as my advocate? Is it likely that he would do so if he believed me really the chief of a conspiracy against his race—as the Mongrels assert of the Klan? Certainly not. Still I do not feel willing to accept his services just at present; not that I have any objections to him personally, nor on account of his color; but for the simple reason that I intend not to solicit any favors from the political faction which has sent me here, and nearly ruined my state by its corruption, robbery and oppression. I am not willing to owe to the men who placed me in the Penitentiary any gratitude for getting me out.

Nevertheless I know quite well that this is about my only chance for liberation.

Jan. 29th. Coldest day of the Season; thermometer 4° below zero! Had a pleasant chat with the Deputy, who can be, when he wishes, very agreeable and courteous. He is certainly a most excellent officer for an institution of this kind: and this ought to be a high compliment to him coming as it does from a prisoner who has had few occasions to ask favors of him.

Today I have been much provoked by Wilcox, the pretended religious lunatic. I am now satisfied that he is a vile cheat, and no more insane than any other small witted, vindictive, and irritable villain. His object is to make the officers think him demented, and therefore be willing to recommend him for pardon. He told a man in the room that his father and his lawyer advised him what to do. So he began singing and praying in a stentorian voice to the great amusement of some of the men, but to the disturbance of others; and when ordered to be quiet, he announced himself ready to give up life, suffer persecution, bear chains and dungeons, etc., rather than give up Jesus. Sent to the dungeon, he informed the officers that he would spend his time praying for them. Such a case was hard to manage and the surgeon pronounced him "cracked." His friends then got the authorities at Washington to inquire of Capt. P. as to his condition, etc., to which the latter replied that he was insane, and recommended pardon. Consequently it is likely he will get out before long. He has numerous scalawag friends at work for him outside. I make this note in my journal, not because it is worthy of note, but merely as a specimen of the petty matters which occupy our time and thoughts in this mental treadmill. Trivialities, of which we should be ashamed elsewhere, *here* give a coloring to whole days and weeks. It is no doubt silly, to allow such trifles to fret us, but it is not uncommon for them to do so. Tonight I am sitting up with a sick darkey. He is destined for a colored climate, I think. Pleasant employment this for a Southern gentleman.

January 31st. The "Annual Dorsey Dinner" failed to come off (or on) today; as the benevolent donor is "down among the dead men." The prisoners are much disappointed; the 31st of January, like the 4th of July and Thanksgiving day, being in favor on account of its big dinner.

February 2nd. Usual Sunday provocation. Let me never forget how I am neglected here! Genl. Pilsbury called me down and gave me his private accounts to put in order; as he does not wish his family or the officers to know the exact amount of his wealth. He is much wealthier than I supposed. When I was leaving the room Mrs. P. handed me a package of cakes to which the Genl. added an apple, thereby expressing their kindness, although I could not but feel a little mortified by the gift, which was rather too much like giving cold victuals at the back door, or a glass of wine to the servant, who brings a message. This, however, I'm sure never entered their minds.

Feb. 4th. Smith, darkey, died 4½ P. M., after a long struggle with his enemy. Geo. S. Wright of York, one of the Ku Klux was pardoned yesterday. The Govt takes good care that those only, who are too ignorant and insignificant to make their wrongs known to the public generally, shall get out. Thus even mercy is made subservient to base political purposes.

Feb. 6th. Y. D. Young of Youngsville, Tallapoosa Co. Ala. was brought up to the hospital this day, sick of Jaundice. He is a grey headed old man of 55 or more and is sentenced to 10 (!) years at hard labor for being a Ku Klux! He was not a member of the order, he says, but had accompanied a party of men who went to the house of a rogue and told him they would give him the choice of returning some leather he had stolen or of leaving the country. The fellow gave up the leather, and no more was thought of the matter until he appeared before the notorious "Dick Busteed," and charged them all with Ku Kluxing. Busteed wishing to get a share of the infamy, acquired by Judge Bond, soon got together a *pliable* jury, and sent these poor men away to this Penitentiary. While at the same time the Northern papers were stuffed with dispatches announcing the discovery of more "bloody Ku Klux" in Alabama! Well may a Southern paper cry, "How long, oh Lord—how long!"

By the way, there is something appropriate for us in

the well known Prayer of Mary Queen of Scots, written in prison, which I give and translate below.

O Domine Deus, speravi in te
O care mi Jesu, nunc libera me
In dura catena, in misera poena,
        Desidero te
Languendo, gemendo, et genuflectendo,
Adoro, imploro, ut liberes me!

O Lord God Almighty, my hope is in Thee
O dearest Lord Jesus now liberate me
In durance repining, in sorrow declining
        I long after Thee;
With sighs never ending and knee ever bending
I worship, and pray Thee to liberate me!

February 9th, 1873.   A few days ago I wrote a letter for Brown, one of the S. C. K. K., to Hon Gerrit Smith, asking him to "use his influence" with Grant in favor of the humble petitioner. Brown sent it, and today received a reply, which as it concerns me to some extent, I here copy.

Peterboro. Feb. 5th, 1873.—Saml. G. Brown, Esq.
Dear Sir:
    I have your letter, a very very proper letter. It is sad that the man capable of writing it should be in a Penitentiary. I lose no time in forwarding your letter to the President and with it a letter from myself in which I say, "If you could find it in your heart to pardon the poor old man, I should be glad." The President may not pardon you immediately, but I trust he will pardon you before long. I hope Mr. Shotwell is in good health. He is a proud man. I wish he would humble himself so far as to apply to the President for a pardon for himself. And I wish he would in his application confess and lament his wrong doing. Never was there anything worse than this Ku Kluxism and all who were implicated in it ought to be punished. Please make my regards to Mr. Shotwell. Your friend, Gerrit Smith."

This is what I call an odd letter; like one of those hard shell Baptist sermons where several birds are killed by the same stone. His allusions to me which occupy half the letter are the more singular, since he could not have been aware that B. and I were in the same room, or that we were even acquainted, still, they show that the old Abolitionist is interested in my case; and that I might easily enlist his services in my behalf. But I am not the man to take such advice as he gives. To purchase freedom at the expense of my honor would rob it of half —nay all—its charms; because *in* confessing I must acknowledge myself unfit or rather undeserving to be admitted to decent Society; and by confessing I should make myself unfit even if I had been clear before, which, of course, would be the case. As for lamenting my wrong doing, he is welcome to his opinion about that. My conscience is easy, and there I rest.
Eo die.

Genl. Leventhorpe sends me the following letter he had from Hon. J. C. Harper.

House of Representatives, Washington, Jan. 31st, 1873.
Dear General

Your esteemed favor of the 21st came to hand in due time & I write to say that on the same day I had occasion to go to the office of the Attorney Genl. in relation to the release of a young man from Buncombe County and while there took the occasion to inquire as to the steps necessary to take to procure the release of Mr. Shotwell. I was informed that a transcript of proceedings in the court is already on file in the Att'y Gen Office and it will not be necessary to procure a copy in his case as usual. I afterwards saw Genl. Ransom and found him quite confident of success, in securing the pardon through the kind offices of leading Republicans in the Senate whose aid he is now trying to secure. If Mr. Shotwell be released he should be careful as to his deportment & conduct for some time as the fate of many others might be affected by any improper conduct on his part. I have just consulted

Mr. Wallace of S. C. on the subject and find he is willing to endorse the application of any for release provided they have not been guilty of murder. Mr. W. says he thinks most of the prisoners will soon be released if those recently pardoned manifest a proper spirit at home. It appears to be feared that they will seek revenge, etc. We think public sentiment is changing in our favor and if our people at home will be prudent for awhile, we may expect justice to resume the reins of government . . . . Very respectfully your

Most Obt. Svt.
J. C. Harper.

The Genl. adds—

"I previously heard from Judge Merrimon who on my suggestion applied to Mr. Phillips.... I think you will agree with me that the sky brightens. If you are released as I believe you will be, for the sake of others I should advise the avoidance of newspaper notoriety. Just go quietly home. I write *en bon ami* and I'm sure you know it; therefore will pardon the counsel of your old friend. Mrs. L. sends kind regards, in which all here join. We are in a whirl of good pleasure at the hope of your release. Ever your sincere friend. C. L.

Nothing could be more kind and thoughtful than this; yet it shows me that my forebodings are true; my friends will expect me to pocket the insults I have received, to be silent about the wrongs inflicted on me, and to continue under constraint after I leave these walls, burying myself in obscurity and scarcely venturing to assert my innocence, in private circles. This I feel would be unjust to my own name and character, to say nothing of my proper resentment for the foul injuries and humiliations that have been heaped upon me. As for newspaper notoriety, I desire to avoid that, except such as I may have from the publication of my own newspaper, which I expect to make the business of my life. But certainly I ought not to be hampered in every reasonable effort to vindicate my name, and show the outrages which under the forms of law have been perpetrated upon our citizens. And, indeed, in so doing I ought to have the countenance of every freeman in the land; for when usurpation and tyranny and judicial pollution are allowed to pass unnoticed, uncensured, unpunished, the last barrier against despotism is broken. "Let me exhort you," says Junius, "never to suffer an invasion of your political constitution, however minute the instance may appear, to pass by without a determined, persevering resistance. One precedent creates another. They soon accumulate and constitute law. What yesterday was fact, today is doctrine. Examples are supposed to justify the most dangerous measures; and where they do not suit exactly, the defect is supplied by analogy. Be assured that the laws which protect us in our civil rights grow out of the constitution and that they must fall or flourish by it."

Perhaps the statements of a single humble individual could effect but little towards the awakening of public opinion against the violence, lawlessness and corruption of the Government; but it might indirectly have some influence on the times. At any rate I hold it to be the duty of every citizen to denounce oppression so far as in his power lies. For unless the people come to their senses, the days of the Republic are few, or there is no truth in the teachings of history.

To be sure I shall, if released, endeavor to avoid prejudicing the cases of those whom I may leave in prison; and on the contrary I expect to go to Washington to intercede for several poor fellows who have no one to speak a good word in their behalf. But afterwards I hope to devote my life to the object of clearing up this Ku Klux Persecution and the restoration of genuine freedom in the South.

However 'tis hardly worth while to speculate about getting out *this* year.

February 10th. Father informs me that Mr. Harper has offered to send McCleary to West Point; but that he shall wait until he obtains a catalogue, etc., which means that he will not let him go! What infatuation! Nothing, no pursuit nor profession in the U. S. is so honorable and suitable for a young man of good birth,

but small fortune, and smaller abilities, than a lieuten-
ancy in the Regular Army. And this is now offered to
McCleary; offered and virtually rejected! It is too bad!
The boy is growing up in ignorance, and with tastes and
manners unfitting him for intelligent society; so much
so indeed, that I saw no way by which he could be ex-
tricated until this offer. But "Mammey's" apron strings
are too strong. I wash my hands of the whole business,
now and hereafter, although I have just written a note
to father begging him to do something at once. Respecting my own situation, he says, "Your letter assures me
we see alike in matters touching your release. Hon.
A. H. Stephens, Judge Fowle, Messrs Strong and
Fuller, with Gov. Vance and Gov. Graham are the persons who will be employed in your behalf, not forgetting
Genls. Ransom and Hunton and Hon. Mr. Harper.
I shall plan it so as to have them move simultaneously
with myself unless they on consultation advise otherwise," etc., etc.

I confess I shall be glad to learn when this skilful plan
shall be sufficiently matured for the "Grand Movement"
to begin. There is something ludicrous in the very idea of
the thing; as if these men would be at any trouble to
consult how to get me out of prison! Why not one of
them would dare to express even a common interest in
me lest he should be accused of friendly relations with
the bloody Ku Klux. I know them better than father;
and I regret to know that he is destined to disappointment in his sanguine expectation of active aid from
them. He may get an answer to his letters, and a promise to do something "When the proper time comes";
but that time unfortunately will not be due until the 22
of September 1876! Meanwhile I should prefer to get
my liberty.

Eo die—Genl. P. Sent for me to come to his drawing
room and gave me his private accounts to revise, as
there has been a rise in stocks. He was very kind and
affable; and spoke flatteringly of father's photograph,
which I rec'd in my last letter.

It is amusing to witness the change in deportment towards me which he manifests in public after a private

interview. In his parlor he receives me courteously, giving me his hand, and having me sit with him on the sofa, etc., etc.; but when about to return to my den, he says, "Watchman, pass this man in!" as if I were an ordinary convict. The former courtesy is no more than any gentleman would do; but the latter shows how strict a disciplinarian he is. Fortunately I am not obliged to feel honored in the one instance, nor dishonored in the other; although, naturally, I am gratified to have the friendship of a man of his character, especially as I am aware he must have been highly prejudiced against me at the start.

Apropos of matters of this sort I must mention something that has more than once given me a good deal of heart burn in the habits of another branch of the "powers that be."

Deputy not unfrequently comes in and takes up any letter I am writing or any book I am reading and always my journal and coolly reads it without the least respect to my feelings. Of course the officers are permitted to examine everything belonging to a prisoner, and it is to be expected that they will so do; but Capt. Pilsbury and the superintendent are more careful not to wound needlessly the feelings of a gentleman. He even passes my letters unopened. [*Passage marked out*] journal is being "viewed with a critic's eye." I mention this, however, more as a specimen of the petty annoyances that befall a penitentiary prisoner than for any other reason. I presume there is no intention to humiliate me.

Feb. 12th. The influx of *detern's* is greater than ever before. Nineteen new arrivals today, coming from all parts of the country. The establishment is now nearly full and many of the lower cells have had double bunks fitted in them, giving me good reason to rejoice that I vacated mine before I was obliged to take a companion. I can hardly conceive of a more disagreeable situation than being shut up in a stone "pigeon-hole," in company with a stranger, perhaps from Five Points, whose temperament, tastes, manners, and position could not have anything in common with mine. Such a position would of itself double the hardships of confinement. And even with a warm personal friend it would be difficult to get on without annoyance, in quarters so constrained.

Feb. 15th, 1873.   Yesterday afternoon the order for release or pardon of the four Sherer Bros. reached here and today they go home. They are poor ignorant youths and so far as I can learn were unjustly sentenced; although that is not to be wondered at since they were tried before a jury composed of *eleven negroes* and one white man of the most worthless character. They were sent here for 18 months, leaving an aged father and mother without means of subsistence. The mother has died since they came here I am told.

Their pardon is the result of their obsequiousness to Whitley. Yet I am glad they are at liberty. By returning home they will keep alive the public interest in others confined here.

Another of the Ku Klux was "released" this morning; but by an higher power than U. S. Grant. J. D. Young died at 3½ A. M. Yesterday he appeared to be improving, and at nightfall he talked quite freely about his home affairs, having just rec'd a letter from his wife and little daughter, giving him the most affectionate assurances of their love and sympathy. But about 3 o'clock this morning the man who was watching with the sick, came to tell me that Young desired to speak to me. I hastened down; but could not understand his last words. Presently with a long sigh he yielded life and was at rest. We stretched him on a sheet on the floor; and this morning a rough box was brought up, the corpse placed in it, and four stout convicts, taking hold of it, carried him away to a felon's grave.

Who can picture the outrage that has been committed on this poor man! For days he has foreseen death, yet he never failed to declare to me that he was wrongfully sentenced.   I know not the particulars of his case farther than I have given them on a previous page, but it is safe to conclude that his degree of guilt had nothing to do with his sentence.   Dick Busteed and a packed jury would be capable of passing sentence on an angel if they could make any money and political capital out of the affair. This man (Young) I consider has been *judicially murdered;* because the sending of him in mid winter from Southern Alabama to Northern New York is the direct cause of his death. Alas! How sudden, how dreadful the shock to his loving family, who were in high hopes of seeing him home in a few days.

Today I have been sick and uncomfortable as can be I think;—doubtless the effect of cold, loss of sleep, and billiousness. "'Tis an hard place" (as Genl. P. says) *to be sick in.*

February 16th. Tonight I am watching with old man Stampers, who after a sharp tussle with Death, seems to have gotten a temporary reprieve. It is hard to see a grey haired man dying in a Penitentiary afar from his friends and family; but in his case, 'tis only just since by his own admission he has been counterfeiting for 16 years or so, among the mountains of Ashe county, N. C.

"Half past ten o'clock! Half past ten, and all's well!" In the room with me are more than a dozen stout sleepers, who are performing such a nasal concert "as never vos." What strange ideas must be coursing through their variegated noddles as they wander in dreamland. Were I asleep, I imagine my thoughts would be "way down South in Dixie." Nobody is a prisoner while asleep. Curious!

> "In slumber, I prithee, how is it
> That souls are off taking the air
> And paying each other a visit
> While bodies are—Heaven knows where?"

February 17th. Winter and Spring are quarreling over the condition of the country, or rather the possession of it. Last night Winter spread his mantle of snow, six inches deep; but today Spring is at work melting it away, unlocking the frozen streams, inviting a-broad the feathered songsters, and preparing to scatter her flowers and fragrance. She is too fast I fear; for I recollect with horror the exploits of the Icy Monarch last March, when he sent the mercury wheezing down to 22 degrees below zero! Still we have our windows up, and are glad to get a breath of unfrozen air.

This morning I sent a note to the family of old man Young, giving particulars of his last moments, thinking they would be somewhat comforted by knowing he had proper attention, and by a Southern man, in his dying hour.

I believe I have mentioned that I am teaching old man Scruggs to read and write. 'Tis slow work, but he is now able to decypher his own home letters by conning them over studiously. So he will go back, if he still lives, wiser than he came; although that can be but a small recompense for his imprisonment.

This morning Hays Mitchell, Stewart, and Lowry, three K. K's from York Dist., were released on pardon papers. They are ignorant and low bred men; and doubtless their being pardoned is due to that fact; although it is a mistake to say that men of that class are entitled to particular consideration because they *are* ignorant, and liable to be misled by more intelligent persons. The truth is that all the "outrages" for which there is any foundation were committed by just such fellows in defiance of warnings, commands, and entreaties of influential members of the community. I know in my own case that two or three of the principal witnesses of Government were the most active and uncontrollable of raiders. These men (of course I am not now referring to the three mentioned above who are personally strangers to me) having gotten into the Klan, too often assumed disguises and harassed persons against whom they had a private enmity. Their conduct annoyed us all, and brought odium on the Klan. Therefore when the Government assumes that these poor and illiterate fellows are deserving of clemency because they are dupes of the designing etc., it does violence to the truth as usual. Still, I am truly glad to hear that Mitchell and the others are free and I would that all were.

February 22nd. Heavy fall of snow. Seeing the long lines of convicts coming from the Workshops through the fleecy showers, called to mind the familiar scene of a regiment under march in a snow storm, or the more familiar picture of "Washington Crossing the Delaware."

And by the way, this is Washington's Birthday—a day that would be more honored if the true spirit of liberty dwelt in the land. I am not among those who eulogise Washington as the "Father" or even the "Deliverer" of his country although no one can read Mr. Jefries "life" of him without feeling satisfied that he was the principal figure of his times in this country. Be that as it may it is impossible not to admire his high toned character and disinterested patriotism; and these qualities are growing so rare that we can well afford to set apart one day in the year to commemorate so illustrious an example.

February 23rd. A furious wind last night piled the snow of yesterday into immense hillocks and longitudinal drifts that almost change the features of the landscape. The view from my window takes in a quarter of the arc of the horizon, and is rather fine for a prison out-look;—embracing an undulating tract of country, dotted with suburban cottages, and showing here and there a grove, a red barn, a rolling meadow, or the unbroken line of a railroad; while afar in the distance arises the blue range of the Catskills, as a background.

It may be imagined how I enjoy this prospect, when I state that all last year when I was in the cell my only view was a whitewashed wall, at about twelve feet from my nose.

Besides the very circumstance that one looks from behind the bars is apt to give a fictitious beauty to the tamest scenery. I recollect that when in Fort Delaware we could by looking through an air hole, see certain grassy meadows and woodlands over in Delaware, and all felt an indescribable longing to be out tumbling "in clover," like the renowned Willyum Weaver, "who when he died, he died all over."

Razor. This morning Deputy asked why I was not shaved. I told him that I was expecting friends and supposed it would do to shave on Sunday in time for church. He said with a frown "No it wont do at all. The barbers ought not to have let you have the razor."

etc. I can hardly say how much I was surprised and humiliated by this rude and undeserved rebuke. The words give no idea of the insolence of his look and tone. I did not get over it all day.

Of course I know that rigid and impartial discipline is indispensable in a Penitentiary and I am satisfied that the system enforced here is as lenient as the design of the Institution will admit. But for all that it is hard to forget that I am a gentleman, the son of a gentleman, and not rightfully held here; and that I have been uniformly careful to obey the rules. It may seem strange that after all I have undergone, I should retain the least sensibility on such subjects. I have received ill treatment and insult sufficient to make me as thick skinned as an rhinoceros: and some time ago, when I had no prospect of getting out, I was almost invulnerable to petty mortifications and rebuffs. But now they wound me to the quick. Philosophy and Patience may carry a man through many grievous troubles; but they are not much consolation during a spasm of toothache, or when set upon by Muschetoo.

February 24th. Excessively cold. Tumbler of water was frozen solid at side of my bed during night although fires were in both stoves, and 13 men sleeping in the room. What must have been the degree of cold outside.

Capt. P. sent for me this morning to inquire about a pardon he had just received, issued to Barton Biggerstaff of Rutherford County, N. C. Here is another specimen of red tape bungling! Barton Biggerstaff has been in Rutherford jail for 15 months or more; and if there is any truth in evidence, ought never to have been sentenced at all. I recollect his case perfectly well, because there was an amusing circumstance connected with it. He was charged with having participated in the whipping of that detestable old vagabond "Pukey" Biggerstaff, his uncle, I believe. Barton offered an *alibi* and proved it by the oath of his sweetheart and that of her parents. The amiable girl, who very likely had never been more than 10 miles from home in her life, went to Raleigh, 300 miles, and on the witness stand testified that she and her lover were "sitting up" on the night of the "raid" and were together when they heard pistol shots and outcry at "Pukey's" house. The counsel for the prosecution, seeing that she was a timid, country girl, tried to embarrass her by insinuations that it was strange she and her beau should be up at so late an hour, but *perhaps they might not have been "up."* "We were sitting by the fire—and—and—courtin'," said she modestly and so straight-forward was her testimony that no unprejudiced man in the room doubted that she told the truth and that Barton Biggerstaff was not on the "Raid," especially as the evidence of the parents strictly corroborated hers. But "proof strong as Holy Writ" could avail nothing against the bent purpose of Jeffreys Bond and his packed jury. Barton was sentenced to two years confinement (if I recollect aright) and $100 fine!

And now after holding him almost his full term, and having accomplished their political ends, the vile wretches agree to set him at liberty. Jim Justice and "old Pukey" Biggerstaff, themselves recommended the pardon (*justice!* I say) the latter by signing his X mark, for he is too ignorant to sign his own name! I presume young B. has humbled himself and begged pardon of the Mongrels; for only those who will abase themselves in this manner have yet been released. But the Administration, or its agents, after signing the pardon, take good care that it shall not be of much benefit to him by sending it off to Albany, which will delay its arrival at its destination, three weeks or a month.

Chaplain R. compliments me on the improvement in order etc., in the Hospital, especially with respect to the suppression of profanity, vulgarity, and obscenity among the convalescents. I have stopped everything of the kind, and while treating all the inmates, sick or well, with gentleness and courtesy, never permit the slightest infringement of the rules, or any noise, or rowdyism. I have not much difficulty in accomplishing this, as I have never allowed any of the convicts to become familiar with me, although all appear very friendly.

Today I have been busy writing up some books—Inventory of the Prison Furniture—for Capt. P. No one, who has no experience in supplying a thousand men with daily rations, etc., would imagine the trouble and outlay of an Institution of this kind. For instance, more than 500 lbs. of fish and a barrel or two of potatoes, and 200 loaves of bread, all go into the pans for a single Saturday's dinner. About 100 gallons of coffee are consumed every day, etc., etc. But the profits of convict labor are large. I am gratified to learn that Capt. Pilsbury has been elected Superintendent, *vice* his father who recently resigned, feeling himself unable to fulfil the duties of the position any longer, as his health confines him almost constantly to his room and his bed. The change has been expected for some months past; but I feared the General might suddenly die, leaving the question doubtful whether his son would succeed him; because at the late election the county was carried by the Republicans, who it was presumed would wish to give some of their own partisans the advantage of the position.

I am told, however, that the election passed off happily and that the Radicals were as prompt as the Democrats, in casting their votes for Captain P. So this settles the matter, and sets me at ease on the subject; for I am sure I shall have fair treatment from him, however long I may be here. And the Trustees of the Institution show uncommon wisdom in resolving that it shall not be made a mere political machine like almost every other public institution in the State. None of the State Penitentiaries pay expenses (I learn) and for the simple reason that the Superintendency has changed with every fluctuation of politics, each temporary incumbent considers himself entitled to "make hay while the sun shines;" to say nothing of the irregularity of system arising from frequent changes—and the outlay resulting therefrom.

Besides these political establishments usually have a number of expensive but *sinecure* offices, created to give place to needy partizans.

Albany Penitentiary, on the contrary, has been for

nearly 30 years in the control of a single mind, who has been fortunate in having little opposition to his plans and arrangements; so that the Institution now moves like clock work. Doubtless it will continue to flourish under the management of Capt. P. who proposes, I believe, to introduce several improvements suggested by his father's observations of the Prisons in Europe.

Both father and son have been so long connected with this institution, that they almost look upon it as family property. Capt. P. was born in State's Prison; and during the 40 years of his life, has been, with brief interruptions employed in various capacities about one. Such experience added to a naturally humane and obliging disposition, peculiarly fit him for the position he now holds. He is married to an agreeable and intelligent lady, and has a son and daughter, both young. His brother acts as an officer of the Prison. To me Capt. P. has been uniformly accommodating and affable; and I consider myself fortunate (since my enemies must send me to a Penitentiary) in being sent here.

"Love laughs at Locksmiths!" and the French aphorism, *"Love and Smoke cannot be hid"* are verified by a little *affaire du coeur* between a couple of convicts—a *she* and a *he*—in this prison. I must premise that all the prisoner's letters are given to me to envelope, and direct, which gives me an opportunity to peruse any of them likely to be of interest.

In the instance alluded to, the sighing lover is in the male department making shoes, while his "ducky dear" enjoys similar retirement among the shirt makers, and chair bottomers, of the Female Department. His name is Smittin, Eugene Smittin; and Eugene is certainly "smitten." Her name is Howe, Martha Howe; and Martha, I daresay, knows how. That the lovers are in sentimental earnest I cannot have a doubt after reading their recent exchanges.

It might be supposed that when a pair of sweethearts had by different roads, and for separate offences, found their way to the seclusion of a Penitentiary, they must find it difficult to keep alive the torch of affection. The gay Lothario must confess 'tis a platonic piece of business to make love, while shivering in the narrow limits of a stone cage, to a questionable maid, in a similar predicament in another wing of the Prison.

But Pyramus and Thisbe osculated (that's a modest word for kissing, ladies) each other through a thick (was it brick?) wall; and as Shakespeare goes on to tell us,

> "Nor strong tower; nor walls of beaten brass
> Nor airless dungeon; nor strong links of iron
> Can be retentive to the strength of spirit"—

Which means, I suppose, pretty much what the Hard Shell preacher (or maybe it was only a deacon) said when he told the young folks all to " 'shake down' among the straw, for there was only one bed, and what is to be will be, anyhow."

At all events the romantic Eugene and his bewitching Martha are resolved that not even the trifling embarrassments of some half dozen walls to say nothing of bolts, bars, chains, dungeons and the like, shall interrupt the course of their true love. For some weeks they have been launching tender missives *"per post office"* in genuine lover-like fashion. The following poetical effusion winged Eugene's latest dart to the soft palpitator of his charmer. *sic*—

1. "I think of Thee
  When day by day
  With downcast mind
  I work my way."

2. "I think of Thee
  When shadows be
  Filling my cell with gloom
  And I suffer sore
  To my heart's core
  With thoughts of Thee and Home.

3. "Oh! Think of me
  Till our union be
  On a better, brighter star,
  When we have liberty—
  Be it near or far."

There is a fourth verse, but *quantum suff*. I am pained (but an historian should be truthful, give the truth, the whole truth, etc.) to add that the amourous swain attaches as a postscript, the remark, "and yet dear Martha, *with all thy faults, I love Thee still!*" Had she responded that the "Pot need not call the kettle black," I should have entered no complaint, nor could her Eugene. But she overlooks—as many better women do—all but the fact that she is loved; and consoles her lover with the following *"original" stanzas:*

"To my dear Eugene—

1.   Our love has been no tender flower
     For joys bright chaplet braided
     Drooping when tempests darkly lower
     By Grief's bleak winter faded.

2.   We have not loved as those who plight
     Their troth in sunny weather
     While leaves are green and skies are bright
     To tread life's path together.

3.   But we have loved as those who tread
     The thorny path of sorrow
     With clouds o'er cast and cause to dread
     Yet deeper gloom tomorrow.

4.   That thorny path—those cloudy skies
     Have drawn our spirits nearer
     And rendered us by holiest ties
     Each to the other dearer.

                    Yours with love, Martha Howe."

Now if the sentimental Eugene don't hammer his shoe pegs like a man after receiving this appreciative missive, his soul must be as tough as the dry soles at which he cobbles. I shall only add that the foregoing is *bona fide* correspondence.

February 26th, 1873. This morning "Squire" Brown of York Dist., S. C., who is permitted to sleep in the hospital, although not relieved from labor, was called out, and measured by the tailor for a new suit of clothes; a very plain indication that the authorities of the Prison are satisfied he will not be released during the present year. They take this impression from an announcement in the Washington *Chronicle* as follows: "The Attorney General declines to issue a pardon to Saml. G. Brown who is in the Penitentiary, under 5 years sentence as a Ku Klux, because he moved in good society, was in fact a leader, well posted, and of good education." Now this statement, so far as relates to 'Squire Brown's being a leader, well posted, etc., and consequently, *guilty,* is utterly void of truth, as most Radical statements are.

As I have never before given a direct account of the old man's misfortunes I will now do so; having been with him in the same room for nearly an half year, during which time I had every opportunity for gleaning the truth about him, from his own conduct and assertions, from the letters of his numerous friends, and from the corroberating statements of other Ku Klux.

Mr. Brown was arrested at his home, nine miles west of Yorkville, S. C., on the 19th day of October, 1871, by a detachment of Federal Cavalry assisted by a number of negroes. He was carried to an adjoining plantation, where he was kept under guard in a stable yard during the whole day, while the soldiers were scouring the vicinity for his neighbors, six of whom were, also, arrested at that time. Having been carried to Yorkville, he was locked up in the county jail, which was already packed to overflowing with respectable citizens. A few days later there were no less than one hundred and eighty-four grown men confined in four small rooms!

The jailer, however, unlike the Mongrel Keepers in Rutherford, did all that he could to alleviate the sufferings of his prisoners, and the ladies of the village kept them supplied with the delicacies of the season. Bail to any amount could have been given, but was not allowed.

On the 15th of December, Mr. Brown was taken to Columbia, where he gave bond of $5000 to appear at court, and to remain in the city meanwhile. Subsequently the court met, Judge Bond presiding. The jury consisted of *eleven negroes* and one disreputable white man, a grog shop keeper!

Of course the negroes considered every Ku Klux a personal enemy; and the white man being perhaps less reliable than his colleagues, there could be no sort of doubt about the issue of any trial in which the defendant was obnoxious to the Radical prosecutors, and the Government officials. . . .

But there was little need for even a corrupted jury in these Ku Klux cases; because there were hundreds of perjured wretches ready to swear so unblushingly and circumstantially against any of the defendants that the most virtuous jury could not avoid finding them guilty if they did not altogether reject the testimony as unworthy of credit. "Worthless judges invariably create a breed of informers around them," says Macaulay.

As the trials proceeded several of the Government witnesses took occasion to implicate Mr. Brown by so-called "confessions" charging him with being at certain meetings of the Order, and with casual remarks about his having a Klan,—all of which was irregular, and injurious to Mr. B., for he was not yet on trial.

Now the truth of the matter is that the old man was not even a member of the order but both of his sons were, the youngest being Chief of a Klan. But Mr. B. had attended one meeting of his son's Klan, his object in doing so, being to use his influence to prevent severe treatment of a young man, who in a drunken frolic had revealed secrets of the Order, an offence punishable with death. Besides he wished to persuade his son to resign the chieftainship of the Klan for the laxity that now prevailed in the Order made its speedy dissolution desirable. He therefore attended the meeting and accomplished both objects—the resignation of his son, and the safety of the young "babbler."

The Government, however, wanted victims; and no one doubted that Brown would be convicted. His lawyers considering his case hopeless urged him to submit his defence, i. e., *plead guilty* and throw himself on the clemency of the court. For Judge Bond had caused it to be generally understood that all who should confess should be let off with merely nominal sentences while those who should demand trial, should be given the full extent of the law if they failed to clear themselves. Major Merrill the military commandant at Yorkville, went further and declared that if Brown submitted he should be at home in a few weeks.   Such a pressure was hard to resist; and finally Brown yielded, and his lawyers plead guilty.   This was precisely as the villains had designed; for they knew the evidence was utterly unworthy of belief; but by getting the old man to submit his case, they had him fast, and stopped his complaints of unfairness at the same time.   Then Jeffreys Bond put the climax to this infamous business by sentencing him to serve five years at hard labor in Albany Penitentiary and to pay a fine of one thousand dollars! In the depth of midwinter he was brought, and sent to the workshops like a common felon, as indeed was done with every one of us!

Since that time he has grown older, greyer, and unnaturally broken; although he is still quite lively, and generally as cheerful as could be expected; considering that he is now above sixty years of age, that he leaves a wife and three daughters without a male protector, that his sons are in exile, from which they cannot hope to return in years, and that he has very little hope of seeing his family in several years, if ever.

That he has been greatly wronged and injured, no candid person can doubt; and that this very fact (as in my own case) embitters the administration against him is equally true.   He has been, however, much comforted (as I never was) by the constant sympathy of his numerous friends, who write to him so frequently that he rarely receives less than three letters per week.   No one who has never suffered an unjust imprisonment, can know how much the time, toil, and privations are lengthened by the receipt of frequent letters from loved ones at home.

The following interesting extract from a Southern paper I copy as a tribute to my friend.

THE CASE OF SAMUEL G. BROWN

The New York *World* contains a communication from Mrs. Westmoreland of Atlanta, Georgia, narrating her efforts to secure Executive clemency in behalf of Samuel G. Brown, of York County, in this State, one of the Ku Klux prisoners now confined in the Albany penitentiary. At the instance of the Rev. David Wills, President of Oglethorpe University, who knew Mr. Brown and regarded him as an honest, upright, law-abiding man, Mrs. Westmoreland determined to address Mrs. Governor Hoffman in Mr. Brown's behalf. The correspondence and the result will be found in the extract we give:

Atlanta, Ga., February, 14, 1872.

Dear Mrs. Hoffman: Although a stranger, you will pardon the liberty I take in thus addressing you when my mission is made known, for I appeal to you in the name of humanity—yea, more, I come to beg you, as a Christian woman, and by those sympathetic and softer feelings which God has implanted in your woman's nature, to befriend the friendless and to console the afflicted. There lies in the State Prison at Albany an old man by the name of Samuel G. Brown, who is sixty-five years of age, almost blind and broken in health. He is from Yorkville, York District, South Carolina, and is a victim of Judge Bond, of Ku Klux notoriety, who was sent to Carolina by Grant, for the purpose, it would seem, of prosecuting the innocent and protecting the infamous. This old man was dragged from his home, brought to Columbia, where Bond's Court sits, and thrown into prison. He was then taken through the mockery of a trial, and notwithstanding he filed an affidavit proving that so far from acting with the so-called Ku Klux he had gone at midnight on a recent occasion to prevent the murder of a negro, was sentenced to five years' hard labor in the State Prison of New York, and required to pay a fine of $1,000. As he had no money to satisfy this atrocious demand the modern Jeffreys has ordered his plantation to be levied upon and sold, and at its sale the poor man's family will be turned adrift upon the world homeless, fatherless, and in poverty. Knowing your husband to be the champion of constitutional liberty, the embodiment of those qualities which make a true man truly great and noble, and believing that you must imbibe his sentiments, I hope I shall not appeal in vain. Now, if the authorities will permit, will you not visit this old man in his loneliness and try to brighten his prison's cell by ministering to his wants. If you have any scruples about his being a Southerner, let me tell you that I fed and cared for many a Union soldier during the war, and that my husband, who was a surgeon, gave the same attention to Union prisoners that he did to our own brave boys—believing that common humanity demanded such a course, and with the hope that our conduct might find its duplicate in some kind but Northern breast. Rev. Dr. Wills, a Presbyterian divine, who has begged me to intercede in behalf of this old man, has known him for years. He says he is an honest, upright man, whose character is above reproach, and that he is innocent of all charges preferred against him. The Carolina people can do nothing for him, for the heel of the tyrant grinds them to the earth, and the same Government which hung a dead woman, and which overrides Congress and the Constitution, plunges old men into penitentiaries in a distant State, and exiles those who would dare intercede for them. Thus it is reserved for a Georgian woman to aid a sister State and to raise her voice against the atrocities, which are daily enacted in her beloved, heart-bleeding, and prostrate South. If the old man needs clothing or comforts, I will at once make up a purse and send it on to supply his wants. Hoping I have asked nothing at your hands which you will find it impossible to grant, and begging you to communicate with me at your earliest convenience, believe me to be, respectfully yours, etc.

Maria Jourdan Westmoreland.

To this letter came the following reply:

Executive Residence,
Albany, N. Y., February 25, 1872.

Dear Mrs. Westmoreland:

I received your letter several days ago, and it has given me great pleasure to assist in any way and relieve the suffering of the innocent. The Governor and myself visited Mr. Brown this morning and had a long and interesting conversation with him. He stated the facts of his imprisonment with great exactness, and I am confident with truth. He says he is not in want of anything; but I am certain if his friends should send him a box of clothing or any comfort, it would be very acceptable. He is troubled with rheumatism, and Mr. Pillsbury, of the prison, said he would see that he had some flannels and other articles, which I told him I would pay for. Mr. Pillsbury says if his friends decide to send him a box he will deliver the contents to Mr. Brown. The Governor is much interested in the case, and has written the President for a pardon, but we said nothing to Mr. Brown on the subject, as it would be cruel to give hope when our efforts may be in vain. If you send any comforts to the old man the box can be expressed to our care, and I will see that Mr. Brown receives it, or to Mr. Pillsbury, the Superintendent of the Penitentiary. Hoping to receive news from the President that will gladden the hearts of wife and children, as well as those who have taken such an interest in the old man's troubles, I remain, yours sincerely,

Mrs. John T. Hoffman.

Many other and more interesting circumstances might be mentioned in connection with this brief history of Mr. Brown's case; but I say no more at present; merely quoting the words of Judge Strong respecting that description of evidence by which all the Ku Klux have been convicted.

"It has been well remarked that 'confessions' are the weakest and most suspicious of all testimony: ever liable to be obtained by *artifice, false hopes, promises of favor,* or *menaces;* seldom remembered accurately or reported with due precision and *incapable in their nature of being disproved* by other negative evidence. To which it may be added that they are easy to be forged and most difficult to guard against."

February 27th, 1873. Snowing. Busy all this day printing (stencilling) copies of hymns for the Chaplain to hang in the Chapel,—that all may see, and sing. The letters are about two inches in length or height; and an ordinary hymn fills a chart of 4x6 feet, in breadth and length, respectively. These charts are plainly readable from any part of the Chapel. The job of printing them is quite tedious and fatiguing, as the operator must bend over his work, and be careful to get the letters in a straight line. I can only finish one hymn of five verses per day. Tonight I wish the hymns were at the devil! (printer's devil of course).

February 28th. Chas. N. Howard and Jas. Blanks of Ala., who came here in July under sentence for 5 years, were released today on pardon papers. I know nothing about their cases except that they plead not guilty and entered a protest against sentence being passed on them. A local paper, also, pronounced them "the victims of Dick Busteed's venom and trickery." How sad to hear these frequent, nay constant, complaints of the Judiciary, which ought to be but is not the real palladium of personal liberty in the land. Is it any wonder there are disorders, and Societies of Regulators (for such, and no more, were the various societies known as Ku Klux) to suppress disorder, in a country where the laws are a dead letter, and the officers of the law mere agents of the government to control elections and establish a base political despotism? Sir James Mackintosh, whose opinion no one will discredit says: "It can hardly be doubted that the highest obligation of a citizen is that of contributing to preserve the community; and that every other political duty—even that of obedience to magistrates, is derived from, and must be subordinate to, it." A sentiment which is more tersely stated in an official letter of Hon. Amos Kendall, Post Master General of the United States in 1835, viz: "We owe an obligation to the laws, but an higher one to the communities in which we live, and if the former be perverted to destroy the latter, it is patriotism to disregard them." "True Oh King!" most true! And here is what is said of *unjust legislation,* by the distinguished Horace Mann (see his Report to Massts. Legislature).

"Unjust laws never stop with merely extinguishing an individual right, or inflicting an individual wrong. They fashion and adapt the general mind to injustice. They bind the foreign substance of error to the heart until the fibres close around it, and it becomes irradicable forever. Erroneous principles in legislation commend the injustice they ordain; they impress the form of right upon the substance of wrong, and they withhold from truth its highest advantage,—the privilege of being seen."

*   *   *   *   *   *

March 1st. "Ah! What have we here?" Said I to myself, says I, when the Deputy sent for me to carry a stout box up to my den, this afternoon. And then I saw some pecans, and the secret was out. It was another Christmas box from one of the best of our Southern girls. One who has done as much as a sister could do to make me comfortable and cheerful since I fell into the hands of the Philistines. May her kindness to the unhappy prisoner be repaid an hundredfold, by those who have it in their power, (if any there be) to add to her present happiness and content! As for me, I can only return my thanks, which is hardly an equivalent to the rich feast of cakes, candies, jellies, peaches, pickles, and other delicacies which fill the box. But I well know I have no grasping creditor; for she is better pleased to give than to receive. To Mrs. N. Y., also, I owe more than I can pay, for attentions of this sort;

which are the more acceptable because they show that though long absent I am not forgotten, nor bereft of the respect and sympathy of that class of our people whose good opinion I most desire to have.

M. M. F. says "I have not written to you since Oct. as it seems utterly useless. You can't imagine how much distressed I was to hear you do not receive my letters, and I think too, I often censured with others for forgetfulness, etc."

Certainly it is a shame that the few letters written to, and by me should be intercepted by a set of vagabonds with unblushing impunity! But it seems impossible to devise any remedy.

When a government coolly undertakes to destroy the liberties or curtail the privilege of any portion of its constituents, the first step is to establish a thorough system of espionage; and from that hour the mails no longer afford any security for private correspondence. I need not add that this being the case at the present time I have no other resource than to accustom myself to silence and apparent neglect trusting that at some future day I shall discover I have more friends than I was aware of.

March 2nd. Genl. L., ever prompt to acquaint me of anything promising release, sends me a letter he had just received from Senator M. W. Ransom who writes from Washington (under date of   ) as follows:

"I am doing all that I can for Shotwell, and will eventually have him released. But it takes *time.*"

To which Genl. L. adds "Ransom is not a man to throw away his words and as you see, he speaks confidently. I don't know to what period the 'time' required may extend, not very remote let us trust. I suppose there are many people to be approached; and some tedious formalities to rencontre. However, I really feel that I can venture the opinion that your bondage approaches its close. Therefore courage *mon ami!* and we shall soon have the great happiness of taking you by the hand," etc.

I can hardly feel any participation in these hopes, although it gives me much pleasure and comfort to know I have a few friends yet.

I answer the Genls. letter as follows:

March 2nd. Thro' courtesy of Capt. P. (our Supt.) I have special permission to write semi-monthly and accordingly am enabled promptly to acknowledge your esteemed favor of 19th inst. to-day recd. as well as those of earlier date. I assure you dear Genl. it gives me great satisfaction to have so true and earnest friend in this hour of mine extremity and I trust I shall never be ungrateful for your disinterested exertions to enlist other influential persons in my behalf. Were the circumstances other than they are, i. e., were the application to be made for anyone but myself, the result I am sure, would be immediately successful. But as things stand, I'm not sanguine, nay I can scarcely aspire to any hope whatever. The same malice and personal and political animosity which actuated the men who thought to ruin me by sending me here still exists to oppose my release, as I have good reason to know. Indeed, should all the distinguished and honorable men of our country unite in an appeal in my favor I doubt if anything would be accomplished against the private remonstrance of a few such mongrels as Caldwell, Carrow, Logan, Justice *et als.*

Besides I have long remarked the administration designs to keep foul hold of every one of us capable of giving the least publicity to the wrongs we have experienced. None but the most ignorant and insignificant are to escape the iron grasp for a long time yet. The question is not whether the prisoner is guilty, but whether he has any influence to exert against the Radical party, or brains enough to expose the injustice of trying a man before a packed jury and a corrupt and partizan Judge. Thus even Mercy, the purest of virtues, is made subservient to base political expediency. Of course it is assumed that the more intelligent the prisoner the greater his guilt, and that the poor ignorant fellows were all dupes of the designing. But this is a false assumption in many cases, in my own particularly. The truth is that every one of those outrages which have cast oppobrium on the Klan was committed by a lot of reckless and insubordinate fellows who could be neither counselled nor controlled; and who, instead of being the dupes of the better informed were a pest and a source of mortification to all right minded members of the Order. And I regret to add that the most desperate and intractable characters among them usually escaped by turning State's evidence.

In confirmation of the foregoing view of the Administration policy I have just seen the following extract from the Washington *Chronicle,* "The Attorney General declines to issue a pardon for S. G. Brown because he moved in good society, was in fact a leader, well posted and of good education." Now there is not a word of truth in this; for B. is a poor old man, past 60, of small property, and only common education; in short, merely an average "small farmer" of upper S. C. and was never in any way connected with the Klan I am satisfied. But as he is about the most respectable of the prisoners from his State, the government intends to hold him until he dies, or turns Republican, or until he will be glad to sneak home and bury his wrongs in silence and obscurity. I mention his case simply to show the barrenness of my own prospects. The same causes will work the same effect to defeat the efforts of my friends in my own case.

However if I could allow myself to hope, I know not any more desirable persons to have the conduct of my affairs than those honorable gentlemen to whom you have written and I beg you to express to them the gratification and gratitude I feel for all that they have done or may attempt. I thought of writing to Messrs R. and H. to give some expression of my sentiments and to mention a circumstance or so that might facilitate but on reflection

I will await your advice about it. I should feel much mortified if the application for pardon, were based on any supposition that I am *humbled* and *repentant* or anything of that sort. I shall remain here to the last minute of my cruel term in preference to confessing that I was justly punished. But I am sure I can trust to your discretion and I only allude to the possibility because I am not personally acquainted with Genl. R. and Mr. H. And I shall never before my dying day forget the humiliation and amazement with which I heard Mr. Fuller, one of my counsel at my trial appealing for "mercy, mercy, mercy," and basing his appeal on the ground that my father, "a poor clergyman with respectable connections," would be much afflicted as he had already been "by the recklessness and indiscretions of his son in these transactions." Conceive the absurdity! Father did not even know that I belonged to the Klan although I presume he expected it and we were of one mind respecting the disorderly element of the Order. But this statement of Mr. F. (prompted I think by a false friend of mine) was a virtual acknowledgement of my guilt and covered me with shame and confusion; besides giving that scoundrel Judge Brooks an opportunity to inveigh in a special tirade against me, as well as to cast reflections on my father. The recollection of that miserable occasion is still an horrible burden on my spirits, etc., etc.

March 4th. Ugh! 'Tis so—so—so cold! Water froze within 12 feet of a large stove last night and that too in a room where there were 14 men sleeping! Who can apologize for such an intolerable climate!

This day on the banks of the Potomac, the most incapable, and undeserving of Chief Magistrates will be confirmed in his *Sinecure* office for another term of four years. Were Grant a man of fine feelings and generous sentiments, we might hope that hence forward he would show some magnanimity towards and consideration for, the down-trodden people of the South. We poor victims of his political policy might, also, hope for a restoration of that precious boon of liberty of which we have been defrauded. It might be expected that now he had secured his re-election, and firmly established his dynasty, he would be more tolerant towards those whose principles taught them to prefer a democratic form of Government.

But from such a man as Grant we can look for nothing. His very election palsied all hope for better things. His stolid soul will accept all the honors that a blind faction can procure for him; and never a thought will he give to the victims sacrificed to obtain for him those honors. Truly he is a President worthy of the fanatics who chose him for their Lord and Master.

March 6th. Bright, clear, and pleasant to *look at* (through a thick pane of glass) is the weather today; although if one should poke his nose into the outer-atmosphere I'm sure 'twould be like running against an iceberg! Down in Dixie, I daresay, the windows are opened—and flowers too—and Spring is fast driving old winter to his Yankee quarters. But up here the old Blow-hard has full sway, and is monarch of all he surveys. I am of opinion that I should refuse the best farm hereabouts, if given on condition that I should farm it all the year round. The climate would put the agriculturist down among his fertilizers in a season or two. No wonder the Yankees are a close-fisted inhospitable race; they are at too much labor and suffering to get their money to permit of their spending it generously.

But this first bright spell of Spring sets me off, wandering beyond prison bounds. My thoughts run strangely to some familiar scenes of youth, and I wonder with Campbell—

Oh when shall I visit the land of my birth—
The loveliest land on the face of the earth—
When shall I, in its scenes of affection explore?
　　Its forests; its fountains,
　　Our hamlets, our mountains,
With the pride of our mountains—the girl I adore?

March 7th. Slept little last night owing to *Les Miserables* whose groaning and yelling was monstrously provoking. One of my patients, a wretched vagrant or "tramp," is afflicted with Bright's disease which has swollen him to the size of an hogshead. His outcries show that his lungs are not affected in the least. Another *miserable* has an abscess in his throat that gives to his breathing a sound resembling a broken wind horse climbing a hill.

It is impossible to feel any interest in, or much sympathy for, these degraded wretches, whose slovenly habits, and utter vulgarity offend every instinct of a well bred person; but I consider it a duty to do all in my power to alleviate their sufferings; and no one, white or black, has ever lacked for careful attention since I took charge of the hospital. Of this I am repeatedly assured by patients themselves; who also tell me that they had far different treatment before I came up. Major Hodge was too indolent or thought himself too good to give any attention to the sick (although placed here for that purpose) and Jones, left to himself had many excuses, and a keen inclination, for the same neglect. Consequently the helpless had to shift as best they could.

For my part I can say without boasting (for 'twas only an act of humanity and duty) that I have fed, lifted, and watched with sick negroes, and still more filthy white men, as carefully as if they were personal friends. And yet I am sent here on the charge of being chief of an organization to murder and exterminate the whole African race in America! Bah!

This day closes with a magnificent sunset. Old Sol, like an immense ball of gold balances on the summit of the blue Catskills, 30 miles distant and every elevated object between is gilded with glory, while the whole Heavens blaze with variegated tints beyond description. And through the open window comes a gentle breeze from the South, the first of the Season I'm sure; and now at last we begin to hope for decent weather. But oh! the longing to be beyond these prison bars! To mingle with the gay, the happy, the fair! To be with the loved ones at home!

Society, Friendship, and love
Divinely bestowed upon man—
Oh had I the wings of a dove
How soon would I taste you again!

March 8th. Have just had instructions to prepare to receive visitors, i. e. to dress up the beds, and all the convalescents to go to their chairs between the beds. They are expected to keep their eyes on the floor or on their books while visitors are present. This is the standing order for state occasions. I wonder if any public institution was ever seen in its every day dress by formal visitors? Invariably the word is passed in front of them, like the signals of the Highland clans, and as they pass from department to department everything that they are permitted to see is ready for inspection.

I do not mean to insinuate, however, that there are here any horrors to hide or any filth to clean up. So far as I have ever seen there has not been a day nor an hour in which a casual visitor would have pronounced the establishment in the least disorder, or unsightly condition; for all such matters are attended to in systematic daily order, without variation of time, weather, or any other circumstances, consequently the appearance of things which each visitor sees is by no means delusive; although as I said, there is invariably a dressing up of all quarters when formal visitors are expected.

P. S. The threatened demonstration failed to take place. "Nobody hurt."

I have been exceedingly provoked all day by the antics of the "Shepherd" (Wilcox), our so-called religious monomaniac. He is a long legged, gaunt, possum-eyed Tennessean, whose sole object in life seems to be to show his own meanness and render uncomfortable everybody around him. This morning he got up cross, and began to make so much noise that I was obliged to take hold of him. He then burst into a terrible passion and became so insulting that I felt like kicking him out of the room. For I am satisfied the fellow is a cheat—a vile hypocrite. Having watched him closely I detected a settled plan to pass for a lunatic, and thus facilitate his obtaining a pardon for which his father is now working at

Washington, through the agency of Brownlow and other notorious scalawags. Wilcox confessed to a chum of his that his father and his lawyers told him how to act. Yet, strange to say, the officers persist in considering him crazy and Capt. P. has written a strong letter recommending his pardon on account of his derangement! The fellow is as sane as any man; but is of a mean, cunning, irritable disposition; and having discovered that he can escape labor, and be as insulting as he wishes under the guise of lunacy, has deliberately chosen that policy, as many other prisoners have done, with less success. He was sentenced for ten years for robbing the mail; but as robbing the mail is a common offense (I beg pardon—'tis an unfortunate eccentricity) among Mongrel postmasters, I suppose he soon will be at liberty, and in office again.

I never see this fellow, in his sanctimonious aspect (i. e. when he is not *mad*) without recalling Whittier's picture of a Puritan (in "Miriam")

> I hear again the snuffled tones
> I see in dreary vision
> Dyspeptic dreamers, spiritual bores
> And prophets, "with a mission."

But Wilcox's case is more aptly described perhaps as follows—

> There are some moody persons, not a few
> Who turned by nature with a gloomy bias
> Renounce *black devils* to adopt the blue
> And think *when they are dismal*—they are pious.

March 9th. Surprised by a couple of letters— A and Aunt's! Both too much like Job's comforters, to be pleasant reading. Addie is arranging to go off on a wild goose chase for fortune in the West, to Texas! What folly! He has neither the education nor the knowledge of the world to give him a chance among Western roughs and having no money but expensive habits, he would soon settle down to the occupation of plow-boy or cow-boy; for I believe the last is the principal opening for penniless youths in Texas.

But I am chiefly saddened by the gradual breaking

up of the family circle. Every day I am more satisfied that a man without a "Home" and family connections is decidedly at a disadvantage in the world. He is the mere drift wood of society. The community regards him as an unsettled man who has little or no interest in local affairs. I recollect that when I was a candidate for the Constitutional Convention, men said, "Why if Shotwell were elected, he would go off to Raleigh, and live there. We should never see him again; for he has no attachments here." This was a mistake; still it illustrates the tendency of people to look at such matters.

Now if Addie goes to Texas, and M. settles in New Jersey, while I am penned in prison, and if father should succumb to his many burdens and trials, our family circle would be utterly broken, and we who have family connections in nearly every state in the Union, would have as little connection with them, as an exiled Arab has with his tribe in the desert. Reflections of this nature cause me a gloomy hour.

Aunt S. intends—tries—to write affectionately; but so deeply prejudiced is she by the Radical lies about the Ku Klux that nothing I could say could change her opinion in my favor on this subject; although she professes the warmest attachment personally. She says, "Your letter was long and interesting and I sent it to Wm. Dwight requesting him to read it. Eliza replied that she had read it and thought it very interesting, but that her husband could *not find time to finish it!*" This means that Dwight, who is editor of the Connecticut *School Journal,* like every other Radical journalist of the North, has abused and misrepresented the South so constantly during the past ten years or longer, that he now accepts every malicious lie against us, as gospel truth, and has educated himself to look for no good thing out of the political Nazareth which he and his colleagues of the New England press, have created (on paper) in the South; hence he had not even patience to read the frank and candid statements contained in my letter to Aunt S. And such is the character and mode of thinking of thousands of Northern men, whose position in society or in politics permits them to shape public opinion; and

thereby to sustain the administration in its most tyrannical usurpations by a show of popular approval. These
manufacturers of false impressions, and pernicious public sentiment are the worst enemies of Liberty in our
Country. The philosophic De Toqueville, [whose] dis-
sertations on American traits are marvelously just, thus
discourses on this very subject.

It is not that I object like other European writers
to the *weakness* of the American government; I
object to its force; not to the extreme of Liberty
that I find there, but that *there is no protection
against tyranny*. Is any one treated with cruelty
and injustice in America, to whom shall he appeal?
To the public opinion? It is that which forms the
majority. To the legislative body? It represents the
majority and obeys it blindly. To the Executive
Power? It is named by the majority and is a passive instrument in its hands. To the public force?
Public force is only the majority under arms. *To
a jury?* It is but the majority clothed with the
power of pronouncing its decrees. The judges themselves in some states elected by the majority; however *unjust or unreasonable your treatment you
have no course but to submit.*

(Again he says) I rest the origin of all power on
the will of the people, and yet I regard as impious
and detestable, the maxim that the majority have
a right to do as they think best. How is this?—do
I not contradict myself? No, for there is a general
law, which has been adopted, not only by a majority
of the people, but by a majority of the human race;
and this law is *the law of justice*. It is *justice,* then,
that forms the right of every people to do what
they choose. . . . When I refuse to obey an unjust
law I appeal from the sovereignty of the people,
to the sovereignty of the human race.

Now I suppose there is not an intelligent man in
America that will dispute the correctness of this position,
since it is the same upon which our forefathers stood at
the Revolution; but while admitting this, they will con-

demn the Southern people for resisting the most unjust legislation known to history!

Eo die. A few hours ago a terrible bellowing was heard in the cells, and just now a man has been fetched into the hospital bleeding like a bull from a severe cut in the forehead. He and his cell-mate having different theories of religion engaged in a controversy, to which the Catholic added a knock-down argument with results as above mentioned. Sunday in prison, like Sunday during the war is commonly distinguished by a battle. The reason is that many of the convicts cannot read or write, and being shut up in their cells all day on the Sabbath, are apt to quarrel, for pastime.

March 10th. Yesterday we had in Chapel instead of a sermon, what is called up here a "Singing (or Praise) service." The hymns I printed recently were hung against the wall in rear of the pulpit; and Mr. Coats, a professional singer, led the music, assisted by the organ. We have these services frequently. It might be supposed that criminals undergoing discipline so strict as is enforced here, would not have much music in their souls, if they had ever known how to sing. But the fact is, as the Chaplain remarks, and my own ears confirm, that the singing in this Penitentiary Chapel is more general, more spirited and almost more correct, than that of many city congregations. These 700 reprobates sing with a will and most of them seem familiar with these hymns—especially all the old Methodist tunes, "Jesus Lover of My Soul," "Rock of Ages," "Greenlands Icy Mountains," etc.

March 11th. Deputy fetched me a letter for Stampers, one of my patients who is very low. It was from Col. Jno. A. Summers of Abingdon Va., to whom I wrote at Stampers' request, urging him to get the old man a pardon. Summers replies that he is confident of success as all the U. S. officials in Abingdon sympathize with Stampers. This is good news for the latter and he seemed to brighten up somewhat when I read the letter to him; but I am of opinion he will not need a pardon from Grant. He is ticketed for the grave; although he may hold.

4:30 P. M. He is dead. Two minutes before the event, he was asked if he did not feel better since he had good news? "Oh! yes, much better," said he, and turning on his side, he died. Query: Is he "better?" Perhaps so, doubtless better so far as mundane happiness is concerned, for life was but misery to him; but perhaps 'twas like jumping out of the frying pan into the fire. Perhaps he is keeping company with Dives & Co. down among the Lucifernians; for his God was the "Almighty dollar," and a counterfeit dollar at that. For 16 years, or longer, he had pursued the business of counterfeiting, I am told; although his lack of intelligence and his mental imbecility seemed to refute the assertion. His name was E. C. Stampers, of Ashe County, N. C. Post Office, "Mouth of Wilson," Virginia. I could not but pity this wretched old man, dying in the hospital of a penitentiary, over a thousand miles from home: but on reflection, although hard, it is *fair;* and as he had all necessary attention, it was as good a place for such a man to die in, as he could have had at home.

March 12th. This magnificent sunshiny morning, tends to increase the poignancy of my monotonous life "behind the bars." Fair weather is by no means the most agreeable to the prisoner in close confinement. When the sky is clear, and the sun and the South Wind making the atmosphere balmy and refreshing, the captive longs to be out, longs to smell the fragrant flowers, to wander in the field, and above all to enjoy the pleasures of charming society. Such a day fills me with desire for active life. I crave the excitement of stirring business. On such a day, too, one can recollect familiar scenes of the past. A thousand beauties of scenery and climate, to which perhaps we gave little heed when they were before us, now recur to memory with unnatural vividness. It is, indeed, only when we are afar from our country that we know the attachment we have for it. Which very clearly shows 'tis true, that "distance lends enchantment to the view."

Genl. Pilsbury was up in Hospital this morning for the last time I fear. He has become very thin and emaciated, and so weak that his step is tottering. I gave him my arm to descend the stairs, but even, when thus assisted, he could make but a short distance without pausing. I trust the warm weather may be of advantage to him.

March 16th. Utterly disappointed as usual not a line from home, or from any of my so-called friends. Let me never forget the lesson I am learning. And never cease to watch for an opportunity to repay my teachers. Commenced the study of Phonography, one hour daily for six months.[1]

Have just finished the "Life of Genl. Geo. B. McClellan," written in 1864 by C. H. Hillard. This book is a marvel in its way; because, although its author is a Massachusetts Yankee, writing at a time when the whole North was boiling and seething with prejudice and fanatical fury, it bears few marks of sectional spirit, few passages of denunciation of the South; and is a much more generous estimate of Confederate valor, skill, and humanity, than I have ever seen from a Yankee pen. Gen. Lee and Stonewall Jackson come in for no meagre praise. To McClellan, himself, the book is a noble tribute, although written without his knowledge (I believe) and certainly without unduly complimenting him. Its dry historic record is sufficient flattering for any ordinary record; while the clear exposition of Abe Lincoln's bungling interference with military matters, and the persistent abuse of McClellan by the Radical leaders and War Committees, fairly forces our compassion for the unfortunate General notwithstanding that we fought against and glorified in his defeat. That McClellan was the first military genius the North produced cannot be disputed by any impartial mind. That he is an head and shoulders above Grant is even less doubtful. Had Grant been in command at Richmond during the "Seven Day's Battle," the whole Federal army would have been captured. In moral character there is no comparison between the men. When McClellan sat down in his tent at Harrison's Landing and wrote his well known letter to Lincoln, declaring that the South must be treated more justly, and the

---

1 This paragraph is crossed out in the manuscript.

war carried on more humanely, etc., he did what not one man in ten thousand could do after suffering so great a discomfiture. That letter alone might serve as McClellan's epitaph; to show the firmness, calmness, integrity and magnanimity of his soul.

Scruggs has a letter telling that we are all expected at home! What bosh! Today I send a letter to Addie, enclosing one to *ma chere amie,* thanking her for the fine box I rec'd recently. I note this because I doubt if she ever gets the letter. It seems useless to write to a Southern postoffice having a Radical keeper.

March 17th. "St. Patrick's day in the morning" comes in like a "March Lion." This building is placed to catch the full force of the wind and today it is shaken as if it were a canvas tent.

I have just had another squabble with our religio-monomaniac. He says he wont obey the rules, that he wont obey anybody but the Lord Jesus Christ, "who died that I might be free—*free!* (Very loud) and I am free! and I defy you to rob me of my Jesus!" (in a yell).

He then proceeds to remark that we are all "hell hounds," "liars," "rogues," and that he puts me especially under his feet (metaphorically speaking). I have endured this sort of thing until I am tired of it. If Wilcox were really deranged I should not care for anything he said; but it does provoke me to be annoyed and insulted by this creature, who would be cured of his insanity by less than 30 lashes.

March 19th. "The Shepherd," seeing two of the patients talking together and laughing, ran towards them and shaking his fists, desired personally to chastise them for laughing at him; but as this was not in keeping with his religious professions I thought proper to stop it. It will be shame to turn this scoundrel loose on the world; yet he will be pardoned without a doubt.

Four Ku Klux from S. C. (Saunders, Warlock, Carroll and McCulloch) were released today on the President's so-called pardon. *They had less than two months yet to serve!* Here we have the key to their release. The Administration, after holding these poor men to the very close of their term, grants them a pardon, and the fact is heralded all over the country as an act of *clemency!* And the Mongrels, no doubt, will lay claim to gratitude of these injured men, for "getting them out." Bah! If I am held to the last few months of my term, the Government need not trouble itself to issue a "pardon" for me.

March 20th. To my great satisfaction we got rid of Wilcox this afternoon; he being marched down, and locked up in a cell in the "Wing" of the Female Department, where are other lunatics, and where he will have much different treatment than he had here. If a couple of weeks in his new quarters does not restore him to sanity, I am mistaken. And now I must regret that I have given this fellow so much notice in my journal; but it goes to show how our lives here are reduced to petty affairs; which become important from the paucity of incident in our daily experience. To a person confined to bed it is a noticeable occurrence when the clock on the mantelpiece happens to strike out of time. So we observe, and are pleased or irritated by trivialities of almost as little importance. A true account of prison life is made up of trifles.

March 21st. Snow 10 inches deep and still falling. Spring where are you? I began this day early, having been awakened at 2 A .M. to superintend the "laying out," of Carter, a negro who drew his last breath a few minutes earlier. He had been failing for some time (consumption) but was not considered in danger although I appointed a man to sit up with him last night. It was lucky I did so for the darkey died while on stool. In the adjoining bed is another negro, going with the same disease. These black rascals from about Washington and from farther South, usually come here with some disgusting venereal disease, upon which the change of climate acts with the effect to throw it into the system, and results in consumption, or some bronchial complaint—fatal almost without exception. I wonder that some negro lover has not gotten hold of this fact, and made a *Jeremiad* of it, to add to the "Book of Nigger." "Southern darkeys ought not to be sent to the Penitentiary to die!" Let this be the cry, and the lucky man who starts it can have a statue in Boston, only he should not say "darkeys" but, "Southern colored gentlemen."

Apropos of these frequent deaths, I am disposed to think the hospital of a Penitentiary is about as effectual as a battlefield for hardening one's feelings respecting the dead. Seeing so many degraded wretches die, and commonly with attendant circumstances having a tendency to diminish the natural instincts of awe and compassion, we become so accustomed to the death bed, that the sight of a stiffening corpse calls up scarcely a serious thought. It is not good for men to be thus calloused. Reverence for the dead is an essential feeling in all genuine piety; and when a man has lost all concern for the great mystery of Death it is hardly worth while to look for the external practices of Religion in his conduct.

March 22nd. Snowing in the morning—making the 50th snow storm this winter; which I learn from the [cut out] prisoners here, who never fail to acquaint the [cut out] falls.

March 23rd. Arose a [cut out] didn't come. Everybody [cut out] except myself. I know not how to [cut out] ther and brothers, who, at least, ought [cut out] As for those who were once ple [cut out] ve ceased to feel wounded at ther [cut out] er forget them; and to help me remember I make this note.

Old 'Squire Brown usually receives from 2 to 6 letters per week, which shows that the South Carolina people are more independent, and undaunted than their North Carolina brethren of the Klan. I, however, knew that before. But unfortunately the 'Squire's letters today bring him bad news. His Mis-Representative in Congress, A. S. Wallace, (who very likely is secretly opposing Brown's release, as they were strongly opposed in several political campaigns) now declares publicly that *"Nothing less than two years will do him (Brown) any good."* Thus this political demagogue, who has done all he can to subject his neighbors and fellow citizens to the domination of the ignorant and brutal negroes, now seeks to keep a grey haired man for years in a distant penitentiary merely to gratify some old political grudge! I told Brown some time ago that he would not get home until he abased himself, and fairly crawled to the feet of Wallace, and so it seems likely to turn out.

But this news is not much better for me; because if the old man is forced to grovel in the dust, confessing himself a sinner and begging pardon, I shall (or should) have to do worse (which I wont).

March 26th. Wilcox, the pretended maniac, was pardoned today. So, another mail robber is out.

Mar. 27th. Very cold and blustery. Printing Hymns to hang up in the Chapel.

March 29th. March didn't come in like a lamb but is certainly marching out like a lion. I am glad to learn that R. S. Gray of Alabama was released a few days ago. He was one of Dick Busteed's victims; and was sentenced for ten years. His release at this early date shows that even his enemies acknowledge the wrong which was done him. They know very well that he and all the other Ku Klux were convicted, by the government, not as a punishment for crime, but to carry out certain electioneering arrangements. The desired end having been accomplished the victims are to be gradually released except those whose further detention is requested by their Mongrel neighbors. This is the truth and nothing but the truth about the matter.

March 30th. My disappointment this morning is inexpressible. Brown has several letters, but nothing new except a cheque for $25 sent him by a friend. I would be thankful for a letter without money.

April 1st. B. Strickland (Spartanburg, S. C.) was pardoned yesterday. He had only about 30 days to serve! Such is Grant's clemency!

Eo. die. Jno. Montgomery and S. Childers just released. Had about 3 months to serve! Small thanks should I give for a pardon issued at this Eleventh Hour.

April 3rd. [cut out]

April 4th. Our surgeon was yesterday in the country to the northward of Albany and found the roads cut through immense snow drifts, 40 feet deep. The ice in the river is frozen to the bottom, 16 feet.[1]

We have now in the hospital a young man dying of congestion of the lungs. His moans and groans robbed me of sleep last night and promise to repeat it tonight. Strange that all men should cry "Oh Lord!" when in agony.

Marshall, a Virginia Scalawag sent here for 10 years for mail robbery, was pardoned today. The Government has not the heart to hold a rogue or mail robber in prison. But its political opponents by scores are left there to rot, if they will.

April 5th. Foreseeing that a darkey (Braden) would die during the night, I prepared to sit up with him, but he saved me the trouble by dying before nine o'clock. This may sound rather flippantly; but really the fellow was so filthy and withal so impudent, refusing to take his medicine, etc., that I could not feel any sort of sympathy for or interest in him. He was what is called an "army nigger," i. e., has been a Yankee soldier; and like all of that class, was conceited, whimsical and insolent. "The colored troops fought nobly" was a pet phrase with the Radical papers during the war, although it would be hard to tell where the noble fighting took place, but whatever their conduct *then,* they have fought nobly ever *since the war* in the way of murder, assault and battery, burglary, arson, rape, and exploits of that sort. It is a fact that nine in ten of the rascals (negroes I mean) who figure in our public courts, or are sent to the Penitentiary are graduates of the "Finest Army on the Planet." And yet, strange to say, Gerrit Smith was, or seemed to be, much surprised to hear that there were any negroes confined here! So blind are these negro-lovers to all that pertains to their blessed pets.

I have just had an amusing illustration of the superstition which prevails among the more ignorant convicts. It has happened by accident that three men in

[1] Aside from the manifest inaccuracy of the statement concerning the thickness of the ice, the current New York papers indicate usual spring weather at this time. The *Times* of April 5 mentions that the ice on the upper Hudson was breaking up in consequence of the warmer weather. The surgeon must have been taking advantage of a Southerner's unfamiliarity with a Northern winter.

succession have died in a certain bed, one of the best in the room. But not one of those convalescents could be induced upon any consideration to sleep in it now!

I am quite disgusted when I glance over my journal and find it a mere record of time wasted in trifles—petty annoyances, squabbles, deaths, disappointments, etc. But these are the only incidents of our lives and taken collectively will show how grievous is the confinement which imposes this monotony on us. They show, moreover, that imprisonment *"in the penitentiary"* is, to a *well bred man,* an heavier punishment than any that the despots of Europe ever invented.

April 6th. "Better bad news than no news," is a saying I frequently have thought of but never realized until this morning. I have just finished the perusal of a letter from my excellent friend Gen. L. which while it depresses me exceedingly, I am glad to get, since it will serve to guard me against future disappointments. The Genl. writing from Rutherfordton, under date of Mar. 17th (nearly three weeks ago!) says:

> I was careful in all the letters I wrote about you to say I was not aware you denied belonging to the Klan, but that beyond this you admitted no culpability and therefore I am sure these Gentlemen in endeavoring to procure your release will not found their application on any plea injurious to your honor. They are actuated by the kindest feelings personally and may use some policy in your case but nothing but what is expedient and of which you would approve.
>
> . . . People who have been wronged as you have and who have been shut out from the knowledge of the changes around understand the movements of the last 18 months, the frequent excitements or new subjects and therefore the apathy about issues that are "past issues" to all but those like yourself who are principally suffering their effects. Yet I am sure that you are more generally known and your fate more generally lamented than that of the other victims. But when released you must not be

surprised to find that the Ku Klux excitement has died out and cannot be revived.

. . . I mention this to show you the temper of the time. And when you are amongst us again I recommend you to study the aspect thoroughly and to make no move at least until you see the changes that have happened and the worthlessness of the actors on the public stage. I make no doubt that the efforts of the administration will be directed towards having Grant in for a 3rd term which of course means the Presidency for life. There is no law against this and nothing but decent custom founded on Washington's example. I don't believe that this will prove any restraint. *Nous verrons.* . . .

What my friend says about the apathy, etc., of the people respecting the prisoners here and Ku Klux matters generally, is but a confirmation of my apprehension on the subject. How often have I predicted that we should be forgotten after the first six months!

And when obliged to choose between betraying my friends or coming (and afterwards of staying) here, I was very well aware that the very persons I befriended, would soon forget and neglect me, and when the danger had passed, would deny that they owed any obligation. I say I knew all this, but 'twas well to be reminded of it by so sincere and reliable a friend as Genl. L. Fortunately I was not guided in the past by any selfish or purely personal motive, and whatever be the result of my misfortunes I hope to retain the dignity of conscious integrity.

Genl. encloses an Act of Amnesty, recently passed by the Legislature of N. C., which I copy here for preservation.[1] It is noticeable that of the eight secret Associations mentioned in the Bill, *five* are *Radical,* and *three Democratic.* The five Radical Klans were in existence long before the Ku Klux Klan, and their members committed "Outrages" which no deed of the Klan can equal or compare to, yet there was never a single

1 The text of the act is here omitted.

Leaguer brought to justice. No charge of conspiracy was made against the Radical Klans and none of their members will ever be sent to the Penitentiary.

*   *   *   *   *   *

The object of this act is to prevent a continuance of the Ku Klux prosecutions by the Mongrels in the State courts. In South Carolina on the other hand all the recently pardoned Ku Klux have been arrested and thrown into jail, to be tried for murder, etc., in the state courts where with negroes on the jury and a scalawag judge on the bench, there is less hope of acquittal than before Bond. In North Carolina the times seem to be brightening. The Mongrels have had everything their own way so long that they are growing tired of their sport, or else they consider they have drawn all the blood from the State, and are now obliged to let her have a breathing spell. At all events the Columbia *Phoenix* contains the following, which I am pleased to hear.

DISCONTINUANCE OF THE KU KLUX CASES

S. T. Carrow, United States Marshal for the State of North Carolina, has issued instructions to deputy marshals not to execute any more *capiases* or *subpoenas* in any cases wherein defendants are charged with violations of the Enforcement of Ku Klux Act. Witnesses are informed that they need not attend. This order has been extended by V. S. Lusk, District Attorney for the Western District of North Carolina, and all persons summoned, recognized, or otherwise bound to appear as witnesses at the United States Circuit or District Courts, either at Greensboro, Statesville or Asheville, against parties indicted under this Act, are excused from any further attendance, and discharged from any further duty as witnesses in any indictments, unless resummoned. We hope that the dragonade is now over, and that the people will be left in peace, to follow their business and support their families as best they may. The persecution has been shameful, and will stand on the page of history to condemn the administra-

tion of President Grant long after his name, which
but for this stigma, would have been forgotten with
his inaugurals.

April 7th. "Weary, stale, flat and unprofitable."
April 8th. Last evening we had an entertainment
in the chapel. The lecturer was the Rev. Mr. Hurlburd
of the Hudson St. Methodist Church, Albany; and his
sayings were entitled "Summer Saunterings in Europe." The speaker so far as I could judge at a distance, is a stout, "muscular Christian" style of man,
with a full and merry voice, like a tickled Irishman's.
His lecture was rather Irish too; and might be appro-
priately called "Summer Skipping in Seven League
Boots." He sailed over the ocean and was sea sick. People who go down for the first time, to the sea in ships
generally are sea-sick. He landed at Dublin, and met
a "fine old Irish gentleman." Perhaps there are many
fine old gents in Ireland; but this was—accidentally
happened to be, the father of Capt. O'Neil of the police force in Albany. 'Twas a most strange coincidence.
Subsequently Mr. Hurlburd and his party visited the
Irish lakes, and inquired for the beautiful Kate Kear-
ney, but could find no female pretty enough to be a de-
scendant of Kate's. He then began to skip; first to the
English Lakes, then back to Ireland, then to Maggiore
and Como, then to the Highlands, then to Geneva, then
to Wales, etc., etc., seven leagues at a breath. All this
was interspersed with humorous anecdotes of a rather
ancient description, as if he had found a copy of "Joe
Miller's Jests," and mistook it for a recent publication.
One of his stories is just a little *doubtful.* When he was
travelling in Ireland the party were importuned by
beggars; and as he had become tired of giving away his
money, he galloped off at full speed. On reaching a hilltop he looked back thinking he had got rid of them at
last, when lo! there was a sturdy fellow holding on by
the tail of his mule!

Now this might have happened twice, but it is a singular coincidence that Charles Lever in one of his nov-
els *tells the same story in almost the same language.*
Truth that moralist's witticisms might have brought the
habit into fashion among the beggars of Ireland; but

I'm afraid the Reverend Traveller drew this anecdote from memory not from his own experience.

Be that as it may the subject matter of the lecture was like pearls before swine to the Penitentiary audience. Not one in a hundred of them cared a picayune for description of lake scenery and foreign travel. Nevertheless after all these critical remarks I must admit that I was interested and pleased by the lecture; and unquestionably Mr. Hurlburd is a ready and entertaining speaker. No doubt too the brevity of time at his command will account for the skipping sketchy nature of his address. Indeed he stated that he had omitted much of his discourse. And we would be glad to have the entertainment even if it were much worse. The Chapel looks finely when lighted by gas chandeliers.

The introduction of weekly evening lectures during the winter, is a new feature in Penitentiary management, and marks a great advance towards the true reformatory policy. Let the convict see that there is a wish to reform and instruct him as well as to punish him for past offenses; let him understand that though punished, 'tis a just reward of their lawlessness and not from any base desire of revenge; let him feel that though in a penitentiary, all the manhood is not to be crushed out of him, and I venture to say he will be easier managed, and will leave the prison a better man than when he entered.

Apropos of this subject, I had a conversation recently with our chaplain, and suggested to him the organization of a "Prison Association" for this particular institution. There is a State Association but it is not very energetically conducted and I doubt if one in a hundred of the discharged prisoners are aware that there is such an aid, nor where it may be found, if they knew it. Now the great benefits to the State, to society, and to the convicts themselves, that such an Association is capable of doing, if rightly managed, are not easily to be described.

When we reflect upon the thousands upon thousands convicted in our courts from year to year; and, the hundreds of thousands of guilty persons, who escape conviction, it is strange that we have not more pity and forbearance for those who fall as it were by accident in paths where our own feet may have often inclined, aye, and been nearer stumbling than we should be willing publicly to confess! Wolves and dogs sometimes turn upon a wounded comrade and tear him in pieces. But men, equally as cruel and unjust go farther and compel their hurt companion to destroy himself.

April 10th. For a long time I have been desirous of getting some writing paper to prepare an article or two for the magazines; that I might sell when released, and thus obtain money to pay my expenses home; but have utterly failed before today when the Deputy fetched me half a dozen sheets. I asked him to purchase two quires. The unwillingness of the officers to allow me writing paper is unaccountable in view of the fact that if I desired to make any improper use of writing material I have a plenty in the leaves of this book and of the coarse book-cover paper.

It may be however, they wish to avoid the precedent of permitting a prisoner to have paper. I am sure I have no desire to carry on any clandestine correspondence.

April 13th. To my surprise I rec'd a letter this morning—three letters—no small event in a life of such wearisome placidity as mine! Better still they contain encouraging news; Genl. L's. letter at least. He says that Capt. D. has been to Washington where he had Grant's promise that he would order a pardon to be issued for me provided Jim Justice, and United States District Attorney—Lusk—would sign an application for it. Lusk had been previously approached by Durham and promised to endorse any petition that Justice should first sign. The latter offered to sign one; which was accordingly drawn up and speedily received an hundred or more signatures. "It simply asks your release," says Gen. L. "and is not *your petition but ours,* who make it, and who put our request on no other grounds than the expediency of pardon in the case of this and all semi-political offenses. It is Durham's be-

lief and that of all others that your release will occur
in less than a month. I need not say with what joy I
shall hear of it. I wrote to Judge Merrimon to remind
him of his promised action; and Jos. L. Carson has also
written to him. He has applied to a good many in your
behalf. *Courage mon ami. tout va bien!"*

This looks promising but promises are a sort of political *mirage,* which office-holders create for the deception of their constituents. It may be that I do Genl.
Grant much injustice in doubting his fidelity to his
promise; but if I do him injustice in thought, he has
done me a far more grievous injustice in deed by sending me here. Durham says in his letter to Genl. L. that
he *found an unreasonable prejudice prevailing against
me in Washington.* Of course! I have been well aware
for years that this unreasonable and unjust prejudice
—hatred rather—existed in the Radical mind in those
circles where North Carolina Mongrel influence is felt.
And with Ex-Govr. Holden, Sam Phillips, Jno. Pool,
C. L. Cobb in Washington there can be no lack of malicious influence against me.

Besides I do not believe that either Justice or Lusk
are willing that I shall regain my liberty, of which they
were actively instrumental in defrauding me. They
might easily sign the petition, and thus gain credit for
magnanimity among decent men; while at the same
time they wrote to Washington protesting against my
release.   Gov. Caldwell was once guilty of this contemptible duplicity in the case of Col B. S. Gaither
and others. He drew up a letter praying that the disabilities of these gentlemen should be removed by Congress and took care that they should see the letter. But
privately he wrote denouncing them as violent Rebels
who should on no account be cleared of their disabilities! His latest letter happened to be read in Congress
by Senator Nye, and afterwards appeared in the Congressional Record, where I saw it; and, having heard of
Gov. Caldwell's villainy, exposed it in my Asheville
paper. From that moment, Caldwell was my enemy;
and during my trial he sat at the *side of the prosecuting
attorney,* almost constantly, and gave me the impres-

sion by his scowling looks and occasional whispers that he was lending "aid and comfort" to the enemy. Think of a Governor of a State spending his valuable time during several successive days to watch the *persecution* of an half dozen of his fellow citizens—poor, humble, and ignorant men, too—before a packed jury and a corrupt and partizan judge!

Now be the result as it may, I shall not forget by whom I was sent here; and while I cherish no vindictive feelings, I shall run into no rhapsodies of gratitude for being released. If Justice and Lusk have signed the petition in sincerity and if I escape through their instrumentality I shall give them credit for all they are entitled to in the matter. But as I have said I have no faith in such promises.

Bro. M., and Jennie write kindly; but the latter, very sadly. Affairs in Rutherford are not improving. Many of the older families are breaking up and seeking more congenial climes. Radicalism, Loganism and Negroism have made a Pandemonium of their once happy village. Erwin has removed the *Vindicator* to Newton, and Jennie says that my friends are of opinion I ought to re-establish my newspaper at home. *Nous verrons.* Wrote to her and Bro. M. by return mail.

April 14th. A convict attempted to commit suicide in his cell last night by eating a quantity of mercurial ointment given him to banish vermin from his body. The fellow has been closely confined for some time, as he is or pretends to be deranged. He was a soldier, tried by court martial and sentenced to wear a ball and chain for ten years; but the ball and chain was remitted through the intercession of Genl. P. Whether the poor man was guilty is hard to say, though I am told he vehemently protested his innocence. To be sure 'tis no new thing for a prisoner to plead "not guilty;" but neither is it uncommon for courts martial to condemn innocent men. I am satisfied that in this country military commissions are the most ready engines of oppression that can be devised; they are no more amenable to Justice and impartiality than the maddest mob, and their power for evil is almost as great. I speak whereof

I know. I have been an officer myself and my *experience* is verified by my *observation,* if it is not a "bull" to say so. No one who has read the trials of *Dr. Mudd, Mrs. Surratt* and others, of Washington and that of *Major Wirz,* and *Champ Furgeson,* and *Lieut J. Y. Beall,* and dozens of other poor prisoners whom this mighty government has doomed to death, no one, I say, can read the published report of these trials without being convinced that a military court is one sham tribunal into which an half dozen prejudiced and obsequious army officers bring the sentence originally pronounced at Head Quarters, utterly regardless of right or reason in the case. Frequently the accused is punished when innocent and sometimes is cleared when truly guilty. I recollect that Lieut. McEwan told me if I had been tried by court martial I should certainly have been hung! And after some conversation he admitted that there was *nothing damaging in the evidence against me,* but everybody considered me the leader, etc. I answered him with a story of a Tennessee jury. A man was charged with murder but proved an *alibi* so clearly that all the spectators thought the prosecuting attorney would drop the case. But he was a smart fellow, and had a grudge against the prisoner. So, after dinner he came into court with an armful of books; and very solemnly began to denounce *the crime of murder;* reading from the Bible, and from many old Reports, etc., to show that murder is so heinous a crime that no mercy ought to be granted the man who had shed his brothers blood. He kept this up for three hours until he had utterly confused the heads of the jury and finally closed by saying, "Now gentlemen you see how the law stands and are bound to bring in this murderer guilty," etc. And to the amazement of all, the foreman presently returned with precisely that verdict! The Judge enraged at such injustice ordered a new trial and the man was speedily acquitted. Meanwhile the prosecutor said to one of the jurymen, "Mr. ———, how in reason did you bring in such a preposterous verdict?" "Well," replied the bright foreman, "there wasn't much agin the prisoner *in the evidence;* but the *law* was *so plaguey strong* we was obliged to hang him."

McEwan then related a case in his own experience in which a soldier of his command was tried by court martial and sentence was about to be pronounced when he was permitted to make some explanation which so far palliated his offense that he was let off with a *reprimand* instead of being shot.

Of course in writing the foregoing, I am not apologizing or defending the man of whom I began to write. I merely give the opinion that a sentence (?) by court martial is not always conclusion of guilt.

April 17th. Snowing all day! Lovely April weather!

Anthony, Mathis, and Moore, were pardoned today. All poor and illiterate men.

Time is hanging very heavily on my hands these days. And my mental miseries may not be mentioned.

Today Captain P. passing through the room with some visitors remarked, *"That* man is in charge up here." "Oh dear!" thought I, "when shall I escape from a place where I am pointed out to strangers as *'this man'* or *'that man;'* or am told, *'Shotwell* come here!' or *'Shotwell* go there!'"

Now I have sense enough to know that I was sent here just as a common convict and therefore must expect the same treatment as the other inmates receive. But that is no alleviation of my sufferings and mortification. It may make me more patient in appearance and conduct; but it does not blunt the keenness of my wounded self-respect. Let people talk as they may about the support of conscious innocence, I am sure the noblest human that ever lived could not undergo the daily indignities of Penitentiary life without being depressed and heart sore beyond telling. The more high-minded and sensible the man, the greater his sufferings from this sort of annoyance. It is not the mere imprisonment, nor the privations, nor the isolation from society, that affects me; it is the degraded position I am forced to occupy, and the constant humiliations arising from that position. Daily I am spoken to, precisely as if I were a slave; until I sometimes wonder if I shall ever hold my head up when I am set free again.

April 20th. Brief note from father, dated 13th gives anything but cheering intelligence. McC. has not been sent to West Point which is exactly as I expected. Father I am sorry to hear is not in good health, and as his letter shows is exceedingly depressed for reasons which I can surmise. I would it were in my power to remedy some of these matters, but it is useless to grieve or fret about it. Respecting myself he says that Jim Justice signed the petition drawn up by my friends and that people believe me certain of release in a few days. The petition does not compromise me in any way, he says. 'Tis well it does not; for I am determined not to yield one jot of my honor and manhood if I never get out of prison.

To add to the unpleasant effect of father's letter, I rec'd one from Aunt Susie, also; who after some extravagant assurances of affectionate sympathy, proceeds to lament my Southern birth, my connection with the Klan, etc., etc., with that persistency of harping on a single string, that characterizes many of the fair sex. She tells of a friend of hers, a minister living South, who was threatened, and whose daughter actually had to make soldiers' caps during the war! Just as if there were not thousands of men abused and injured because they were opposed to the war *up North!* I could relate to her some anecdotes of persecution and mob violence which occurred in Media and Phila. before I went South, that would cap the very best of her stories. But what *can* I reply to such a malicious lie, as that she was told by Wm. Dwight, i. e., *that a Northern man in North Carolina was called into an hotel by persons in disguise—told that he must retract his opinions or die, and on his refusal, had his throat cut from ear to ear! The murderers only allowed him to go to a window to see his little child playing in the yard, before they severed his* "jugular." She does not say that the Ku Klux then drank his blood but that we may (if we choose) add to the story.

Now in the name of common sense how can intelligent people *believe* such monstrous *canards,* which fairly disgrace human nature? It seems to me these abominable lies ought to refute themselves at the bare recital. And yet I daresay the whole Yankee nation has heard, and credited this identical story, and perhaps many others of even greater atrocity!

But possibly it may all turn out for the best. Let this sort of defamation, and unceasing misrepresentation continue; let the government be encouraged by the popular voice to heap fresh and increasing oppression—still heavier burdens—on the Southern people; let liberty be taken away from the whites that political supremacy may accrue to the negroes; let all honorable men in the South feel themselves at the mercy of the vile local agents of the Administration; let things go on as they have been going for half a dozen years; and mark the consequences! Sooner or later the opportunity will come when the South may throw off her yoke if she will. And then the smouldering resentment of years will spontaneously kindle the fires of strife such as America has never seen—black as is her record. Then, when the North is divided, and hostile fleets sweeping her coasts, with fire and sword, the "Southern cross" will blaze in the Heavens, and a fearful debt will be paid in blood of our enemies. *I do not wish this day may ever come; I love the Union, and am proud of the name of American Citizen;"* but I *hate* and *despise* those who are leading public opinion in the North; in approbation of the detestable despotism of the present administration. And every day is making me more and more willing to resume the sword. Only a day or two ago I found the following slip of an article I wrote for the Newbern Times in 1865, just after the War. If my sentiments are changed, 'tis not my fault.

The War, with all its terrible drama of marches, battles, victories and retreats, has been numbered with the past. The thunder of artillery—the crash of musketry—the sharp crack of the skirmisher's rifle, and the steady tread of troops marching to battle, are heard no more in our land. Our lines

are broken, our flag lowered and furled, and with
sorrowful hearts we have turned back from the
hill sides we went forth to defend.   Alas! there are
many who cannot return.   The shadow of death
has entered the door of many a homestead, and the
vacant chair in the fire-side circle marks the spot
where once sat a form that perchance now sleeps
in a grave whose only monument is the dark-hued
grass his blood has enriched.

But we have accepted the fiat of events. Firmly and resolutely we made the arbitrament of the
sword, and yielding to its decision we have ever
endeavored to comply with the requirements of our
new position.   Yet, while we shall never, by word
or deed, encourage a renewal of strife in our land,
we feel that the disinterested self-abnegation that
led so many thousands of our boyhood's friends to
sacrifice their lives for a cause we called our own,
deserves the sorrowful reverence of every Southern
heart.

April 21st.   I often blush for the letters of my Ku
Klux comrades which I see each week, and cannot help
feeling mortified to find myself in such company, notwithstanding they are not acquaintances of mine, and
all of different grade of society.   But this week's mail
is peculiarly rich in odd and illiterate expressions.   One
K. K. rejoices to learn that his wife is *"fat as a pig and
purty as a pink, and Oh hunny, how I'd like to squeeze
you."*   Poor fellow, he is badly off no doubt!   Another,
sends his *"best respects to all the nabers."* Another
wishes his brother, "Tomus" to write him, and let him
know if *"the guse hangs hy."* Another invariably calls
his wife *"Lizziean,"* meaning I suppose, Lizzie Ann,
etc., etc. Nearly all "wright" letters. And it is upon
this class of ignoramuses that the government conde-
scends to pour out the vials of its wrath! *imprisoning
them* with the intent to *intimidate the more intelligent
people* of the South.

Have just seen Capt. P., who relieves me of some
anxiety by promising to have me provided with shoes,
etc., if I should be pardoned; and that he will do what he

can to assist me in carrying out some other private arrangements I have in view. He doubts, however, whether I shall be released as soon as my friends expect, because it is reported at Washington that no more K. K. are to be pardoned for some time. I am entirely of his opinion; notwithstanding Grant's promise to Plato Durham.

April 22nd. Williams, negro, died this morning. Yesterday I predicted his death in 24 hours, and told him he had better get his thoughts in good order for the business. "Yes, I guess I'm 'bout played out"—said he, and ate a very hearty breakfast—to march on I suppose. His lungs were congested or one was; the other being entirely gone. For several days the pulsations of his heart were all on his *right side.*

Having no more serious cases in hospital we shall now get a little sleep.

April 24th. Deputy gave me the match board to fix. I fixed it well, neatly and correctly. When I carried it to him, he said "Why did you not bring it to me before you finished it? You ought not to have fixed it till I told you to," etc., etc. Now in this matter I was not in the least in the wrong, for I had been told to do a certain thing, and I had done it. I was not told to wait for further instructions; and it is not discovered that I have made any mistakes. But as there is a possibility of some slight error, I was thus censured for not calling on some of the officers to inspect my work. I feel that this is unjust to me; but the censure and mortification of being roughly reprimanded is none the less galling because undeserved. I am aware that it is unwise to yield to irritation from such a source but I cannot help it. I should prefer a blow, when free, to an insult, when unable to resent it.

April 27th. Usual Sunday morning disappointment. Very blue all day. Brown has a letter containing a confirmation of the ill tidings concerning the intention of the Administration to issue no more pardons to the Ku Klux for some time. The organ of the Cabinet at Washington, on the 9th inst. announced that no more pardons would at present, be granted to the K. K. prisoners at Albany, as they were "convicted of *direst complicity in the deeds of the Klan* and while it is the intention of the President sooner or later to pardon all the prisoners convicted under the enforcement act, he does not deem it proper to extend to this class Executive clemency until they have *realized by imprisonment* that the government is determined to enforce *law* and *order* in every section of the land!!!"

It is hard to do justice to such a piece of base fabrication as the foregoing.   It may well excite the deepest indignation in the breasts of all who know the truth of the matter.   Here are many prisoners—dozens perhaps—who were not even charged in their indictment with any overt act of Ku Kluxism; but merely of having at one time belonged to the order.   Five men I can name; Brown, aged 62, charged with being a member of the Order (which he was not); Scruggs, aged 50, charged with lending his gun to a party who demanded it; DePriest, who was not on the "Raid" but said he would like to go; Rev. John S. Ezell, 66, who was a member of the Order, but opposed to violence; Geo. Holland, who was not on the Raid but knew of it, etc., etc. How many others there are here, who are free from "actual complicity" in the deeds of the Klan, I know not; but as there are about 40 Ku Klux prisoners, besides these, I am satisfied that a dozen or more of similar cases could be picked out. And yet Grant tells the world that he has pardoned all but the actual participants in the so-called "outrages," and that the remainder must lay in prison until they realize that the government is determined to enforce the law!

Now the object of this announcement is very plain; the President takes credit for having pardoned all *who are worthy of pardon*.   He deceives the North with the idea that none but *violent desperadoes* are still imprisoned; while at the same time he *discourages our friends* in the South, from making any effort in our behalf.   "And they will all be pardoned, after while, without our intercession," they say.

In all this we see verified a remark of Sir James Mackintosh that Imprisonment is the *safest,* most quiet, *most convenient,* and *often the most cruel punishment an Oppressor can inflict. "The Prisoner,"* he says *"is silently hid from the public eye; his sufferings being unseen speedily cease to excite pity or indignation, and he is soon doomed to oblivion."*

Sir James might have added that the oppressor has it in his power to justify and commend his own cruelty by calumniating and misrepresenting his victim. The prisoner is voiceless, while the government commands its agents to disseminate falsehoods, which an obsequious partizan press takes care to impress upon public opinion. The history of the Radical Administration, beginning in 1861, is full of instances of this sort. Men have been arrested by Seward's "little bell;" or Stanton's detectives; or Grant's artillerymen; and having been tried by courts martial, special commissions, or the sham tribunals called "Federal" Courts, have been hurried away to linger for years in the dungeons of Northern forts, or die upon the feverish sand of the Dry Tortugas; while the government took good care to explain each step of its iniquitous proceedings to be necessary and entirely justifiable. The victims can only say like Emmet,"let no man write our epitaphs until our country is free."

History to be useful, must be true and this can hardly be said where rolls and records speak not truth but falsehood; and where contemporary history is written after bloody conflicts when one party is reduced to silence, and the other possessed of every organ of publicity, makes it to suit his own views: when the writer is he whom the spoil has enriched, and the hand that guides the pen is red with the blood of the calumniated victim. Then *vae victis:* then venal tongues and mercenary pens will herald forth the triumphs of successful wrong, and the name of the patriot who felt and bled and dared for his country will be consigned to obloquy or oblivion: none will then dare to breathe his name, nor throw a flower on his silent grave, till Time the great detector, brings truth to light, restores to virtue her true lustre, and to humanity the most precious of her interests, the heart stirring and inspiring examples of generous martyrs, whom in the gloomiest seasons of their country's fortunes, bribe could not tempt, nor torture move, nor Death's worst terrors daunt."

April 28th. Deputy came up and demanded to know what I had done with two stamped envelopes. I said I hadn't had but 50, and those I sent down. He looked at me for a minute and then said "Well I suppose I must have made a miscount." But there was something insinuating in the tone that made me miserable for hours afterwards. As if I would steal an envelope! I do not know that there was any intention to wound my feelings; but the remark was successful whether or no.

April 30th. Today expires the month allowed to Durham for my release; and here I am. Got up in a bad humor, and didn't improve all day, which was silly but natural.

May 1st. Much disturbed during night by ravings of maniac brought in yesterday. I have learned a variety of lessons since I lost my liberty, but this business of looking after crazy people is a little worse than any.

*   *   *   *   *   *[1]

May 2nd. Sat up last night with Pat Hoy, a sick Irishman. His time expires on Monday, and I was instructed to give him as much stimulant as he could stand, to keep him up if possible. But 'twas a lame race. Death came in ahead this morning about daylight. His sister wrote him last mail, telling him how they had new clothes ready for him, and intended to make merry over him, etc. Their joy will be painfully disappointed tomorrow, when "Poor dear, dear Pat" is carried home in his coffin. Some of his friends here took him away this morning. Many of the convicts complain that they (the sick) are left in their cells until just about to die, before they are brought up to the hospital. Complaints of course would be made if the prisoners were supplied with every luxury. But I must think that there is some-

---

1 A discussion of Dixon's "Life of Lord Bacon" is omitted.

thing wrong or there would not be so many fatal cases. Fourteen men have died in about five months, which is an average of nearly one per week, from a whole number of near 500 men.

Raining, damp, and disagreeable all day. Have thought of (Hari Kari).

May 4th. It would be hard to describe my feelings this morning, and perhaps they would be very little to my credit were they known. Hence I shall only say that I am realizing the truth of the old saying, "Dead or in prison soon forgotten." It is but natural that men who have been sent to antipodes, and cut off from communication with their people should gradually drop out of the public mind, but to be utterly neglected by relatives and friends so soon is hard.[1]

May 6th. For a number of days I have employed my leisure in composing short articles and miscellany to sell when released, but can get no paper on which to copy them. Such are the trivial annoyances that go to make up the dreadful whole of Penitentiary life. And the nerves having become shattered and unstrung by long confinement, renders one more than naturally fretful about such trifling deprivations.

Chaplain Reynolds has just fetched me two quires of paper, on which he desires me to write another batch of letters for the Albany Agency of the State "Prison Association" of which he is corresponding secretary. I am not willing to do anything to help forward this work, because I am satisfied that only a small proportion of the discharged convicts would return to their former haunts of vice, if they had immediate and remunerative employment elsewhere. See my views on this subject on page 356.

May 8th. Somewhat indisposed; and decidedly out of spirits. Raining and very gloomy.

May 10th. This day is generally observed in the South as a memorial occasion for the decoration of the graves of the Confederate dead; a beautiful custom which I trust may continue, at least until the South es-

---

1 This paragraph is crossed out in the manuscript.

capes from her oppressors and thoroughly vindicates her fallen sons. May the day soon come.

The Chaplain came in to get the letters I wrote, and brought bad news. There have been political troubles in Louisiana, and the government is sending troops there rapidly. Reported that 300 negroes were shut up in a barn and burned! So much for the Radical rumors of the affair.

Now even Mr. Reynolds, Abolitionist and Radical, as he is, doubts the truth of these telegraphic dispatches; but more prejudiced and less intelligent minds all over the North will accept them for facts, and thus the hostility to the South will be inflamed, and the growing sentiment of the country in favor of peace, and the restoration of Southern liberties will be checked. And indirectly this affair will affect *us:* for the government can excuse itself for holding us, asserting that the Ku Klux are "still murdering Union citizens in the South." So marches the coming man!

May 11th. Exceedingly dark and gloomy. Recd. a very affectionate note from Bro. M. to which I reply, "Nothing you can think of will be *stale* to me. I doubt if you will ever experience the *soul-thirst* the perpetual craving for something to break the monotony of ideas which becomes habitual to an intelligent prisoner. For six weeks I have not had a line save yours from any quarter, and I have sunk to that condition which Sidney Smith terms a 'state of suspended vitality.' I live, move, and eat my rations, but this told, you have the sum of my existence . . . etc."

Accompanying this I sent a letter to Genl. L. as follows:

"Dear Genl. Your kind letters of 17th and 31st March were so full of sympathy and good cheer that I could not but feel comforted by them, although I cannot think my liberation so near at hand as is believed at R. For 2 or 3 weeks I kept my trunks packed and paid great attention to having my horses shod (at least I asked for a pair of shoes) in expectation of receiving orders to march at a moment's warning. In the meantime I lived on Hope; a very light diet after the 2nd week. At length, however, the dream is at an end and I am full of disgust with myself for dreaming with my eyes open. Was it Chateaubriand who said *'L'esperance tient lieu des biens qu'elle promet?'* If so, he didn't know anything about it. The true policy (for one in my situation, at least) is *Nil admirari,* and be hanged to them!

You are aware I suppose that the administration organ at Washington announces that the govt. has exhausted its stock of clemency, that all the prisoners have been pardoned except a few desperate characters who were actual participants in the so-called 'outrages,' etc. The falsity of this statement will appear when I assure you that to my knowledge there are half a dozen men here who were not even charged at their trials with any overt act beyond a nominal connection with the Klan. But the effect of the announcement is to give people of the North the impression that only a squad of desperadoes are confined here: while on the other hand our friends will consider that it would be useless to make any further effort in our favor. Well may Sir. Jas. Mackintosh describe imprisonment as the safest, most quiet, most convenient, and often the most cruel punishment an oppressor can inflict. 'The prisoner,' he says, 'is silently hid from the public eye, his suffering being unseen, speedily ceases to excite pity or indignation and he is soon doomed to oblivion.' Sir James might have added that the oppressor always has it in his power to apologize for his barbarity, while calumniating his victim; the prisoner is voiceless while the govt. flings falsehoods broadcast by means of a mercenary partizan press. This has been the policy of the Radical administration from the very close of the war. Men have been tried by courts martial, by special commissions and by Star-Chamber Courts, and the victims have been hurried away to linger and die in distant prisons in the cold North or at the Dry Tortugas; while the govt. by means of its paid writers and obsequious newspaper organs has been able to justify its violence at each successive stage of the proceedings. But why expatiate on this subject? You have witnessed these things yourself. Jefferson foresaw them half a century ago when he predicted that the tyranny of Congress would first endanger the Republic and afterwards would come the despotism of the executive. We have already had some experience of both evils; but I doubt if we have seen the worst. You will notice, my excellent friend, I say nothing of my release of which you wrote me. Having had no intelligence since yours of Mar. 31st I am unable to form any opinion of the matter, altho' I confess I feel an intolerable anxiety to know what has been done and what are the prospects. . . . I am wonderfully curious about these trivial matters of which no one would be likely to write me. Even father has ceased to write me, or at any rate I have ceased to receive his letters. I begin to feel very much like Topsy who 'never was born and never had any friends or relatives.' However I shall always feel proud and confident of your generous friendship, etc."

May 12th. Wrote a long "Temperance Tract," showing the results of intemperance as recorded here, etc. Nine in ten convicts confess to hard drinking when outside. Another Ku Klux was discharged this evening and one will go tomorrow, having served their term, I believe. Murphey and Martin are the names; both poor whites. I have, also, heard of the pardon of Dr. E. T. Avery which merits mention here. He was arraigned at the same time that 'Squire Brown was, and would inevitably have been sent here for a long term. But he forfeited his bond and fled to parts unknown. Half a dozen negroes swore that he was a "Raider," a leader, etc. His property would have been sold but his wife raised the $3000 and satisfied the bond. And now after two years, when the government has satisfied its desire for convictions, one of the government witnesses comes forward and swears that Avery was not on the raids, etc., and Grant has signed an *unconstitutional pardon!* Whether the Doctor will recover his $3000 is doubtful although if he was an innocent man he ought not to have been arrested and therefore ought not to have given bond or forfeited it.

But what I most think of is this, that by running away he escaped coming to the penitentiary and is now fully cleared of the charge against him. Had I fled the country when warned to do so, I should have escaped in like manner. Had he stood trial as I did he would now be here and might never obtain pardon. From this may be seen the unfairness, and vindictiveness of Hugh Bond's Political Tribunal, so-called the Federal Courts!

May 14th. In despair of obtaining any writing paper, I wrote to Capt. P. asking *him* to issue orders that I might be permitted to purchase a couple of quires. He promptly replied by sending me the quantity asked for; but marked "no charge." This is not exactly as I wish; but as it may be against the rules to allow prisoners to buy paper, I take it, and am obliged to Capt. P. For now I can go on with my literary compositions, which I find is the most efficacious plan to *forget time.* Weather is disagreeably cold and wet this morning.

Lynch, one of my patients, is very low and had written to his mother to bring him the picture of the "blessed Virgin Mary." She came today, a poor, pinched, dried up, Irish woman but full of affection and tenderness for her "by." It is really touching to witness her distress over the bed of her vagabond son. She is now gone for the Priest.

May 17th. Have been reading De Toqueville's "Democracy in America," or trying to read, but the day is so chilly that I can scarcely hold a book. This horrid climate appears to be utterly void of the spring season; 'tis winter until July; and people wear overcoats the whole year round.

May 18th. Addie writes that he gave me all the news in his *last* letter! This is intolerable. The letters containing "news" *always* contrive to not reach me. I sometimes doubt whether they ever get out of the portfolios of the writers.

May 19th. Two rascals released together on Saturday came back together today. Their little financial arrangement was interrupted by the police I suppose. One fellow came in the other day in his bare feet although the weather was hardly endurable to me in heavy clothing! He ought to be glad to get in.

May 25th. During the past week I have been much out of spirits, but hoped to have something interesting if not encouraging by today's mail; instead I am, in spite of good resolutions, left a prey of feelings in which disappointment, mortification and indignation are about equally divided. I am disappointed in getting no letters, mortified that I have not inspired my friends, so-called, with a warmer attachment, and indignant that I should be so utterly neglected by all, even those who took a solemn oath to aid, comfort, and assist brethren in distress. I try to banish these occasional ebulitions of irritation, but 'tis not easy to do so; especially when I see many poor, degraded, and insignificant creatures warmly sustained and encouraged by their people from week to week. Upon the whole, however, I think my liver is out of order, and that I am rather bilious.[1]

Capt. P. has been in with Col. T. C. Calicott, whom he introduced to me as a "brother editor." The latter was recently connected with the Albany *Argus,* but is now publishing a new paper of his own. He is a pleasant appearing and speaking gentleman of about 38 years of age, and is reputed to possess an high order of intellect. He was elected speaker of the New York House of Representatives when a very young man, and bade fair to ascend rapidly in public life. But being appointed Collector of Customs at New York City, he became involved in some irregularities (of which I know nothing) and was sent here for two years. He spent a great deal of money in prosecuting the court for false imprisonment, but was pardoned before the expiration of his term. While confined here he held my situation (Steward of the Hospital) and employed his leisure in acquiring knowledge of French and Spanish. His Penitentiary sentence does not appear to have greatly affect-

---

1 This paragraph is crossed out in the manuscript.

ed his social *status,* and his newspaper is said to be rapidly gaining favor in Albany. Col. Calicott was considerate in proffering his sympathy, saying that it is generally understood that political persecution had much to do with our prosecution, etc. I was pleased to meet him; since it facilitates certain arrangements I have in view for remaining North a few weeks after my release, if it occur soon. Capt. Pilsbury told him, I had more friends in N. C. now than I had ever before. His wife had just received a letter from a former friend, the wife of Lafayette or Dick (I forget which) Twitty of Spartanburg, S. C., who wrote that the reason she had said so little about the Ku Klux heretofore was because they were living under a reign of terror, and her husband was in great danger of coming here himself as, indeed, all respectable men were, etc., etc. The testimony of this Northern lady writing to her Northern friends from the very centre of the Ku Klux district, ought to remove some prejudice from the minds of those who hear it. But what is a single voice, against the daily, the persistently repeated, misrepresentations of the Radical presses? This casual visit, which was not wholly to me, is an agreeable interruption of my monotonous life; although it awakens the keenest desire for liberty.

Monday, May 26th. Rev. Jno. S. Ezell, one of the K. K. prisoners from S. C., has had a visit from some of his brethren of the Northern Baptist church; and gives a most amusing account of it in his letter today. I say "amusing," because it is so to me, not because he had any intention to ridicule his visitors. On the contrary he seems highly gratified by their proceedings. They were respectively, the Revd. Dr. Fulton of Boston, Rev. Dr. Simmons of New York, Rev. Dr. Brooks from somewhere else; and Rev. Dr. Somebody whom he couldn't remember. They questioned him closely and then prayed for him, so fervently that his "Soul overpowered itself." They then assured him they should do all in their power to get him out, etc., etc., and finally *counselled him to repent and "confess his crimes!"* How hard is it for these Yankees to believe that their pet

President would consign an innocent gray-haired
preacher of the gospel to the Penitentiary merely because he was opposed to his own political principles!
Yet this in effect is a true statement of the case. The
old man held up his hand and protested in sight of God
and man that he was innocent of all crime, and had
been only nominally a member of the Klan. But I
presume the delegation took counsel rather with their
prejudices than their reason, or his asseverations.

Nevertheless they will get him out. For Ezell professed the deepest humility, and promised that if pardoned he should go home, and try to befriend the negroes, preserve peace, etc., which was equivalent to
acknowledging the justice of his punishment! These
gentlemen then prepared a petition to send Grant, and
will push the matter to a successful issue. But I am
sorry the old man abased himself in that manner; and
he is sorry too; for he says in today's letter, after reciting the facts, "let not this be known outside of the family—burn this letter." Of course there is nothing
censurable in this conduct on moral grounds, for doubtless he will do, and has always been doing, just what
he promised to do. But it is too bad for our men thus
to cringe before the tyrannical villains who robbed
them of their liberty. Each week the letters show that
weakness of backbone is spreading among prisoners.
Men are yielding or professing to yield their life long
principles for the poor bribe of a few months, or years
of liberty. Thus W. L. Hood and Capt. J. W. Mitchell in their letters of today send messages to A. S. Wallace, the despicable Scalawag member of Congress from
S. C., assuring him that they are *very much his friends*
and *always were his friends,* and *if pardoned they intend always to vote for him,* etc. Is this not enough
to disgust even so degraded a creature as Wallace himself? True, these men have long terms, and their families need their support and Wallace seems to hold the
destinies of all the Ku Klux from his section in his own
hands. But I would much prefer to see every Southern prisoner patiently awaiting the freedom which
Time is sure to bring instead of purchasing a semblance

of liberty by surrendering their principles and manhood.

May 27th. The gong was struck two taps; which being the signal for me, I hurried down, and found that Aunt Susie and Dr. Schneider were come to visit me. Capt. P. had conducted them into his private drawing room, whither he carried me to meet them, as the office was lumbered up with a new safe he had just received. This was an unusual courtesy on his part, for all visitors are taken to the guard room to meet their acquaintance among the prisoners. But Capt. P. went farther and after I had saluted Auntie and shaken hands with the Doctor, told me to talk as much as I pleased, and left the room; his wife, being my only guardian for the time. He, also, declined to examine a package of articles fetched me by Aunt Susie: all of which shows that he is a gentleman, and knows how to treat a gentleman, even if the latter is an unfortunate prisoner in his custody. Aunt and Uncle are just from Valatie, where they arrived an Saturday on a visit to Uncle Alexander, but being called by telegraph to Boston to deliver an address, the Doctor hurried Aunt to see me before going east. She is better looking than when I saw her last, 15 years ago. He much more broken. Both will return to Asia Minor in a few months; but speak of seeing me again. They are as affectionate as any one could wish, and Auntie's eyes were rarely free of tears during the interview; yet such is the force of prejudice, and the influence of repeated misrepresentation that it is utterly impossible to reason them out of the belief that the Government is perfectly justifiable in all its usurpations, injustice, and tyranny. Grant they think one of the best men of the age, and scrupulously honorable, etc., while the Klan was a wicked conspiracy to break up the Union, slaughter the negroes, etc. They do not, of course, insinuate that I was guilty of all this; but they are *so so* sad I got into such bad company, that I ever went South, that I had the misfortune to be Southern born, etc. Consequently we were obliged to do as the doctors, "agree to disagree" and drop the subject. The interview lasted about an hour (double the usual time) and then they were obliged to go to catch the afternoon train for Boston.   Altogether I enjoyed their visit very much, and I hope and believe dear Aunt will think better of me hereafter; whatever her view of the Klan, and the South, generally.   And I feel a sincere regard for her. After the withdrawal of my friends, Mrs. Pilsbury bade me keep my seat, and entered into conversation, telling me about the letter she had from Mrs. Twitty who had just seen Mrs. Dr. Craton, and appears to have expressed herself generously in my favor.   To which Mrs. P. replied next mail, and as she remarked—"said a good deal more about you than the Captain would have allowed if he had known it," etc. I was much pleased to have a little chat with a lady, after having been so long deprived of sweet society.

Mrs. Pilsbury is about 35; is good looking, intelligent; and a good Democrat in political opinions; though much of an aristocrat in her private sentiments I suspect, as indeed all women who have nothing to do, usually are.

June 1st.   Aunt Susie sends me a little package of chromatic prints of flowers beautifully executed by a new process of which I forgot the name.   'Tis quite a novelty to see even the counterfeit of a flower. From Genl. L. I have another encouraging letter. It encloses the following from Plato D.

Shelby, May 23rd, '73.   Dear General—I don't think Capt. Shotwell needs be out of heart about his release.   When I carried the petitions to Washington the President was absent on a Western trip and returned only a few days ago.   If any one is interfering to prevent his release I am not aware of it.   *Big* men, though, you know can't be hurried and take their own time to do things.   If the President had been in Washington when I was there I think the prisoners would all have been pardoned; but it is impossible to get men to take an interest in such matters, and work, unless one can be present to urge them up.   I hope to hear something favorable in a few days, and I will write you at once. I am urging them by letter almost every mail. Very truly yrs.

P. Durham.

To which Genl. L. adds, "I feel certain that you have a staunch friend in Durham who will let no occasion slip to further your release by his action with the authorities. I have also heard from Judge Merrimon, who is as you know a man of much energy in all he undertakes. He is working for you and will in time do all he can to shorten official and other delays. I must say that I confidently hope for your restoration to liberty."

Ah! *mon ami,* 'tis kind of you to wish it, but alas! We too often take for granted that which we only very strongly wished should happen.

I regret to learn that sickness has prevailed in our family, and that father is still indisposed, although improving. His illness perhaps accounts for his long silence. The Genl. says he supposes I hear from him often! How much mistaken he is!

Another piece of intelligence is that the Mongrel thieves have already begun to quarrel and as a consequence honest men are coming by their own. Wallace, the post master at Rutherfordton, having been removed to give place for Scoggins' niece, turns State's evidence against both Andy, the marshal, and Nathan, the commissioner, and showed them guilty of such malfeasance in office that they *have been suspended, pending their trial.*

These are the men who ordered my arrest, confined me in a cage in company with murderers and negroes, and subsequently carried me to Marion in handcuffs before I had been even examined! Retribution already overtakes them! But they have made so much money by persecuting their fellow citizens that they can afford to *buy the Judge* and get off for the time. The infamous Jim Justice is a witness against the Scogginses, and they now threaten to expose some of *his* rascality and bring him and many others into difficulty. In short, it is *"a very pretty quarrel,"* as Capt. Mac Turk would say, and is likely to lead to exposures, highly beneficial to the public, if damaging to the actors. I must confess this information gives me great satisfaction. Nothing can so materially assist to vindicate my reputation as these criminations and recriminations of the principal emissaries of the government in the Ku Klux prosecutions, and who were the immediate workers of my own wrongs.   In South Carolina, also, the Scalawags have fallen to squabbling among themselves and are exposing their own corruption and lawlessness in fine style.   If it be true that a rogue makes the best of detectives, we may look for some extraordinary developments.

June 8th.   Letters from Geo. R. Valentine of New Bedford, Mass., requesting to see a copy of my paper, the "North Carolina Citizen."   Unfortunately I am not now in the newspaper business.   Bro. M. writes that he has been down to Philadelphia, and spent a day with Governor Pollock, who is a distant cousin of ours, and has a charming daughter.   M. is so disgusted with the South that he is resolved not to return home but go West, and is now trying to get a position on one of the Chicago R. R.'s where he will study law.   I am exceedingly sorry he don't go South and be with father in his old age, as well as take advantage of the family influence to advance his own fortunes.   But he has lived so long among the Yankees, he has become partly "Yankeeized;" and considers the South too slow for him I suppose.

June 12th.   A real, or pretended, lunatic was fetched in yesterday, and is giving me a great deal of trouble. He is a negro, and an old offender.   The surgeon told me to watch him closely and be ready for an outbreak; but I soon became satisfied that the black rascal is *shamming,* that is, no more insane than I am.   He cried, and raved precisely like a half-witted creature, so long as the officer was present, but became quite rational immediately after he withdrew.   This evening, however, after he heard me tell the deputy that he was a fraud he began to put on airs, so outrageously that we were obliged to handcuff him with his arms around one of the stout pillars in the room.   A couple of hours of this confinement cured him; so that when I asked him if he would behave himself he promised to be quiet as a lamb if released. He has given no trouble since. Yet, strange to say, the Deputy still thinks him crazy.

June 14th. About 9 o'clock last night two officers came in, dragging an huge Irishman in a fit of *delirium tremens.* He is quite a giant, and being very violent at times, I was obliged to set a constant watch by his bed-side, taking it myself during half the night. Deputy soon afterwards brought me a bottle of chloral, which, in an hour or two, I exorcised the "devil," and laid Pat in a comfortable slumber; although he never ceased to talk in his sleep, keeping nearly everybody else awake in the room. The counterfeit lunatic was so frightened by the ravings of the Irishman that he forgot his cunning, and talked as rationally as could be wished. I shall soon have a miniature Insane Asylum up here; I have three deranged men already, and a promise of others. Pleasant situation for a gentleman isn't it? But misery and the Penitentiary make strange bed fellows.

Three more Ku Klux were brought in today: Jno. Wallace sentenced for eight years; H. M. Moore, and Robt. Riggins for three years each. The last named was tried more than a year ago, but contrived to be kept in jail at Yorkville. His coming here now is no very promising indication of our getting out. Wallace deserves to come here, as he was one of the first to turn State's evidence, and swear against his friends and neighbors. But, having subsequently incurred the enmity of some of the Mongrel leaders, he was arrested on a new charge; and here he is where all traitors, and perjured witnesses ought to be!

Brown has letters containing newspaper extracts telling of the rapid organization of the negroes into military companies, and predicting the most direful consequences in S. C. if the movement is not checked through the good sense of the more intelligent of the colored people themselves. Here is one more feature of Grant's Ku Klux crusade; the negroes are to be incited to a servile war, which will lead to the military interference of the Government for carrying the South for Grant's *third term,* or a life dictatorship. The same policy is being carried out in Arkansas and Louisiana

I am told:—the government as usual supporting the negroes in all their atrocities.

June 15th. Got up before daylight to look after my crazy chaps, and could not sleep for thinking about the news I should get in the mail. But 'twas a waste of time; there was nothing for me. And yet——.[1]

June 16th. The negro (sham) lunatic turns out to be as sane as anybody; just as I predicted. But he did mimic madness "mighty muchly."

By the letters today I see that old preacher Ezell is in high hopes of a pardon. His Baptist brethren have been at work to get him out, and Judge Bond has written a letter to his son, Landrum, telling him that he is going to Washington to explain his case to the authorities, etc. Of course, Bond, who sent him here can get him out; and doubtless will make a merit of doing so, now that he sees that public sympathy is being awakened in behalf of his aged victim.

June 17th. Capt. P. informs me that old Mr. Ezell's pardon has been signed and doubtless will be here in a few days, which I am glad to hear.

It is reported that a widow lady and her daughter, 12 years old were *raped* by negroes in *Rutherford County*. The citizens caught one of the villains, and hung him;—another "Ku Klux outrage" of course.

This is no more than I expected, no more than the Mongrels encouraged by their shameful persecution of the white citizens of that county. The negroes have been taught that they are masters, and will be supported in any atrocity by Grant's bayonets. This very crime of rape of white women by brutal negroes was the origin of the Ku Klux Klan in the original instance.

Capt. P. mentions that he has just received a telegram telling him to hold one Bowen, and not commit him to the Penitentiary because a pardon has been signed by the President, and is on the way to him. Bowen is, I believe, the Scalawag postmaster of Mobile, and was convicted of embezzlement of large sums of money; but he proved that he used it in *electioneering for Grant,* so he is pardoned before he reaches the Penitentiary!

---

1 This paragraph is crossed out in the manuscript.

Can anything exceed this for open and unblushing partizanship. Here is the President compounding a felony merely because the thief applied the proceeds of his robbery to electioneering purposes! Thus the public treasury is robbed to carry the election of a partizan and corrupt President! But what of that? May it not be said of Grant's partizans—

> "Each hour dark fraud
> Or open rapine, or protected murder
> Cry out against them!"

I frequently wonder whether, in after years when I shall read these pages, I shall perceive that I was wrong; unduly biased against individuals; and erroneous in my judgment concerning the action of the administration? I am well aware that at times I write gloomily, and too often under the spur of bitter and indignant feelings. But have I exaggerated in any respect? Is not the cruel cunning of the administration shown in its acts, and illustrated by a thousand instances? Have I given too dark a tinge to the story of my own wrongs and sufferings? It is possible that Time may mitigate, and further information "explain away" much that now oppresses my soul, with horrible reminiscences. But in all candor and fairness I declare that I doubt if I have painted the depravity of the Mongrels, and the crafty corruption of our Military government in colors black enough to do them justice. I know that respecting myself I have stated only the truth. But who can tell what outrages of a similar nature may have been perpetrated on our Southern citizens since I came here!

June 18th. Rev. Jno. S. Ezell's pardon having arrived, he has just come in from the work shops for the last time. It will be a joyous afternoon for *him.* No more of wearisome prison life afar from his loved ones and in a strange land; no more drudgery in the shops under a captious overseer; no more dreary nights in a solitary cell; no association with vagabonds and cut throats. Liberty like the enchanter's wand will in less than an hour put all of these things out of sight, only to be remembered as the hideous creatures of some distempered dream! Thus terminates (let us hope) a persecution as foul and merciless as the decrees of the Spanish Inquisitions. This aged and earnest (tho' it may be uneducated) preacher of the gospel, has been tried, convicted, sentenced, and imprisoned among the offscouring of the earth—for no offense whatever; but merely because his principles were opposed to the wicked and usurping policy of the government. He at last is pardoned at demand of the public voice speaking through a number of the most respectable ministers of his own branch of the Church, North. He goes home in glee, and will there be more esteemed than ever. Even his Yankee brethren are satisfied of his innocence; for I notice that Dr. Simmons invites him to spend a day in New York with him; to meet other friends.

I rejoice that the old man is free. He personally was nothing to me but surely the Northern people who hear of his case must begin to reflect that if this *preacher* could be so treated how small the chance of escape for more insignificant men who were of less consequence in their communities.

I was in hope that old 'Squire Brown would have been released before now, as he is fast breaking with age and infirmity: but I suppose the government considers him not sufficiently humbled and disgraced for its clemency. Not until he abases himself utterly in the dust, will he be restored to his rights,—if it be not an Irish Bull to say that a man must give up one right —that of being truthful—to obtain another—liberty.

There is one thing in connection with the release of prisoners here that does not seem exactly just. A pardon may come in the 8 o'clock mail, but the prisoner knows nothing of it until 2 o'clock or later; the interval being used in the washing of his linen, etc. Now five or six hours is not much to a free man but to a miserable captive, toiling in the shops, this time is of no small importance. Five dollars *an hour* would not tempt me to stay in such a position, after I had a right to quit it. And surely the prisoner is entitled to his liberty the moment the pardon reaches the hands of the Superintendent. Of course it is as well that the man should know nothing of his good fortune for the time until he is put in possession of it; but I think he ought to be allowed to stop working.

The case of Leander Spencer, one of the K. K. from S. C., as I have heard it, shows much of the usual injustice of Jeffreys Bond's sentences.

Spencer and White were farm hands of a man named Wm. Smith, the chief of a Klan. The latter proposed that they three should whip a negro (Goode) who had threatened to violate some white women in the neighborhood, and who had also made himself very obnoxious to the whites by fixing old guns (he was a gunsmith) and furnishing new ones to arm negroes.

The party took Goode into the woods, and Smith then ordered Spencer to shoot him but Spencer recoiled from the murder, and utterly refused to have anything more to do with the business, notwithstanding their threats to kill him, too, if he drew back. Finally White shot the negro, and failing to kill him, deliberately beat out his brains with the butt of his gun.

And now we come to the injustice of the matter. When the arrests in York had frightened many of the Ku Klux into "confessing," and joining to hunt down their late friends and neighbors, White went to York, and turned State's evidence; thereby escaping himself (though he was the leader and *actual murderer*) and sending Spencer (who protested against it) and Caldwell, who merely assisted to bury the negro, to the Penitentiary for ten years, and compelling them to pay $1000 fines! These poor men are ignorant, and have no family influence; therefore they must serve full term, while White, the guiltiest of the party walks at liberty and fills his pockets by perjury. Such is the unfairness and injustice of these Government persecutions. Smith fled to parts unknown. Caldwell was not present, but was called in next day to help bury.

Today my "wild Irishman" was sent down to his cells, "Sound in mind and body." To him, as to many others, it is a blessing that he was arrested and sent to prison, for his hard drinking was carrying him to the grave at a gallop. He confesses that he has had three spells of delirium tremens in three months! As soon as released from bed he resumed his debauchery. Here he will be sober for six months, during which time Nature can rejuvenate his constitution somewhat though she can never restore it to aboriginal health. (N. B. I shouldn't like to have the rhetoricians criticise the foregoing sentences.)

*   *   *   *   *   *

Our surgeon is Dr. H. R. Haskins, (office 689 Broadway, Albany) who is (I'm told) the Professor of Anatomy of the Medical College in this City. He is a short stout man of about 36 years; dark hair and moustache; and apparently a good physician. Does he give proper attention to the sick? So far as I can see, he does. He visits the institution four times a week (Mondays, Wednesdays, Fridays, and Saturdays) and sometimes oftener. Patients able to work are called to the Deputy's desk in the Hall. In the hospital, the Doctor visits each bed. He uses very little medicine, chiefly opiates, tonics and astringents. Many convicts complain that he is sparing of his drugs, i. e., that is is *stingy,* but I am of opinion that he follows his professional judgment without regard to pocket. One hundred dollars is allowed by the institution for the purchase of medicines and surely ought to suffice for a year and I believe Dr. Haskins to be too honorable a man to defraud the sick convicts as is insinuated. In truth the position he holds is not a desirable one; or at least, it is one in which he will get no thanks from those he cures. I have never had a patient who gave the Doctor any confidence, and who did not profess to know better than anybody what kind of treatment he needed. Most of the convalescents clamor for bitters, patent pills, etc. One day the Doctor sounded a man's lungs to see if they were affected. When he retired a growler sneered, "'Spose he thinks he cured Williams by patting his belly!" Another man complains every damp day that the Doctor "won't give him nothing to cure his rheumatism," a chronic case which all the drugs in Albany could not alleviate.

It is possible that Dr. H. sometimes slights a man who really needs medicine, but this arises from the daily attempts to "play off sick" (to escape labor) which make him skeptical where the ailment is not actually perceptible.

June Nineteenth! A day memorable in American History; for on this day the first skirmish of the Revolutionary War, and the first in our Civil War (the attack on the Massachusetts Regt. in Baltimore) took place.

It is also memorable in my own personal history as the day on which I was released from Fort Delaware Military Prison in 1865, after 13 months confinement. Strange enough I have this morning found a sketch of our Barracks as they were then. The buildings were of rough planks, making one continuous hall subdivided into "divisions" for 100 men, each. The black looking space in the picture is to represent water, a slimy filthy "back water" from the river which gave an offensive odor in summer, and was frozen in winter; and being the only fluid allowed us for washing purposes, was execrated by all the prisoners. On the fence may be seen the sentinel who occasionally fired on us, sometimes for throwing water in the ditch after using it, and sometimes for not doing so. The yard contained about two acres, but was full of holes, the breathing places of huge Norway Rats, which many of the prisoners daily caught, skinned, and ate! I once tried to take a bite of rat soup; but could not accomplish it; although the cooked rodents looked as white and nice as squirrels.

During this long imprisonment I suffered much from hunger, thirst and cold; for we received but six crackers per day, and a morsel of spoiled meat; and were often without palatable drinking water, and few of us had more than one blanket, and very little underclothing; to say nothing of other annoyances. Yet Fort Delaware life was happiness in comparison to my existence here. For there were 2500 of us (officers) and no bar to amusement so far as we were capable of originating amusements among ourselves; and there was the stimulant of the feeling that we were undergoing hardships for the good of our Country, and to our own future honor.

And ah! what satisfaction, what pleasure, we promised ourselves *"when this cruel war is over!"* Then should we all go home and "fight our battles o'er again" around the friendly hearth. But the poet explains how all these fond predictions and anticipations were realized.

> "Ah me! what changes time has wrought
> And how predictions have miscarried.
> A few have reached the goal they sought,
> And some are dead, and some are married,
> And some in city journals war,
> And some are pleading at the bar,
> For jury verdicts, or for liquor!
>
> And some on trade and commerce wait
> And some in school with dunces battle,
> And some the gospel propagate
> And some the choicest herds of cattle,
> And some are living at their ease,
> And some were wrecked in the 'Revulsion,'
> Some 'serve the State' for handsome fees
> And *one* I hear *upon compulsion.*"

Brown was sick today, and at my suggestion did not go to work. I think any old man like him ought not to work unless he is able. Deputy came in and asked why he was not out at work? Brown said he was not able to go out today. "Pshaw! you should have taken a pill and gone to work! I don't stop work every time I feel a little weak!" etc., etc. The tone and manner in which these remarks were made was worse than the words. Poor Brown was quite cut to hear about it. This is no uncommon occurrence, and I am liable to the same abuse myself although I do not give the Deputy as many chances to pick at me as Brown does. Yet I can't help feeling worried and humiliated when I see an old man like Brown insulted by a lowborn hound like the fellow I speak of is.

Saturday, June 21st. The variableness of this climate accounts for the prevalence of consumption and pulmonary complaints. Yesterday on rising I was oppressed by the sultriness of the atmosphere; whereas today we are all shivering, although still wearing our winter flannel! "I wish I were in Dixie."

I mentioned a few days ago the sentence to this place of the Scalawag Post office Thief (Bowen) of Mobile Ala. and the probability that he would be pardoned, as he proved that the stolen money was expended in *electioneering for Grant*. He arrived here three days ago under sentence of *12 months* (other poor devils get 12 years) but was *pardoned and released this afternoon!*

The barefaced iniquity of the Administration in this transaction surpasses even anything in the former history. It should bring the blush of shame to the cheeks of every honest Republican in the land; for why is this rogue pardoned? Simply because of a political party! Grant or his agents in the Cabinet having done the same thing (though under the pretense of paying the expenses of the Ku Klux Courts) they feel obliged to screen an humble disciple who follows their example. So when Grant is up for his 3rd term (or life) I suppose we shall see all good Republican postmasters doing their best to spend the public funds in his favor.

Sunday, June 22nd. It was some consolation to hear from dear Aunt Susie this morning, and be assured by her that *one* at least, has not forgotten me nor ceased to feel affectionate interest in my welfare. Strange that I, a *Southerner*, and *suffering for my Southern principles*, should be left to languish, alone and uncared for, except by one friend, and she a genuine *New England* lady! A father I have; and brothers, sisters, friends (so-called) in the South; and they profess to feel indignant at the oppressions and villainy of the men who sent me here. But on this Sabbath morning (as usual) I am without a line from the South while even the poor devils whose friends have to get the neighbors to write their letters for them, receive their budget of home intelligence regularly almost every week. Thus have I been mortified and pained Sabbath after Sabbath for 12 months or longer! Surely I shall not forget this if Fortune ever restores me to mine own again. Scruggs' wife writes that she *walked twenty miles* to borrow the money to send him for his expenses home! this is *hero-ism,* but she does not know it. Brown's letters tell him that the negroes are being organized and armed in S. C., and serious trouble is anticipated. The "irrepressible nigger" seems to be resolved on his own destruction. Nothing can save him; and the longer the Radicals rule the country, the faster his march to extermination. Jefferson knew the negro well when he wrote, "The slaves are to be free, but it is no less certain that the two races equally free cannot live together in the same government. Nature, habit, opinion have drawn indelible lines of distinction between them." And Jefferson is called the Great Apostle of Freedom!

June 23rd. It is hardly possible to describe the petty mortifications I am obliged to undergo from day to day in this wearisome confinement. Yesterday I felt sad and depressed because I failed to *get a letter,* and to-day I am brought to the same gloomy feeling because I failed to *write one.* Two weeks ago, I asked for an half sheet of paper to answer a letter which I expected to receive from home; and as I did not get the expected missive, I retained the half sheet until I should hear from home. Today the Deputy wanted to know what I did with the half sheet. I produced it. "Well, now here-after when you ask to write a letter, go write it, and don't put me to this bother another time." I naturally felt hurt and humiliated by this speech; for I had in-tended no breach of the rules; and as Capt. P. allows me to have 2 quires or more of paper at once, I saw nothing improper in retaining the half sheet until I could hear from those who profess to consider me a relation.

But in spite of my earnest endeavors to comply with the regulations, and show courtesy towards the officers, I am constantly being cut up with these petty reproofs which wound my feelings much more than a blow could do if I was in a position to resent it.

It is astonishing that Capt. Pilsbury should treat me courteously and considerately while his subordinates are permitted to do exactly the reverse.

One thing certain I shall not ask for any more paper if I never write another letter.

Another mail robber (I. J. Hamlin) was pardoned today. Grant seems determined that all the rogues in the country shall owe him obligations. The tyrants who overthrew the Roman and Grecian Republics did likewise; pardoned the public offenders and cultivated the gratitude of the rabble, until they saw fit to assume the purple; after which they leaned towards the patricians and trampled on the populace.

June 24th. R. B. Clark, another counterfeiter pardoned today. Political friends in New York forced Gov. Dix to solicit his pardon of Grant, and the latter was glad to oblige his supporter, as well as to lay under obligations a fellow who may be of some service as an electioneer among the denizens of Five Points. Clark was considered one of the worst men here.

I do not grudge these men their liberty; and indeed, I think they ought to have been released sooner; for three years are surely enough to punish a man for a first offense. But how monstrous is that cunning policy which retails clemency to convicted criminals, who promise aid to the dominant faction; but forbids it to innocent men whom the conspirators have robbed of their rightful liberty.

Deputy came up to inquire about razor of C's. I did not know any thing about it. But for all that he must search my box as if I would steal it. Of course he did not find it. No one can tell how much incensed I am by these insinuations, notwithstanding my resolves to the contrary. However one can't be a philosopher when racked by the toothache and such small matters.

I have frequently remarked that military courts, and special commissions to try State prisoners, are the most convenient and most arbitrary instruments of our Republican (so-called) Government for the perpetration of the foulest injustice and persecution. Let me now record an instance of which I have been informed for a considerable time but which is now brought forcibly to mind by the approaching death of the victim.

Saml. O. Berry (the son of a man in humble circum-

stances) born at Liberty, Clay Co. Mo. in the Spring
of 1839. When 6 years old he lost his mother and was
then removed by his father to Kentucky where he was
bound apprentice to a good old Shaker in Shaker town,
Mercer County. In his 13th year he ran away from his
straitlaced guardians and went to Louisville but subsequently returned to the country, and rejoined his father.
In 1862 Berry joined the Confederate Army—Grigs-
by's Ky. Cavalry. In 1864, when the Confederates
evacuated the Kentucky borders, he was sent into that
State to bring out deserters, and stragglers, and to damage the enemy in every way in his power consistently
with the laws of war. Kentucky was full of absentees
from the Confederate Army who were unable to rejoin
their commands owing to the vigilance of the Federal
outposts; and among these Berry soon arranged a system of depredations on the enemy which gained him a
wide reputation for daring and activity, as well as for
cruelty. Respecting this portion of Berry's career I
know nothing more than he tells me; but as he is aware
that his end is near at hand, and as he professes the sincerest piety, I am disposed to credit his asseverations that
he never countenanced the excesses which disgraced the
partizan warfare of the "dark and bloody ground" nor
did he permit of such excesses by the men under his
immediate command. Many crimes were, however, attributed to him; and when the war closed his friends
counselled him to fly from the country. He considered
himself protected by his Confederate commission; and
Genl. Palmer (the Federal Commandant of the District) was evidently of the same opinion, as he admitted
Berry to the regular *parole* on the 30th day of May
1865, and sent him word that he should not be molested
so long as he behaved himself. Yet on the 7th of December, 1865, a squad of cavalry under Maj. Wilson, led
by a false friend of Berry's surprised him, and carried
him to Louisville to be tried for murder. The court met
in January and consisted of Maj. Genl. Palmer and
Jeff C. Davis, Maj. Collins, Lieut Burns, and others,
with Major Wm. Coyle, acting Judge Advocate. There
were 17 different charges against Berry, but the evi-

dence was of the most unreliable character, while several Union citizens, including a colonel of volunteers whose life had been saved by Berry's interference, came forward voluntarily to testify to his magnanimity to prisoners. But the court (excepting General Palmer) was deeply prejudiced against the prisoner, and nothing could save him. On the first of February 1866 he was sentenced to be hung; and the inhuman jailor erected his gallows directly in front of Berry's windows where it stood for weeks to remind him of his approaching doom. But the victim was not to perish so quickly. President Johnson commuted his sentence to ten years in the Penitentiary, dating from the 3rd of March 1866. He came here soon afterwards; and as evil report had preceded him, was regarded as a perfect desperado by the officers. Nor was he long in getting into trouble; for on breaking the rules in some slight particular he was reproved so harshly that he made an angry reply, and was punished for it. This made matters worse, and he was locked up in his cell where he remained for nearly *seven years!* He confesses that he was wrong in yielding to his anger; but I can very well see how a high spirited young man who felt that he was unjustly imprisoned; might forget himself when unduly provoked by his keepers, especially when they were imbued with a strong prejudice against him. Of this, however, I have only his own statement.

Time and sorrow and close confinement did their work, and now at 32 years of age Berry is dying an *old gray-haired man!* His young wife died of a broken heart, leaving him a son whom he has never seen. His father also, died since he came here. And Berry will be in the grave with them in a very few weeks. He was fetched up to the hospital some time ago but his health and spirits are so utterly broken that no medicine or nursing can save him. Even liberty could not benefit him now. His intellect is almost as weak as his body; and he has no energy whatever. He cares for nothing but to lie and sleep; and yet sleep he cannot without opiates. There has been unaccountable opposition to this poor fellow's pardon. No less than ten times has his

case been reveiwed by the Attorney General and always
with an adverse report; although the petition for pardon
was signed by such men as Maj. Gen. Thomas, Governor Palmer, (of Illinois), Gov. Stevenson (of Ky.),
Ex. Gov. Bramlette, Genl. Ward, Maj. Genl. Rous-
seau, Geo. D. Prentice, Hon. J. J. Guthrie, Powell
Clayton, etc. The last named who married a cousin of
Berry's has exerted himself to the utmost to effect the
pardon; but in vain. The Government can pardon murderers, robbers, and all sorts of desperadoes; but a
Southerner who has dared to signalize himself by deeds
of successful audacity, must linger and die in Northern
dungeons!

Now in summing up this statement, I know not what
degree of guilt truly attaches to Berry; but there is no
doubt that he was a *Confederate officer* and had a right
to *kill, burn, and plunder,* as best he could, those who
were invading the soil of his state. And his magnanimity to prisoners seems to be well established; for Governor Palmer (who presided on his trial) recommends
him for pardon *on that very ground*. And Berry declares he never killed but one citizen, and that was in a
melee after he had been shot himself.

Be that as it may, he has been for years in so wretched
and sickly a condition that it was inhumanity to torture
him to death by holding him here. Yet this is precisely
what has been done; and the end is not far off.

A LONELY NIGHT WATCH

1873.

July 1st-14th. The past fortnight has been one
of the most distressing of my prison experience. There
has been so much sickness and night watching, so much
irksome duty in connection with the dying, the dead,
and the lunatics, that I have many times wished myself
back in my solitary cell, where at least I could sleep at
night, and have my thoughts to myself without such dis-
cordant interruptions as continually distract me in this
crowded hospital. Let me speak of the death of Oscar
Berry, the one-armed Kentuckian of whom I gave an
account in a former entry. He had been confined in a

cell for nearly seven years, when at the eighth brought up to this place to die. Never have I seen a similar spectacle; for although only about my age, still under twenty-eight, his white hair, wrinkled features, and dejected air, made him appear an old man tottering on the verge of the grave. Nevertheless I believe he would have recovered, and perhaps lived many years, but for the malice and meanness of two Yankees. The effect of the change from his silent cell to the lighter, warmer, and bright surroundings of the Hospital, with the companionship of a number of convalescents, was very perceptible; and, in a few days he picked up sufficiently to sit in a chair and talk with old Mr. Brown and others. I felt sympathy for him as a fellow Southerner, and sufferer, a brave Confederate soldier, and a victim of vile Radicalism; therefore made every effort to arouse and invigorate his shattered mind and body; and, for a time, with much success. He even began to *hope,* and have appetite. Unfortunately his cot adjoined that of S. O. Crawford, of Saugerties, New York, a young lawyer, who had been convicted of embezzling money from Insurance companies. Crawford was handsome, (though *cunning* and trickery shone in every feature) and so plausible that Genl. P., on promoting me to take charge of the Hospital warned me against the sleek young Yankee as one who would give me more trouble than all the other inmates. I felt very much tempted to ask the General, in response whether during the eighteen months I was drudging in the work-shops I had ever shown any disposition to affiliate with the convicts. But on second thought I thanked the old gentleman as if I had taken his advice very greatly to heart. And perhaps I was the better for it, as Crawford needed constant watching. He seemed to have no conception of honor or moral principle. He saw that Oscar Berry was weak in mind and body, and instead of feeling pity for a youth of his own age, thus terribly wrecked, he exerted all his blandishments to secure an influence over him in order that he might wheedle him out of his money, provisions, (sent by friends) extra clothing, etc.; for

Berry had wealthy relatives who kept him well supplied with everything the prison rules will admit of.

I saw from the first, the "little game" of the swindler; but as Berry needed nursing and coddling, all of which Crawford gladly performed in order to ingratiate himself with his victim, I did not interfere. About a month ago Crawford was discharged, and left Berry under the belief that he should hasten at once to Washington and exert all the influence of his "Uncle," Gen. Crawford of Phila., and others, to get a re-hearing of Berry's application for pardon. So great was Berry's belief in the truthfulness of Crawford's marvelous tales and promises that he presented the latter a fine pair of cavalry boots (cost $18) and also, a variety of smaller articles, books, etc. sent to him during the long years of his solitary confinement.

Berry's hopefulness was so confident I thought of warning him against disappointment; but had I not been doing all I could to cheer him, and would not this be counteracting my own efforts?

Disappointment came soon enough. During the first week after Crawford's departure, Berry watched the door like a cat at a mouse hole, expecting the Deputy to enter with a box, or package. It never came; and at the end of two weeks he began to realize that he had been again deceived. For several days he tried to conceal his chagrin, but it was easy to see he had relapsed into his listlessness.

Then came two other disappointments. His friends in Missouri had sent him two boxes of edibles. One was entirely lost: the other came and was opened by Berry with great impatience. *Every article was mildewed and decayed;* the box having been delayed for weeks on the road! The other disappointment was a letter from Congressman Powell Clayton who married Berry's cousin, stating that the tenth, and final effort to obtain a pardon for him had failed utterly, as Secretary of War W. W. Belknap was even more embittered against him than was Jo. Holt.

I tried to rouse his drooping spirits, by telling him he had only 18 months yet to serve, and though his wife, and his father were dead, he had still his young son to live for, and a brother's home to go to; and above all he had his own name to vindicate, and his enemies to punish. But he was now too far gone to feel the influence of any appeal whatsoever. He admitted that he ought to try and live, but said there was no longer any hope of surviving his term of service, therefore the sooner he were out of the way the less he should suffer.

One day he remarked, "It is not long now until the Fourth of July. But then what does it matter? I've seen my last Fourth of July dinner." I made some jocose reply; but he persisted in a melancholy tone that he should never live to see another 4th of July; and strange to say his words were prophetic! On the first of July he went to bed, and shortly afterwards relapsed into a comatose condition, alive and breathing heavily, but unconscious. I watched by his bedside all night on the 1st, half the night on the 2nd, and again all night on the third, my assistant being himself sick. This night was a sorrowful one, indeed! Outside the prison all was jollity. The uproar, the banging of guns, pistols, and fire-crackers began at sunset on the 3rd, and was kept up all the night long. The echoes of the great city, rioting in its annual saturnalia of saltpetre, fire works, shouting, shooting, drunkenness and demagoguery, were strangely in contrast with the sad scene in this prison hospital, where I sat watching the death throes of two men. The other patients had all fallen asleep, the lights were toned down, and I sat on the broad window ledge, clinging with one arm around the bars, to hold myself in position, for the night was warm and there was little draught in the hospital when the doors were all locked on us at night. But the room being on the upper story had full access for the sounds and explosions of the surrounding suburbs; very different from the cells into which nothing less thundering than a cannon could penetrate.

Slowly the hours crept past, and the clock on the city tower pealed the noon of night. As the chimes ceased, a strain of superb music (vocal with instrumental accompaniment) swelled upon the night breeze with thrilling effect. A large company of singers, probably some Glee Club, had taken position on a flat roof of a very high building in the centre of the "Hill" section of the city to greet the dawning anniversary with anthems and carrols. The voices were very strong and through the high, sashless windows, accompanied by instruments, and, as it were, scented by the perfumes of the rich gardens of the adjacent residences, it seemed unreal, supernatural! Certainly I never was so affected—spell-bound—by any kind of music before. The anthem was grand, the carol delightful; and for the moment I forgot that I was clinging in the third-story window of a Penitentiary hospital to listen to it! But when silence came there was a painful revulsion. A low moan from the beds caused me to glide noiselessly to the two sick men; and lo! Oscar's eyes were open (for the first time in three days) and his head turned as if listening to the strains of music! Did he mistake it for celestial harmonies? We cannot know. For even as I watched his haggard face, he breathed a long sad sigh and breath passed forever from his lips!

He had spoken truly; he did not live to see the dawn of another Fourth of July, though very nearly thereto.

Ascertaining that Berry was really dead I aroused my assistant, and we proceeded to perform the disagreeable duties so often required of us this year. (The body must be stripped, wrapped in an old sheet, and lifted out upon the floor of the hospital, and straightened: there to be left until six o'clock next morning, when the doors are unlocked and a coffin can be sent for).

Considerable time was taken in paying these last duties to the dead (for I wished to show all the respect to poor Berry that would be allowed me, and therefore had him dressed in a new suit of underclothing, and not sent away as are the generality of the dead prisoners, nearly nude) so that the grey glimmer of dawn crept in as we were composing the corpse on the floor. A tremendous explosion of artillery, accompanied by clashing cymbals, drums, brass-bands, and all manner of reports of burnt powder, together with the clangor of an hundred church bells at this moment shook and roused the city to greet the "Anniversary of Freedom," the "Glorious Fourth," "The Day We Celebrate!"

Amid the uproar I stood looking down upon the mutilated remains of the young Southerner, who had given, first, his time, his services, his right arm, for the cause of his countrymen and now, at last, after eight years of suffering, in ignominious solitude and confinement, yielded up his shattered remnants of life! What a savage satire was this death amid the shouts and rioting of the blind and prejudiced people of the North, in so-called celebration of "Universal Liberty," "National Independence," "The Best of Governments!" To think, too, that on this day, we, helpless prisoners (I refer to the Southern political prisoners)—should be forced to attend services in the Chapel (such as I described in connection with the last year's Fourth) and sit, surrounded by hideous malefactors, to listen to silly speeches in panegyric of "Our Noble Rulers," "Our Grand Republic," "Our wise, just, paternal, and peerless government!" Yea, and our "great and good President, Ulysses S. Grant!" What mockery! What a shame!

At breakfast time four convicts came into the Hospital with the usual pine box by courtesy called a coffin. Would it not be well, I asked the Deputy, to hold the body until Berry's friends can be notified? "Never you mind about that!" was the gruff answer, as the men scraped a few shavings into the end of the coffin as a pillow, stretched the body thereon, and nailed it down, and bore it away.

Meantime the other sick man, (Dwyer) who had watched us lift Berry's body from the bed, became so frightened at the scene, and the realization of his own approaching end, that he fell into convulsions, and began to struggle and rave, screaming that "I aint agoing to *die!* Oh! I *aint* a-going to die! Berry's got the *box!* . . ."

[*Two pages are here cut out.*]

After being taken abed he called me and said, "I never have bothered you much have I?" "Not much,

Dwyer; what do you want?" "Well, you see, Steward,
I'm on my last pegs, an' its a tight race betwixt me an'
the capting over yonder who'll die fust (alluding to
Berry), but it looks like I wus gwine a leetle ahead.
Now, you see, my wife, she sent me here, 'cos she
wanted to live with another feller (this was the truth I
suspect) an' she wouldn't never come a nigh me all these
whiles, but I hear she's a coming ter-morrow, 'cos she
knows my time is out in nine days, and she's afeard I'll
come and play smash 'round her an' her feller. But I
reckon I won't git ter live a-til my time's out, so I want
you ter promise, steward, you'll bundle up my clothes,
especially this yer new undershirt, an' either burn 'em,
or give them to that black nigger what brings the dinner, 'cos my wife, she'll be a-comin' ter git my clothes,
and it would a-most kill me ter think of that feller o'
hern wearing my shirts an' things!"

I should have been amused at the poor creatures
anxiety to prevent his effects from going to his wife's
paramour had I not so plainly perceived the sign of
Death's shadows in his eyes. It seemed a terrible and unnatural thing that such thoughts should occupy a human
mind at the very moment of the passage behind the veil
of Eternity. But these waifs from the slums have no instincts higher than a brute's.

*   *   *   *   *   *

1873.
July, 14th-15th. The gruffness and rudeness of
the Deputy Superintendent makes me almost constantly miserable. He doesn't like to see me *studying,*
strange as it may seem; and often times he slips up
stairs in his noiseless cloth-slippers to surprise us and
if possible to catch me in some infraction of the rules
or some negligence of duties, so that he may have an
excuse for depriving me of my books, paper, and pencil. Do I do him injustice in this? I think not; for whenever he finds me poring over my law books, or studying
French, or practicing Phonography, he perceptibly
frowns, and never fails to order me to attend to something; or he scolds me for not doing this or that. It is
rarely he finds things as he wishes them and no matter

how I might arrange them, he would not want them that way. For example, he just now has ordered me (having found me immersed in my grammar) to turn the blankets on the whole row of cots, putting the under side uppermost. It is not at all probable that he really wants them thus, because they are not meant for it, but he thereby breaks up my studying, and gets a chance to hurt my feelings by his gruff, "See that you attend to it right away; and keep this place looking more in trim."

Often and often I am tempted to pitch my books into the fire, and give up all thought of saving myself from the insanity which must surely overtake me during the dreary years before me if I do not seek to strengthen my mind by study, and at the same time divert it from the gloomy brooding over my wrongs which every moment would return and take possession of my soul. But if I give up books and pencil shall I not also give up all hope of teaching my enemies that they may slander, villify, and imprison, but cannot crush or ruin? I must go on, and try to endure all things that good may come.

'Squire Sam Brown received a letter on Sunday which depresses him greatly: so much that he has taken his bed fancying himself sick. The circumstances are certainly aggravating. It will be remembered that an unprincipled demagogue named A. S. Wallace holds the seat (to which he was not elected) belonging to the congressional district of which York County is a part. Wallace, therefore, is Representative, in fact, though not in right, of Brown's district and is looked upon as one of the most prominent of the villainous coalition of Carpetbaggers and Scalawags who have so long plundered the Prostrate State. Wallace is still further strengthened by the office of United States Marshal for South Carolina; the title being held by his son, but the power (and it is an autocratic power much greater than Queen Victoria ever exercises) is virtually in the hands of the unscrupulous old rascal in York. The latter, it may be remarked, is a neighbor of 'Squire Brown, and is indebted to him for many friendly deeds in former days when Wallace was one of the bitterest of "fire-eaters," and slave-drivers. Yet no man has shown a more vindictive spirit in pursuing and persecuting his neighbors. Several months ago Brown's friends recognized the power possessed by "Ass" Wallace (as he is almost universally styled in South Carolina) through his stolen seat at Washington, urged the old man to make overtures to Wallace, and seek to propitiate him, etc. Finally in a fit of homesickness, the 'Squire wrote a very humble letter appealing to the fraudulent Congressman to remember old fellowships, and not bear hard feelings, but lend his influence in behalf of the efforts now being made to secure his own release from prison, as his family were sorely distressed and in need of his assistance. Members of Brown's family also, went to Wallace almost upon their knees. Each time the old thief became very voluble in "promises," but always had some excuse for delaying immediate action. Of course none was taken. About three weeks ago, Brown received a letter from one J. D. Ottz, a secret service agent, well known at Raleigh and Charlotte, stating that he had seen President Grant and held his explicit promise that if Brown's friends would get up a petition and have it signed by the neighbors, he would issue a pardon for him. Ottz suggested the petition be sent to himself by the 1st of July, and he would lose no time in reminding Grant of his promise. Squire Brown was now in high feather. His friends speedily got up the petition, and had a number of well known Republican's names on it. Hearing of the movement, the wily Wallace called on Brown's friends, expressed great gratification, and, of course, got possession of the petition; promising to forward it by next mail accompanied by private recommendations, etc. All these details were promptly written to the old man, who for the first time yielded implicit credence to the assurances of his family that he would be *at home in a fortnight or so!* Weeks went by, and nothing was heard of the release. Finally after the *"1st of July,"* (the limit which Ottz had set as the latest date at which he could be able to assist in the matter),

Wallace admitted he had never sent the petition, and really could not think of signing it, as it *"might cause a fuss among* his Party!" Could anything be more base, treacherous, and malicious? The result is that all the 'Squire's dreams of speedy return to his grieving wife, and unprotected daughters, have melted in thin air, and the disappointment is very severe upon him; especially as he has been roughly treated of late, by the Deputy and his Overseer. He is a good hearted, easy-dispositioned, old man, accustomed to a good deal of petting among his friends and relatives and it seems impossible for him to recollect that he is an utter stranger here, a prisoner on the footing of a felon, and as much subject to the strict discipline as the vilest negro or thief in the Prison gang. This forgetfulness causes him many a moment of pain and mortification; for the understrappers nearly all dislike him.

Another crazy negro has been brought into the hospital to give trouble. I shall soon have a small mad-house under my charge. Large numbers of demented creatures are unjustly convicted every year, for instead of being sent to the Penitentiary they ought to have permanent confinement in an insane asylum. Surgeon Haskins tells me there is no question that many magistrates send half-witted men to this Prison solely to get rid of them. The law requires that when a prisoner shows signs of insanity he shall be placed in the prison hospital under treatment of the Surgeon, for a stated period; not less than three months I believe. Thus it is that we have at all times, two or three lunatics among the inmates; for there are new victims of dementia every month or so.

1873.

July 16th. At noon today the engine blew off steam, the great wheels ceased to revolve, the roar of the machinery grew still, the convicts were marched to their cells, and locked within; and the noisy prison suddenly became as quiet as the Sabbath!

This half-day of rest was in respect to the obsequies of the late Superintendent, old Genl. Amos Pilsbury, who died yesterday morning. He had been in ill-health for a long time, suffering from internal disorders which gave him no ease except when under the influence of morphine. The last time he visited the Hospital he asked me to lend him my arm to descend the long flight of stairs leading to the Main Hall and remarked as we passed down that he should never ascend them again. It seems his utterance was prophetic.

It is perhaps unusual for a prisoner to feel any special interest in the lives of his keepers, particularly under a rigid discipline such as prevails here, but I certainly very greatly regret the loss of the old General; for he was, I think, really well intentioned towards me and would gladly have set me free at any moment, if he might; or would grant me many privileges if he could have done so without relaxing the impartial discipline essential to the system of the Institution.

He possessed many noble traits of character; and one of the greatest was his confidence in human nature, notwithstanding his forty five (45) years as a Prison-Keeper, during which time he must have seen more of the wild, wayward, and wicked side of society than any other man of the time.

Yet his latest public appearance was at an International Congress for the Reformation of Prisoners, and his latest publications were written in behalf of the same object. His views were so just and compassionate, I draw large extracts from them in my articles on "Prisoner's Aid Associations."

July 17th. Began the day with a severe struggle with one of my crazy negro patients. The Deputy directs me to make him stay in his bed. At breakfast time, the darkey, who I sometimes think is by no means so crazy as he pretends, sprang out of bed, and galloped round the hall like a wild man. I ordered him back to his bed, and on his refusing to go, took him firmly by the arm to lead him. Instantly the negro seized me by both arms and tried to bite me with a very formidable set of grinders. He was not so large as myself, but had better muscles, and probably derived the unnatural strength of frenzy which makes lunatics dangerous. However I succeeded in mastering him after a prolonged struggle in which my clothing was much torn, and my temper almost torn to tatters also. Having securely tied him hands and feet I placed him in bed, set another negro to feed him with a spoon; and then spent half an hour trying to get rid of the peculiar *odor d'Afrique* which tainted hands and clothing from contact with the fellow. Then, for an hour I deliberated whether it were not better to take the vial of prussic acid which was among my medicine stores, and get rid at once and forever of these terrible humiliations—nursing filthy felons, all the night, and tussling with negro lunatics by day! True, it was only doing my duty according to the requirements of my situation; but unfortunately duty is merely moral whereas the sense of mortification, indignity, and disgust is natural!

A NARROW ESCAPE

July 18th. A very disagreeable night. I sat up till midnight, and I was rather afraid to leave my brace of crazy men so long as they were awake. Indeed until near midnight there was no sleep for any of us, as the lunatics were alternately singing, screaming, praying and cursing in a fearful manner. Several times the guards came up the stairs from the Main Hall to demand the silencing of the outcries, but I told them nothing could be done save killing them, and there was no "Rule" for that, even in Albany Penitentiary. However about twelve o'clock A. M. I went to my cot. The gas was turned low, but not so much so that I could not see the other beds. Every inmate was quiet, and from the sounds of snoring all were asleep. Wearied by repeated night watching, I quickly fell into the same condition. It was not "so very" far from being my last long sleep. For towards morning I became conscious of heavy breathing near my face, and at the same moment heard an outcry from one of the convalescents. The crazy negro, Johnston, had slipped his handcuffs, loosened his straps, and slipping down to the sinks got one of the twelve-pound iron "dumb bells," which I had, as I thought, securely concealed! With this fearful weapon in his hand, he crawled on all-fours under the long row of cots until he came to mine, which was at the upper end of the Hall. He then crept upright, and was about to make a cat-like pounce upon me, perhaps to brain me at a blow with the heavy bolt, when simultaneously I opened my eyes, and he was diverted by the cry of the men at the other end of the room.

I sprang out of bed, and partially dressed myself, while telling Jones to arouse old Squire Brown, and two or three of the convalescents. As soon as they were up, I went to the lunatic, who had gone to the side of the Hall, and was hammering at a window. Seeing there was no use of wasting words I seized him, and the others rushed in to help me; and their assistance was needed, for the fellow seemed made of iron. However we overpowered him, and restored his shackles; and strapped him to the bed. During the entire procedure he raved and cursed frightfully, declaiming against me as *"that Damned Steward,"* whom he meant to kill at the first opportunity!

After this delightful midnight episode I did not feel composed for a renewal of my nap; and today I feel weak, sick, and worn out. And yet, with these sights and sounds before me, how grateful I ought to feel for the *mens sano in sano corpore,* the sound mind, in a sound body!

July 19th. Deputy Scripture ordered me, if the lunatics gave trouble to handcuff them with their arms around the pillars in the center of the Hall. I did this once, but the poor creature thus bound seemed to suffer so much from his constrained posture that I disliked to repeat it. I determined to strap him securely in bed, hoping he would soon fall asleep. (I refer particularly to the darkey Johnston, as the others gave trouble only at intervals of several days) Johnston is very cunning—so much so that I sometimes doubt his insanity —pretended to go to sleep at once. Nevertheless I watched him for a long time, resting on my elbow on my own cot in a position to see his. Sleep eventually overpowered me, and the darkey began to free himself. He gnawed his arm ropes, slipped his handcuffs, untied his feet, and gently slid down upon the floor. He first

devoted himself to hiding his handcuffs, and succeeded
so well that we haven't yet found them. He then unlocked the key of the Pantry and was hunting for a
knife when one of the convalescents who had been afraid
to give the alarm previously called me to the front.
I now resorted to the more severe measures of tying his
arms *behind his back,* and strapping him as before. It
was, of course, not possible for him to rest easily in such
a posture, but it seemed more humane than to force
him to sit on the hard floor with his arms around a post.
Perhaps I ought to say here that it is not the fault of
the prison authorities that these poor creatures are thus
treated. They were sent here by the legal authorities,
and must be confined in some manner, else they will
surely kill some one, perhaps themselves, perhaps myself, perhaps some helpless sick man in the adjoining
cots. The real blame and shame consists in the original
conviction of such men.

Have just been down to the guard room to see Aunt
Susie, Cousin Lizzie Dwight, and Rev. Dr. S. who had
written to notify me they were coming; but as their
note was *not given me,* I knew nothing of it, and was
taken so unawares that I felt rather flurried. However
they seemed so affectionate I was soon at ease, though
it was hard thus to meet my Northern relatives after
fifteen years of non-intercourse, I in the striped jacket
of a convict and with an armed guard standing over me
throughout the interview. I must say, though, that Deputy Scripture showed some courtesy in pretending to
be busily looking over the books as we talked, instead
of watching us. He also "passed" to me several books,
pictures, etc., which Auntie had brought for me, without searching through them for notes as he usually does.
Cousin Lizzie is the same jolly, plump and pretty little
woman whom I first met in Penna. in my school days.
She pressed me to make them a visit on my release, if
that ever should happen, but it is not at all likely I shall
ever do so. Her husband she says is a strong Republican
and "all the Dwights have been Abolitionists." She
need not have told me so much; it was enough to say
that William Dwight is *editor of a New England Re-*

publican journal! All birds of that feather have a professional doctrine which binds them to abuse and denounce the South, and Southerners, "regardless!"

Notwithstanding, I was gratified at the visit, and I think I showed them a feeble glimmer of the truth. For if they came to compassionate me, as a convict, or wrong-doer, they soon learned I would accept no sympathy which was not based on a full acknowledgement that I am suffering from political malice, and not from any crime of my own.

Sunday.

July 20th. Another of the crazy men slipped his handcuffs last night and gave me a great deal of trouble. I have twice spoken to the Deputy about these men, who ought to be sent to the Asylum, or placed in the cells specially fitted for them. There are four of such cells in the "East Wing," but it is reported that all are full! The negroes seem to furnish the majority of new cases, and the reason is easily understood by physicians.

"No letters" again this week! It seems useless for me to vow I will not yield to disappointment; for each Sunday morning finds me on the alert as usual, and perfectly *certain* of some word from some friend *this* time! But, of course, it is merely repeating the pang of disappointment and chagrin. It is not easy for one at my age to bring himself to admit that he has no friends, nor any to feel an interest in him; but "Out of sight, out of mind." So be it; I'll learn in time to measure as is now meted to me. After all, the main motive of my craving for letters is to obtain news from "home," to give me something to think about, and divert my mind. And do I not have the advantage of old 'Squire Brown's large correspondence? He has had quite a bundle of them to-day, and there is an item of good news for all of us. The Democrats, i. e., the decent citizens of "York District," South Carolina, have sent a delegation of prominent personages to intercede with Grant for the release of the South Carolinians now in this Prison. This is a good move. Not that any direct result is likely to come of it; but it will tend to attract public attention thitherward and will keep us from being utterly forgotten among our friends.

From the hospital window as I write may be witnessed a spectacle rarely if ever known down among the "Savage slave-holders," notwithstanding their oft denounced "Barbarity," "Lawlessness," and "Selfishness." The sight to which I refer is, that of *an whole field of reapers cutting grain on the Sabbath day!* The field is said to belong to the County Poor-House, which stands at one end of it, and from the appearance the harvesters are inmates of that institution. I suppose they are forced to desecrate the Sabbath, or seek other homes, which are not easy to find in this section. But whether these particular reapers are compelled or not, there are others who do likewise without compulsion. A few weeks ago when the hay was being cut, we saw men at work in several fields on Sabbath; and I have seen one farmer building fence while the city church bells were ringing within plain hearing!

Now, I suppose, these fellows would give some excuse, pretending to fear a storm, or the injury of the crop, but were such a scene to be witnessed down South, a thousand preachers and papers would make it the text for severest denunciation of Southern ungodliness!

Services in the chapel this morning were in memory of Genl. Pilsbury. The pulpit, and the large arm chair usually occupied by the old Superintendent, on the left of the desk, were draped in black. Chaplain Reynolds devoted his discourse to the moral, religious, and philanthropic traits of the deceased; mentioning many incidents of his large-heartedness. Unfortunately there is little opportunity to exhibit the softer side of a man's nature when he has a thousand or so fierce outcasts and outlaws (the majority I mean) under his control watching for the least chance to throw off that control. Still, as far as I can judge, the convicts regarded Genl. Pilsbury as a *just man,* and more than usual stillness prevailed among them as the Chaplain narrated instances of his generous faith in human nature. At the close of the services, a musical amateur from one of the city choirs sang the hymn "Home of the Soul," which the

General requested should be sung after his death. What a people!

NO CHANCE FOR ESCAPE

July 21st. It would seem, from the marvelous escapes of noted characters from both civil and military prisons, that a determined and desperate man can break out of any prison that man can devise. But if such narratives be examined it will be found that in nearly every instance the successful fugitive had a plenty of leisure at his disposal, or in other words, was simply a *prisoner,* not a galley-slave, or confined in a treadmill. Albany Penitentiary appears to be proof against even the most desperate efforts; for not only are the physical obstacles unsurmountable, but there is, also, a much more serious preventive in the prison system. There is not a moment of day or night when the captive is free from the watchful eyes of officers who are themselves closely watched.

The cells, as heretofore stated, are honey-combed into a massive block of masonry, which is surrounded on all sides by a wide corridor or Hall, and the whole enclosed by an huge shell or brick walls. The building, also, stands within a large court-yard surrounded by high walls, so that the prisoner must break out of three sets of walls. The following is a ground plan of the Main Hall, or block of cells where the convicts are locked in at night, and on Sabbath.

It will be seen that half of the cells open into the "East Corridor," and half into the "West Corridor." The block of cells is four tiers high and the three tiers above the ground tier, have narrow iron galleries running along in front of them, suspended on brackets and braces. Each cell is lighted and warmed through the door, which is made of bars of iron, the size of a broom stick, latticed together by cross-bars. Now, each tier of cells has its overseer, who is furnished, by the "Hall Warden," a list of cells, and is held accountable for his men.

Every morning at 6 o'clock, at the tap of the bell, each overseer passes from cell to cell, unlocking his men: after which, having formed them in single file, he marches them to the work shops where every man is narrowly watched throughout the day. Each overseer reports the number of men in his gang to the Deputy who is furnished the exact number of men in the prison, therefore instantly detects any absentee. Moreover in the workshops the men are divided into "teams," each man being assigned to a particular piece or part of the work. If he should quit his post for a few moments his absence must be detected by the disarrangement of the team. But why leave his post merely to be arrested at the door, or shot by the guards on the parapet of the outer walls? Even a pair of wings would not facilitate matters, as the sentries are each supplied with two double-barrel shot guns loaded with slugs, and could hardly avoid bringing down the fleeing lark. At night the overseers march their men in single file as before back into the main Hall, and every man to his cell. The door of each cell is carefully locked. The overseer reports the number of men in his gang to the Deputy who also has his list. When all the overseers have reported, the Deputy pulls a lever in each corridor, which draws a long heavy, bar of iron in front of the whole row of cells, so that no cell door can be opened even if it had been left unlocked by the overseer. This outside bar is also locked into position and the Deputy pockets the key. Thus the doors are all double locked. And now all the officers, and overseers, retire from the Main Hall into their guard rooms, leaving two "Night Watchmen" whose duty is to keep constantly walking along in front of the cells looking in at the men. They wear slippers made of heavy listing, so that their steps are inaudible on the smooth flag-stones of the floor; and they seem to be shadowy beings as they glide from cell to cell peering through the door of each to see if the inmates are quiet. These watchmen are forbidden to speak to a prisoner except to reprove him, and they are closely watched themselves by the Deputy who also slips about at night with cat-like steps, and has also two little windows, or apertures, as large as this book through which he can look down into the Main Hall at any hour of the night to detect the watchmen in any suspicious movements, or whispering to the prisoners.

It is apparent, therefore, the prisoner has no possibility of escape save by miracle, or by bribery. And even a scheme of bribery would need miraculous aid, together with unlimited money to succeed. For the routine is so strict that each officer is a check upon every other officer. To bribe one would be useless unless nearly all were bribed; and the amount would have to be heavy in each instance as the escape could be traced almost unerringly to the negligence or corruption of the officers. And the latter would do well to leave with the fugitive, else he might soon exchange the inside for the outside of the cells.

Another safeguard against escape is the law which *doubles* the original sentence of any prisoner attempting to escape! Thus a man must be very desperate indeed, when he can make up his mind to *burn his ships* behind him by engaging in an attempt wherein the chances of failure are as a thousand to one, and not to succeed is ruin!

Nevertheless there are not infrequent attempts by the short term men who are usually employed about the yards, laundry, etc., and being generally from Albany, or vicinity, have better means of communication with friends. Tradition, also, tells of one escape from the cells. . . .

The weakest point in the Prison, if *any* can be called *weak,* is the hospital, where I now write. It is on the third floor, but its windows open upon the yard, and only a set of iron bars defend them. Three hours of any night would enable us to saw off one or two of these bars and with the ropes from the beds all might descend in safety. Or we could cut through the walls, a mere double partition of lath and plaster, into the hallway of the Superintendent's residence, where there are no bars to the window. It is my belief I could escape any night.

But, of course, having given my *parole of honor* not to attempt to escape nor to permit any of the convalescents to do so, I am as securely confined as if I were back in my cell, where for 18 months I slept. Capt. Pilsbury told me one day he felt perfectly at ease respecting the Hospital, and should continue to do so as long as I remained. We are locked in at 7 P. M., and remain thus until 6 A. M.

July 22. Gloomy weather and gloomiest—darker spirits. The petty vexations and humiliations to which I am daily subjected keep me in continual harassment. It is strange how these petty troubles distress and mortify me. It would be far easier for me to endure actual physical pain than to be hectored and insulted by the lowborn, vulgar, under-strappers in authority over us. Sometimes I think they purposely seek to annoy me. One of the overseers has never forgiven me for my having my pencil returned to me (by Genl. P.) after he had ordered me to give it up. The Deputy doesn't like the way Capt. Pilsbury comes occasionally to bring me paper (writing), and talk with me; as it is his aim to become the go-between the prisoners and the Superintendent in all things; thus having all complaints or appeals within his own discretion either to grant, or *forget to tell Capt. P.*

I dare not write as I should like to do, for the Deputy has more than once picked up my books, and read the notes I had made from time to time. But he cannot read my cypher. Unfortunately it requires so much trouble to spell out that I rarely use it.

Later: Two of the Rutherford men who were brought here in the party with me were today released at the expiration of their two years sentence. They were George H. Holland, and Adolphus DePriest. Poor young men! They were both innocent of any participation in the Raid on Rutherfordton as I am assured by respectable men, and by their own statements. Both admit they knew the affair was in contemplation, but one was unwell, and the other had no horse.

It is but a repetition of the old story to say that while these young men who had no hand in the Raid were sentenced to Albany Penitentiary for two years, the real leaders and concocters of the Raid were graciously received as special pets of the government, their pockets filled with gold, the price of perjury, and their lies used to blacken the reputation of honest men!

Holland has a wife and child awaiting to welcome him home; that is unless they have succumbed to trial and suffering. They were greatly distressed even before the trial ended.

Adolphus DePriest is a young unmarried man, not 19 years old. He has been a good deal threatened with consumption, and we can surmise the effect of confinement in the damp cell of a prison in this inclement latitude.

July 23d. By a singular coincidence three of the negro lunatics are named Johnston, or Johnson; all from the District of Columbia (whence nearly all the negro convicts come; owing perhaps to the demoralizing influence of Grant's Administration, and the Radical Congress which is almost constantly in session); and all deranged by their unbridled passions. The coincidence goes farther. Johnson No. 1, *sings,* rehearsing quite an extensive repertoire of camp-meeting hymns, or tunes; Johnson No. 2, *prays,* very long, very loud, and very fervently (especially when he invites a blessing on that *"hard-hearted Steward, who wont give me but three meals a day!"* while Johnstone, No. 3, *curses,* outrageously, and makes so much noise that I am momentarily expecting the Deputy to pounce in upon us, and give me another hectoring for not *gagging* the fellow, though he came so near to choking to death the last time it was done I shall never authorize it again. If the Deputy orders it in person that will be *his* act, not mine. I shall take no discretion in the matter. Nevertheless between them, the creatures make a Bedlam of the place. Poor Louis Myers, the white patient, seems as much disturbed at the antics of the darkeys as if he too were sane. He walks continually day and night, perfectly silent, with arms folded behind his back, and head lowered on his breast (and he has a large intelligent head), as if in deep thought. But he never gives trouble, is unusually cleanly, and at times seems almost master of himself. Yet the least allusion to Germany or the Rhine, or above all, to his own wife and children, throws him into a moody moroseness, followed by evident signs of derangement. I asked Capt. P. if something might not be done for Louis's release. "Yes," he replied, "His term is almost expired, and I could release him under the act allowing reduction for good behavior. But it would be a pity to turn him loose as he is. The sharpers have gotten all his money: he has no friends in America, is incapable of self-support, and it is altogether certain he would fare worse outside than where he is. We do not require him to work, and perhaps in a short time he will recover his reason." He certainly has greatly improved since I came up into the Hospital, as at first we had to force food into his mouth. I have stated the particulars of his case heretofore.

July 24th. During the night a large owl flew in at the window, blinded by the light, and aroused every one by its frantic dashes against the walls to escape the cat, which leaped and chased it with surprising agility. I watched the pursuit for a time with some interest. It illustrates two things. First, how *groundless* fear may be. The owl with all its reputation for wisdom could not compose itself sufficiently to see that its hideous enemy was without wings and could not possibly reach its flight around the lofty ceiling—unless in its mad fears it should cripple itself against the walls.

Second, how savage is the instinct of the whole species of cat kind, how unfeelin' are all varieties of felines! Our gentle Tabitha, dreamily dozing at the stove, ordinarily as gentle as the limpest of lambs, was in a moment transformed, by the advent of the bird, into the counterpart of a tiger! Were the cat photographed in its full vigor of glistening eyes, ravenous jaws, bristling beard, and every hair on its back erect and quivering with passionate cruelty, as she bounds like an elastic ball from bed, from table to desk, seeing nothing, heeding nothing, but keenly intent upon tearing and rending the fluttering victim; were this photographed, and the picture enlarged to many times its natural size, the result would show a blood-thirsty tiger or jaguar or puma, or panther, as fierce and formidable as ever was seen amid Asiatic jungles, South American forests, or California cliffs! I was so disgusted at this savage instinct that I allowed the men to catch the owl and make it give Tabby a good whipping, which the bird easily did after getting "claw-hold" on the cats fur.

But humanity is little improvement on the beast. The patients wanted, some to kill, others to cage and pet, the owl. I bade them remember they themselves had food, raiment, shelter, medical attendance, etc., etc., yet would gladly live on crusts, and sleep in the street, with no covering save their rags, rather than remain shut up as prisoners. Why then should they rob of its liberty a harmless bird to whom liberty was everything? With that I took the bird by the window, bade it carry a message for us to all the great world of the free, and set it outside the iron bars.

Sunday.

July 26th.   It is a *Sunday* without Sun for me! The morning distribution of the weekly mail always brings disappointment; and when we go to chapel the singing of familiar hymns awakens old memories; and then the Chaplain indulges in remarks which show how utterly outcast a man in a Penitentiary is; no matter what his act, or how unjustly he be imprisoned. There are, as even the preacher admitted, worse men, with blacker stains on their souls at this moment sitting in the costly churches of the city and the land, respected and honored. But they are *not yet caught,* maybe never will be detected and exposed, or they may have the wealth and influence to do with impunity what would send a poorer and purer man to this Penitentiary. Nevertheless all this, though recognized fact, does not at all relieve the "Penitentiary Convict" from an indelible stigma which no former, nor after, purity of life can eradicate. It were better for many a youth that he were hanged the day he was sentenced to this Pen.

TRAVELING AT PUBLIC EXPENSE

'Squire Brown has had visitors. Being called to the Supt's office he found Dr. J. Neagle, the carpet-bagger Comptroller of the State (So. Ca.) but at present out of office having realized "a large fortune" from the Rogue's Ring at Columbia. Wishing to make a Northern tour during the hot mid-summer, he had Gov.

Moses (his confederate in former stealing) to appoint him a roving commissioner to visit Northern Public institutions and enjoy himself at public expense. He and wife were just now on their way to spend a week at Niagara Falls; and seeing a chance to manufacture a little credit for himself, free of cost, the wily doctor having glanced through the "Model Penitentiary," sent for Brown and one or two others of the South Carolinians to make a pretence of inquiring as to their health, condition, etc. Old Man Brown knew his man, yet could not repress his elation at the promises Neagle freely made to intercede with "my friend Grant," and "get you out."

A more encouraging piece of news leaked out amid the conversation to wit, that a delegation consisting of Genl. J. B. Kershaw (of Kershaw's old Division) Hon. W. D. Porter of Charleston, Rev. Dr. Martin of Columbia, and Col. R. M. Sims, of Rock Hill, have been sent to Washington to ask the release of the 80 "Ku Klux" prisoners from South Carolina, now toiling as felons in this miserable place. Neagle says his friend (I should be ashamed to name the Dictator, the brutal butcher of his own men, and the lawless foe to Southern freedom as my friend, or even acquaintance, much less political bedfellow!) Grant is not at the Capital, but spending the hot weather at the sea-coast, where he has a cottage among the gold-puffed nabobs who thrive upon the Grant regime. "Birds of a feather *will* flock," etc. It matters little to the stolid Gift-Receiver that his absence from the Capital disarranges public business; not to speak of such instances as the South Carolina delegation sent so far, and so humbly, to beg his clemency! Really I am glad *my* friends, nay, the people I used *once* to think my friends, have made no such appeal. It is most humiliating to suffer years of foulest injustice at the hands of Grant, and his Grantizaries, and at last to give him the opportunity to gain a false credit by *magnanimously* (!), condescending (!) to put a period (not to repeal or restore past wrongs) to his outrages by generously (!!) turning loose the humble victims of his fiendish plots to secure a second lease of power and plunder!

For my part I long for liberty with frantic wishes, as if, as sometimes I fancy, I can hear my own heart crying for freedom from this terrible captivity and ignominy; but shall I, after all the outrages heaped upon me without one provocation, one threat, or taunt, or any manner of refractory resistance, now kiss the hands that smote me? God forbid.

Wednesday.

July 30th. Had a miserable night. The crazy negroes gave much trouble. One of them tried to kill a patient in an adjoining cot and his strength being almost supernatural while in the rage of frenzy, I had to call the convalescents to my assistance. It required all the effort of four of us to hold him down on his bed, while we handcuffed and shackled him. His ravings against me were terrible, and I could hardly repress my anger, especially when seeing that a number of the convicts, who dislike my enforcement of the Rules, and the coolness with which I treat them, were furtively snickering over the negro's abuse of me.

Of course I could easily retaliate, and send them back to their cells, as able for duty in the workshops, but, after all, why make such a confession of my own weakness and irritability?

The crazy fellow, by the by, is another illustration of the injustice often done under the forms of law, and in the so-called courts of justice. He was storing ice at Sing Sing when a large piece slipped and fractured his skull, since which he has never been wholly responsible for his actions, consequently instead of being sent to the Penitentiary he should have been *restrained* in some safe manner, perhaps in an insane asylum. As it is, he is stigmatized as a felon, and when not too violent, is made to toil as a felon, by reason of having suffered the accident of Providence.

Have just seen a queer sight. A well dressed white man, accompanied by quite a party of visitors, passed through the prison, and came as is customary to view the Hospital. Thus far there was nothing different from

the hourly visitations that annoy us, by standing for
five minutes to stare at us, and make remarks about us,
and *how well treated we are!* But to my eyes it was a
curious thing to see leaning on the arm of the well
dressed white man a lolling, flaunting, *woolly-headed
negro* wench, as black as the fellow's stove pipe hat, and
as impudent as Old Nick! Holding up her dress to dis-
play a pair of white kid *brogans,* she clung to his arm,
and made many giggling remarks, one of which caused
a laugh after the party left. It was, *"Oh dear! If there
aint a whole pass-el ob men right thar in bed!"*

The turnkey who acted as guide for the party seemed
not to fancy them as he brusquely called, "Come along!
There's other folks a-waiting!"

August 2nd. Capt. Pilsbury came up into the Hospital for the first time since his father's death. He is
now Superintendent, and therefore the Deputy watches
him as closely as he did the old General, lest the prisoners should get a chance to make some complaint. The
"less said soonest mended," is a good maxim for here!
But Captain P. gave me one bit of comfort in mentioning that he or his wife, had received a long letter from
Mrs. Doctor Twitty of Spartanburg, South Carolina,
speaking very warmly of the wrong done to our poor
men, and sending personal regards to myself. Mrs. T.
is a native of Albany, and a schoolmate of Mrs. Pilsbury; therefore her testimony in our behalf must be of
service in off setting the miserable falsehoods about the
Klan, and Ku Klux outrages, that have filled the Radical press. He also gave me a clipping from a newspaper
containing a telegram announcing that "Landaulet"
Williams had graciously recommended for pardon
D. S. Splawn, Wm. Scruggs, Dover, and—Murphy,
Ku Klux convicts now in Albany Penitentiary." Be-
hold how the "Best government the world ever saw,"
dispenses mercy! Murphy served his sentence and was
released months ago! The three others are almost on the
eve of release, having served the term of their sentence
minus the 30 days reduction for good behavior! How
magnanimous to pardon the last half a dozen days of a
two years sentence, and claim credit therefor! But this

was quite like the sending of a pardon to the Alabamian, Porter, six-weeks after Death had unlocked his prison doors, and led him away to a quiet resting place amid the bones of Potter's Field! Or, like the sending of a pardon for Barton Biggerstaff, who was never at this Prison, but had been long awaiting it in Rutherford jail! Of course these were "mistakes." But what dependence, or confidence, can be felt in a government which thus trifles with the living and mocks the dead, by its shameful and utterly inexcusable *"mistakes?"*

Sunday. Disappointed as usual. Feeling almost certain that the renewal of rumors concerning a general release of the Southern Prisoners here confined (of which mention is made in the letters of both Brown and Scruggs, the only two Ku Klux now in the Hospital), would cause some friend to drop me a line this week, I arose at day-break, visited each patient, arranged the beds, performed my usual duties, and sat by the window, pretending to read, but in reality watching the door through which the Deputy must enter. He came, as the cat comes, stealthily, until with a sudden movement he opened the door, and glanced round the hall in hope of catching some infraction of the rules. All was quiet and orderly! Then he passed from cot to cot distributing the mail. Every one seemed to have some one in the world who still remembered them, no matter how vulgar, vile, and villainous they were. Even the negroes receive numerous letters, frequently averaging one or two a week the year round. It requires almost an whole day for one person to read the weekly mail of the Prison; and I suspect a good many letters are merely glanced at and thrown into the fire if found too long, and apparently unimportant.

Not much trouble have my letters given the examining clerk. There have been intervals of three and four months when I was as utterly forgotten as if I were dead. Poor father would gladly send me a letter every week, I feel sure; but even he seems to have become discouraged by the continual interception of his letters.

And this puzzles me; where can the Radical Rogues get their fingers on my correspondence? Numbers of letters come safely to Squire Brown and to Wm. Scruggs, by the same route Northward, after reaching Charlotte. So, the embargo must be *at Charlotte, or at some point between it and Rutherfordton.* Oh! that we had an honest Post Master General that I might have these iniquities laid before him! But now, every post master and mail-messenger, is a politician, in league with the Radical managers and all would approve the *stealing* of my letters in order to get, if possible, some clue to our prominent leaders.

It shows that the stealing is done on the above named route, because Genl. Collett Leventhorpe's letters come safely, as do, also, my brother's letters from Princeton, and Aunt Susie's from Connecticut and Massachusetts. Ah! well, 'Tis folly to worry over the unavoidable! And yet!

> "All blank and meaningless is life
> In this foul spot! One eternal Present,
> Rayless as Lapland Winter, wraps my soul;
> One ceaseless wrong—affording but one sense
> Of cruelest agony—makes up my life,
> Stretching from day to day, its sole event!"

Two years! Two years dead and buried! what a thing it is. How many strange occurrences must have occurred! How full of news will be the newspapers if I ever see them again! There has been a war between France and Prussia and Napoleon slain; thus much I have heard; but what of the battles etc.? There have been great conflagrations at Chicago and Boston; this much I know. Grant has been re-elected and Greeley is crazy; these events I have foreseen. But what a mass of fact, of folly, of accident, of casualty and crime, must be hidden behind the curtain of ignorance drawn before our eyes by the discipline of this "model prison!" Surely this policy is all wrong. The purpose of Penitentiaries as their name signifies is to cause men to repent and re-form—not merely to *punish.* If offenders were punished merely to *retaliate* on them for crimes against society it would be better to kill them at once, and be done with them; for after society became satisfied with *retaliating* on the prisoner he would return to *revenge* himself, and *his* retaliation would be apt to cost heavily.

Then if the purpose of imprisonment is to *Reform* as well as punish, why treat the man as if he were expected never again to re-enter the world? Why dwarf his intellect, and narrow his range of thought, (until he has only his own dark thoughts, recollections, schemes, etc., to brood over) as if he were no longer within the scope of human existence?

There are men now in this prison who are like *great grown up babies*. Ten, fifteen, twenty, some twenty-five, years ago they came to the big gate, glanced gloomily backward at the green fields which then surrounded the prison, entered, heard the iron doors banging behind them, and have never seen nor heard anything of the great world since! Perhaps they have never heard more than some vague allusion to the Civil War! It is doubtful if they know that Albany has extended its suburbs until the Penitentiary is surrounded by residences, and has paved streets to the outer gate of its beautiful grounds! Why should this barrenness of mind be required? No wonder the released convict finds himself overwhelmed by the sense of ignorance of the mighty march of the nation, and despairs of regaining an honorable foothold in life! Books, to be sure, in limited allowance, and very *Sunday-schoolish* character, but a prisoner who is weary with toiling from dawn till dusk, and perhaps fired by needless mortifications on the part of his keepers, is not much interested or instructed by stories of "Mary's Little Lamb," or "Jack's Playmates," or "Missionary Voyages," etc. Surely an allowance of one newspaper per week could do no harm.

August 11th. A note from Bro. M. at Princeton College mentions a rumor that I am to be shortly released! Indeed! I fear "all signs fail in dry weather," and 'tis dreadfully dry at this writing. Have so written him. He says that Col. C. who was himself a political prisoner at one time. . . .[1]

August 14. Rainy, dark and disheartening! I have wandered up and down the floor until I imagine I can see a path worn in the planks. Sitting up half the night

---

1 A line in the manuscript is blank.

to watch with the sick, and constantly disturbed during the remainder by their coughing or wheezing, naturally tends to render me nervous, and easily annoyed. But were it otherwise I could not but be unhappy in the existing conditions.

Dover and Splawn, the latter an old grey haired man of 65! have just been released! They were tried in South Carolina, but live not far from the line between Rutherford and Polk Counties, I believe. What the accusation against them was I do not know, but it matters little. They were caught in the dredge-net thrown out by the Grant manipulations and have had to pay the penalty of not voting the Radical ticket.

August 15th. It is surprising the difference between this climate and our own. Last night, in this tightly constructed room, occupied by a dozen men, I slept under two heavy blankets, and wished for as many more. This morning is as cold as *any November,* or many *December* mornings at Raleigh, though only the middle of August!

Jones, my assistant, says he was down in the Main Hall when the two North Carolinians were released yesterday. Old man Splawn was so agitated he could hardly stand, and was helped to change his convict garb for his citizens dress. Every moment he would cry out— *"Good Lord! Good Lord! Am I goin' ter git out et las! Good Lord! Jes' to think! Goin' ter git out, an go home! Oh! I'm all a-trimble!"* And still making these exclamations the old man tottered out into the world again! Good Lord, indeed! Will He ever make Bond and Grant, and Wallace, and Logan, and Company, to be "all a-trimble!" It is the thought of the injustice and wrong done to innocent men, to the principles of liberty, to the right of individuals, and to my own name, family, father, and future prospects, that fixes me in my determination to return to North Carolina, and devote the remainder of my life to vindication and justice. But for this, I should humbly plead for pardon, release, or banishment, anything to get out of this fearful place; and when free, I should go very far "over the border" nevermore to return. Of course no one would care, (excepting father and brothers) what became of me; and doubtless the world is right; a man who is not missed is generally not worth missing. And yet I fought four years for my people, not by compulsion as many did, but from principle and I battled four years for my party, not for office or profit but because I regarded its success as utterly indispensable for peace, prosperity and good government; and finally I have given up four more years of my life—three of them already spent—to uphold those same principles, to preserve order and morality in the State, and to protect our noble women. Surely, then, I have meant well, however unfortunate. Bah! it matters naught! Queer if there be not meat and bread for one more man out in the "wide, wide, world," and as the French say, "If the house cannot be made to be comfortable, it can be abandoned!"

August 17. No letters this week, as usual! 'Squire Brown received *four*, and came to me with eyes glistening even behind his eyeglasses as he related the contents, and for the five hundred and fifty-fifth time grew enthusiastic over the prospect of "immediate release" held out by the kind-hearted friends, his correspondents. It appears that Messrs. Porter, Sims, and Kershaw obtained from Grant a promise there should be an end to his lawless raids on the Southern people. Under pretense of enforcing the unconstitutional Enforcement Acts, Grant directed "Landaulet" Williams to make an announcement which might be accepted by the thousands of young men in exile as an intimation that they might return home without fear of molestation. But Williams issued a letter so full of quirks, and quibbles, and ambiguities that no one can place the least reliance on it. His language is framed to allow him to break faith with any man who ventures within his grasp. It says, "there may be exceptional cases of great aggravation where the government would insist upon conviction and punishment. Persons who have absented themselves on account of complicity in Ku Klux offences are at liberty to return, and *unless their crimes belong within the above named exceptional cases,* they will not be prosecuted." Now, as all the acts done by the Klan date three years ago, and all such exceptional cases must be already well known, the object of the phrases quoted is clearly to allow him to pounce upon any man who may have means to pay for his own plucking, or whom the Granti-zaries may wish to punish for personal spite. In short the whole letter is a trick. When I was confined in the cell I read a letter written by a female lawyer of Washington City to B. which contained a remark very near the truth. The Attorney-General, she declared, had treated her disrespectfully, but that was nothing new. He was a pettifogger on horseback. He had come from the wild woods of the far West where he learned to play the part of Prosecutor, Judge, and Jury, all in one; and if the thing wouldn't make too much talk, he would like to include the part of hangman also!

And I say—"All *so!*" to the remark. Like Edwin M. Stanton, he is cruel and cunning for party purposes; like Jo Holt he is cruel and atrocious from the sheer maliciousness of his narrow soul.

Aug. 18th.   In addressing the letters (written by the convicts on Sunday) every Monday morning I have an opportunity to get an insight to the thoughts, feelings, hopes, fears, and affections of the majority of the occupants of this great human hive, both male and female. One thing noticeable is that nearly all the family letters begin with "Dear Mother." Occasionally it is "Dear Brother," or "Dear Sister." But very rarely does the convict address "Dear Father."

Several deductions might be drawn from this singular fact, but one thought will immediately occur; no child can sink so low as to lose all hold upon the mother's heartstrings. He may be as one dead, to his father, and to all the family, but he can never hesitate to make new calls on "Mother."

Among today's letters was one from Amos Owens of Rutherford, in which occurs this sentence, "How did you hear that *Shotwell is pardoned?*" 'Tis a pertinent question. I should like to hear of it myself. I happen to be acquainted with that poor fellow, Shotwell, and it would be very gratifying for me to inform him that he needn't tarry here abouts any longer. Just now he is more than ordinarily tormented.

Of all tortures the mental "rack" of suspense is most fearful. It is one of the chief ingredients of Milton's poetic "Hell." As Miss Jane Porter says, "In its hot and cold regions the anxious soul is alternately tossed from the ardor of Hope to the petrifying rigors of Doubt and Dread." It is one of the nerves whence agonies are born. The mere talk of possible release renders me so restless that I cannot read, or sit still, or sleep; though I know by experience of an hundred disappointments there is scarcely the shadow of a shadow of Hope! And yet.

> "Because it *may* be so,
> My credulous heart whispers it *is;*
> And fondly fosters the feeble glimmerings of
> A sickly Hope!"

Aug. 22nd. For five days we have had not one hour of sunshine—nothing but rain, and lowering clouds. At this moment, (10 A. M.) the fog is so dense one cannot see across the Prison Yard. Such weather in North Carolina would arouse fears of the Deluge. The natives hereabout do not mind it, in the least. Not less than a score of well dressed women visited the Prison yesterday, regardless of the rain. Two and three in a gang, with skirts elevated showing whole acres of gum-shoes, they tramped through the sloppy grounds, giggled at the coatless convicts, made notes in well-thumbed note books, poked the turnkey with their parasols to attract his attention and made themselves altogether at home, causing me to remark for the forty-leventh time, *"What a People!"*

Aug. 23d. Having been called down to the Superintendent's Office I was met by Horace R. Hudson, a young gentleman holding the position of Assistant Editor of Col. T. C. Callicott's paper, the Albany *Evening Times.* He came at the suggestion of Capt. Pilsbury to whom I had written a note asking if he would assist me to sell some articles to the city press in case I should be released. Mr. Hudson states that he has seen a telegram from Washington announcing the order for the release of *"R. A. Shotwell and W. M. Fulton."* Fulton is a South Carolinian, and having no Scalawag enemies to interfere, was *immediately released!* He *left the Prison yesterday evening!* I do not know why my name should be coupled with his; but the fact that they were thus coupled and that Fulton *is already a free man* gives grounds for Hope! But reflect! The so-called pardons were said to have been issued on the first week in the month; why this delay? I cannot forget how poor Scruggs was tantalized; his release ordered, the news published, his friends stirred to send him money for travelling expenses, (obtained by a long journey and sale of his wife's cow!) and then the pardon revoked at the instance of some vile scoundrel; notwithstanding the fact that a more harmless little man than William Scruggs does not live anywhere!

August 24th. The day is exceedingly dark and gloomy, symbolizing my own feelings and fortunes. It is clear that Grant has again disappointed those to whom he gave his promise. Three months ago he gave his pledge to Capt. Plato Durham that if Virgil S. Lusk and "Jim" Justice would sign the application for my release he should grant it. He had been informed, of course, that neither Lusk (whom I had caned in the street), nor Justice (whom I had so often exposed and denounced for his deeds) would sign it. But by some strange freak or foresight, both, as I have heard, did sign it. Nevertheless Grant refused, or neglected to keep his pledges. True, I never applied for pardon, and shall never do so, no matter if I die in this terrible place; but he should not have given his word if he meant not to keep it, as no doubt he did mean.

However, there is no use of my brooding over these troubles. All my indignation amounts to naught. I am in the power of my enemies and there is nothing I can do but to show them the firmness of true manhood. Thank God it is my high prerogative to live as truly and nobly within these prison walls, surrounded by felons and all the attributes of felony, and forced to stand before my keepers with folded arms, and downcast eyes, as if I were in a palace surrounded by obsequious dependents.

I shall once more take up my studies, and prepare to endeavor to distract myself as little as possible by passing rumors of release. Why should I worry? Fortune has done her worst! Can a man get lower in life than be convicted, sent to a distant penitentiary for years, forgotten by his friends, lost his health, have his teeth destroyed, have not a penny, or a decent suit of clothing, with which to go forth into the world? Surely there is no lower round so far as physical and pecuniary, and personal situation is considered.

But there is no need to become embittered. Devotion to Southern principles brought me here: advocacy of the same kept me poor, and having reached the bottom-rack of ill fortune, I can henceforth look on frown or favor with equal equanimity. Unfortunately I can never be enough of a philosopher to regard my own losses and sufferings with indifference: but I can do the next best thing namely to endure them as a matter of principle and necessity.

1873.

Aug. 25th.   Night was so cool we slept uncomfortably under two blankets. This would seem incredible at Raleigh in August.

My lunatic patient gave a great deal of trouble. The black rascal sleeps all day, and prevents our sleep at night, by his howlings and prowlings. Whenever the monotonous growling ceases I awake by sheer habit, having learned by dear experience that such cessation signifies the madman is loose, and prowling in search of weapons. These Yankee-born negro convicts are as cunning as an Indian, as plausible an an Italian, and as impudent as a Spanish beggar. One of them, I have already stated, deceived the Surgeon, and also a brother physician called in specially to examine him; making them satisfied that he was crazy. Every feature of lunacy was manifest in his actions and appearance. But I one night caught him off his guard; and knowing the fear which sane negroes have of madmen, I suggested to Dr. Haskins that the negro be locked into the cells in the basement where the more violent lunatics are kept.

At this the scoundrel suddenly recovered his senses and is now at work in the shops.

A note from Bro. M. at Princeton says, *"I see a telegram from Washington announces your release. Cannot understand the delay. There was great rejoicing in Rutherford when the news arrived."* Indeed! Seems to me there is another instance of shouting inside the woods!

AN INFAMOUS PROPOSAL

'Squire Brown's letters confirm the previous report that the foul hearted A. S. Wallace upon being urged by Judge Mackey to permit the old gentleman to be pardoned, (his signature being all that was required), brutally replied that Brown should be released on one condition; namely, that he reveal the location of his two sons (who had sought safety in exile) and assist to have them exchange places with him! Could anything more vile and brutal be suggested! The villains arrest an old grey-haired citizen, convict him without a shadow of foundation for the charges, drag him to a distant penitentiary, and after breaking the old man's spirit by years of drudgery, meet the tears and appeals of his lonely wife and daughters by a proposal to let him come home to die if he will act as stool-pigeon to betray his own sons into chains, slavery and perchance even death; for all things are possible with a negro jury and Bond as judge! And this shameful proposal comes from a public thief, who holds a seat in Congress belonging to another!

CHAPTER EIGHTEENTH

Back to North Carolina—Free

Notwithstanding I invariably assured my correspondents that there was no likelihood of my release, and although my journal shows how little reliance I placed on the rumors of my release I must have cherished a latent spark of trust in them; for when, at length, the important document came, it had no such effect on me as is common in cases of men suddenly turned loose after long years of "Hope Deferred." Hope, I think, was incorporated among the human faculties for the sake of the miserable, the sick, and especially, the imprisoned. To all men it is a good gift, but to the wretched and the prisoner it is the mainspring of life. Without it one half of mankind would seek self destruction before attaining the age of 40 years; and four fifths of those who survived that age would end life in a similar manner. Hope acts as the safety-valve of human suffering, raising the spirits to a living temperature even amid circumstances when all earthly surroundings seem created for our special destruction, loss, suffering, and self-imolation! Surely there had been little to keep alive my spirits during the long period of my sojourn within the walls of Albany Penitentiary; yet now that my days therein were to terminate it seemed as much a matter of course as if I had been expecting to stay the even 800 days, and no more. Capt. Pilsbury seems to have expected a scene, as he called me down into his private parlor and mysteriously closed the door before drawing from his pocket the official document which was to unlock the outer gate. But I did not tremble, nor weep, nor break down, nor make a scene, but simply remarked, that I was rather surprised to see it, though I supposed they would get tired of keeping me, after awhile. He laughed and said he was sorry to lose me, on some accounts, for he didn't know where to get a good man to take my place as Steward of the Hospital.

The paper given me was a large double sheet of parchment, sealed with the "Great Seal" of the "Universal Yankee Nation," and signed by the autograph of Ulysses (Hiram) S. Grant; countersigned by J. C. Bancroft Davis, Acting Assistant Secretary of State. It announced that whereas one R. A. S., had been "convicted of conspiracy (against *what?*) and whereas he has "now been imprisoned more than two years," therefore, "be it known that in consideration of the premises, and divers other good and sufficient reasons, me thereunto moving," do "hereby grant full and unconditional pardon," etc., etc.

But mark! "Done at the City of Washington this *ninth day of August 1873,*" etc., etc.—nearly *one month* ago! think of it!

The time required for the order to go from Washington to Raleigh would be about twelve hours, a single day. To return to Albany two days; or say *four days* after the signing of the document. Instead of this time it was nearly four weeks on the road! Nay, not on the road, but *purposely delayed* at Raleigh! When I pointed to the date of the paper, Capt. P. smiled and said, "Your Republican friends down South were not in a hurry to see you back."

My own feelings were the reverse of pleasant on the subject for some of the most harassing experiences of my three years' prison life had occurred during those last weeks. One might suppose there would be some slight relaxion of rigor by the prison officials after it became known to them (as it was known) that my "Pardon" (so-called) had been issued, and was on the way. But there was not the slightest relaxation even *after its arrival!* The order came in the A. M. mail but I heard nothing of it until 11; and was not released until 3½ P. M. In this is seen the wonderful system of the place. The individual prisoner has no consideration whatever; there can be no deviation of the daily routine no matter how it effects him. His life might depend on his getting out at a certain hour, but if he got out at that hour would depend on whether the

Deputy was disengaged of the regular programme of duties.

Besides if the prisoner whose pardon comes at daybreak is kept until four or five in the evening the contractors have to pay for an whole day's work supposed to be done by him!

At the noon hour, 'Squire Brown came in from the work shops in rather better spirits than ordinarily, and began to tell me how many pairs of shoes he had finished when I whispered to him that I should take leave of him at some hour during the afternoon. It was much of a surprise, and the old man nearly broke down, probably with the feeling that all the Southern men were getting out while he remained. I sought to encourage him by showing him how largely he gained by my release, as I should do everything possible for his release. And I would make a special effort to get Capt. Pilsbury to appoint him to the vacant stewardship which would relieve him of the drudgery of the shoe shops.

At 3½ P. M. I took my departure from the Hospital forever. It may be allowable to mention that many of the convalescents expressed regret at my going, and said they had not had any such care and attention for years as I gave them when sick, tho' I held them to strict order and quietness when able to leave their beds, and sit up.

Down in the Main Hall I found Wm. Scruggs who was released by expiration of his sentence. His route lay with mine as far as Charlotte (he going on to Spartanburg, S. C.) and he seemed very anxious to travel with me as he had never been so far from home in his life before; but he had funds to go directly home, and I had to stay until I "made" it in some way. Here observe the generosity of the "glorious," "best government;" a Southern gentleman is dragged from his home and business without warrant, is convicted by bribery and corruption, and is dragged a thousand miles away into an inhospitable climate, kept in a felon's cell for two years, then turned loose without a decent suit and without money to pay his fare home, much less to buy food *en route!* An allowance of $10 is made to each prisoner regardless of the distance he may live from the prison. In our cases it would pay railway fare as far South as Baltimore without food!

On unrolling the bundle of my citizens clothing it was found to consist of funky rags white with moths and mildew, and so in tatters. It will be remembered Marshal Carrow instructed us to wear only our commonest clothing in coming here, and that we arrived in a drenching rain. The wet clothes were rolled into a bundle, labeled, and tossed into the "clothes-vault," together with the filthy rags of all classes, Negroes, Chinese, Malays, Fejies, Turks, Modocs, etc., etc., most of which were infested by all manner of vermin. The moths had helped the mildew, and my coat was literally in *shreds,* pantaloons like sieves, waistcoat, *wasted!* As for hat and shoes, they were an insult to any blind beggar! The thought of going out in the world in such attire made me feel almost sorry to be released—so silly is supersensitiveness!

At 4 P. M. came the last humiliation within the walls. I had not seen any of my fellow-prisoners from North Carolina during the whole two years term; and, while I had no personal acquaintance with them previous to my arrest, I felt that in view of the similarity of our sympathies and sufferings it was but proper to make an effort to see them, and carry home any messages they might desire to send. I asked the Hall Warden to ask Capt. P. if I could have this privilege. *"No!"* said he gruffly, *"Put on your clothes! I can't be foolin' round here all evening. Them fellers is out at work anyhow."* Then he fumbled over my satchel, books, etc., to see if any notes were concealed and called to the Deputy, *"These here fellers is ready to get out!"* The Deputy said, "Come along!" and we marched to the great gate in the outer wall. Then he seemed to relax somewhat, assumed an half smile, and remarked: *"Well!—now— you're all right!"* and put out his hand. I felt no pleasant response. Looking abroad over the beautiful grounds, with their flowery terraces, rustic seats, miniature suspension bridges, and other charming features of a city park, I mentally contrasted it all with the life of gloom, darkness, dullness, drudgery I had led within those walls since that iron gate clanged behind me two years before; and I recalled all the slights, rudenesses, oppression of the life of which this man was the cast-iron personification; and it was hard not to do as so many prisoners have sworn to do, viz: signalize the first moment of freedom by cursing their keepers.

Happily I was able to restrain myself from this folly, and I took his hand saying gravely, *"It was not 'right' to send me here!* The Deputy mumbled something, slammed the great gate, and thus closed the *third year* of my captivity in Grant's Military and Political Prison.

HOOTED BY YOUNGSTERS

Passing down the gravelled avenue, winding amid the shade trees and shrubbery, which cause the Prison's outward appearance to resemble some splendid private mansion, we found a large party of city urchins playing on the grass just outside the Park gate. Seeing us with our ragged garb, and shorn heads, and carrying carpet sacks, they set up a chorus of *"Here's yere con-wicks."* "Here's your Tenny-Pentiary fellers! Sa - a - a - y, fellers wot you'ns put in fur? Look's like you went in 'bout time the ark went down Hudson!" and then, "Bet you them fellers killed somebody!" "Look at that big feller!" together with such and similar pleasing epithets common among the unwashed *gamins* of a great city. It was hard not to feel mortified of this first greeting from the outside world, notwithstanding our long training in all manner of humiliation, and, for all that we knew, the boys mistook us for real convicts.

Accompanying Scruggs to the street leading down to the steamboat landing, (he expected to meet a friend at the wharf in New York) I bade the little man adieu, and saw the last of him.

Then I sought a very cheap, fifth-class hotel, knowing I could not be admitted to a better house in my dilapidated garments, as the people of Albany are accustomed to seeing released convicts on the streets every day, and would perhaps make a similar mistake as did the *gamins* at the gate.

No one can know, nor is there any need of telling, the mortification and misery of such a situation as was mine at this time. To a late hour I walked the streets of Albany, looking in at the long rows of lighted windows, and repeatedly reminded of some incident in Dickens's writings, whose wonderful fidelity to nature in certain phases of life cannot be too highly extolled.

[*A blank of several lines here occurs in the manuscript.*]

I opened the letter and found a piece of delicate kindness on his part that was totally unexpected, and must ever close my lips from saying anything harsh of him or his; whatever I may say of the prison system or the understrappers who alone came in contact with us.

The subject of the letter was an order on Messrs. Wilson, Crafts & Co, No. 90   street, to supply me until such time as should be convenient for me to repay it! Conceive what a Godsend this was to me, as I could not take the first step towards making any money until I got a decent outfit of garments.

It will interest no one; it pains me to tell of the difficulties met with in realizing my wishes and needs. Suffice it I found a kind friend in young Horace R. Hudson, of the *Daily Times,* associate editor with Col. T. C. Callicot, who also showed a disposition to befriend me. Hudson had me to take tea with him, and to go with him (he having free passes) to the theatre; besides other civilities. He also secured the acceptance of my articles on "Masonic Incidents of the Civil War," "Prison Glimpses," etc. These articles Col. Callicott said, attracted a good deal of attention and comment. I sent one or two of them to Genl. D. H. Hill who wrote as follows:

> *R. A. Shotwell Esq.*—Randolph Shotwell has sent us a copy of the Albany (N. Y.) *News, in* which he is writing a series of Confederate incidents of the war. The bearing of Mr. Shotwell in the Al-

bany Penitentiary has been very noble. He was
offered a pardon, if he would come home and can-
vass for Grant, but refused. Again he was offered
a pardon to betray his associates and indignantly
refused. All honor to the man, who can't be bought!

ONCE MORE AT THE PENITENTIARY

Having resolved to wait no longer, but trust to the
good fortune which sometimes assists in the darkest extremity, I attired myself with all possible neatness, borrowing a pair of gloves, and a cane, from Hudson, and
walked out to the Penitentiary to fulfill my promise to
Squire Brown. I had previously (when first handed my
release paper) asked Capt. P. to appoint the old man to
the vacancy but had obtained no positive answer. Subsequently I told Brown I would make another effort.

Slowly strolling up through the shady walks, and
looking at the handsome facade of the building, with
the office windows and Superintendent's portion dis-
playing rich curtains, flowers in vases, and canary cages
swinging in the arches, I thought how vast a difference
in the view to one who approaches as a prisoner, and
one as a visitor. Doubtless many persons, visiting the
place, on a balmy spring day would fancy it a pleasant
home until they entered, passed through the luxurious
private apartments, passed through the Guard Room
with its long tier of muskets in racks, and entered
through doubled, muffled doors into the gloomy Prison
proper. Then would be seen the iron hand under the
glove. But how little could any casual visitor appreciate the real severity of the iron-grip unless they were
crushed under it, and we had been for many a melancholy day!

Capt. Pilsbury being absent, I sent my card to Mrs.
Pilsbury, who at once hastened into the office, and invited me to the private parlor. While awaiting her appearance, however, several of the under-officers had
gathered near the Hall door, and were in quite a state
of wonderment, as was shown by the muttered inquiry
—"Aint that the feller what was cribbed in No. 9, first
tier, an' worked in shoe shop 4?" "Yes," was the reply,

"I know'd he'd get out, as soon as he got up in the Hospital. None of 'em stays more'n a while or so after they gits up thar."

Probably their mystification grew stronger as they saw Mrs. P. take a seat with me, chatting pleasantly, and I was glad of it, as the effect could not but be beneficial for the other poor Southerners still subject to the authority of these understrappers. It would open the eyes of the latter to the fact that our men were in prison and wearing convict garb, but not as felons.

Mrs. Pilsbury is a pleasant-faced, well-preserved, little woman, mother of two handsome children, of whom she is very proud, and also, of her husband; not forgetting, either, that she lives in style, and rides in her carriage, and will be mistress of some hundred thousand dollars in a few years, as her husband inherits the bulk of the old General's property, which was above $120,-000, in stocks, bonds, etc., when he died.

Nevertheless the lady was very kind, as well as courteous, in her demeanor, and expressions to me, and mentioned how anxious she had been frequently to send me something nice to eat, but was imperatively forbidden by her husband, who did not wish the precedent to be set. Nevertheless she had once put a piece of pie in my supper pan, and once a small glass of strawberry jelly. I supposed at the time that they had gotten into my pan through some mistake.

It appears she knew nothing of my case until we had been in the cells more than twelve months; her interest in us being awakened by the letters written to us, and by us, (she assisting her husband to open and examine the weekly Prison mail, in those days) and particularly after receiving the letters from her old acquaintance, Mrs. Doctor Twitty of Spartanburg, S. C. The latter lady being of Northern birth, and only a few years in the South, was better able to speak dispassionately of the outrageous conduct of the Federal officials; so that her statement had great weight and were of benefit to us.

Shortly after my arrival, Mrs. Pilsbury called for her young sister Miss Belle Hendricks to come into the parlor, and meet me. The younger lady seemed quite averse to coming, but on entering the room, and being introduced, she became entirely affable and agreeable. She has passed one or more winters in Florida, and expressed much fondness for Southern customs and modes of living, so different from the Northern ways. She was a pretty and stylish girl of twenty. While we were conversing, Deputy Scripture bustled into the room ostensibly to inquire for Capt. Pilsbury, but really to see if it were true that I had come back to the Prison—by the front entrance—and what I came for. Seeing me, genteelly dressed, sitting with the ladies, he was amazed, and made an exclamation equivalent to *"Ah! is that you?"* and he half stepped towards me, as if to shake hands. But just then, at that very instant, I happened to feel like asking Mrs. Pilsbury something about the gigantic oleander which occupied a tub in the corner, and my back was turned to Scripture. It must be confessed I felt a boyish pleasure in thus disconcerting the man, for he had given me many a browbeating and heartache. Scripture mumbled some remark about not waiting and left the room.

Capt. Pilsbury came after a time, and greeted me courteously, but not without an elevation of the eyebrows and a curious look as if to ask why it was I yet lingered in Albany, instead of hastening home. And I did not feel like explaining to him the necessity.

However he answered my appeals, in favor of old 'Squire Brown by a promise to make him, at least, an assistant steward, which would relieve him of drudgery in the shoe-shops.

HOMEWARD BOUND

Early next morning, Horace Hudson walked with me to the train, where I made an hasty adieu, leaving him to think me rather ungrateful, I fear, as I momentarily forgot his kind attentions in the flood of recollections connected with the weary period of my stay in Albany. Beside I was half sick. Long confinement had rendered me subject to torpidity of the liver, and instead of taking medicine for relief I took stimulants to sustain (fearing a spell of sickness) and thus only aggravated the ailment.

The long and dusty ride down the Hudson, the coaches swaying as much as on a North Carolina road, naturally produced *sea-sickness* in my bilious condition; so that, on arriving in New York, I could scarcely sit up, much less walk. I called a cab, and was driven to the Southern Hotel, where I had telegraphed for brother to meet me; but the begemmed individual who condescended to stand behind the desk, and look stylish, declined to accept me as a guest, because of my suspicious looks, I suppose; or perchance 'twas my lack of Saratoga baggage. Luckily the National Hotel clerk, a less gorgeous representative of the Retired Millionaires' Club, gave me a room. It was time. Half an hour later I was in bed almost unconscious.

Next day Bro. M. came over from Princeton College, and thenceforth I had every attention that his energy and affection could procure, though confined to bed for two days or so. Ah! those wretched days! Trial and suffering and mortification had left me crippled in body, and mind; so much so that all the world seemed strange and different to me. I thought, while in prison, I was bearing up bravely, becoming quite philosophic and hardened, but at the first breath of free life I realized how far I had retrograded in all respects. It may illustrate the feeling to say that I shrank from going to the hotel table, was bewildered on Broadway, and could not walk half a mile without as much tremor as a weak invalid. It could hardly have been otherwise. Human nature is not constituted nor meant to endure a continuous strain such as I had been going through.

AMONG THE NEWSPAPERS

As soon as able to sit up on bed I began the preparations of some articles, which I hoped to be able to sell to the daily papers. Green as grass, I knew not how hopeless was any such effort in the great city where hundreds of sharp-witted, well-trained journalists are constantly failing in similar endeavors, owing to the plethora of more interesting *news*-matters. Three offices

we visited, two, or three times each before we found
the managing editor. The *Herald* had not time to read.
The *Sun* didn't want the articles, but *might* use a spicy
sketch of the Klan, if I would write it. The *World* accepted one of my articles, but when I went next day to
inquire when it would appear an editor could not possibly say; perhaps not for several months; meanwhile
"would I accept a trifle?" viz: *a dollar!* I bowed, and
walked down the stairs so blind I missed my way and
came out on another street. Then hastened back to my
little room at the hotel utterly out of heart!

AT PRINCETON

Next day, Bro. M. took me to Central Park, with
which he was perfectly familiar from his frequent visits in vacation time, and the effect of the day in the open
air and sunshine strengthened me sufficiently to undertake another stage of my homeward journey. At 6
P. M. we took the train for Princeton, N. J. where I
spent the Sabbath, the major portion of the time in bed,
as I was still quite sick.

During Sunday evening, however, we walked out to
see the College buildings, and other objects of interest,
as Princeton is our family college. Father himself graduated at it, and also at the Seminary. Bro. Hamilton
and I both "prepared" to enter, and had the war held
off two months longer I should have been duly enrolled
as a Sophomore of the Pater's *Alma Mater.*

Bro. M. had spent three years at Edge Hill Prepar-
atory School in the suburbs, and afterwards four years
in the college proper. His seven years in the place had
made him quite a citizen of it, and he had numerous invitations by friends to bring me to see them. Among
these was Mrs. John R. Thompson, the gay young
widow of the well known literateur.

But I was not in a mood to pay a visit though a Queen
had besought it. Bro. M., having assisted me, to the utmost of his ability, accompanied me to Phila. next evening, where we parted, en route for Bryn Mawr where
he expected to join a party of eight couples of young
ladies and gentlemen, invited by the daughter of the

Supt. of the Eastern Division of the Penna. Railroad, to go on a pleasure jaunt into the mountains. The party travelled in two Pullman Parlor Coaches, with kitchen car, etc., including a settee fastened in front of the locomotive for smoking room, etc. It was a delightful trip, especially so to him, from several cirsumstances.[1]

BALTIMORE

Leaving the West Phila. Depot at $11\frac{1}{2}$ P. M., very sleepy and weary, I arrived in the Monumental City at 4 A. M. before daybreak yet too near it for me to waste one of my few dollars in taking a bed. Besides I had already had a surfeit of investigation by the New York and Albany specimens of the gorgeous creature who entertains the dignity and mock-diamonds of hotel clerk: therefore I hunted a soft spot on the rough plank bench in a corner of the car-sheds, and waited for dawn; and not without fear that I should be arrested for a trespasser by some stupid specimen of the police.

Sitting thus, crouched in a corner, amid the grime and smoke of the depot, I felt not a little annoyance, nay mortification's the word, at being forced to resort to all these makeshifts to reach my home after being dragged away in so wicked a way; but there was no help for it.

After a cheap breakfast (including use of wash-basin, etc.) I hunted up a directory and hunted down the only friend in the city of whom I knew, viz: Capt. Matt Manly, son of Judge Mathias E. Manly, of Newbern, U. S. Senator in 1866-7 but not permitted to take his seat. Matt is an high bred, courteous, gallant gentleman; without an equal in some respects, among the young men of my acquaintance. He commanded a battery of artillery during the war with skill and valor, notwithstanding his youth. He was now associated in the commission and brokerage business with Bart S. Johnston. Both members of the firm happened to be at their warehouse, corner of Lombard and Frederick streets, and gave me a cordial welcome. Matt, at once, sent for my valise, and escorted me to his room, insistent that I should spend a day with them. At his com-

---

1 This paragraph is crossed out in the manuscript.

fortable rooms, after a bath and change of garments, I felt as one who suddenly steps out of the darkness and rain into a warm room. Do these minutiae seem trivial? Far different they seemed to me at the time; and I record them because details of kindness ought never to be forgotten, and in these particulars of suffering and ill usage are illustrated the injustice and outrage of my enemies.

By invitation of Capt. Johnston I took dinner at the St. Clair House together with some fifteen or twenty North Carolinians doing business in Baltimore. All were very cordial, and urged me to go to their houses and have a chat with them; but I had not time, nor ————. Among these were Capt. W. C. Coughenour of Salisbury; M. A. Bencini of the same town, with C. S. Beebe, 94 Lombard; C. E. Mills, 242 West Balt. St., Capt G. W. Clayton;   Merrimon; P. A. Dunn; Tom Gash of Brevard, Jas. Erwin of Hendersonville.

AFTER DARKNESS LIGHT

After tea a party was made up to accompany me to the theatre to witness the play of "After Dark," then making considerable stir. The scenes were well-mounted, and realistic, so *real* as to result in a *finale* not anticipated by the players. The closing scene represented the hero, bound hand and foot, stretched across the rails of a railway-track in a tunnel. The roar of a lightning train, coming at full speed was heard. The rattle of the wheels was very life-like, and at length the glare of the locomotive headlight appeared in the tunnel. At the precise nick of time, the heroine rushed in to release her lover, who rolled off the track just as the ponderous train rushed down through the tunnel, the wheels ringing along the track, the steam hissing, and the sparks flying precisely like a real locomotive. Unfortunately it was *too natural* and the shower of sparks fell among the heavy curtains, there to smoulder until the theatre became deserted, when they leaped into flames, seized the drapery of the boxes, and the dry wood seasoned by successive coats of paint until like a tinder in inflamability, and there could be no suppressing them!

The "Old Holliday Street Theatre" was one of the best known in America. It had witnessed the acting of all the great players of the past century of the American Boards.

It was a narrow escape from a great panic, as the theatre which was crowded at 11 P. M. was in ashes at midnight; together with the St. Nicholas Hotel, Baltimore Commercial College, and other buildings.

DOWN THE BAY

On the following morning Matt accompanied me to the steamboat wharf but was not able to obtain the transportation he sought for me. Fortunately Capt. Johnston had a friend in the superintendent of the rival line and after several long walks succeeded in finding him. Supt. Smith cordially granted the "pass," and at 5 P. M. I boarded the vessel. Before doing so, Matt Manly handed me a sealed note to "look at, at your leisure." It was his delicate way of loaning me a sum for my homeward journey. The money I have long since returned, but the thoughtful kindness remains unpaid, and I fear must so continue indefinitely.

As we swung down the Bay on the "Gude ship Adelaide," at sunset, I stood under the awning on the rear-deck watching the magnificent scene, the distant shores, the countless sailing vessels, and the broad expanse of gold-tipped wavelets; and wondering how soon I should pass over this route again, and under what circumstances! In August, 1861, I had passed down as a school-boy, flirting with the captain's daughter, and bound for Beauregard's army at Manassas. In July 1864, I had passed up as a prisoner, cooped in a filthy hold of a rocking steamer, with a thousand fellow-prisoners, suffering the torments of the condemned.

Again in 1865, I had gone down, in rags, penniless, subjugated, with all the future blank, with all the losses of the war, and eleven months of close confinement wearing upon me.

And then the melancholy return Northward, in irons, under sentence of six years at hard labor, in 1871; and now once again—back!

Strange, sad milestones in the years of my youth were these! But how little hope of the next ones being any brighter!

A TERRIBLE TEMPTATION

Capt. Bart. Johnston had introduced me to Capt. A. B. Andrews, Supt. of the Raleigh & Gaston R. R., who chanced to be going down on the Adelaide. He proved to be a very courteous gentleman whose kind attentions under the circumstances were invaluable. Seeing that I sat on deck, he insisted that I should take a state-room, and have meals regularly, regardless of my pocketbook. His heartiness finally overcame my sensitiveness, and I went down to tea. By a singular co-incidence I was given, by the steward, a seat at a separate table at the head of the others. Two men were already at this table, but I was somewhat blinded by coming out of the darkness into the glare of the dining room and did not recognize in the short squat figure across the table, the American counterpart of Brutal "Jeffreys"—*Judge Hugh L. Bond!* 'Twas the very creature, sleek and slippery with the fat proceeds of many a vile deed in the service of his lawless master!

And, as was fitting, in his travelling companion I recognized a secret service spy, who, if I mistake not his smirking face, accompanied the "Safe-Burglary Plotter" Whitley to Albany to brow beat and vilify me, because I would not sell myself to them.

Bond recognized me before I him, and on catching my eye gave me a very marked bow of recognition, at the same time raising the butter-dish for which I had extended my arm. It is needless to say I had no recognition for him, nor accepted any civility at his hand. Had I taken the dish before recognizing him I must certainly have thrown it into his face; and I confess this piece of rudeness seemed too tempting to resist.

Recall if you can what misery this man had imposed upon me, and how trying it was thus to meet him before reaching home! It was, therefore, with real thankfulness I saw him get up and leave the table; for the spirit of resentment was strong upon me. Had I attacked him, knife in hand, it would have been a serious business for one or both of us.

Returning to the grand saloon I was joined by the genial and handsome commander of the Adelaide, Capt. Mayo, an whole souled Southerner, who expressed warm sympathy for me and speaking of Bond, said, "Well, I'm for peace as a rule, but after what you've suffered you're entitled to some satisfaction, and if you whip Bond it wont matter. He's got no jurisdiction on board this boat!"

Capt. Andrews, however, urged me to make no demonstration as my conduct would be watched, and an outbreak affecting one so great a favorite with Grant would destroy all hope of release for the poor men still at Albany. The Grantites would say, "No use of asking any more pardons. We released Shotwell and before reaching home he fell upon Judge Bond and beat him to jelly!"

BACK TO RALEIGH

Capt. Andrews proved to be a very thoughtful *comrade*. Arrived at Portsmouth, he whispered to Conductor Cromwell who thereupon forgot to call for my ticket, aware perhaps that I had forgotten to get one. On reaching Weldon, Capt. A, being now on his own road, passed me on to Raleigh. Nay more, he telegraphed to several points in Virginia to find Col. H. A. Buford, of the N. C. R. R., who replied by the same means to the agent, to pass me on to Charlotte. Agent Geo. Jones made haste to bring me the pass, and to express his pleasure in being allowed to do so. I had known him casually at Goldsboro.

Arriving at the Raleigh depot we found quite a number of friends, though it had been reported I had gone by the Danville route. They generally came to speak with me, though I knew only the faces of Mr. Kingsbury, Dr. Blacknall, and one or two others. Dr. B. at once gave me a pressing invitation to stop with him for a day or two, and was very clever in his attentions. It was necessary for me to wait until the next day's train (there was but one daily) to get the pass from Col. Buford; so I accepted the Doctor's invitation, and took a room at the Yarborough.

During the afternoon, evening, and following day I was closely besieged by persons—I suppose I may say friends—anxious to hear all about my imprisonment, etc., etc. Popular sentiment was wonderfully changed since the day I marched down the street in front of the Yarborough manacled to poor Teal, and surrounded by a gang of Yankee bayonets and a hooting rabble. People had gotten over their uneasiness, had gotten to see more clearly the true inwardness of the Ku Klux prosecutions; and perhaps to see that all the oaths of perjured witnesses could not make a man degraded if he were not a criminal. Among those who came to talk with me were Senator Matt W. Ransom, Gen. W. R. Cox, Col. D. M. Carter, Maj. Blount, Pulaski Cowper, Sion H. Rogers.

On Friday afternoon, at 5, I took the train for Charlotte. Rev. Dr. R. H. Chapman, and wife were on the train, and Mrs. C. was exceedingly enthusiastic and sympathizing. Some of her expressions were too kind to repeat; for she has the real Irish vehemence of *like* and *dislike!* Other friends were on the train. Col. Webb of Hillsboro, Vorhees, *et als.* Some curious manifestations of sympathy were offered. Mr. W. L. McGee, of Franklinton, gave me a pair of sleeve buttons, of imitation coral, representing a Ku Klux "Death's-Head and Cross-Bones." Mr. P. Lyon, of Durham, offered me a dollar greenback!

CHARLOTTE

At Charlotte as at Raleigh I registered my name as "R. A. Shotwell from Albany Penitentiary;" not in any unseemly spirit of bravado but simply and solely because I wished to let people understand from the onset that I had no shrinking nor shame facedness over the fact that I had been confined in the Radical Bastille. Perhaps had I known the public sentiment I should not have registered as it was liable to mislead persons into supposing I wished to attract attention or be lionized; whereas I preferred just the opposite. How easily are the best of intentions misconstrued to one's disadvantage.

During Sunday I wrote a long letter to Mrs. 'Squire Sam Brown of York County, S. C. telling her many particulars of her husband's situation and life at Albany that she could not learn through his letters, restricted, limited, and watched as they were by the prison authorities.

Mrs. Brown replied very heartily, thanking me, in the highest terms, for "the earnest efforts put forth by you to secure my husband's release. I need hardly say it though I repeat, you have the heartfelt and sincere thanks of myself and daughters for the very kind interest you manifest and the kind sympathy you express for us all, and your earnest effort in behalf [of] one who is near and dear to us," etc.[1]

I also wrote to Genl. B. Kershaw.

I also wrote to Col. S. D. Pool thanking him for his congratulatory telegram though I had not forgotten his thoughtless comments on my conviction which had cut me to the heart at a time when I needed all my strength for the inevitable rigors of my situation. But he only had followed other examples.

Among others who called on me were Mr. W. J. Yates, whose thoughtfulness in sending me a copy of his paper containing the impeachment of Judge Logan, had made me warmly his friend; Joseph P. Caldwell, whose kindly mention of my return will appear on the following page; and also Genl. D. H. Hill, the Hero of "South Mountain Pass," or "Boonsboro Battle" who had spoken very kindly of my articles in the Albany *Times*. His visit gave me a special encouragement as he mentioned to me that he had accepted a Professorship in the Carolina Military Institute, (in which he had formerly been Superintendent) and should need an assistant editor for his paper, the *Southern Home*. I as-

---

1 In Shotwell's scrap-book, under date of Jan 5, 1874, appears the following clipping:

S. G. Brown, Esq.—We are truly gratified to learn that this old gentleman has got home to York, S. C. in safety.

It is terrible to reflect that an aged and highly respected citizen has been two years an inmate in Albany Prison, as one of the victims to re-elect Gen. Grant. We trust that the malice of the donkey-Congressman has at last been satiated, and that Mr. Brown will be permitted to spend the remainder of his life in the bosom of his family. (Gen. Hill)

sured him it would give me great pleasure to take such a position were it not that I had set my heart on getting control of a paper either at Rutherfordton, at Shelby, at Lincolnton, at Marion, or Morganton—some point within easy reach of the scene of my sufferings in Rutherfordton but if not able to effect any such arrangement, I should be glad to join with him.

SHELBY

From Charlotte to Rutherfordton is about sixty miles by direct line, but the distance by rail is greater, and requires two days travel, spending the night in Shelby, twelve miles beyond the (then) terminus of the Railroad, Cherryville. From Shelby to Rutherfordton, a rickety old buggy carries the mail, and any stray passenger, a distance of twenty-six miles, counted by geographical measuring rods, perches, or poles, (principally poles): but a full day's journey counting by the slow crawling of John Peter Eaves's "government mule."

At Woodlawn, Iron Station, and at Lincolnton a number of friends were at the depot, not specially to see me, for they had been expecting me a week before and had concluded I was gone around by Morganton, or Spartanburg either of which were about as near; but they expressed much pleasure that I was free. I had hoped to see quite a number of friends at Lincolnton; and I made special inquiries for Capt. John Justice, who had spent a night with me not long before my arrest; David Schenk, the well-known lawyer, whom I had regarded as a faithful Klansman; Vardry McBee, Ben S. Guion, *et al.* In truth, it seemed a little singular that Mr. Schenk, against whom I had been repeatedly urged to testify and for whom I remained two years in durance vile, the vilest that ever man bore, should not even walk one or two hundred yards to welcome me, after all my sufferings. But the fact that my coming had been announced for several previous days no doubt accounted for his absence *now:* he possibly came before, and had given up looking for me. How ignorant of the man, and his character, I was in thus excusing his ungrateful negligence! But of this, more anon!

A cordial welcome awaited me at Shelby. As soon as I alighted from the hack, the citizens came in numbers and congratulated me heartily. Perhaps no county in Carolina is more unanimously Democratic and seven in ten had been members of the Klan. Moreover they were specially friendly to me because my father often visited them, and preached for them, helping to establish a congregation among them. The people of Shelby, it will be recollected, were the only ones in the State to give me practical evidences of sympathy and esteem. The ladies had made a contribution of $65, for the seven sufferers by the Logan-Scoggins handcuffing spitefulness. It was the Shelby Literary Society which had elected me their honorary member at a time when I was toiling from dawn till dusk in a felon's cell, wearing felon's garb, and doomed to years of such life. Here, too, was the home of Plato Durham, who had proven himself so truly my friend, when to be a friend at all was to be a "a friend indeed."

Needless to say I was sincerely glad to meet each and all of these friends. They knew of the "Reign of Terror in Rutherford;" they knew the vile character of the men who slanderously swore against me; and they knew the pressure I had to bear.

Capt. Plato Durham, I was most anxious of all my friends to see, and talk with, and we had a long conversation; a sad one for both. He was very nervous and irritable, having lost much of the calmness which made him, in 1868, like a tower of Truth and Manhood surrounded by snarling, snapping, sneaking spaniels, yelping at him because he threw light upon their scoundrelly schemes and stealings.

Many things, in some his own fault, in the majority the fault of others, and illustrating the *meanness* and *ingratitude* of politicians, had led him into drinking more freely than his deep, impassioned yet reserved nature could bear; and between the irritability born of these habits, and a sense of injustice and ill-treatment, he became politically reckless doing and saying things which weakened his hold on the Democrats without adding to his strength among the Radicals, as indeed he did not desire.

HOME

At dusk next evening, Bro. Addison, who had come to Shelby for me in the buggy, drove me over the brow of the "Mile Hill" whence the village of Rutherfordton may be seen stretched along a ridge, but so surrounded by higher hills that it looks like a platform of an amphitheatre. Prominent above all other buildings were the once handsome courthouse where the Scoggins mockery of a "Commissioners Court" was held, at $5 a day for commissioner and Marshals, besides bribes from the accused; and the three story, tumble-down jail where I had been locked for months with murderers and thieves! It was not pleasant nor *peaceful* emotion they excited. There was scarcely a single pleasant memory connected with the place. It had been the ruin of my father's life for from the day of his settling there until now, he became buried from the world, his learning and talents misapplied, because utterly unappreciated, save by a very few cultivated people; and his usefulness nullified by his inability to suit himself to the requirements of such a situation, and surroundings.

My own life, in the place had been as thoroughly wasted as if one had burned a roll of bank notes, or had been asleep all the time.

Fortunately there were exceptions to the rule, as I have already pointed out in speaking of this region; and there were those whose friendships I shall evermore prize, and for whose kindness I shall ever be grateful. Among these friends there had been considerable talk of giving me a public reception, illuminating the town, ringing bells, etc., etc. In my letters home I discouraged all such demonstrations, "even if there were any likelihood of their occurrence," *which there was not,* as the wishes of a few kind-hearted ladies are not always the will of the townsmen. And I knew the effect would be disastrous to the hopes of the poor men still at Albany.

So, I came home quietly, receiving many warm welcomes from friends; and even from the better class of Republicans like John McFarland, John Eaves, John Allen, and others.

JIM JUSTICE SENDS A MESSAGE

A few days after reaching home a friend came to me with a verbal message from Jim Justice to the effect that he hoped I wouldn't cherish any hard feelings toward him; and he would like to speak to me if I would allow it. Old Mr. Carrier told me something to the same purport, and said Justice wished to shake hands with me.

These messages and overtures gave me much perplexity. Justice was too low, in moral and political character for me to recognize him (beyond, perhaps, a nod in answer to his salutation) even *before* the attempt to ruin me through his connivance. and *NOW!*

But, per contra, the man had compelled me to treat him with at least formal courtesy; for had he not signed the application for my release when the government declared his signature necessary or requisite to any hearing of the case?

And did not the fact that he had signed without a request from me, and in ignorance as to my future course towards him [constitute an obligation?].

True, there were those, who knowing the man and his physical shipwreck, which was now almost equal to that of his moral degradation, argued that he foresaw I should get out soon, and felt that this was his best chance to disarm my resentment. But I prefer to think he acted from natural, if irregular, generosity and compunction of conscience at having done so much to destroy me. Be that as it may he had signed, and cheerfully, and had most humbly made his advances, and I must not reject them else I should show myself more ungenerous than he.

When, therefore, a day or two later he crossed the street, and came up to me with hand outstretched nervously, I gave him my hand, saying gravely, in answer to his expressions of gratification at my return, that I was glad to get back, but as for "letting by-gones be by-gone," as he requested, I should do so only so far as a resort to personal vengeance was concerned; but that I felt a life-long duty had been imposed upon me of exposing and holding up to the scorn of the world many deeds of the Ku Klux Crusade against our people," etc., etc.

Justice replied that he was "very sorry," and "There was so much excitement, you know, a good many things was done on both sides that wasn't right." I passed on, and those were the last words I recollect of hearing from the miserable creature.

And here I may as well mention the termination of Justice's career.

JIM JUSTICE'S TRAGIC DEATH

For his own name and memory it had been a fortunate thing if Jim Justice had been hanged by the Klan. He would have been pitied, and his vile conduct over looked, by even the extreme Southerners; while with his own party his fame would have been that of a "martyr to his principles," and it is very possible his family would have been cared for by Congress. But he escaped as if Providence meant to give him a few more years for reformation. Alas! his career was ever downward, and during his last days it was very rapid.

Judge Logan, having lost his prestige even with his own party, no longer assisted to keep Justice on his feet. His drunkenness and vagabondage grew more marked. He had no longer any influence even among his old associates, and his daily associates were low whites and negroes. He openly abused his wife on the street. . . . Finally he was forced to leave the village and go to Hickory Nut Gap to a small farm owned by Logan. Justice drank and played cards day and night, until nearly killed in a row.

[*Several pages of clippings follow in the manuscript.*]

TO WORK AGAIN

Mention has been made more than once in my journal of my fixed determination to get control of a newspaper at Rutherfordton or, if unable to do so there, at some point nearest adjacent thereto, and to devote my

life to exposing the atrocities which were allowed to pass
in so little notice at the time, owing to the suicidal policy of the Democratic leaders in trying to hush up matters lest they too should become involved. Miserable
policy! Many a poor man suffered imprisonment, torture, and financial ruin, because there was no determined effort by prominent Democrats (who had often
besought his vote, and profited by it) to demand justice
for the innocent.

It needed but a few days to show me how little could
be done at Rutherfordton, as there was no press, and
the people were not only poor and hard pressed to live,
but almost hopeless. Father, of course, begged me to
stay at home and read law, but too well I knew the
waste of years that befalls a young man who sits down
in a small, back-country village to wait for employment
or opportunities. They never come, and he becomes
utterly unable to go elsewhere to seek them.

Besides I could not think of remaining as an additional burden to father.

Looking around, however, I saw no better field. The
Piedmont Press, and the *Newton Vindicator,* covered
all the Western Railway line, above Statesville, which
had its *Intelligencer.* Asheville had two papers, Shelby
one, and Lincolnton one. True, the proprietor of the
last named paper, the *"Progress"* wanted an editor and
had started to the Depot to meet me, and offer me the
position, but was turned back by David Schenk of which
more anon.

One place remained; Shelby: and it was the location
I preferred above all others, for not only were the people of the town and county strongly Democratic, and
Klansmen, but the village was the centre of a large
wagon trade and traffic from all the surrounding regions including the upper counties of South Carolina
which had been co-sufferers with our own people from
Grantite Rule.

The *Cleveland Banner* was still alive, and floated the
name of Capt Plato Durham; but he rarely wrote anything for it, and report said was anxious to sell. Its circulation had become merely nominal, and I thought

454 THE NORTH CAROLINA HISTORICAL COMMISSION

likely there would be no difficulty in my getting it. It appears, however, he had personal motives for keeping it going, and keeping other papers away.

Unaware of his feelings about it, I wrote to several gentlemen of Shelby expressing my wishes to get a paper there. All replied favorably; but Mayor W. P. Love interested himself so far as to agree to help me raise the $700 or $800 which I deemed indispensable to starting a successful paper. He was about to take a trip to South Carolina, and would see what the people thought of the project, "over the Border."

On his return he wrote me he had been assured on all sides the paper would secure thousands of subscribers; and to show the popular confidence therein, he had already raised $400, to start me, and could easily secure the remainder. This was good news, and I was highly elated at the prospect of going immediately at work.

Unhappily all the Mayor's efforts were thrown away. For close on the heels of his letter came Capt. Durham on a business trip to Rutherford, and soon I heard he was worried about my coming to Shelby. I straightway sought him out, and asked if the report was true. He seemed much troubled, and offish, but after I assured him I was not ungrateful for his past kindness, and would do all that was right and honorable to oblige him, he replied that he had strong reasons for wishing I would not settle in Shelby, at least not for six months, or so, as my paper would, of course, utterly ruin the *Banner,* which was a very small, badly printed sheet. Nor was this all. He had another serious objection to my settling in Shelby. He had been obliged to work very hard, and make great concessions to get myself and others (with himself) out of the clutches of the Grantites, and if I were to come to his own town, and start a red hot Democratic paper, denouncing the Radicals, etc., it would be alleged he had been instrumental in setting me up and the result might be serious to him, etc., etc., etc.

If I would go somewhere else for six months, all would blow over, and he would then be glad to have me take the *Banner.* I felt both surprised, and saddened by this conversation but assured him I should at once give up all my plans and write to Mayor Love not to proceed farther in the matter.

And this closed all the circle within which I hoped to have settled.

I had no means of my own, and though every friend expressed the wish to see me get a comfortable position, *wishes* do not *help,* nor buy meat and bread, nor give a man a chance.

Nothing remained but to abandon, for a time, and probably forever, the hopes I had fostered during the long days of my toil at the shoe-bench; and go to Charlotte. Accordingly I wrote Genl. Hill, and subsequently met him at Shelby Court where we arranged for me to enter upon my duties as assistant editor of the *Southern Home,* Oct. 13, 1873.

The salary was small, the position secondary, and uninfluential, for of course as Gen. Hill was editor and proprietor he would control the course of the paper (not making me write as I disapproved, but excluding matter of mine which he disapproved; if he wished); still it was a support, and an honorable business, and the prospects of Charlotte were brighter than almost any other town in North Carolina at that time. And Genl. Hill's political and general views were more nearly my own that almost any other paper, as the *Home* had a reputation for outspokenness.

ADIEUX TO RUTHERFORDTON

Although the scene of much suffering and humiliation to me though seemingly covered with the deadly blight of Loganism and Grantism, making the whole region seem blighted like the valley of the Shadow of Death, Rutherford had been my abiding-place for several years, had been the home of my father for nearly sixteen years, was the resting-place of my martyred brother Hamilton, and I had still within the boundaries many warm and faithful friends, such as few men gain in this life.

Therefore it was with unfeigned reluctance I made my decision to settle in Charlotte, and leave Rutherford.

My friends appeared sorry of my going, and for the

last fortnight I was almost constantly visiting them at their homes, receiving hearty welcomes from all.

Promptly to my agreement I arrived in Charlotte, and entered upon my duties; my first article being devoted to a sketch of the outrageous treatment of Captain Oscar Berry. Genl. Hill wished to introduce me with a somewhat exaggerated *resume of my past record,* but I chanced to see a 'proof' of the article, and begged him to suppress it, as I wished to go quietly to work.

The Charlotte papers gave me cordial welcome. The people, also, made me welcome giving me frequent invitations to dine, or take tea, with them, though as usual I managed to be always busy or pre-engaged on such occasions.

Now and then I met a Job's comforter whose ears I decidedly desired to pull. It was not pleasant to be patronized, in such style as this: "Now Shotwell come and see us! Don't feel in the least backward. Don't worry about the Penitentiary business: What if you were convicted: everybody knows all about it, and they don't look down on you at all," etc., etc. What could I answer to a speech like this evidently dictated by real friendliness, but so shockingly deficient in tact, or delicacy or consideration that I could have returned a blow to the invitation!

In other cases these ill-bred persons went so far as to *assume that I felt some humiliation* (!) by saying as follows: "Captain why in the world don't you stir about more! There aint no use of your feelin' down-hearted about that Ku Klux affair. All o' us wuz Ku Kluxes, and so far as I'm concerned I ruther think better of you now than I did afore!" Bah! 'Tis sickening to think of! A *woman* would never be guilty of such want of thought, delicacy, tact, and sensibility.

Usually I replied quietly that I had done as I believed to be my duty in the past, and should continue to do; but occasionally I lost temper and exclaimed that any man who fancied I felt ashamed of the life at Albany was not only a *fool,* but ungrateful: for I had suffered for my principles, and not from any personal cause or

purpose! Even had I led the raid on Justice I should
not have done so from any *personal* object or motive.
What had I to gain? What could the Klan do for me?
Bah! Get behind me! I want none of Job's comforting.
I appreciate sympathy, and rejoice to have it from good
people who believe me wronged for my principle's sake,
but I want no pity, nor any sympathy which is not based
on thorough recognition of the foul wrong done to me.

THE END[1]

---

1 There is more of the Shotwell manuscript dealing with conditions in North
Carolina in the 1870's and 1880's, but, written long after the recorded events had
taken place, it is less valuable than that published in the three volumes of *Shotwell
Papers*. The unprinted material is easily accessible in the archives of the North
Carolina Historical Commission, Raleigh.

INDEX